ANNALS OF THE NEW YORK ACADEMY OF SCIENCES
Volume 323

Expanding the Role of Women in the Sciences

Edited by Anne M. Briscoe and Sheila M. Pfafflin

THE NEW YORK ACADEMY OF SCIENCES
NEW YORK, NEW YORK
1979

Copyright © 1979 by The New York Academy of Sciences. All rights reserved. Under the provisions of the United States Copyright Act of 1976, individual readers of the Annals are permitted to make fair use of the material in them for teaching or research. Permission is granted to quote from the Annals provided that the customary acknowledgment is made of the source. Material in the Annals may be republished only by permission of The Academy. Address inquiries to the Executive Editor at The New York Academy of Sciences.

Copying fees: *The code at the bottom of the first page of each article in this* Annal *states the fee for each copy of the article made beyond the free copying permitted under Section 107 or 108 of the 1976 Copyright Act (If no code appears, there is no fee.) This fee should be paid through the Copyright Clearance Center Inc, Box 765, Schenectady, N.Y. 12301. For articles published prior to 1978, the copying fee is $1.75 per article.*

Library of Congress Cataloging in Publication Data

Main entry under title:

Expanding the role of women in the sciences.

(Annals of The New York Academy of Sciences; v. 323) Papers from a conference held by The New York Academy of Sciences and cosponsored by the Association for Women in Science Educational Foundation on March 6–8, 1978. Includes bibliographical references.

   1. Women in science—Congresses. I. Briscoe, Anne M. II. Pfafflin, Sheila M. III. New York Academy of Sciences. IV. Association for Women in Science Educational Foundation. V. Series: New York Academy of Science. Annals; v. 323.

Q11.N5 vol. 323 [Q130]   508'.1s [331.4'81'5]   79-11142

CCP
Printed in the United States of America
ISBN 0-89766-014-5 (cloth)
ISBN 0-89766-013-7 (paper)

ANNALS OF THE NEW YORK ACADEMY OF SCIENCES

Volume 323

EDITORIAL STAFF

Executive Editor
BILL BOLAND

Associate Editors
BEATRICE H. RADIN
WERNER SIMON

The New York Academy of Sciences
2 East 63rd Street
New York, New York 10021

THE NEW YORK ACADEMY OF SCIENCES
(Founded in 1817)
BOARD OF GOVERNORS, 1979

JOEL L. LEBOWITZ, *President*
PARITHCHERY SRINIVASAN, *President-Elect*

Honorary Chairman of the Board of Governors
I.B. LASKOWITZ

	Honorary Life Governors	
SERGE A. KORFF		H. CHRISTINE REILLY
I. B. LASKOWITZ		IRVING J. SELIKOFF

Vice-Presidents
MERRIL EISENBUD

| CRAIG D. BURRELL | | HEINZ R. PAGELS |
| DOROTHY CUNNINGHAM | | LUCIE WOOD SAUNDERS |

Recording Secretary
MORRIS H. SHAMOS

Treasurer
ALAN J. PATRICOF

Corresponding Secretary
ALLAN GEWIRTZ

Elected Governors-at-Large

1977–1979
FLORENCE DENMARK   EVELYN E. HANDLER   WILLARD J. JACOBSON

1978–1980
BENJAMIN BEDERSON   WALTER N. SCOTT
MARY J. MYCEK   BABETTE B. WEKSLER

1979–1981
WILLIAM T. GOLDEN   DOROTHY T. KRIEGER
HAROLD GRAD   SIDNEY UDENFRIEND

Past Presidents (Governors)
CHARLOTTE FRIEND   PHILIP SIEKEVITZ
HERBERT J. KAYDEN   PHILIP FEIGELSON

SIDNEY BOROWITZ, *Executive Director*

*Expanding the Role
of Women
in the Sciences*

ANNALS OF THE NEW YORK ACADEMY OF SCIENCES

Volume 323

April 20, 1979

EXPANDING THE ROLE OF WOMEN IN THE SCIENCES*

Editors
Anne M. Briscoe and Sheila M. Pfafflin

Conference Organizers
Anne M. Briscoe, *Chair*, Sheila M. Pfafflin, and Anneta Duveen

CONTENTS

Introduction. By Anne M. Briscoe	1

Part I. The Future of Women in The Sciences
Estelle Ramey, Session Chair

Research Challenges and Opportunities. By Richard M. Krause	6
Women in Academe: Why It Still Hurts To Be a Woman in Labor. By Bernice Resnick Sandler	14
Women in Science-Related Activities. By Philip H. Abelson	27

Part II. The State of the Art: Current Status of Women in The Sciences
Dorothy Cunningham, Session Chair

Women in Physics and Astronomy. By Vera Kistiakowsky	35
The Changing Status of Women in the Geosciences. By Theresa F. Schwarzer	48
Women in Psychology in the United States. By Florence L. Denmark	65
The Peak of the Pyramid: Women in Dentistry, Medicine and Veterinary Medicine. By Amber B. Jones and Eileen C. Shapiro	79
Women in Engineering Revisited. By Naomi J. McAfee	94
The Status of Women in Mathematics. By Gloria C. Hewitt	100
Women in the Biological Sciences. By Elizabeth M. O'Hern	110

Anneta Duveen, Session Chair

Scientific Sexism. By Lilli S. Hornig	125

* This series of papers is the result of a conference entitled Expanding the Role of Women in The Sciences, held March 6, 7, and 8, 1978 by The New York Academy of Sciences and cosponsored by The Association for Women in Science Educational Foundation.

Part III. Opportunities for Professional Advancement
Janet Welsh Brown, Session Chair

Expanding the Role of Women in the Biomedical Sciences. *By* ALEXANDER G. BEARN 134
Changing Attitudes Toward Women in the Profession of Chemistry. *By* ALAN C. NIXON 146
A Certain Restlessness. *By* ESTHER A.H. HOPKINS 173
Careers in Industry for Scientifically Trained Women. *By* IVY M. CELENDER 179

Part IV. Altering Attitudes: Strategies for Change
Sheila M. Pfafflin, Session Chair

Implications of Equality. *By* ANNA J. HARRISON 190
Redress of Grievances. *By* HELEN C. AND ROBERT E. DAVIES 197
The New Feminism and the Medical School Milieu. *By* MARY C. HOWELL 210
Development of Feminist Networks in the Professions. *By* ARLENE KAPLAN DANIELS 215
Strategies for Change: A Summary. *By* JUDITH A. RAMALEY 228

Part V. Government and Academic Policy
Marie M. Cassidy, Session Chair

Introduction to Part V. *By* MARIE MULLANEY CASSIDY 234
Filters for Women in Science. *By* JEWEL PLUMMER COBB 236
Feminism in Academia: Its Problematic and Problems. *By* RUTH HUBBARD 249
Implications of Giving Women a Greater Share of Academic Decision-Making. *By* ELLEN C. WEAVER 257
Innovative Approaches: Meeting the Needs of Women Faculty in the Eighties. *By* DIANE IDA MARINEZ 268
The Role of the National Science Foundation. *By* F. JAMES RUTHERFORD 276

Part VI. Experiences in Achieving New Directions
Neena B. Schwartz, Session Chair

How a Scientist Who Happens To Be Female Can Succeed in Academia. *By* DIANE HADDOCK RUSSELL 283
From Clerk-Typist to Research Physicist. *By* SHIRLEY A. JACKSON 296
Academics, Bluestockings, and Biologists: Women at the University of Chicago, 1892–1932. *By* DIANA LONG HALL 300
Psychological Challenges Confronting Women in The Sciences. *By* RUTH MOULTON 321

Part VII. Summation
Ethel Tobach, Session Chair

An Agenda to Further Expand the Role of Women in Science and Technology. *By* ETHEL TOBACH 336
Equal Opportunity for Women in Science. *By* SHEILA M. PFAFFLIN 341

Financial assistance was received from:

- American Can Company
- Amoco Foundation, Inc.
- The Association for Women in Science Educational Foundation (Conference cosponsor)
- Burroughs Wellcome Co.
- Campbell Institute for Food Research
- Corning Glass Works Foundation
- Exxon Corporation
- General Mills Foundation
- Gulf & Western Foundation
- Hoffmann-La Roche, Inc.
- Merck Sharp & Dohme Postgraduate Program
- Merck Sharp & Dohme Research Laboratories
- Mobil Oil Corporation
- Pfizer, Inc.
- Sandoz, Inc.
- Smith Kline Corporation
- Syntex (U.S.A.) Inc.
- Warner-Lambert Research Institute

The New York Academy of Sciences believes it has a responsibility to provide an open forum for discussion of scientific questions. The positions taken by the participants in the reported conferences are their own and not those of The Academy. The Academy has no intent to influence legislation by providing such forums.

Introduction

ANNE M. BRISCOE
Harlem Hospital Center
Columbia University
New York, New York 10037

THE CONFERENCE on which this book is based was held six years after the historic first: that is, six years after the Conference on Successful Women in the Sciences: an Analysis of Determinants, sponsored by The New York Academy of Sciences. This one had a cosponsor in addition to The Academy, the Educational Foundation of the Association for Women in Science, or AWIS, as it is called.

AWIS was founded in 1971 at about the same time as the 1972 conference was in the planning stage. Its Educational Foundation was organized in 1974 by Estelle Ramey. AWIS was among the first of the activist women's organizations that emerged onto the national scene in the 1970s. Its purpose has been "to promote equal opportunities for women to enter the professions and to achieve their career goals." Features of AWIS activism are a national bimonthly newsletter, a triweekly job bulletin, a computerized talent bank of women scientists available to employers, establishment of local chapters for mutual support and career development, annual graduate scholarship awards by the Educational Foundation, and support of such conferences as this one.

The 1972 conference had examined the careers of twelve unusual women who achieved success before the advent of the laws and executive orders outlawing discrimination in education and in employment on the basis of sex. The proceedings of that conference also included analyses of the institutional and societal practices and traditions which largely excluded women from careers in the sciences or relegated them to professional oblivion.

In 1976, the recently established Ad Hoc Committee on Women of The New York Academy of Sciences, chaired at that time by Kathleen Prestwidge, requested, and was granted a follow-up conference. The Organizing Committee for the conference consisted of Sheila Pfafflin,

Anneta Duveen, and myself. We began by asking a question to provide a focus of the initial planning stage: Is six years a sufficient time interval to permit visible signs of internal changes in institutional practices? Specifically, if accurate data of the status of women in 1976 were compared with those of 1970 (allowing for the time lag for data-collection and conference-planning), would it demonstrate that there had been substantial changes in policy with regard to 1) admission of women to professional training programs, and 2) recruitment and promotion on the basis of merit without consideration of the sex of the individual?

Because these questions were answered in the negative, the Organizing Committee designed a conference to present, publicize, and record the most recent data on the status of women in the sciences. Next, the conference was intended to bring together some of the policy-makers in government, academia, and industry to review these data. And finally, the participants were to explore together strategies to combat the continuing, pervasive, intractable phenomenon of sexism in the American scientific community, one facet of the larger problem of sexism in society. We decided to focus on Ph.D. and M.D. careers in the sciences except for engineering and industry, where advanced degrees are not necessarily a prerequisite for upward career mobility.

This does not represent an elitist attitude per se. Women have had few problems in entering and working as laboratory and technical assistants and as nonphysician health-care professionals such as nurses, dental hygienists, and physical therapists. If the emphasis is on that level of opportunity for the greatest creativity, prestige, and financial reward in the sciences, this necessarily concerns Ph.D.s and M.D.s. It is at this, the doctoral level, that career tracks for women and men diverge from graduation onwards. In fact, with respect to personal guidance, professional development, or career sponsorship of doctoral candidates by their professors, men enjoy a distinct advantage even prior to graduation. Thus, the conference was aimed at those with high-level credentials who hope to avoid professional stagnation due to forces beyond an individual's control.

We therefore limited the focus and invited 39 resource people to participate and present data or preside over sessions. The response was enthusiastic. Thirty-six accepted immediately, and two others did so after being assured that the conference was to be held in 1978, not in 1977. A few additional speakers were invited later to replace two who had to withdraw and two more to complete the program, but essentially the affirmative responses permitted little revision of the preliminary program. That first plan was for a two-day conference with two simultaneous sessions. This would have required the participants to choose between topics and would have reduced the size of each audience. The Academy Conference Committee, in its wisdom, insisted on a three-day, single-session symposium.

Thus, the three-day conference was held from March 6th to 8th and was attended by more than 500 scientists, students, and distinguished people from all over the United States and abroad. The participants were women and men from the universities, government laboratories, and the private sector. There were heads of government agencies, distinguished professors, present and past presidents of professional societies, members of the National Academy of Sciences, fellows and members of scores of professional societies including fellows of the Royal Society, the Royal College of Physicians, the American College of Physicians, the American Institute of Chemists, and The New York Academy of Sciences. Distinguished speakers included Rosalyn Yalow, 1978 Nobel Laureate; Helvi Sipila, the Assistant Secretary General of the United Nations for Social Development and Humanitarian Affairs and originator of International Women's Year and Decade; and Frank Press, Director of the White House Office of Science and Technology Policy. Recruiters from government agencies, industry, and academia came to announce immediate positions for women scientists and science administrators for senior-level appointments. The great interest generated by the conference was evidenced by the large attendance at the sessions, the official luncheon and dinner, and by the numerous news articles which appeared afterwards. The conference was given television coverage on the evenings of March 6th and 8th when Frank Field of News Center 4 invited me to appear with him, and on March 31 when Sheila Pfafflin and Lilli Hornig joined me on a local New York television station to discuss the conference and the problems and objectives of women scientists.

Among the organizers and speakers of the conference were sixteen women who are now or have been leaders of activist organizations of women scientists or presidents of professional scientific organizations. The latter include the 1978 President of the American Chemical Society, Anna J. Harrison; the 1977–78 President of both The New York Academy of Sciences and the Harvey Society, Charlotte Friend; the 1979 President-Elect of the American Psychological Association, Florence L. Denmark; and the 1978–79 President of the Endocrine Society, Rosalyn

Yalow. The emergence of women's activist organizations in the 1970s has been reported recently.* Participating in this conference were the following leaders of a few of those, listed here in terms of their status at the time of publication: three Past Presidents of AWIS, Neena B. Schwartz, Estelle Ramey, and myself; the current President and President-Elect of AWIS, Judith A. Ramaley and Sheila M. Pfafflin, respectively; a Past President, President and President-Elect of the Federation of Organizations for Professional Women, Janet W. Brown, Marie M. Cassidy and Naomi J. McAfee, respectively; the Founder of the Association for Women in Psychology, Ethel Tobach; the Past Chair of the Ad Hoc Committee on Women of The New York Academy of Sciences, Kathleen J. Prestwidge; a Past President of Women in Science and Engineering, Vera Kistiakowsky; a Past President of Sociologists for Women in Society, Arlene K. Daniels; a Past President of the Society of Women Engineers, Naomi J. McAfee; and two Past Presidents and the President of the AWIS Educational Foundation, Estelle Ramey, Ellen Weaver, and myself, respectively.

Almost all of the answers to an evaluation questionnaire by the participants were enthusiastic and favorable. A few noted the lack of an international focus and also the absence of official representatives of the nursing and elementary and secondary school professions. The Committee expects that these areas will be covered in a subsequent conference. We realize in retrospect that the generous corporate and foundation support of the conference might have included travel funds for many young scientists who wanted to attend. No such budget request was made because the Committee (regretfully) did not anticipate the extraordinary interest the program would evoke all over the country.

The purposes we defined at the start seem to have been accomplished. The papers which follow will document the inadequate nature of affirmative action as a remedy for the social disease, sexism: not affirmative action per se, but as it is ignored, bypassed, flouted, and distorted. Our speakers will provide the data that in academia and government, affirmative action has neither diminished sexism nor lowered any standards nor created reverse discrimination. Even if it were inherently favorable to the latter, it has never had wide enough application to make any difference. Before a serious attempt to implement a remedy for sexism is likely to

---

*Briscoe, Anne M. 1978. Phenomenon of the Seventies: The Women's Caucuses. Signs 4(1):152–157.

occur, continuing exposure of its multiple manifestations is needed as well as an ongoing dialogue with the decision makers. The conference should add a step along this route.

On behalf of the Conference Organizing Committee, the Women in Science Committee of The Academy (now a standing committee), and the AWIS Educational Foundation, I wish to express our deep appreciation to the Board of Governors of The Academy for supporting our efforts and to The Academy Conference Committee and its subcommittee, both of which gave us valuable advice and criticism. We are very much indebted to Ellen Marks, Conference Director of The Academy, and her assistant, Renée Wilkerson, for their invaluable efforts and expertise.

Our sincere thanks are expressed to Bill Boland and his staff: India Trinley, Beatrice H. Radin and Werner Simon for their skillful preparation of these proceedings for publication. A special word of appreciation is owed to Ann Collins, whose public relations management of the conference accounted for its success in terms of attendance and in the news and media coverage. Finally, to all the speakers and participants, you were great to give your time, talent, and energy: thank you from the Women in the Science Committee and AWIS.

PART I. The Future of Women in The Sciences

Research Challenges and Opportunities

To Bertha, in whose library, after teatime,
I came to know Of Six Medieval Women

RICHARD M. KRAUSE
*Director, National Institute of Allergy and Infectious Diseases
National Institutes of Health
Bethesda, Maryland 20014*

... *March amazes me! The lawn is full of south and the odors tangle* ...
Emily Dickinson in The Belle of Amherst

JUST SEVERAL WEEKS AGO, on a bright cold Sunday afternoon, spontaneously and without forethought, I dropped in on the Kennedy Center for the production of Handel's "Alexander's Feast." It is a robust oratorio, yet lyrical, and the choruses are vigorous and majestic. As my mind wandered into the music, what struck me about the production of an oratorio was the harmonious blend of the sexes. Indeed, the music would lack texture if this were not the case. There is more than symbolism in this observation. Just as with the performance of great music, every aspect of our culture prospers with this participation of both men and women.

There is, of course, a long, if sparse, history of women who have participated fully in the affairs of society. We can begin with ancient Egypt—with Nefertiti, or with Hatshepsut, who ruled as pharoah with an artificial beard.

Even in the Middle Ages—a grim time for women and almost everyone else, for that matter—there was a small number of remarkable women. And here I am not making reference particularly to those women who achieved sainthood, although they are not to be neglected.

Quite by accident I recently came across a small volume entitled *Of Six Medieval Women*, by Alice Kemp-Welsh. I say "quite by accident" because it truly was that, one of those chance occurrences which happen while browsing in a friend's library. Let me say just a word about two of these medieval women. There was Roswitha, a tenth century nun who wrote plays, and remarkable plays they were. There is a resemblance between one of her plays and a later masterpiece, *Romeo and Juliet*, in the drama of passion, the frenzy of the soul and the senses.

Another of these six medieval women was a fifteenth century feminist, Christine of Pisan. Christine was not only a forerunner of true feminism, but also a great champion of the creative power of women when they have opportunities equal to those of men. In judging the sexes, Christine holds the scales evenly. As Ms. Kemp-Welsh writes, "She stands before us, at the dawn of the fifteenth century, Janus-headed, looking to the past and to the future, a woman typical of a time of transition, on the one hand showing, in her writings, a clinging to old beliefs, and on the other hand asserting, in her contact with real life, independence of thought in the discussion of still unsolved questions."

Born in Venice in 1663, Christine and her family soon moved to Paris and the Court of King Charles V. There she had unlimited access to the King's remarkable library, including many books that had been translated from Greek, Latin, and Arabic. Even, mark you, as a child Christine showed extraordinary capacity for learning, and this her father zealously fostered and developed. She married at fifteen and married for love. But within ten years her husband died, leaving her with the need to provide both for herself and her children. "Men must work and women must weep," says the poet. But life reveals that men and women alike must, indeed, do both, and this is what Christine set about to do. She turned to writing. She says, "I betook myself, like the child who at first is set to learn its A B C, to ancient histories from the beginning of the world—histories of the Hebrews and the Assyrians, of the Romans, the French, the Bretons, and diverse others—and then to the deductions of such sciences as I had time to give heed to, as well as to a study of the poets." In a miniature from the beginning of one of her manuscripts we see her seated in the library of the University of Paris working on a folio.

Christine's fame spread as a poet and essayist. To her belongs the honor of introducing Dante to France. Scattered in her poems and essays are illusions to the Divine Comedy. But all was not comedy, and all was not poetry. She was versed also in the science of her time, including astronomy. She saw order in the firmament, where all matters obey physical laws, so that harmony ensues "like sweet melody," to use her phrase—"like sweet melody." And this reminds her of Pythagoras and Plato and suggests to her what life on earth might be if good laws were made and observed.

In later life Christine wrote *The Golden Book of Heroines*. It was her masterpiece and her favorite subject. In it she counsels the education of women, and condemns those who suggest that this will lead to unseemly ways. She says, in regard to education, that if boys and girls are taught the same subjects, girls can, as a rule, learn just as well, and just as quickly, as can boys. In truth, her wonderful sense of justice leads Christine to a glimpse of the Promised Land.

We move then from Christine's version of Utopia to the evolution of opportunity for women in this country since the American Revolution for Independence. Have we arrived at Christine's Utopia? Hardly that. But I perceive currents of change which will overcome the historical limitations that have minimized the research challenges and opportunities for women. And I propose here to examine these currents of change in a historical context. The challenges and opportunities for women in science stem from two social developments which are converging at this time. First, science and technology are still expanding their influence throughout the cultural and social fabric; and women are now moving into this arena, particularly in the medical and biological sciences. Second, the role of all of us—men and women—is being questioned today because of the reemergence of skepticism and negativism which borders on anti-intellectualism. The assault is broad-based, and science is included in the sweep. With the "Tiger at the Gates," there is challenge and opportunity for all of us. None can be spared in this arena.

Before developing these two points, it is useful, I think, to identify the origins of the limitations of opportunities for women in this country. To do this we must consider the place of science in early American society, on the one hand, and the role of women in that society on the other. In these origins are the seeds of our discontent. What was science like in the early days of our republic, and what was the role of women? Both were meager, at least so it is recorded by Alexis de Tocqueville, who described our society in 1830, nearly 150 years ago.

A recent edition of De Tocqueville's book *Democracy in America* runs to 705 pages. But only one chapter—six pages long—is devoted to a discussion of the sciences in America. In fact, the picture was so bleak for science—and for the arts—in early American life, that De Tocqueville felt compelled to entitle his chapter, "Why the Example of the Americans does not Prove that a Democratic People can have *No* Aptitude or Taste for Science, Literature, or the Arts." He goes on to admit that few of the civilized nations had made less progress than the United States in the higher sciences. Some Europeans, struck by this fact, considered it the natural and inevitable result of the movement for equality. But as a friend of Democracy, De Tocqueville disagrees, and he gives several pages of reasoned arguments for his view that people living in a democratic society are not necessarily indifferent to science.

Incidentally, I might pause for a moment and say that we find in De Tocqueville's book an unusually perceptive description of those several compartments of science that we now term "research and development" and "technology transfer." For example, he writes that science can be divided into three parts:

"The first comprises the most theoretical principles and the most abstract conceptions whose application is either unknown or very remote.

"The second comprises general truths which, though still based in theory, lead directly and immediately to practical application.

"Methods of application and means of execution make up the third.

"Each of these different aspects of science can be studied apart, although reason and experience teach us that none of them can prosper for long if entirely separated from the other two."

De Tocqueville then states that in America the purely practical side of science is cultivated admirably. But attention is given to the theoretical side only insofar as this is necessary for application. Hardly anyone in the United States, he notes, devotes himself to the essentially theoretical and abstract side of human knowledge.

So on this barren plain, in the early 1800s, there is little scientific opportunity for either men or women, and of the two, certainly even less for women.

But what about women in America at the time De Tocqueville wrote? Three pages in his *Democracy in America* are devoted to a general description of the position of American women in society, two pages are devoted to American women as wives (an interesting omission for a Frenchman is any mention of a mistress), one page is devoted to the trials and tribulations of women on the Western frontier, and two pages are devoted to the education of women. Eight pages in all. And that was that. No women in science, nor indeed in any of the other professions.

Seventy years later, by the turn of the century, opportunity for a life in pure science was still remote for either men or women. Young men left this country for a European education in science only to return and find few opportunities. For example, when the Rockefeller Institute for Medical Research was established in 1901, several of those recruited to its initial staff had returned previously from Europe and had gone into medical practice because there were at that time no research opportunities.

But now, in the last half of our twentieth century, opportunities in science have grown beyond all expectation; surely De Tocqueville would see our recent course as a vindication of his judgment that science *can* flourish in a democracy. Beginning with World War II, both our society and our government made a new commitment to science.

Let me give you an example of this expansion from my own personal experiences. When I entered Case Western Reserve Medical School in 1947, the doors to medical schools were opened more widely than ever before to various segments of our society. The GI Bill that paid the cost of education for veterans was responsible for this egalitarian access to medical training. Many of my classmates had never anticipated a career in medicine. Now this was possible. But these open doors did not swing widely enough. There were only a few women in that entering class in 1947—only six in a class of 78—5 percent. But in September, 1977, at Case Western, this number had risen to 50 women in a class of 143: 35 percent.

So there has been movement and some progress, although we have still not yet reached the millennium. In 1977, throughout the country, women made up only 27 percent of the first-year medical school classes. At least my "alma mammy"—to use F. Scott Fitzgerald's phrase for his Princeton—my "alma mammy," Case Western Reserve, with 35 percent in the freshman class of 1977, is a touch ahead of the national average. Although this represents an improvement over the last thirty years, it does not equal the rapidly closing gap between men and women enrolled in higher education. Some filter, to use Jewel Cobbs' phrase, some filter of a social and cultural nature seems to create a blockade between this large reservoir of women who have received baccalaureate degrees and their enrollment in medical school.

It may be that we should not make too much of an expanding opportunity for women in medicine. Because of cultural and social forces the nature of which escapes our comprehension, there is historical evidence that medicine has been, since early times, one of the few professional guilds open to women. One early and famous woman was no ordinary physician. In ancient Egypt she was a Chief Woman Physician—a sort of *geheimrat* professor. Her name was Peseshet. She was, as I said, one of the famous and eminent ladies of antiquity, and the hieroglyphs representing her name clearly contain the feminine determinant. The glyphs for a doctor are an arrow and a pot and, again, the semicircle symbol representing the feminine determinant. Her status as a chief physician of some importance is indicated by the glyphs representing overseer: an owl and an eye.

Another historical example of women in medicine is recorded by Ms. Kemp-Welsh in her book *Of Six Medieval Women*. She calls attention to the important role of women in the Medical School of Salerno in the Middle Ages. When the Salerno School of Medicine was at its zenith in the eleventh and twelfth centuries, women played a key role both as professors and practitioners. These women left behind them, as evidence of their exceptional learning, treatises that are of interest today because they show medieval methods of medicine. One book of special interest was written by a woman named Trotula. This book was a famous forerunner of a modern text on obstetrics.

Yet, in all fairness, these early examples of women in the forefront of medicine are beacons that shine in a void. So we must examine the extent and the meaning of the progress in the last thirty years which has seen an increase in the percentage of women who enter medicine. Will it last? Will it endure? And perhaps the most crucial question of all: What is the future role in science for these women who now enter medical school with a brisk cadence in step with their male classmates? What opportunities await them? To what medical careers do they now have access? Do they have free access to those first steps that lead to a career in either research or medical practice—in a specialty such as internal medicine or surgery? Again, we need more data. But it is interesting to follow the progress of the 33 women who graduated from Case Western Reserve University School of Medicine in June, 1977. Of these 33 women, at least 17 are interns in university hospitals, including the University Hospitals of Harvard, Yale, Cornell, New York University, and Case Western Reserve. So more than one half of these 33 women have internships in university hospitals. Not bad, actually, not bad at all. These women are on their way. An internship in a university hospital is an essential first step on the ladder of opportunity in either research or a specialty such as internal medicine, surgery, and the like. But we must follow closely the progress of this cohort to determine if they move freely out of internship into either research or specialty practice, or will they be "filtered out" at some further stage in the postgraduate process?

Is this a significant trend, this flow of women into the medical sciences? And is it now a permanent feature of our social fabric? My guess, and of course it is no more than that, is that this trend is indeed irreversible. But the whole enterprise, we must admit, remains a premature creature, and safe delivery will require attentive midwifery.

Now, let me turn to the second historical development, to which I already referred. In my introductory remarks I indicated that these times pose a special challenge and opportunity for women in science as well as men. This challenge and opportunity stem from the erosion of confidence in scholarship. And science is included in this assault on scholarship—an assault that is broadly based. There is current today a general complacency concerning the search for knowledge, abated perhaps by the impact of television's commercialism. Perhaps we already know enough, it is said—or even too much. For some of our youth, there is cynicism or despair, a condemnation of progress and aimless growth. We must recognize the justifiable elements of this social criticism, particularly the criticism of the technological authoritarianism that has gained sovereignty over our lives. And this criticism has proliferated new creeds by new theologians, for example, "small is beautiful," by Mr. Schumacher, who sees the virtues of a latter day postindustrial society; or the maladaptation of the industrial civilization, as proclaimed by the anthropologist Gregory Bateson.

In no way can we ignore these attacks on a society that has been born of the scientific revolution. There is no doubt that we must take heed of these substantive criticisms and reorder, where appropriate, the priorities of our cultural life. At the same time, we must find a way to focus these criticisms on those commercial ventures which exploit science and distort the ethical values of our social fabric. It is when these criticisms include science and the search for knowledge in their sweep that they ferment an antiscientific counterculture.

It is my suspicion that there is really nothing new in this antiscientific counterculture. In discussing these issues, Dr. Joshua Lederberg has said that the historical roots of this ideology are numerous and complexly interwoven, and indeed they are. Certainly the Roman stoics held fast to cultural values in the midst of gross and vulgar materialism. And it is worth noting here that these stoics were among the first to see the justice in equal rights for slaves and women as well as for men.

We have already touched on the low estate of science and the arts in America in the early days of the Republic. De Tocqueville noted America's concern for the application of science rather than the pursuit of knowledge, and the elements which formed such early attitudes surely feed the anti-intellectualism in our time. But the picture is far from bleak. In recent times a prosperous government and an optimistic people have been lavish with resources. One result is a biomedical research enterprise without equal in the world. The people have supported that. They have instructed their government to create this enterprise, and if there are periods when our people falter in their resolve, these depressions will surely be followed by a new burst of enthusiasm in the search for knowledge. Women must play their part in that. The search for knowledge is far too critical and far too central to the salvation of our society for this work to be the domain of any exclusive male club. I believe in that. I believe that conditions are changing and that new destinies are impending. I believe what De Tocqueville stated in his introduction to the first edition of his *Democracy in America*. In this introduction he stated that "the gradual progress of equality is something fated. The main features of this progress are the following: it is universal and permanent; it is daily passing beyond human control and every person, every event, helps it along."

So I see our society changing shape, and I welcome that. I welcome the research challenges and opportunities in science that will be generated out of these changes for men and for women, for black and for white, and for all those other people who represent the pluralism of our society.

The seasons bring new life, new vision, new hope. In spite of snow, winter gives way to spring. Let me end with a quote from Emily Dickinson in the *Belle of Amherst:*

> I've had a curious winter, very swift, sometimes sober. I haven't felt well, much—and March amazes me! I didn't think of it, that's all. I hayed a little for the horse two Sundays ago, but it snowed since. Now—the full circle of seasons—spring has come, though delayed. But I would eat evanescence slowly. The lawn is full of south and the odors tangle, and did you hear today for the first time the river in the tree? Spring is a happiness so beautiful, so unique, so unexpected, that I don't know what to do with my heart.*

---

* Luce, William. 1976. *The Belle of Amherst*, p. 75, Houghton-Mifflin. Courtesy of Dome Productions, 9200 Sunset Blvd., Los Angeles, Calif.

Women in Academe: Why It Still Hurts To Be a Woman in Labor

BERNICE RESNICK SANDLER
Project on the Status and Education of Women
Association of American Colleges
Washington, D.C. 20009

I'M GOING TO TALK about issues in higher education and how they are affected by what happens in Washington. The subtitle of my talk is "These are times that truly try men's souls." Of course, the word "men" applies to "women" as well, for these are times that indeed try our souls as well as those of men.

But since The Academy is an organization dedicated to science, I thought I would start off with something "scientific": a description of the famous Peter Principle, and how it applies to women. As you know, the Peter Principle has been widely hailed as a theoretical explanation of how men get promoted. Essentially, men are promoted upward until they no longer function effectively, i.e., they are promoted upward until they finally reach their level of *incompetence*, at which point they no longer get promoted.

Women, however, and to a large degree, minorities, have been *exempt* from the effects of the Peter Principle because they do *not* get promoted to their level of incompetence; indeed, they hardly get promoted at all. Study after study, whether in academe, industry, or government, shows that women and minorities, no matter how well qualified, simply do not move up the promotion ladder with the same speed as their white male counterparts.

This often means that at any given job level, where both men and women work side by side, the women *seem* to be far more capable than the men—not because they are brighter, but simply because the men who are their equals have been moved upward and above to their level of incompetence, and the men who are at the same level with the women have moved up from below to their level of incompetence. We are all familiar with the female assistant dean who keeps things going, the woman who really runs the office, the middle-management woman who keeps things going for her male boss.

Well, now that we have affirmative action, women, like white men, may finally get promoted to their level of incompetence. This may have profound social impact upon the management of academe and industry, for if women, along with men, get promoted to their levels of incompetence, then who indeed is going to carry out the day-to-day functions, effectively if *everyone* is promoted to his/her level of incompetence?

Such may be the cost of equal opportunity. Women as well as men may finally have the opportunity to make fools of themselves, but that is precisely what equal opportunity is all about. Equality will come when a female "schlemiel" can go as far as a male "schlemiel."* Since women are exempt from the Peter Principle because promotional opportunities "peter out" for them, one might conclude that women are unprincipled. That, however, is not the case.

First, let me tell you some of the things that are going on in Washington; the good news and the bad news. We have had about eight years of affirmative action, depending upon when you start counting. Enforcement of the Executive Order (which prohibits contractors from discriminating in employment) started in 1970, which is about a hundred years ago in terms of progress for females.

Title VII of the Civil Rights Act was amended in 1972 to cover employment in educational institutions. The Equal Pay Act was amended in 1972 to cover executives, professionals, and administrators, including women on faculties of higher learning institutions. Also enacted in 1972 (a banner year for sex-discrimination legislation) was Title IX of the Education Amendments, which covers employment and students in all federally assisted educational programs.

I am not sure if we have just finished seven fat years or seven lean years. Certainly it is a myth that women are being hired in droves, that the problems of discrimination have been solved, and that the major problem is simply a shortage of qualified women. (I am also reminded that the word "qualified" is used in "qualified women," "qualified blacks,"

---

* Yiddish word for an untalented person.

"qualified Hispanics," "qualified minorities." No one is ever looking for a "qualified" man. They would either like "a man to do the job" or a "qualified minority woman." There seems to be some amazement that women are qualified at all.

There has indeed been a slow, slight increase of women at the assistant professor level, at the lecturer and instructor levels. By contrast, the number of women at the level of full professor and associate professor shows very little increase. As a matter of fact, in some instances there has been a drop at the higher levels as the older women in those ranks retire.

There has been a very slight increase in the number of women in administration, although the overall numbers are very small. Most of these women belong to the "Triple A" club; they are Assistant to the Dean, Assistant Dean, or Associate Dean. We have a visible president here and there. However, women, like minorities, are seen as representives of their sex. *One* woman is successful, and everybody says, "Women have made it." Or, conversely, *one* woman fails, and we hear something like "Women just can't cut the mustard." When I hear that kind of comment, I am always tempted to say, "I once had a man work for me, and he was terrible. Therefore, I'll never hire a man again." There is indeed a good deal of truth to the old saw which says a woman has to be twice as good to get half as far and get paid half as much as a man.

The salary gap between men and women faculty continues, despite increases that have gone to women in many institutions. Nevertheless, the gap between men and women on the campus is not getting narrower; it's actually getting wider.

Most promising, I think, is the marked increase of women going back to school and the increase of women at the graduate level, and in medicine, science, and law. Additionally, we have a national policy in place, and that is a major accomplishment. Although there may be some chipping away here and there, there is no way that the Congress can eliminate this legislation. It is probably the most comprehensive national policy in the world regarding discrimination against women in the workplace and women and girls in the schoolroom.

Perhaps the most progress has been made in the area of eliminating overt discrimination. Rules, for example, which used to keep women out simply because they were married to men who worked for the same institution, are becoming a thing of the past.

We have had a shift in the types of discrimination problems. We are going away from overt discrimination, which is far easier to recognize, and is gradually being eliminated. Virtually no one in academe says aloud any more, "I won't hire a woman." I have a letter in my file from a prestigious institution which must be nameless, written about eight years ago to a woman. The letter states, "Your qualifications are indeed excellent, but we already have a woman in this department."

That kind of overt discrimination is disappearing. More and more, it is the subtle forms of discrimination which we are fighting now, and these are harder to identify, far harder to prove, much harder to deal with and to remedy.

One problem is that very often traditional activities are not seen or viewed as discriminatory. For example, private all-male clubs are perhaps places not many of us would have an opportunity to join, but they are indeed clubs where deals are made, where professional information is exchanged. In the state of Maryland we just had a ruling from our Attorney General saying that the Burning Tree Country Club (which is where many past presidents and other notables played golf) can remain an all-male club because it was set up to be predominantly male and therefore is not discriminatory. In Washington, many members of the local educational establishment belong to a particular club where information is often exchanged informally. The two criteria for admission to this place, the Cosmos Club, are intellectual achievement and a particular set of reproductive organs. Lacking the latter, women cannot join and are thus deprived of an important channel of information.

Let me tell you some of the things that are happening with regard to enforcement of the extensive national policy that we now have. It has not been very good. Indeed, it has been so bad that several organizations, spearheaded by the Women's Equity Action League (WEAL), and including the Association for Women in Science, sued HEW because of that agency's poor enforcement of the Executive Order and Title IX, and the women won that suit.

What did we win? We have a series of procedures to ensure that the government is going to investigate complaints, which they were required to do all along but hadn't been doing. Additionally, the government will follow certain time frames; it will notify institutions when complaints are received.

We have a commitment from HEW for more staff. There is an enormous backlog of cases, and it will take two to three years to get rid of it. Some of the cases date back to 1970 and 1971. Certainly justice delayed is justice denied.

As part of the President's reorganization plan there will be a transfer of the Executive Order from HEW to the Department of Labor. The Department of Labor has always had responsibility for Executive Order policy, but HEW had responsibility for the actual investigation. In October, 1978, HEW will lose that power. Women's groups are supporting the change because HEW certainly hasn't been able to do its job very well (what we don't know is whether the Department of Labor will really do it any better). In the spring of 1978, following the settlement of that WEAL suit, there was an increased amount of activity from the Office for Civil Rights at HEW. That office is conducting pre-award reviews, which they had not done before even though they were required to do so. However, women's groups and the Department of Labor are very unhappy with conciliation agreements HEW is developing. Instead of enforcing compliance with the Executive Order and affirmative action requirements, what HEW is coming up with is what the Labor Department calls "plans to plan." For example, institutions that should have been collecting data since 1970 are now saying, "Yes, we plan to collect that data. Yes, we *plan* to have someone in charge of affirmative action."

A major problem with HEW has been policy inconsistency. It is important that the government make consistent decisions and get them out. For instance, under Title IX, athletics is a major issue, and it is important to know whether a particular sport is a contact sport or noncontact sport, because they are treated differently. Contact sports can be limited to men. Soccer is a relatively new sport in schools and it became important to find out whether soccer was or was not a contact sport. Depending on whom one asked at HEW, you could get different answers. One answer was "Soccer is *not* a contact sport." If you didn't like that answer you picked up the phone and called another official, and you got this answer, "Soccer *is* a contact sport." If you wrote to a third official, the letter came back saying, "HEW has not yet decided whether or not soccer is a contact sport." And if you wrote still another official, the letter said "HEW doesn't make that decision; it's up to the individual institution."

Now, this story is not apocryphal; it is true. The National Coalition for Women and Girls in Education went to the Secretary of HEW with this story and obtained a promise from Secretary Califano that OCR would get its policies in order and develop a dissemination system by

September 30, 1977. September 30 has come and gone, and so has March, 1978, and we are still waiting to find out what the policies are (and we hope they would be good policy decisions), and what procedure OCR will use so that people will know what the policies are.

As part of the Carter administration's reorganizing of civil rights enforcement, a plan has been submitted to the Congress that will transfer the Equal Pay Act (currently in the Department of Labor) to the Equal Employment Opportunity Commission (EEOC), which enforces Title VII of the Civil Rights Act. The plan is to make EEOC a superagency and eventually put all of the antidiscrimination employment legislation under EEOC. Women's groups are supporting the transfer of the Equal Pay Act but only lukewarmly, because EEOC in the past has been an agency with many problems. However, Eleanor Holmes Norton, the chairperson of EEOC, is a dynamo and a ray of sunshine in Washington. She has been meeting with women's groups quite regularly. She is shaking up EEOC and trying to make it a viable functioning agency, something long overdue.

Many new issues are emerging. Some of them are going to be settled by the courts, some of them will be settled by the executive branch, and some by Congress. Those settled by the executive branch and the Congress will often be most vulnerable to political pressures from institutions and women's groups. Among the issues to be decided is the question of due process *for institutions* (not due process for individuals): If the government is about to cut off funds from an institution, how should it be done? What constitutes a fair process? I want to point out that *no dollars have ever been withheld because of failure to comply with Title IX; no dollars have ever been withheld under the Executive Order for sex discrimination in institutions.* Despite the myth that the government is pulling money away from institutions, it has never happened.

In a few instances the government has *delayed* federal funds going to institutions but not because of sex discrimination. Money has been delayed only when the institution has refused to provide data or somehow was not in compliance with the *procedural* requirements of the Executive Order.

Another question is whether all funds would get cut off, or merely some. Although the question has never been put to the test, it is nevertheless an interesting one which will probably be ultimately solved by the courts.

Another issue is whether Title IX covers employment as well as students. There are mixed decisions in the courts. In the Romeo case in Michigan, and in the Seattle University case, the courts said Title IX does not cover employment. Both cases are under appeal by the government.

Of critical importance is whether an individual can go into court under Title IX and sue an institution directly. The law does not say specifically whether individuals have a private right to sue. However, Title IX is patterned after Title VI, under which courts have allowed individuals to sue in cases involving race and bilingual discrimination. Similarly, the handicapped have the right to sue; yet the right of women to do the same in cases involving sex discrimination is not at all clear. The cases are mixed. One case is now before the Supreme Court, asking for review of a decision stating that there is no private right to sue under Title IX. If we had the Equal Rights Amendment it would be very clear that women have the right to sue under Title IX.

Having the right to sue, however, does not guarantee good decisions from the courts. Many of the employment suits under the laws are indeed going very badly. Women's groups are no longer encouraging women to sue as a means of dealing with discrimination. It costs a good deal of money; it takes several years; and the chances of winning are not good. The courts have been very reluctant to interfere with academic judgment. Somehow academic judgment is not seen as an employment procedure but as something mysterious and not to be tampered with. The argument is made that academic employment is unique and very different from other employment settings; thus, academic institutions should be treated somewhat differently than other employers. We will see this argument arise again and again in attempts to weaken regulations and legislation that have given academic employees the same rights and protections as other employees. Women's groups oppose having different rules for academic employees; treating people differently usually means less than equal.

Another issue currently before the Supreme Court is the pension question. Women as a group tend to live longer, and thus get smaller pensions than men because their money has to last longer. In a case against Los Angeles where women have been paying more for their pensions, the Circuit Court said that it was discriminatory to have different rates. The Supreme Court has heard the case and is expecting to rule upon it shortly. Although the case involves nonacademic pensions, it will in all likelihood affect academic pensions such as TIAA-CREF.†

---

† *Manhart v. City of Los Angeles,* 46 U.S.L.W. 4347 (April 25, 1978). Subsequent to this speech, the Supreme Court ruled in favor of the women.

The Bakke case is another case everybody is watching. This case involves racial preference in medical school admissions. I want to point out here that the preference given in the Bakke case would be prohibited if it had been an employment case, unless that particular institution had been discriminating previously.

Quotas in admissions for men or women are prohibited by Title IX, so that the Bakke case should not have any impact on women's admissions at all. *Required* affirmative action is not at issue in the Bakke case. What the University of California did was voluntary, and not required by an federal law or regulation.

If the court rules that preference in admissions is illegal, i.e., if Bakke wins, it is likely to be overinterpreted by the press as the end of affirmative action, even though required affirmative action was *not* an issue in the case. I think it will be important to read the decision and see exactly what it says rather than rely on press accounts. It is not likely to be the end of affirmative action no matter what the court rules, but symbolically it may well have that effect.

The blacklash is indeed increasing. The anti-ERA movement, the antiabortion movement, the antiregulation movement, and a piecemeal chipping away of Title IX are all indications of increased backlash and increasingly well-organized backlash. Some of it occurs because women have indeed been successful. The backlash is a compliment to women, although it's a compliment we could well do without.

Some of our early successes (such as getting all that legislation through the Congress) were based not on an understanding of the issues but simply "let's give the little ladies their due." Many people did not think through the implications of the legislation in terms of a whole host of activities. For example, nobody realized that Title IX was going to cover sports. People did not think antidiscrimination would affect pensions or discrimination on marital status.

The backlash seems to come from three basic groups. Although what follows may be somewhat oversimplified, it may help put the problem of backlash into a more orderly context: One group consists of the traditionalists. Our society is changing very rapidly because of increased technology, and other reasons as well. As society develops new ways of dealing with the stresses caused by such changes, it's a time of uneasiness for many people who would like to return to an easier, more simple time.

The women's movement, which is in part *a response to the changes in society*, is instead seen as the *cause* of many changes. Thus some of the backlash, particularly against ERA, abortion, and other feminist goals comes from those who believe that such notions threaten the very fabric of our society. The arguments are virtually identical to those used to oppose women suffrage more than 50 years ago: the whole family would fall apart if women got the vote, and now the whole family will fall apart if the ERA is passed, despite the fact that the Equal Rights Amendment would do much to strengthen the family.

A second group consists of the anti-Washington, antiregulationists. These people also have difficulty in accepting change, but the language is different. They believe in equal rights, they are all for affirmative action, but they don't want Washington to do anything to accomplish it. They want the federal dollars but without any strings attached. They believe that affirmative action and nondiscrimination can be achieved best on a voluntary basis.

They are concerned with the *effect* of the law, particularly when it requires that procedures change. After all, they know best which procedures work in academe. These people also talk about the vast amounts of paper work, and I will say that some of these complaints are legitimate. However, they rarely talk about the benefits of having adequate data for sound management and fiscal planning, the benefits of having due process for employees as a result of federal action, or the necessity to develop procedures that truly insure that all persons are hired and promoted on the basis of merit.

Currently in place is a group called the Sloan Commission, funded by the Sloan Foundation, which is looking at the impact of federal regulations on the academic community. Women's groups are very concerned that that commission will look at the difficulties which regulations pose to institutions without looking at the benefits that occur to institutions, and the benefits that occur when discrimination is ended.

The third group of opponents can be called the antiaffirmative action crowd. These are people who are convinced that goals and quotas are identical, that universities and colleges are giving sweeping preference to women and minorities despite contradictory data. It's beyond the scope of this paper to discuss the differences between quotas and goals, but certainly confusing the two has hurt a good deal.

Backlash never occurs without creating an "antibacklash," and so there is some good news to tell. Women are banding together all around the country. I read recently that in Cleveland (which is hardly considered a bastion of change), there were more than 50 women's groups started last year. That tell us something about what's going on in the nation.

Similarly, women in Washington are banding together. There is a National Coalition for Women and Girls in Education, which includes traditional groups such as the American Association for University Women, the Girl Scouts, Business and Professional Women, the League of Women Voters, my project at the Association of American Colleges, and the project on women at the American Council on Education.

We meet with people as high up as the Secretary of HEW and the Department of Labor, as well as people who do a lot of the work at lower levels. The Coalition monitors federal activities and has been responsible for many changes in government (not as much as we would like, but certainly less would have happened if the Coalition had not been in existence).

One of the trends that has not been written about is that the women's groups are working informally with the traditional civil rights groups. Increasingly there is a concern for minority women's issues, and increasingly minority women are concerned with women's issues. Black, Hispanic, handicapped, and women's groups worked together successfully to turn around a proposed regulation that would have substantially weakened enforcement procedures.

Coalitions on women's issues are springing up all over Washington. The education coalition is one of the oldest and best organized. There are two health coalitions: one on pregnancy discrimination in employment; and on women in development, women in the military, women in employment, women in federal appointments, the abortion issues, and the Equal Rights Amendment. Women who work on Capitol Hill have a caucus. The congresswomen themselves now have a women's caucus. The women appointed by the Carter administration have also begun to meet and exchange information. There are more women in government than previously, but not enough. They have been helpful when policy is being developed because they give us access to information and they do indeed have impact on policy.

Women are also watching the Congress. The Women's Educational Equity Act, which provides money for demonstration projects, is coming up for reauthorization. Women are trying to get it funded at a much higher level than previously so that money will be available for technical assistance to institutions.

Senator Kennedy has introduced a bill to increase the number of women in science. When he introduced that bill he noted that in 1920 the number of women working as scientists and engineers was about 10 percent. Fifty-seven years later, years of supposed progress, the percentage of women working as scientists and engineers is still about 10 percent.

Another very serious issue is nondiscriminatory female participation in athletics. The transition period for athletics and physical education in secondary schools and colleges ended July 21, 1978. We expect some last-ditch attempts to amend the legislation to exempt revenue-producing sports in some manner.

Sports involve big dollars, big power, and all the stereotypes about how women are or ought to be. Sports are very important because it is in sports that men have learned leadership. Women and girls need to learn the same kinds of things that men have learned—teamwork; learning to play with someone who is good even though you don't particularly like the player; learning how to set a goal; developing strategies for meeting that goal; learning how to persevere in the face of failure; learning how to win; and learning how to lose. Finally, in many ways the sports issue could be seen as a cutting issue, because it will teach our young women so much of what they need to learn.

Over the past few years one of the major changes has been in the legitimacy of women's issues. When I get depressed I like to look back a few years and acknowledge changes that have occurred. For example, few public officials make nasty cracks about women any more in public. I don't know what they do behind closed doors and I really don't care, but in public they are very careful to say, "Some of my best friends are women," or "my daughter is going to law school," or "My wife is going back to school." Even when men oppose us they are very careful to say, "I'm not against women's rights, but. . . ." Women increasingly are being seen as a genuine advocacy group. We are beginning to act like a power group, and we need to act that way even more.

There's much more awareness of women's rights, and we are beginning to see the institutionalization of these issues. In HEW there is a Women's Action Program which looks at women's issues; there is the Secretary's Advisory Committee on the Rights and Responsibilities of Women for HEW; there is a presidentially appointed National Advisory Council on Women's Educational Programs; there is a Women's Program staff in the Office of Education looking at the role of women in the department; and there are sex discrimination provisions in the Vocational Education Amendment of 1976 and in the Career Education Act.

Despite a lot of lip service the most active opponent of affirmative action has been the world of higher education. Universities have found it easier to support programs for minorities (and sometimes not very well), partly because the minorities are fewer in number. If educational discrimination and the educational handicaps of minorities were to disappear tomorrow, minorities would rarely represent, in the long-range future, more than 10–15 percent of academe, assuming that all discrimination had ended. Because women are a larger group, we represent much more of a threat. If women were given equal opportunity we might be 50 percent of the power structure within academe, and that makes many people uncomfortable. Indeed, we threaten the relationships of men with their wives, with their lovers, with their sisters, with their daughters, for there is one of us in almost every house.

Yes, there is increased backlash. Yes, there is increased opposition. Nevertheless, women across the country and men, too, show increasing support of women's issues whether the question is, "Would you vote for a woman president?" or "Are you sympathetic to women's rights?"

Even with increased backlash there is no turning back the clock, and progress goes forward at the same time that the backlash increases. We may indeed lose on a few issues. I'm worried about the Equal Rights Amendment and I'm worried about the anti-abortion backlash.

But we women and men are concerned about the lives that our daughters will lead. (One of the best potential indicators of support from men is if they have daughters.)

We are embarked on a long journey that will take perhaps a hundred years or more—a journey that will lead to a more decent world, where opportunities and options in education and work are related to capacity and potential and not to the particular kinds of reproductive organs that one was born with.

I want to close with a quotation which has become my favorite. I've been using it on almost every speech I give. It's a newly "discovered" revelation from the Bible; it was supposedly discovered by a woman archaeologist, with an all-woman team of archaeological students, and it is now being passed around the country. I want to share it with you because it symbolizes the new mood of women. Though we may get discouraged, it still symbolizes what's going to go on:

And they shall beat their pots and pans into printing presses,
And weave their cloth into protest banners,
Nations of women shall lift up their voices with nations of other women,
Neither shall they accept discrimination anymore.

That may sound apocryphal, but I suspect it may yet prove to come from the Book of Prophets, for what women are learning is the politics of power; they are learning indeed that the hand that rocks the cradle can also rock the boat. And the campus, and Washington, and the nation, and the world will never be the same again.

Women in Science-Related Activities

PHILIP H. ABELSON
Editor, Science
American Association for the Advancement of Science
Washington, D.C. 20005

A LARGE PROPORTION of the young people of this country are attending colleges and universities. Most of them hope or believe that the experience will confer great economic and other advantages on them, no matter what courses they take. However, many of the graduating seniors, both men and women, are sure to be disappointed. In some fields, such as the humanities, job opportunities are very limited. Prospects in the sciences are much better. Potentialities in the physical sciences, and especially engineering, are particularly favorable. Today, engineers are avidly recruited, and their starting salaries are high. The starting annual salary of a Bachelor of Science in Chemical Engineering is typically more than $17,000, and that of a petroleum engineer, over $18,000.

Even among the favored professions, opportunities are not widespread. Graduates with degrees in the biological sciences are less sought after than those with degrees in the physical sciences. The outlook for teachers is poor at all levels.

Secondary education in this country seems to be in process of a strong swing toward emphasis on reading, writing, and arithmetic. Meanwhile, the teaching of science is likely to be a casualty. I have been informed that curtailments of science requirements are being made. Thus, the present status of secondary school science teachers is likely to get worse.

The outlook in higher education is not much better. During the 1960s there was a real expansion of science faculties at the universities. At that time many young men received tenure. The expansion has ceased, and there is little turnover in faculties. Beyond that, faculties at many of the major universities have resisted giving tenure to women.

Betty Vetter, of the Scientific Manpower Commission, has provided some statistics about proportions of women on university faculties. These figures show that despite Equal Employment Opportunity legislation, the universities have not significantly changed their behavior. Thus, in 1972-73 at public universities, six percent of full professors were women. Three years later the fraction was still six percent. At private universities in 1972-73, six percent of full professors were women, but in 1975-76 that figure had dropped to five percent.

Betty Vetter also was a source of a striking statistic with respect to chemistry faculties. Today, women constitute an increasing fraction of graduates receiving doctorates in chemistry. This has now reached 15 percent. Although the women tend to rank higher scholastically than the men, their performance has not been correspondingly recognized. For example, the chemistry department at Berkeley, with its 60 professors, includes no tenured women professors. There are 27 other major universities with faculties of 28 or more professors that have no tenured women. These universities are turning out large numbers of women Ph.D.s. Yet they claim they can find no suitable women applicants for professorships. It would appear that major universities have been able to disregard Equal Employment Opportunity legislation as far as tenured faculty is concerned. They comply with respect to blue-collar employees.

Recently, a top-ranking university encountered trouble regarding its personnel policies. It had not one tenured woman on its faculty. A woman in the English Department was denied tenure. She sued. The spotlight was suddenly on the university. Its budget is heavily dependent on federal government grants and contracts. There followed a sudden change in university perceptions of the desirability of having women faculty members. On the other hand, no contracts were canceled and the university was not penalized for past misdeeds. As long as the game is played that way, most universities will be slow to change their practices.

The situation is different in industry. In 1973, the American Telephone and Telegraph Company came under heavy pressure with respect to Equal Employment Opportunities. As a result, the Bell System agreed to give 26,000 women and minority employees immediate wage increases amounting to $36 million in the first 12 months. Another $15 million was distributed to cover past claims of job discrimination.

Other companies, such as United Airlines, the National Broadcasting Company, and the Reader's Digest Association, also have made settlements of more than $10 million each to women and minority employees who had complained of job discrimination. Note that in contrast to the universities, industry has been subject to substantial retroactive penalties.

Managements are not happy at the prospect of bad publicity combined with financial penalties. In one company, the president directed his chiefs of divisions to make a special effort to recruit women for professional and managerial jobs. For a while nothing happened. The chiefs reported that no qualified women were available. The president responded by letting it be known that when the performance of managers was being judged, important weight would be given as to whether they had succeeded in recruiting competent women. A miracle occurred. Suddenly many qualified women could be found.

To many people, and especially to young men and women, the thought of having anything to do with industry is repulsive. In part, this is because students are brainwashed at the universities. Professors too often bolster their own egos by denigrating those who are not professors. They also spread the word that scientists of quality stay in the university. Only second-class, beyond-the-pale creatures go to industry. To my knowledge that kind of talk has been going on for at least forty years. If there is any difference, women are influenced by it more than men. Some of them have spoken of clanking machinery, dirty and vulgar laborers.

If they were to visit Bell Laboratories and major research centers such as those of General Electric, IBM, and DuPont, they would come away with a different impression. Beyond that, if they looked into the facilities for research work, they usually would find that in general these major laboratories have available better equipment and better support staff than do universities. Finally, they would be free of the hassle that today goes into getting federal grants. That is not to say that conditions are perfect, but rather to make the point that they are not inferior to those of academia.

I do not pretend to have comprehensive knowledge of industrial laboratories and industrial personnel practice. I have, however, visited a number of the major industrial research installations and have had opportunities to gauge the quality of their work. In preparation for this occasion, I talked to key research managers at Bell Labs, General Electric, IBM, Exxon, and General Foods. I spoke with other people at these companies knowledgable about personnel policies. In addition, I had conversations with women actively participating in industrial research and development.

Among the managers there was unanimity on two major points. All said that the performance of women in engineering and scientific tasks was as good as that of men. In fact, they said there was no difference. All said they were trying to increase the number of women professionals on their staffs.

The one minor negative comment was that women were not as mobile as men. This is understandable when the woman is married, but I was told that it also is true of single women. There are, of course, major differences among companies and occupations with respect to the need to transfer. Engineers are more likely to be moved about than are scientists. Among the most mobile groups are the earth scientists and engineers.

There is direct and indirect evidence that the companies seem eager to improve their practices regarding employment opportunities. For example, there is increasing willingness to arrange for part-time work. There are special educational opportunities. Exxon has sponsored a club of women for after-hours discussion of the business environment and the sharing of learning experiences.

Much of the effort at industrial laboratories involves teamwork. This is especially true at General Electric, where the emphasis is on engineering. But it is also true at the Bell Labs, where an effort is made to have smooth and continuing interactions between research and applications. Thus, one has the impression that people-people interaction is more important in industrial research and development than it is in academic research. When a number of people are involved, the individual's potential contributions will be minimized unless he or she is willing to speak up. I was informed that the management of the Bell Labs provides assertiveness training for women employees.

There are substantial differences among the various companies, arising in part from different product lines but also from different policies. The organization that comes closest to having an academic environment is Bell Labs. Its primary goal is to improve communication, and the big payoff is in better, cheaper equipment. However, good research is recognized and rewarded. At General Electric there is less interest in research. The emphasis is on engineering.

The women scientists and engineers to whom I talked were engaged in a wide variety of projects. They also tended to have had experience in a number of different fields.

At the Bell Labs a woman physicist had worked in materials science, re-entry physics, plasma physics, and chemistry of the lower atmosphere. Another had worked on the degradation of polymeric materials. Another had done extremely important work in experimental development of low-loss glass fibers. Another woman who was trained as a organic chemist has been doing research on semiconductors, seeking more efficient light detectors. Another woman told of the many ways in which mathematicians interact at the Bell Labs. They participate in projects in psychology, operations research, marketing, chemistry environmental studies, engineering, and physics. One of the young women had a Ph.D. degree in electrical engineering, conferred in 1974. She has been working on means of improving the performance of the telephone network during periods of overload, such as at Christmas time or on Mother's Day. Her work involves computer simulation of how the network performs and study of the effects resulting from addition of various types of equipment.

Most of the women I talked to at General Electric were engineers. They were proud to be engineers, and they enjoyed participation in team efforts. The one scientist I talked with was an organic chemist. She had gone to G.E. in 1973 to provide nuclear magnetic resonance analyses. She is now acting manager at the Analytical Branch of General Electric. About 40 people work for her, including ten Ph.D.s in thirteen laboratories. The equipment involved includes electron microprobes, transmission electron microscopes, and various kinds of equipment for elemental analysis. She must interact with a host of different people, advising various people from other divisions of the company how best to solve their analytical problems.

I asked her if she had had any problems with male subordinates. She said no. She had known everyone before she took the job. She said, "When people know you they will judge you on your capabilities." When asked to compare academic and industrial work, she said: "There is a broader array of opportunities in industry. People wind up in completely different fields." She went on to say, "People have to look for their own specific opportunities. You can't sit down and wait for people to bring them to you. You don't get unearned favors."

The research director at General Foods told of a different set of challenges. The staff there includes microbiologists, enzymologists, protein chemists, food scientists, toxicologists, physical scientists, mathematicians, and engineers. The staff has been growing at the rate of 15–20 percent per year, thus creating new positions. He also suggested that there might be openings at other companies engaged in food processing, including General Mills, the Kellogg Company, Ralston Purina, and Proctor and Gamble. He said that within his own company it had long been the policy to recruit women. In the central research laboratory, about six of the twenty scientists in the very senior grades are women.

My brief survey leaves me with the impression that many openings exist in industry for qualified women. The atmosphere and objectives are generally different from those at the universities. There is more need to be prepared to interact with others. There are basically more opportunities for interdisciplinary work. There are more occasions to display managerial talents. The value systems are quite different.

The federal government is another major employer of scientists and engineers. In addition, local jurisdictions have been increasing their reliance on technically trained people.

The performance of the federal government with respect to equal employment opportunities has been uneven. Citizens outside Washington seem to have the impression that their government operates in a unified, coordinated way. While the hundreds of different agencies and other entities may give lip service to unity, in practice there are as many employment policies as there are agencies.

Consider the example set by the Congress, which enacts the laws that others must follow. The Congress voted itself special privileges. It is exempt from the Equal Employment Opportunities legislation.

The example set by the Carter administration is different. A determined effort has been made to recruit women and minorities. In the area of research and development, perhaps the most important post is in the management of nearly 100 laboratories and development centers, with a total annual budget of millions of dollars. Dr. Ruth Davis was chosen to direct this effort.

Dr. Davis is a well-recognized expert on computers. She was among the pioneers in the field. She is also broadly knowledgeable about other areas of electronics. She has no problems in dealing with men. She is at all times poised, and her judgments are well considered and sound.

Prospects for women trained in biology are not so good as those for women with a degree in the physical sciences and engineering. A major source of opportunities for them is the federal government. The most prestigious federal organization in the biomedical field is the National Institutes of Health. Its policies have been relatively favorable for women. A recent survey of employment at NIH showed that 1,434 people there had a status comparable to that of tenured faculty. That is, the individuals had either the rank of commander or above in the Public Health Service, or a civil service rating of GS-13 and about. The starting salary for a GS-13 is $26,022. There are 175 women at NIH having the rank of GS-13 or better.

Customarily, scientists are chosen for GS-13 rating when they are about five years beyond the Ph.D. degree. At present at NIH there are 369 postdoctoral and nontenured employees who will be feeding the GS-13 pool. Of these, 94, or about 25 percent are women. Among young bioscientists generally, women constitute 16.6 percent of the total. Thus it appears that NIH now is recruiting more of its share.

The picture at NIH is not all roses. Critics point out that the proportion of women in top management is low. However, when I queried one of the most successful women scientists at NIH, she told me that she had no interest in taking on the headaches of management. It was more fun to do research.

Many of the opportunities for women in science-related activities are in circumstances other than those of academia, industry, or government.

One example that is generally known is the medical profession. Medical schools have substantially increased the proportion of women in their classes. A decade ago the fraction of women in the entering class was nine percent. In 1977 the fraction had risen to 25.6 percent. Experience has demonstrated that women are as successful as men in completing medical school.

Betty Vetter has told me of a program at the University of Miami for converting Ph.D.s to M.D.s. The conversion is accomplished in two years. The program started modestly with fourteen Ph.D.s from the physical sciences. The program has been a great success. There have been no dropouts.

One of the rapidly expanding fields is the legal profession. Increasingly the law is dealing with issues that involve science and technology. An individual with training in the sciences and with a law degree enjoys many opportunities. Recently I talked with a woman who had obtained a B.S. degree in chemistry thirteen years ago. She had decided that she did not wish to spend five years getting a Ph.D. degree. She was then not sure that she would enjoy academic life. She worked for nine years in industry, but with her level of education had only limited responsibilities. One of her supervisors encouraged her to go to law school, which she did. By December of her third year she was besieged with job offers. At present she is a patent attorney, but she has virtually an infinite number of interesting options including positions leading toward top management.

Another set of opportunities for women scientists lies in the publishing field. Quantitatively the area is probably not as large as some that have been mentioned. However, because I have had some experience in the field and a chance to observe women engaged in it, I will provide some impressions. At *Science* women are engaged in all aspects of the production of the magazine. Each week we prepare for publication and print more material than that which appears in *Time* or *Newsweek*. About half our reporters are women. The news and comment editor is a woman. The style editors are women, as is the production manager.

Our chief style editor had her Ph.D. degree in bacteriology many years ago. After working a few years she dropped out of science to mother a family. When the children were grown, she came to *Science*. She enjoys her work, and we are delighted to have her.

One of our best reporters for Research News obtained a Ph.D. degree in biochemistry about ten years ago. She was married and went with her husband to a place where only a second-rate teaching position was available. Her talents were not appropriately used. Since she came to *Science* she has enjoyed a much more interesting and satisfying life. She has reported on important developments in cancer and heart research and is co-author of two books. Today she is one of the best informed people of this country with respect to biomedical research, and she receives recognition and a good salary.

During the course of preparing this presentation I talked at length with about twenty professional women. It was an interesting, rewarding experience. I was left with the impression that they were enjoying life and finding much satisfaction in their work. My guess is that as time goes on they will be joined by others who will find similar satisfaction.

PART II. The State of the Art: Current Status of Women in The Sciences

Women in Physics and Astronomy

VERA KISTIAKOWSKY
*Department of Physics
Massachusetts Institute of Technology
Cambridge, Massachusetts 02139*

THE EARLY YEARS

THE SITUATION of women scientists today is much more understandable when viewed from the perspective of history. In the United States, this history begins with a botanist, Jane Colden (1724-66), but there was a gap of nearly a century before our second well-known woman scientist, the astronomer Maria Mitchell (1818-89), became internationally recognized. Higher education, unavailable to women in the eighteenth century, began to include them as the need for schoolteachers and the words of the first feminists touched the educational world; simultaneously, science ceased to be an avocation for the well-to-do and began to be taught and practiced in the universities. After the Civil War, college education of women blossomed and Maria Mitchell was followed at Vassar by her student Mary Whitney (1847-1921), also an internationally recognized astronomer. At the Harvard College Observatory, Williamina P. Fleming (1857-1911) was followed by Annie J. Cannon (1863-1941) and Henrietta S. Leavitt (1868-1921),[1] a concentration of internationally recognized female scientific talent, due to the influence of Professor Edward C. Pickering, director of the Observatory, who was also important in the career of one of the few notable women physicists of this period, Sarah F. Whiting (1847-1927).[1] She took a physics course with Pickering while he was still at M. I. T., which strongly influenced her later work at Wellesley. Only one woman, however, was among the physicists who were awarded stars indicating international recognition in the 1906 to 1921 editions of "American Men in Science": Margaret E. Maltby (1845-1926), a Barnard professor.

Margaret Rossiter[2] has given us a very detailed picture of the situation at the beginning of the twentieth century. Two and six-tenths percent of physicists and 6.4 percent of astronomers were women. Approximately half these women (11/23 of women physicists and 11/21 of women astronomers) received their undergraduate education at women's colleges, and virtually all the women physicists (21/23) were employed in women's colleges at some points in their careers. The majority of both women physicists and astronomers was employed in academia (18/23 and 21/21), a situation which was also true for the men in these fields, but half the academic women astronomers (10/20) were employed in observatories, and not as professors, and most of the professors were at women's colleges, not universities. Three of the 23 women physicists in Rossiter's study were secondary-school teachers, whereas this was true of none of the men. It is also interesting to note that with the exception of two (10 percent) of the astronomers, none of the physicists or astronomers was married.[2] Pursuit of a scientific career required dedication and determination that precluded marriage, which, until the 1920s, generally enforced a subordinate role for the woman.

At the end of the nineteenth century a Ph.D. degree began to be a requirement for professional recognition. In Rossiter's sample, 65 percent of women physicists (vs. 71 percent of men) and 24 percent of women astronomers (vs. 41 percent of men) had Ph.D.s.[2] The participation of women in these fields after 1920 is closely linked to the doctorate degree awards, and one may trace this through the next five decades. FIGURE 1 shows that the number of physics doctorates awarded to women increased steadily from 1920 to 1969, but the percentage of participation dropped from the 20s to the 50s because of the more rapid increase in the number of men. It is interesting to note that in 1920, nineteen percent of the physics doctorates were awarded to women (4/21), whereas in the 50s this was true of only 1.8 percent of the doctorates.[4] The numbers in astronomy fluctuated about 15 up to the 1960s and then rose to 37. However, the percentages dropped from 27 percent in the 20s to 6.5 percent in the 1950s. The large increase in the 1940s is due to a small total number of astronomy doctorates, presumably associated with the war years. The decreases in percentages can be traced to the breaking of the first wave of feminism with the achievement of suffrage and the changes brought about by the 1920s. Neither The Depression nor World War II was a good climate for increased scientific participation by women, and the back-to-the-home enthusiasm following the war was devastating.

The renaissance of feminism in the late 1960s led to, among other things, a desire to understand and improve the situation, and this

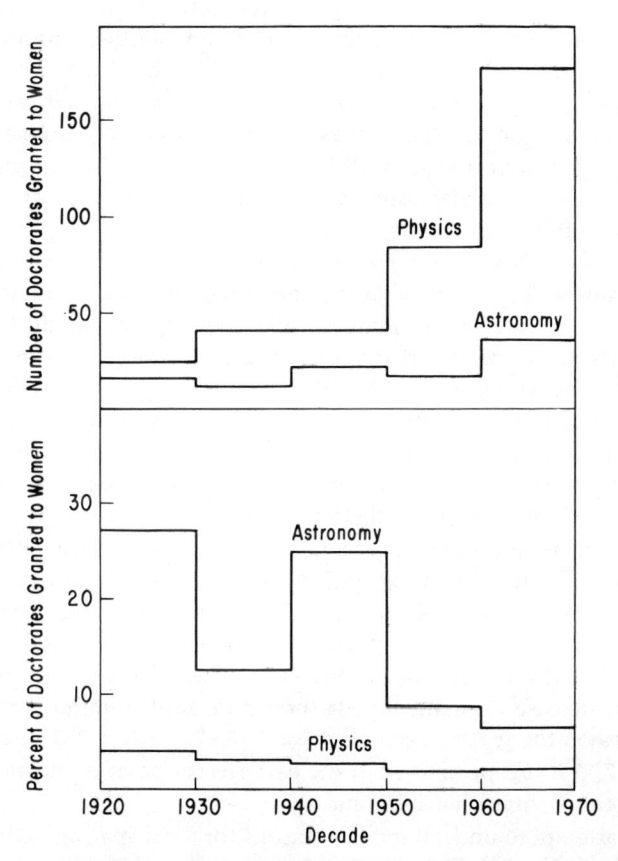

FIGURE 1. The number and percentage of doctorates granted to women in physics and astronomy in each decade from 1920 to 1969.[3]

resulted in studies on the participation of women by committees of the American Physical Society and the American Astronomical Society in the early 1970s.[4,5] Both studies described a situation that was little changed from that described by Rossiter's study for the period before 1920. Women physicists were still employed mainly in academia and still were found more frequently in the lower faculty ranks and nonfaculty positions and at the less prestigious institutions. Both studies found that a larger percentage of women than of men suffered from involuntary unemployment and underemployment and that the average salaries of women were lower. An interesting difference from the situation before 1920 is that the majority of women physicists and astronomers in the studies was married, although the percentage of unmarried was greater than the norm. The conclusion was drawn that overt discrimination had played an important role in the differences observed between women and men, as well as prevalent societal attitudes and practical problems of combining career and marriage.

The early 1970s were marked by the beginnings of affirmative action, and it is interesting to see what changes have occurred in the last seven years. FIGURE 2 shows the number and percentage of the doctorates in physics and astronomy/astrophysics awarded to women in this period, as well as the averages for the 1960–69 period. Because of the small numbers, the data for astronomy and astrophysics are not presented separately, and because of the overlap between these fields, astrophysics is presented with astronomy rather than as part of physics. (Astrophysics was recorded as a separate doctoral field for only a few years before 1970.[3]) The numbers and percentages for physics exhibit overall increases, the difference between 1975 (5.0 ± 0.7 percent) and 1976 (4.0 ± 0.6 percent) not being statistically significant. In astronomy/astrophysics, the numbers are approximately constant until 1975 and 1976, when there is a significant increase, whereas the percentages drop and then increase dramatically. It should be kept in mind that the uncertainties on the percentages are large (in 1975, 9.2 ± 2.6 percent, and in 1976, 7. 3 ± 2.2 percent), but the patterns for physics and astronomy do seem to be somewhat different.

In an attempt to understand the reasons for participation patterns, one can ask whether participation by women is related to the overall popularity of a field. TABLE 1 presents the percentages of doctorates in the various subfields of physics awarded to women in 1960–69 and 1970–76, as well as the percentages of all doctorates awarded for work in those subfields. Astronomy/astrophysics are also shown, and the total number of doctorates awarded per year in astronomy increased by 139 percent, whereas that in physics increased by 47 percent. The average percentage of degrees in physics awarded to women rose by 79 percent, whereas that in astronomy/astrophysics remained constant. The change in physics is seen to be due to increases in most subfields without any signficant correlation with the changes in popularity. The percentage of astrophysics doctorates awarded to women is seen to lie between those for physics and astronomy, and this gradation can be explained by the

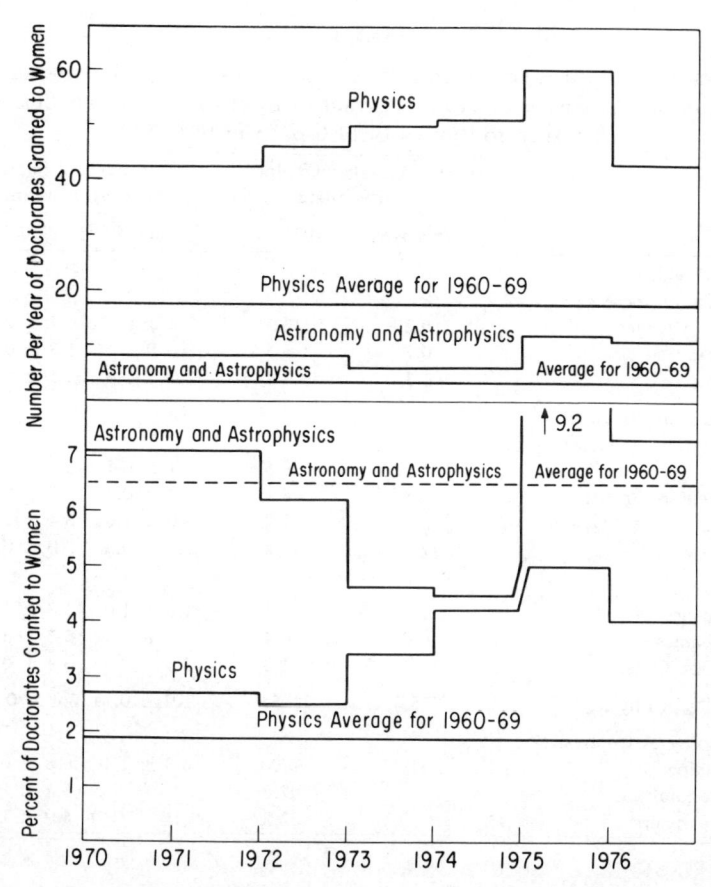

FIGURE 2. The number and percentage of doctorates granted to women in physics and astronomy/astrophysics in each year from 1970-71 to 1976-77, compared with the average values for 1960-69.[3,6]

greater attraction that descriptive fields, rather than the purely quantitative, have had for women. Certainly in the past the so-called "hard" sciences have been considered unfeminine in this country, and it is well documented that there have been powerful societal pressures on young women to avoid such studies. The recent increase in the percentage of physics doctorates awarded to women apparently does not come from an increase in the number of women entering graduate study, but rather

TABLE 1

Percentage (Number) of Doctorates Awarded Subfields of Physics and in Astonomy/Astrophysics and Percentage of Doctorates in Given Subfield Awarded to Women in 1960-69[3] and 1970-76[6]

	Percentage of Total in Subfield		Percentage of Subfield Awarded to Women	
	1960-69[3]	1970-76[6]	1960-69[3]	1970-78[6]
Physics Fields in which Participation Increased				
Physics, General	6.2%	12.5%	3.2 ± 0.7%	4.4 ± 0.6%
Plasma	0.7	5.5	0	1.3 ± 0.5
Optics	1.1	2.4	2.0 ± 1.4	2.6 ± 1.1
Physics Fields in which Participation Decreased				
Atomic	11.0	9.6	2.1 ± 0.5	2.4 ± 0.5
Elementary Particle	16.8	14.1	2.3 ± 0.4	3.8 ± 0.5
Fluids	3.0	1.7	3.0 ± 1.0	3.1 ± 1.4
Nuclear	17.1	12.8	1.6 ± 0.3	3.0 ± 0.5
No Change				
Acoustics	1.0	1.1	1.0 ± 1.0	1.8 ± 1.3
Mechanics	0.7	0.4	0	5.3 ± 3.7
Physics, Other	11.2	11.3	2.3 ± 0.5	3.4 ± 0.6
All Fields of Physics	(9285)	(9584)	1.9 ± 0.14	3.4 ± 0.19
Astronomy/Astrophysics				
Combined	(538)	(900)	6.5 ± 1.1	6.6 ± 0.9
Astronomy		47.8		8.4 ± 1.4
Astrophysics		52.2		4.9 ± 1.0

from a greater percentage who persevere to the doctorate level. In the past, women were twice as likely to stop with a master's degree,[4] perhaps perceiving no reason for continuing in the limited employment possibilities open to them.

TABLE 2 gives the numbers and percentages of doctoral scientists employed in physics and astronomy in 1971, 1973, and 1975 who were women. Both numbers and percentages have risen steadily. It is seen that somewhat more of the women were foreign citizens than was true of the men. TABLE 3 gives the employment status for these scientists in 1971 and 1973. In both surveys, the percentages of women who were part-time or unemployed are significantly greater than those for men, and the

TABLE 2

PERCENTAGE (NUMBER) OF DOCTORAL SCIENTISTS EMPLOYED IN THE FIELDS
OF PHYSICS AND ASTRONOMY WHO WERE WOMEN, BY
CITIZENSHIP AND YEAR OF SURVEY

	1971[4]	1973[7]	1975[7]
Native-Born U.S. Citizens		2.1 (281)	2.4 (334)
Foreign-Born U.S. Citizens		2.1 (39)	2.4 (50)
Foreign Citizens		3.5 (59)	3.0 (46)
Citizenship Unknown		4.0 (6)	4.9 (10)
Total	2.1 (347)	2.3 (385)	2.5 (440)

latter percentages are greater in 1973 than in 1971. Furthermore, if one combines the percentages of those unemployed seeking employment and part-time seeking full-time, it is seen that in 1973, 14 percent of the women (vs. 2.5 percent of the men) were looking for jobs. Comparisons of the data for doctoral scientists and engineers in all fields in 1973 and 1975 carried out by Maxfield et al.[9] and by Gilford and Snyder[7] have indicated a substantial decrease in the unemployment rate for women in this period. The percentages of doctoral scientists and engineers desiring but not holding full-time employment in science and engineering were

TABLE 3

PERCENTAGE (NUMBER) OF MEN AND WOMEN DOCTORAL PHYSICISTS AND
ASTRONOMERS BY EMPLOYMENT STATUS IN 1971[4] AND 1973[8]

Employment Status	1971[4] Men	1971[4] Women	1973[8] Men	1973[8] Women
Full-time	95%	73%	94%	66%
Part-time	2.0	16	1.7	16
Seeking full time			0.8	7
Not seeking			0.9	9
Unemployed	1.3	9	2.1	13
Seeking employment	1.2	5	1.7	7
Not seeking	0.1	4	0.4	6
Retired, other	1.5	2	2.6	5
Total Number	(16,284)	(347)	(17,481)	(471)

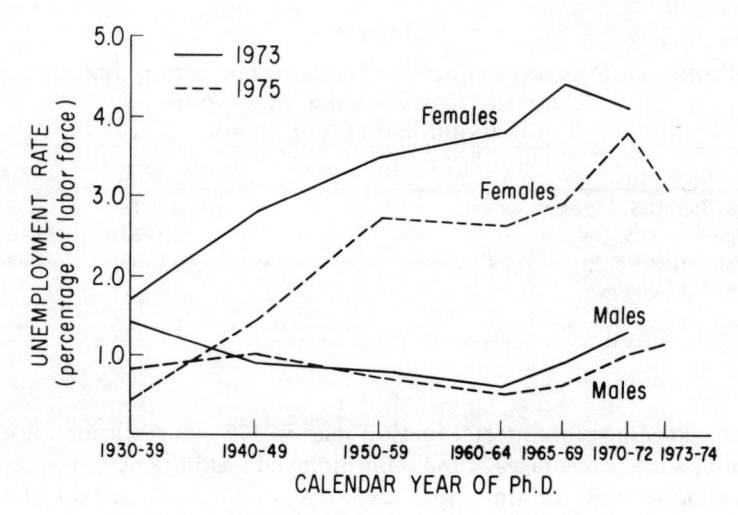

FIGURE 3. Unemployment rates by calendar year of Ph.D. for male and female Ph.Ds.[9]

1.8 percent and 1.6 percent for men and 8.8 percent and 6.4 percent[7] for women in 1973 and 1975, respectively. Thus, in spite of the decrease, the percentage of women seeking employment remained four times that for men. FIGURE 3, taken from the Maxfield et al.[9] study, gives the percentage of the science and engineering labor force that was unemployed and seeking employment as a function of calendar year of doctorate. It is interesting to note that the largest involuntary umemployment rates pertain for women three to five years away from their doctorates and thus presumably just completing their first postdoctoral positions.

TABLE 4 gives the distribution of men and women physicists and astronomers with respect to type of employer. In both fields the percentage of women in educational institutions is greater than that of men, and the 1973 percentages are greater for astronomy than for the combined fields. The percentages in educational institutions for the combined fields decrease between 1971 and 1973, with corresponding increases in the percentages in government and nonprofit employment. Furthermore, the percentage of men in industry decreased, whereas that of women increased very slightly. It should be noted that the percentages of doctoral women in these fields who taught in junior colleges and secondary schools in 1973 are larger than those for men. However, the study of Law

TABLE 4

PERCENT (NUMBER) OF MEN AND WOMEN DOCTORAL PHYSICISTS AND ASTRONOMERS BY EMPLOYER IN 1974[4] AND 1973[5,8]

	Physicists and Astronomers				Astronomers	
	1971[4]		1973[8]		1973[5]	
Employer	Men	Women	Men	Women	Men	Women
Educational Institution	60%	77%	56%	67%	62%	77%
Ph.D. Granting			41	44		
University					56	65
M.A. Granting			5	4		
4-Year College					4	6
B.A. Granting			9	15		
Jr. College			1	3	2	6
Secondary School			0.3	1		
Government	9	9	15	16	18	10
Industry	26	9	21	10	6	2
Nonprofit	3	3	5	4	9	4
Other	2	2	3	3	5	6
Total Number	(15,867)	(308)	(16,689)	(387)	(510)	(49)

et al.[10] of women high school physics teachers showed that such individuals are a small minority and, in fact, most women high school physics teachers do not have any physics degree.[10]

TABLE 5 gives the mean salaries for men and women for the various types of employers, and the salaries are consistently lower for women. In both the physics and astronomy studies it was found that further sub-

TABLE 5

MEAN SALARIES OF MEN AND WOMEN DOCTORAL PHYSICISTS AND ASTRONOMERS BY EMPLOYER IN 1971[4] AND 1973[5,8]

	Physicists and Astronomers				Astronomers	
	1971[4]		1973[8]		1973[5]	
Employer	Men	Women	Men	Women	Men	Women
Educational Institution	$13.5K	$12.2K	$19.1K	$16.6K	$17.0K	$12.9K
Government	19.8	18.4	23.2	21.1	22.5	*
Industry	20.0	18.4	23.8	21.7	20.3	*
Nonprofit	19.2	13.1	21.0	16.2	19.4	*

* Too few individuals to be significant

division of the sample did not remove the differences,[4,5] and an examination of the 1975 data for all fields combined showed that this was still true for all age groups at this later date.[11]

Since the major employer of physicists and astronomers is the educational institution, it is interesting to examine the situation there more closely. TABLE 6 presents the number and percentage of women in various types of physics departments in 1971-72[4] and in 1977-78.[12] It is seen that the changes in percentage either have been slight or, where they appear substantial, are so because of a very small number. Furthermore, the overall effect is a decrease. It should be noted that except for the "Top

TABLE 6

PERCENTAGE (NUMBER) OF FACULTY IN PHYSICS DEPARTMENTS WHO WERE WOMEN, BY RANK IN 1971-72[4] AND 1977-78[12]

Department Type/Rank	1971-72[4]	1977-78[12]
"Top Ten"[13]		
All Professors	0.8 (4)	2.1 (10)
Full Professors	0.6 (2)	0.6 (2)
Associate Professor	1.1 (1)	5.8 (3)
Assistant Professor	0.9 (1)	5.5 (5)
Ph.D. Granting-Number of Departments	(158)	(220)
All Professors	1.5 (74)	1.4 (77)
Full Professor	1.0 (23)	0.9 (28)
Associate Professor	1.8 (24)	2.0 (30)
Assistant Professor	2.0 (27)	2.5 (19)
M.A. Granting-Number of Departments	(133)	(126)
All Professors	2.3 (28)	2.0 (23)
Full Professor	1.9 (7)	1.5 (8)
Associate Professor	2.2 (9)	2.1 (9)
Assistant Professor	2.6 (12)	3.2 (6)
B.A. Granting-Number of Departments	(743)	(602)
All Professors	5.4 (144)	4.2 (103)
Full Professor	5.8 (55)	2.9 (26)
Associate Professor	4.9 (33)	3.4 (32)
Assistant Professor	5.2 (56)	7.4 (45)
All Three Types-Number of Departments	(1034)	(948)
All Professors	2.8 (246)	2.3 (203)
Full Professor	2.4 (85)	1.4 (62)
Associate Professor	2.7 (66)	2.5 (71)
Assistant Professor	3.3 (95)	4.5 (70)

TABLE 7

PERCENTAGE (NUMBER) OF FACULTY IN SELECTED ASTRONOMY DEPARTMENTS WHO WERE WOMEN, BY RANK IN 1972-73[5] AND 1977-78[12]

Department Type/Rank	1972-73[5]	1977-78[12]
"Top Five"[14]	0%	2% (1)
Professor	0	0
Associate	0	0
Assistant Professor	0	12 (1)
"Top Fifteen"[15]	4	5 (9)
Professor	4	4 (4)
Associate Professor	5	2 (1)
Assistant Professor	0	11 (4)

Ten" category, the institutions in the various categories are not the same in the two years studied, and thus the changes in percentage and number are a composite of changes in degree granting type and changes in the employment of women. TABLE 7 presents similar data for selected astronomy departments, and again the big change, that at the assistant professor level, is due to small numbers.

Thus, the overall impression is that statisically the situation of women physicists and astronomers has not changed very much since the beginning of this century or during the last seven years, but this is not quite true. The increased percentages of physics doctorates awarded to women now correspond to respectable numbers, and it will not be long before they become commonplace enough in physics so that most physicists will know a competent woman as a colleague. Furthermore, affirmative action has caused a reversal on the acceptable reasons for discriminating against women, which once were readily and even righteously voiced. Even though this does not mean that discrimination has ended, the perceived change in climate will make it easier for women to take themselves seriously as competitive scientists. This in turn will result in a new generation of male scientists who are much less likely to be prejudiced on the basis of sex.

Equally important are the changes in the societal views of appropriate roles for women. Admittedly, the progress here is uneven, but I do not think that there can be a preteenage girl whose family owns a television set who views marriage and motherhood as her sole exclusive option, even though this may be the only option of interest to her. She knows that, like her male counterparts, she has a choice. Coupled with this is a widening of the possibilities open to a high school girl which should result in increases in the numbers who take physical sciences and advanced math in high school and who can therefore consider such majors in college. Again, the changes are slow, but coupled with the trend toward a society in which the majority of women are employed outside the home for a major part of their adult lives, they should lead to much more substantial participation by women in physics and astronomy.

It is tempting to end this paper on the optimistic note of the preceding sentence. There is also however, a pessimistic factor that must be mentioned. This is the combination of the increasing cost of scientific work in these fields, due to the dependence on rapidly changing technology, together with the much slower increase or lack of increase of funding for basic science. In my opinion, the result of this situation will not be unemployment as much as changes in employment patterns as the competition for prestigious university positions and others permitting basic research becomes increasingly fierce. In this competition women will still be handicapped to some degree by surviving discriminatory attitudes, and to a much greater degree if they are not single-minded in their pursuit of a career. Roles in marriage are currently being rethought and changed, but even if the responsibilities are divided equally between both partners, each is still at a disadvantage with respect to the individual who has no responsibilities outside of his or her career or who has a completely supportive partner, situations which, I believe, will continue to be much more common for men than for women. However, the saving facet of this situation is the growing awareness that many young physicists and astronomers will have to turn to applied and nontraditional fields for employment, together with a simultaneous increase in the possibilities. Employment in these fields may initially be considered much less prestigious than becoming a younger edition of one's doctoral thesis adviser and consequently lend itself more readily to a lifestyle in which personal relationships are an important component. There will always be women who manage to combine brilliant and highly competitive careers with happy families, but I think the less demanding situations will continue to attract many women, particularly those with young children. And I think that this is as it should be. Women scientists should not all be required to be superwomen, just as the majority of men scientists are not required to be Einsteins.

Notes and References

1. JAMES, E.T., Ed. 1974. Notable American Women 1607–1950. Belknap Press of Harvard University Press. Cambridge, Mass.
2. ROSSITER, M.W. 1974. Am. Scientist 62: 312.
3. NATIONAL ACADEMY OF SCIENCES, U.S. 1973. Doctorates Awarded from 1920 to 1971 by Subfield of Doctorate, Sex and Decade. Washington, D.C.
4. COMMITTEE ON WOMEN IN PHYSICS. 1972. Report, Am. Phys. Soc. Bull. Am. Phys. Soc II, **17**: 740.
5. REPORT ON THE COUNCIL OF THE AAS FROM THE WORKING GROUP ON THE STATUS OF WOMEN IN ASTRONOMY—1973. 1974. Bull. Am. Astro. Soc. **6**: 412.
6. NATIONAL ACADEMY OF SCIENCES, U.S. Summary Report (Year). Doctorate Recipients from U.S. Universities for 1972–73, 1973–74, 1974–75, 1975–76, and 1976–77. Washington, D.C.
7. GILFORD, D.M. & J. SNYDER. 1977. Women and Minority Ph.D.'s in the 1970's: A Data Book. Nat. Acad. Sci., U.S. Washington, D.C.
8. Kistiakowsky, V. Women Doctoral Scientists in the United States (1973). Unpublished.
9. MAXFIELD, B. D., N. C. AHERN & A. SPISAK. 1976. Employment Status of Ph.D. Scientists and Engineers 1973 and 1975. Nat. Acad. Sci., U.S. Washington, D.C.
10. LAW, M.E., J. WITTELS, R. CLARK & P. JORGENSON. 1976. A study of women high school teachers. Bull. Am. Phys. Soc. **21**: 888.
11. NATIONAL ACADEMY OF SCIENCES, U.S. 1976. Doctoral Scientists and Engineers in the United States, 1975 profile. Board on Human-Resource Data and Analyses. Washington, D.C.
12. Data compiled from the 1977–78 Directory of Physics and Astronomy Faculties. 1977. Am. Inst. Phy.
13. The top ten in 1970 according to the American Council on Education: Berkeley, California Institute of Technology, Chicago, Columbia, Cornell, Harvard, Illinois, Massachusetts Institute of Technology, Princeton, and Stanford. The same institutions were included in the 1977–78 study.
14. The top five in 1973 according to Ref. 5: California Institute of Technology, Princeton, Berkeley, Chicago, and Harvard. The last four of these were included in the 1977 study, since the Cal. Tech. astronomy faculty could not be identifed.
15. The top fifteen in 1973 according to Ref. 5: those in Ref. 14 plus Arizona, Cornell, Maryland, Massachusetts Institute of Technology, UCLA, Columbia, Texas, Michigan, Washington, and Yale. M. I. T. was not included in the 1973 study, and neither M.I.T. nor Cal Tech was included in the 1977 study, since the astronomy faculty could not be identified.

The Changing Status of Women in the Geosciences

THERESA F. SCHWARZER
Exxon Production Research Company
Houston, Texas 77001

THE CURRENT STATUS of women in the geosciences is changing—and improving—rapidly.

1. Women are entering the geosciences in unprecedented numbers. In 1974, only four percent of working geoscientists were women. Currently, women constitute about 20 percent of all undergraduate geoscience students.

2. Women geoscientists are now actively recruited—and hired—by employers, particularly by energy companies, the single largest employer of earth scientists.

3. Starting salaries for men and women geoscientists are comparable, although median salaries for women at all experience levels are about 75 percent of those for their male colleagues.

4. Women geoscientists are moving away from their historical concentration in academic jobs and into employment areas and work activities in industry and government where salaries are higher and overall career opportunities are greater.

5. The timing of these changes is coincident with a high-demand market for geoscientists generated by our increasing energy needs and environmental concerns.

Past energy consumption in the U.S. and our projected energy demand through 1990 are shown in FIGURE 1.[1] Our appetite for energy is staggering in its magnitude. Although we in the U.S. represent one sixth of the world's population, we consume one third of the world's energy. Currently, we consume about 39 million barrels of oil equivalent energy every day. To put this into perspective, consider the fact that our vast Prudhoe Bay reserves, which run about 15 billion barrels of oil equivalent, would last us only about a year if it were our only energy source, and oil fields of this size are rare. An even more sobering thought is the fact that we are currently importing about 44 percent of

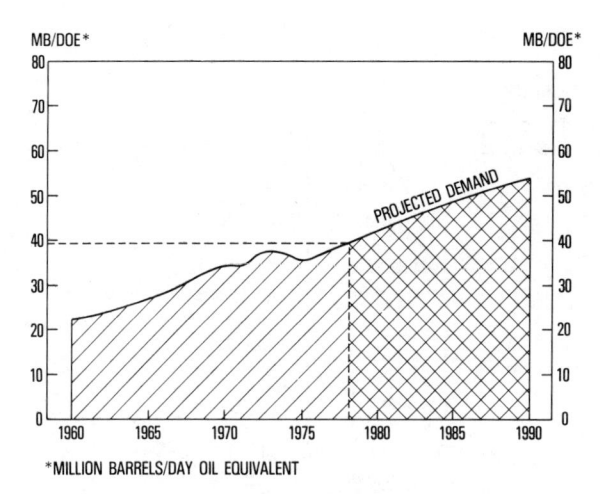

FIGURE 1. United States energy demand projected to 1990. (From Exxon Co., U.S.A.[1])

our energy, although we were an energy exporter as recently as 1969. This dependency on foreign energy sources has strained our national balance of payments and weakened our national security position.

These factors have emphasized our need for domestic energy independence and have intensified our efforts in domestic oil and alternate fuels exploration. Our position on certain other mineral commodities is similar. However, our need to utilize the mineral wealth of nature seemingly puts us into a head-on conflict with our need to preserve the quality of our environment.

Fortunately, geoscientists are comfortable wearing both exploration and environmental hats simultaneously. They have the training and skill to perform both jobs competently and harmoniously, and this dual ability has put them in high demand. The November 14, 1977, *Houston Chronicle* reported the ten most promising professions through 1985. Geologists were ranked fifth after medical doctors, veterinarians, systems analysts, and dentists.

It thus appears that geoscientists will be in high demand at least for the next five to ten years. This factor is critical to the expanding role of women in the geosciences and may be partly responsible for it. The National Science Foundation (NSF) in Washington, D.C., has made projections of the supply of scientists and engineers through 1985 which

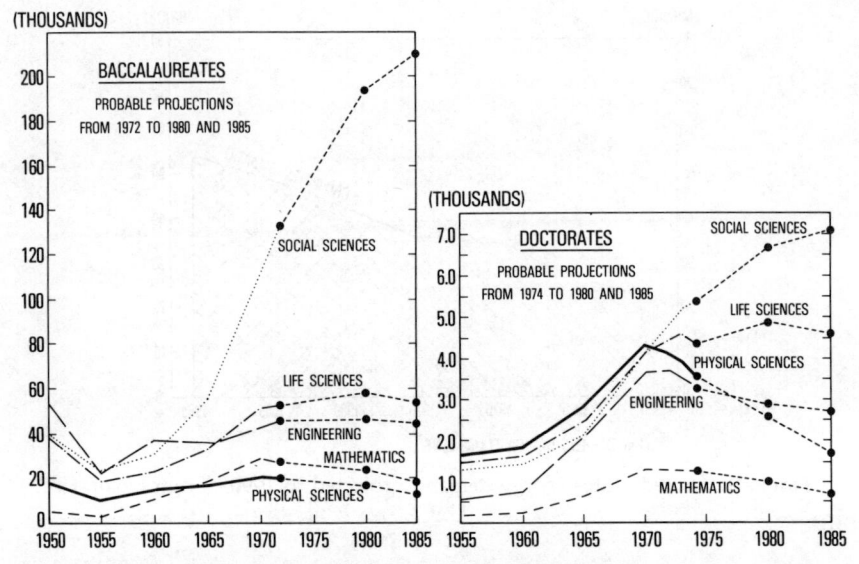

FIGURE 2. Projection of baccalaureate and doctoral degree recipients to 1985. (From National Science Foundation.[2])

indicate that the numbers of physical scientists graduating have taken and will continue to take a sharp downturn. Such projections have prompted Dr. George Handelman, Dean of Science at Rensselaer Polytechnic Institute in Troy, New York, to stress the need to recruit more of the already-increasing numbers of women into science and engineering. In a parallel development, recent data from the American Geological Institute (AGI) in Falls Church, Virginia, suggests that despite a high-demand market, the numbers of geoscience students, mostly men, have declined in recent years. At the same time, the numbers of women earth scientists have increased.

These trends are shown in the following sequence of figures. FIGURE 2 is abstracted from the 1975 NSF publication "Projections of degrees and enrollment in science and engineering fields to 1985."[2] The number of baccalaureate degrees received in five major science and engineering fields is shown from 1950 to 1972 and are projected from 1972 to 1985. The number of doctorates received in the same fields is shown from 1955 to 1974 and is also projected to 1985. The respective curves for the physical sciences have been emphasized. Although earth scientists are not broken out separately from this larger category, they constitute about 20 percent of all physical scientists, and I am presuming parallel trends with physical scientists as a whole. Following a peak observed in the early 1970s, physical scientists are expected to experience the greatest percentage decline of the five major science and engineering fields and to drop by 1985 to levels as low as those experienced in the early 1960s. Doctorates of physical science in particular will take a sharp decline.

FIGURE 3, based on an American Geological Institute survey of student enrollments from 1971 to 1976 in several hundred geoscience departments,[3] suggests that this downward trend is currently being experienced in earth science. Predominantly male student enrollments at all degree levels from 1971 to 1976 have declined from a peak during 1973–1974. Simultaneously, the numbers of women students and degree recipients have increased during the same period, as illustrated in FIGURE 4.[4] The data

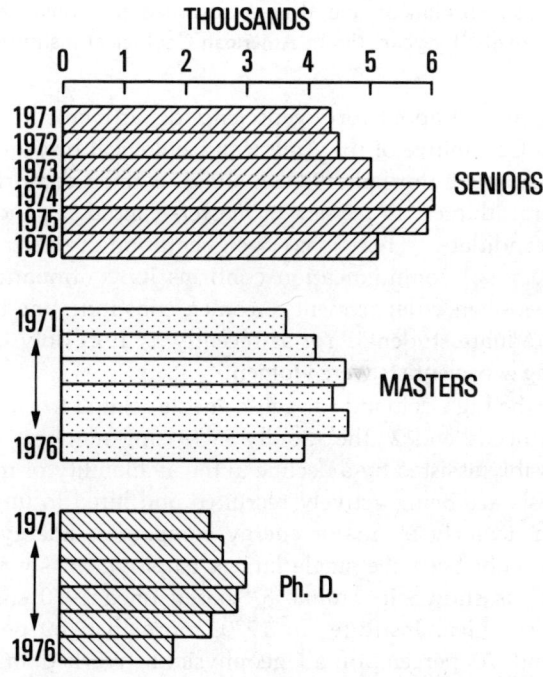

FIGURE 3. Annual student enrollment in earth sciences, by year. (From American Geological Institute.[3])

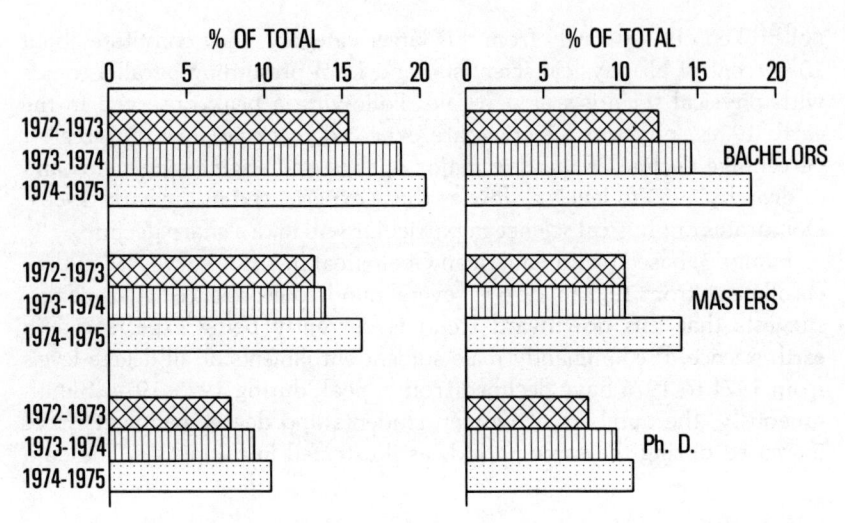

FIGURE 4. Annual enrollment and degrees awarded to women earth science students, by year. (From American Geological Institute.[4])

are from a survey of about forty geoscience departments by the Women Geoscientists Committee of the American Geological Institute and cover academic years 1972 through 1975. In 1975, women comprised 20 percent of undergraduates, 17 percent of masters candidates and 11 percent of doctoral candidates. There is no documentation of this trend beyond 1975, but personal communication confirms its continuance. In some prestigious geoscience departments, women constitute one third to one half of all graduate students. Yet as recently as 1974 only four percent of all working geoscientists were women.

Due to 1, the high demand for geoscientists related to energy and environmental needs and 2, the rapidly increasing numbers of qualified women, possibly assisted by a decline in the availability of men, women earth scientists are being actively recruited and hired in unprecedented numbers, particularly by major energy companies. Energy companies have traditionally been the single largest employment source for male geoscientists, as shown in FIGURE 5,[5] based on a 1970 survey of the American Geological Institute. In 1970, more than 60 percent of all geologists and 70 percent of all geophysicists worked in petroleum-related industries. On the other hand, in 1970 more than half of all

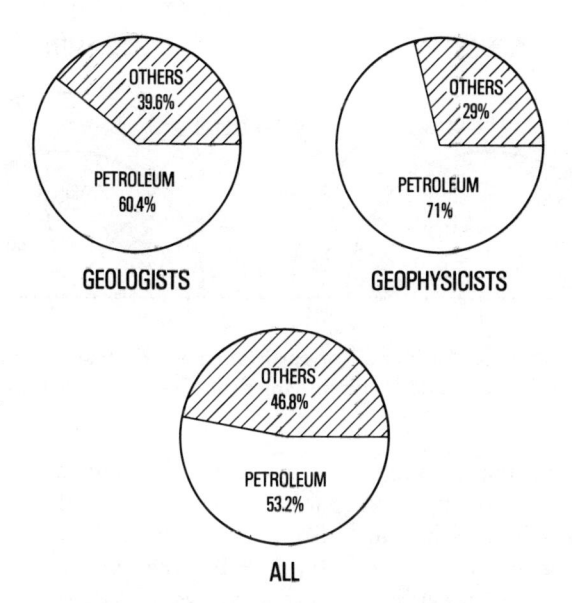

GEOLOGISTS — PETROLEUM 60.4%, OTHERS 39.6%
GEOPHYSICISTS — PETROLEUM 71%, OTHERS 29%
ALL — PETROLEUM 53.2%, OTHERS 46.8%

FIGURE 5. Petroleum industry employment of earth scientists, 1970. (From American Geological Institute.[5])

women earth scientists were in academia, either at the college or secondary school level.[6]* This discrepancy is not due to differences in educational level, since American Geological Institute studies indicate that both men and women geoscientists have similar degree breakdowns, i.e., 40 percent baccalaureate, 40 percent masters, and 20 percent Ph.D.[6]

However, a comparison of the distribution of women and men in 1974 vs. 1970 by employer (FIGURE 6)[7] suggests that women are moving away from the academic sector and largely into industry. The percentage of women geoscientists in industry increased from 12 percent in 1970 to 18 percent in 1974, while their percentage in academia decreased by about the same amount from 1970 to 1974. This fortuitous turn of events has occurred at a time when many college faculties are retrenching in their hiring and tenured promotions are becoming more difficult to obtain.

Women are also redistributing by work activity. They are moving

---

* The specifics of survey populations used from the remaining references are tabulated in TABLE 1.

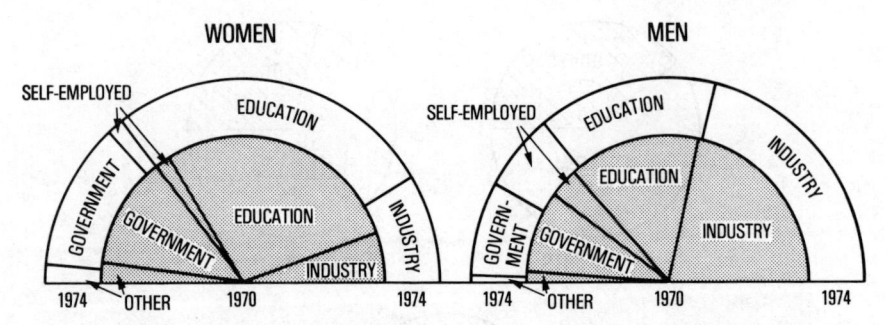

FIGURE 6. Percentage distribution of earth scientists by type of employer and sex, 1970 and 1974. (From American Geological Institute.[7])

from lower paying teaching jobs in academia, especially at the secondary school level, to higher paying jobs in petroleum exploration and in private consulting. They are also increasingly entering research and development activities in industry and in government, especially the United States Geological Survey. While still underrepresented in management relative to men, there are indications that government agencies and oil companies, in particular, are actively pursuing a policy of not only hiring women but of promoting them to levels of administrative responsibility.

Management responsibility and other career opportunities, however, are a function of experience, and an enlarged experience pool of women earth scientists has just recently begun to grow with their increasing entry into the profession. FIGURE 7 shows the age distribution of women geoscientists in industry in 1974.[8] The distribution is obviously skewed toward ages less than 30. The median age of a woman petroleum geologist in 1974 was 29 and this age is probably even younger in 1978, since most of the recent hires are baccalaureates and masters in their early to mid-twenties. By contrast, men geoscientists have on the average about 15 years more work experience than women. This is illustrated by a comparison of work experience for all men vs. women geoscientists in 1970 (FIGURE 8).[6]

These factors of age, experience, employer type, and work activity interact in complex ways to generate one of our most widely used yardsticks of success: salaries. For proprietary reasons, current salary data

SCHWARZER: THE GEOSCIENCES

TABLE 1
SURVEY STATISTIC,* BY REFERENCE

Reference No.	Source	Survey Date	Survey Group	Scientists/Engineers Survey Sample Men	Women	Survey Response Men	Women	Total Population Represented by Survey Men	Women	Survey Response Total Population M.	Fe.	Earth Scientists Survey Sample Men	Women	Survey Response Men	Women	Total Population Represented by survey Men	Women	Survey Response Total Population M.	Fe.
(6)	AGI†	1970	All									31,700	1140	23,750 (75%)	850 (75%)	36,500	1300	65%	65%
			Ph.D.									6,300	230	4,750 (75%)	170 (75%)	7,300	260	65%	65%
(7)	AGI	1974	All									3,000	785	2,370 (79%)	650 (83%)	38,000	1,500	6%	43%
(9)	NSF†	1974	Bachelors, Physical and Science Earth	3,400	340	3,000 (88%)	300 (88%)	75,000	750	4%	4%	750	38	660 (88%)	35 (88%)	17,000	750	4%	4%
(10)	NSF	1974	All	50,000	5,000	44,000 (88%)	4,900 (88%)	1.1 Million	100,000	4%	4%	2,000	85	1,825 (88%)	75 (88%)	38,000	1,500	4%	4%
(11)	NSF	1974	Ph.D	50,000	5,000	44,000 (88%)	4,400 (88%)	280,000	28,000	4%	4%	400	20	360 (88%)	18 (88%)	8,000	300	4%	4%
(12)	AGI	1974	Ph.D									600	95	461 (79%)	78 (88%)	8,000	300	6%	43%
(13)	NSF	1974	Ph.D	50,000	5,000	44,000 (88%)	4,400 (83%)	280,000	28,000	4%	4%	2,000	85	1,825 (88%)	75 (88%)	38,000	1,500	4%	4%
(14)	AGI	1974	All									2,000	785	2,370 (79%)	650 (93%)	38,000	1,500	6%	43%
(15)	NRC†	1975	Ph.D.	58,000	5,800	44,000 (75%)	4,400 (75%)	280,000	28,000	4%	4%								

*Numbers are rounded off and, in some cases, are approximated. The numbers are intended to convey the general magnitude of the survey base.
†AGI = American Geological Institute. NSF = National Science Foundation. NRC = National Research Council.

NO. OF WOMEN

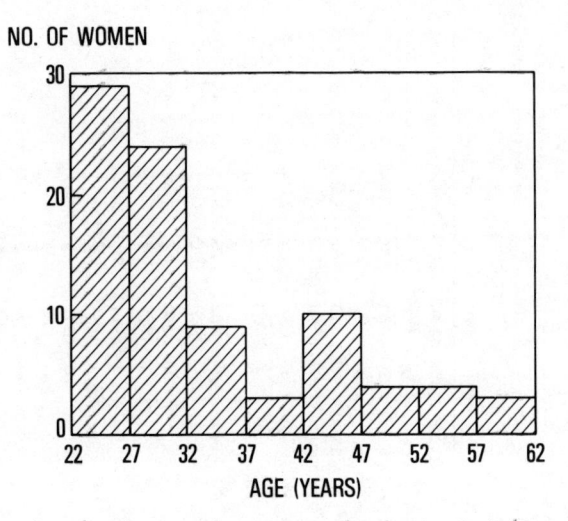

FIGURE 7. Age distribution of women earth scientists in industry, 1974. (From American Geological Institute.[8])

from private employers are not available and, unfortunately, public sources are two to three years out of date. However, some recent trends and patterns in salary treatment of men vs. women geoscientists have been pieced together from 1970-1975 government surveys of a national sampling of about 44,000 scientists and engineers representing a total population of about 1.1 million, and a 1974 survey by the American Geological Institute based on a sampling of about 4,000 out of 40,000 earth scientists.

Starting salaries overall for both men and women earth scientists hired in the past few years are generally equal, at least at the baccalaureate degree level. FIGURE 9, based on NSF national sampling of about 3,000 out of 75,000 physical and earth science baccalaureates for 1974 through 1976,[9] demonstrates that in 1976, women physical and earth science baccalaureates were earning 99 percent of their male counterparts' salaries. In 1975, this ratio took a dip to 89 percent after reaching 98 percent in 1974. Since these baccalaureates are primarily hired by industry and government, this favorable comparison of starting salaries would seem to be a strong indication of recent affirmative action policy on the part of these employers.

However, when salaries for men vs. women at all levels of work experience are compared, the historical lag of women's salaries behind men's becomes apparent (FIGURE 10).[9,10] Government studies indicate that for the national sample of 23,500 earth scientists at all degree levels, women were earning 70 percent of men's salaries in 1970 and 73 percent in 1974. Unfortunately, more recent comparative data are not available. It should also be pointed out that these older salary ratios for men vs. women earth scientists are similar to those in most other scientific disciplines.

Unfortunately for women Ph.D. earth scientists, government studies and those of the American Geological Institute on a sampling of about 500 of 8,000 geoscience Ph.D.s further indicate that women doctorates overall actually lost ground salary-wise from 1970 to 1975 (FIGURE 11).[6,11-13] In 1970, the ratio of salaries for women to men Ph.D. geoscientists was

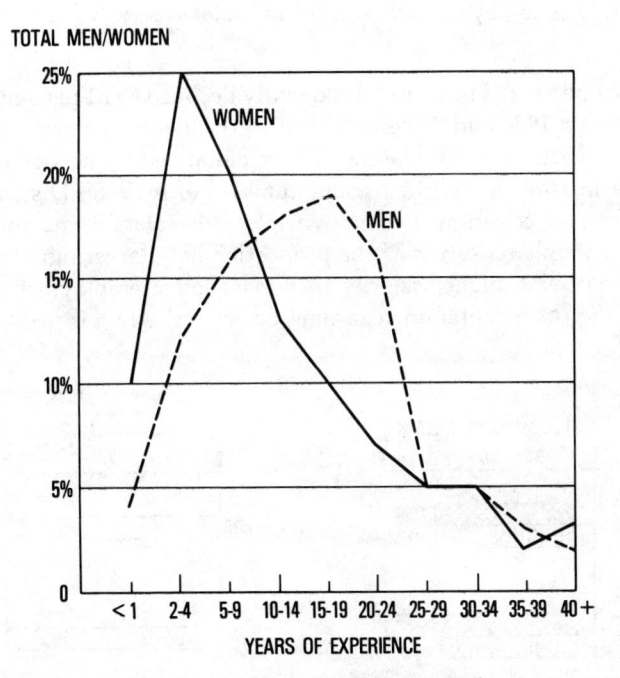

FIGURE 8. Work experience of women and men earth scientists, 1970. (From American Geological Institute.[6])

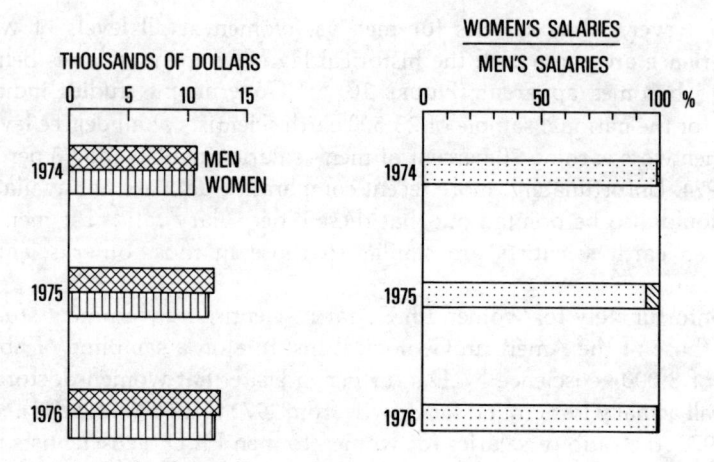

FIGURE 9. Annual salary offers to bachelor's degree candidates in physical and earth sciences, by sex and year. (From National Science Foundation.[9])

almost 87 percent. The ratio subsequently declined to 81 percent in 1973, 78 percent in 1974 and 77 percent in 1975. While the majority of women Ph.D.s in earth science, like men, were employed by academic institutions during this period, increasing numbers of male Ph.D.s entered oil company and government employment. This salary trend may therefore be a simple reflection of the proportionately larger number of men Ph.D.s receiving higher salaries in nonacademic employment. But although the documentation regarding cause and effect is not available,

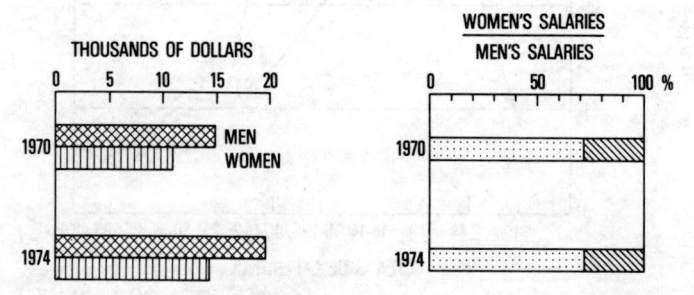

FIGURE 10. Annual salaries of all earth scientists, by sex and year. (Source: 1970- National Register of Scientific and Technical Personnel. From B.C. Henderson[6], National Science Foundation.[10])

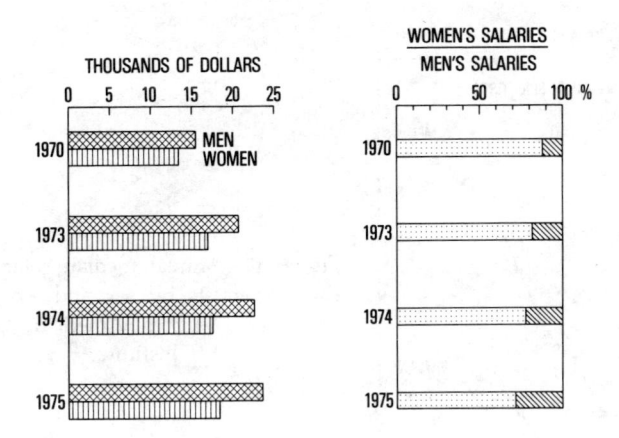

FIGURE 11. Annual salaries for Ph.D. earth scientists, by sex and year. (From B.C. Henderson,[6] National Science Foundation,[11,13] American Geological Institute.[12])

the trend may also indicate that the salaries of women Ph.D.s in universities decreased relative to men's salaries during that period.

An examination of 1974 median salary distribution on a sampling of all earth scientists by years of experience and sex emphasizes that while the gap between starting salaries for men and women is closing, the historic lag of women's salaries behind men's is apparent and actually increases with years of experience (FIGURE 12).[14] The data are based on a 1974 survey of the American Geological Institute and represent responses from 650 women earth scientists (presumed to represent about 43 percent of all 1,500 working women geoscientists in 1974) and a random sampling of 2,370 men (representing 6 percent of all 38,000 working male geoscientists in 1974). The data are compiled for all employers, but subpopulations according to industry, government, and academia each show similar trends. For instance, in 1974:

1. Overall, the salary curves for women earth scientists were below those for men.
2. The salary curves tend to converge for recent hires. Although subdivisions by degree are not shown, women in the sampling who had baccalaureate degrees and less than one year of experience actually reported salaries slightly above those of their male colleagues. In 1974,

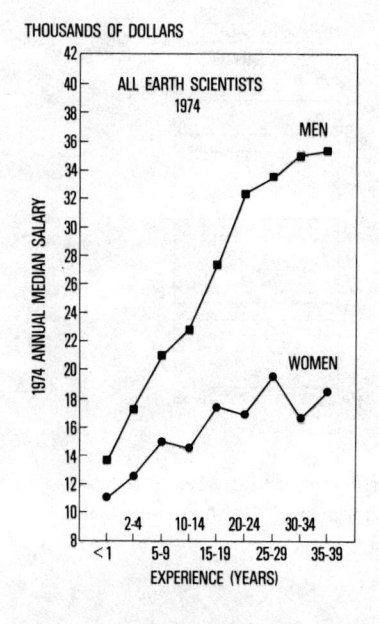

FIGURE 12. Annual median salaries of all earth scientists by sex and work experience, 1974. (From American Geological Institute.[14])

salaries of women with less than ten years of experience were greater than the median salary ratio of 75 percent for all men vs. women, whereas women with more than ten years of experience were earning less than this median salary ratio.

3. The two salary curves diverge with increasing number of years of experience. Although salary curves are not shown by degree level, after 15 years of experience there is total separation of the highest paid group of women (Ph.D.s) below the lowest paid group of men (Masters).

These salary trends as a function of work experience for men and women earth scientists are similar to those experienced in other scientific and engineering disciplines. A point of comparison can be made for the AGI sample of 461 men and 78 women Ph.D. earth scientists in 1974[14] vs. about 40,000 men and 4,400 women Ph.D. scientists and engineers from the national sample in 1975.[15] FIGURE 13 indicates similar salary levels and similar salary trends for men and women doctoral earth scientists relative to other doctoral scientists and engineers. It is anticipated, however, that more current data will show a significant improvement in diminishing these salary differentials.

As the status of women in geoscience is changing, stereotyped images are fading, not only in the minds of men, but those of the women themselves. Geology, like other so-called hard sciences, historically has been a male domain and has been considered an unfeminine discipline. The geosciences have indeed had a long-standing image of rugged masculinity: the field geologist living and working under primitive, physically demanding conditions or the shipboard geophysicist handling heavy equipment and living in cramped, impersonal quarters. In such a "physical" world, women, if not discouraged from pursuing the profession, were largely seen as teachers, librarians, and mapmakers. In fact, many geoscientists work almost exclusively in the laboratory or classroom. The physical image of geoscience and misconceptions regarding a woman's ability or willingness to participate fully in virtually all aspects of geoscience explains why, until very recently, women entered the profession

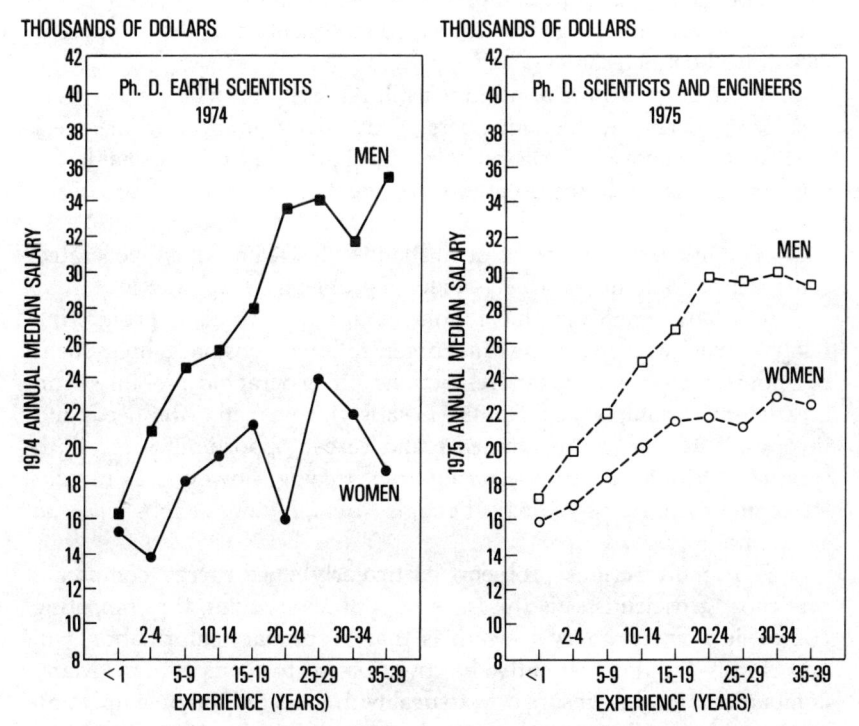

FIGURE 13. Annual median salaries for Ph.D. earth scientists, 1974, and all Ph.D. scientists and engineers, 1975, by sex and work experience. (From American Geological Institute[14], National Research Council.[15])

in small numbers and tended to advance relatively slowly when they did pursue a geoscience career.

But as attitudes are changing, women are increasingly entering work activities that not long ago would have been largely closed to them. Increasing numbers of women are demonstrating their ability to perform in the field, underground in the mines, on the drilling rig, or in the boardroom. Women are publishing more frequently and assuming a greater visibility within the profession. As a result, most of the prior stereotyping of geoscience as an unfeminine discipline has fallen away. Women geoscientists can now look forward to careers as fulfilling and rewarding as their male colleagues.

I have emphasized the positive, but some challenging problems remain:

1. While employers generally consider their women geoscientists (many of them young) as competent as men, employers are concerned about the women's long-term career commitments and their apparent lack of well-defined career goals.

2. Women professors at all ranks still represent only about two percent of geoscience faculty members. Since many younger women feel the need for "successful" role-models, especially at the educational level, this continuing underrepresentation of women professors is a serious concern.

3. The increasing numbers of husband-wife "teams" have generated some complex and not-so-easily-resolved problems:

   A. Many employers have policies against nepotism prohibiting relatives from working in the same organizational division. Employment of spouses, especially given restrictions on geographic mobility, can greatly limit a company's flexibility in satisfying its manpower needs and in optimizing the job assignments and career opportunities for both spouses. Attitudes on spouse hiring are softening, however, as rapidly increasing numbers of geological couples are applying for jobs with the same employer.

   B. A more serious problem, particularly since energy companies hire most geoscientists, is the issue of spouses working for competing companies. The primary concern is that proprietary information will consciously or inadvertently be transferred to competitors. Many companies are either unsure how to deal with this situation or simply will not consider it. Even so, a small, but steadily-increasing, number of spouses are finding employment in competing companies.

4. Professional women geoscientists, like other professional women,

must weigh in the balance career vs. family commitments. Marriage and children can put limitations and additional stress on pursuit of a career. Because of these conflicts, a considerable number of women geoscientists get divorced, do not marry, or if married, do not have children.

In conclusion, while some problems remain, current and future career opportunities for women in geoscience are unprecedented. The number of women geoscientists is increasing rapidly, they are generally actively hired and promoted, salary discrepancies are disappearing, women are moving into work activities in which they were previously underrepresented, and they are shifting toward higher paying employment with improved career opportunities. Such advances are expected to continue as the current and projected demand for geoscientists remains high.

We shall follow with interest what we hope is a continuation of the rapidly changing and improving status of women in geoscience.

References

1. Exxon Company, U.S.A. 1977. Energy outlook 1977–1990:5.
2. National Science Foundation. 1975. Projections of degrees and enrollment in science and engineering fields to 1985. NSF 76-301:2-3.
3. The American Geological Institute. 1977. Student enrollment in geoscience departments:81-82.
4. Crawford, M. L., J. B. Moody & J. Tullis. 1977. Women in academia: students and professors. Geology 5 (8):502-503.
5. The American Geological Institute. 1971. Manpower supply and demand in earth science:28.
6. Henderson, B. C. 1972. Women in geoscience. Geotimes 17(9):24-25.
7. Henderson, B. C. 1975. As you might guess, men are paid more. Geotimes 20(3):30.
8. The American Geological Institute: Women Geoscientists Committee. 1976. Women in geoscience:11.
9. National Science Foundation. 1977. Women and minorities in science and engineering. NSF 77-304:11.
10. National Science Foundation. 1976. Characteristics of the national sample of scientists and engineers, 1974. NSF 76-323:197.
11. National Research Council. 1974. Doctoral scientists and engineers in the United States, 1973 profile:27.
12. The American Geological Institute: Women Geoscientists Committee. 1976. Women in geoscience:5.

13. NATIONAL SCIENCE FOUNDATION. 1975. Characteristics of doctoral scientists and engineers in the United States, 1975. NSF 77-309:61.
14. THE AMERICAN GEOLOGICAL INSTITUTE: Women Geoscientists Committee. 1976. Women in geoscience:7.
15. NATIONAL RESEARCH COUNCIL. 1976. Doctoral scientists and engineers in the United States, 1975 profile:12.

Women in Psychology in the United States

FLORENCE L. DENMARK
The Graduate School and University Center
The City University of New York
New York, New York 10036

STUDIES ON WOMEN in psychology date as far back as 1947 when Bryan and Boring[1] found positive discrimination against women. As you might expect, women were paid less, were promoted rarely—if ever, were less likely to be employed full time, were practitioners rather than researchers/teachers, and came from higher socioeconomic status backgrounds. Have times changed? The answer to this question is what this paper is about. We will first consider the number and distribution of women in psychology, then examine their participatory activities in the American Psychological Association (APA), followed by their employment and salary, and conclude with barriers faced by women in obtaining doctorate degrees.

NUMBERS AND DISTRIBUTION

It is practically impossible to determine how many psychologists there are today. The 1977 Directory of the American Psychological Association (APA, which includes Canadian psychologists) lists 44,650 members and associates.[2] Of that number, 11,929, or 26 percent are female, as shown in TABLE 1. Of course, many American and Canadian psychologists are not members of APA. A best guess is that there are twice as many American and Canadian psychologists than are listed in the APA Directory. This "guess" was arrived at by examining a survey of recent doctoral graduates from 1972 to 1976 from 132 Ph.D. programs in the United States.[3] The survey indicated that 52.2 percent of the 9,292 recent Ph.D.s did not join APA. Since approximately one third (rather than one quarter) of these recent Ph.D.s are women, and since 55.5 percent of the women compared to 49.7 percent of the men did not join

TABLE 1
1977 APA MEMBERSHIP STATISTICS

		Fellows	Members	Associates	Total
Men	N	2739	24,697	5285	32,721
	%	85.7	75.3	61.0	73.3
Women	N	456	8100	3373	11,929
	%	14.3	24.7	39.0	26.7
Total	N	3195	32,797	8658	44,650
	%	100	100	100	100

APA, it is possible that more than 26.7 percent of all psychologists in the United States are female.

In any event, the total number of psychologists has increased significantly, and the number of women in psychology has also increased significantly. However, as of 1978, existing and available records indicate that the *percentage* of female psychologists has hardly changed over the last 25 years.

An important source for obtaining this data was Jane Hildreth of the Membership Office of APA. She reported that 25 percent of the 8,554 APA members were female in 1951, even though no gender breakdown was officially kept. In 1951, women APA members were asked to list their husbands' names in the directory along with their own. Fortunately, this practice was discontinued shortly thereafter. Similar data were reported for 1968, although membership in APA had increased to 27,250. The total percentage of female psychologists does not tell the full story. Psychologists include both "scientists" and "professionals." Thus, some psychologists carry out research and others serve as mental health professionals, and still others do both. It is impossible to look at numbers and figure out exactly who belongs in one camp or the other, but a look at the 1977 divisional membership is of some help in this regard.[2] Total divisional membership is greater than total APA membership, since even though some APA members do not affiliate with any division, many members belong to more than one division. As shown in TABLE 2, women tend to be clustered within a relatively few areas, while men are dispersed throughout the discipline. In 1977, 19.7 percent of the psychologists in Division 12 (Clinical Psychology), and 23.2 percent of the members of Division 29 (Psychotherapy) were female. Many, if not most, of the members of these divisions are at least part-time mental health professionals. In contrast, only 11.5 percent of the membership of Division 6 (Physiological and Comparative Psychology) and only 12 percent of Division 3 (Experimental Psychology) were women. These divisions are among the more "pure" research-oriented ones. A still smaller percentage of women are in Industrial and Organizational Psychology (6.3 percent), Consumer Psychology (6.9 percent), Engineering Psychology (4.6 percent), and Military Psychology (4.1 percent). These figures may reflect the "business world" where women at higher managerial levels are still few in number.

Division 7, the Division of Developmental Psychology, provides some interesting figures. Although primarily research oriented, 40.3 percent of its 1977 membership is female. Women are not only more welcome in the helping areas of psychology, they are also more welcome in and choose to enter areas where the target of inquiry and investigation—in this case, children—is considered appropriate for females. Similarly, Division 16, School Psychology, has 39.7 percent females in its membership. Interestingly, Division 35, also referred to later in this paper, a division established in 1973, entitled and devoted primarily to research in the psychology of women, is 92.5 percent female. The recognized importance of developing and expanding knowledge in this field and of moving into the public arena by applying this knowledge to society and its institutions was, as the first president of the division wrote, "an idea whose time has come".[4] Many women belong only to this division and report that at last they have found a home in organized psychology.

Areas of psychology that involve extensive and expensive laboratory equipment are less likely to welcome females into their domains. Only universities offering doctoral degrees, rather than colleges, and certain well-funded research laboratories are likely to have such equipment, or are willing to invest in it. Individuals with tenure and higher ranks or those likely to obtain them (primarily males) will become the recipients. Thus women are frequently deterred from obtaining Ph.D.s in physiological psychology; those who do receive the Ph.D are often forced to switch fields when the technological support, equipment, and/or space to house such equipment is denied them.

In 1968, there were only 29 divisions, no division on the Psychology of Women, and there was no gender subcount. However, by hand count,

TABLE 2
1977 APA DIVISIONAL AFFILIATIONS

Division	Men N	Men %	Women N	Women %	Total N
1. General Psychology	2,171	78.6	591	21.4	2,762
2. Teaching of Psychology	2,022	81.0	474	19.0	2,496
3. Experimental Psychology	1,220	88.0	166	12.0	1,386
5. Evaluation and Measurement	780	85.1	137	14.9	917
6. Physiological and Comparative	531	88.5	69	11.5	600
7. Developmental Psychology	626	59.7	422	4.03	1,048
8. Personality and Social	3,311	78.8	892	21.2	4,203
9. SPSSI	1,705	76.8	514	23.2	2,219
10. Psychology and the Arts	284	73.4	103	26.6	387
12. Clinical Psychology	3,462	80.3	851	19.7	4,313
13. Consulting Psychology	590	85.6	99	14.4	689
14. Industrial and Organizational	1,545	93.7	104	6.3	1,649
15. Educational Psychology	2,593	75.2	854	24.8	3,447
16. School Psychology	1,551	60.3	1,023	39.7	2,574
17. Counseling Psychology	2,060	82.2	446	17.8	2,506
18. Psychologists in Public Service	702	82.4	150	17.6	852
19. Military Psychology	469	95.9	20	4.1	489
20. Adult Development and Aging	419	68.7	191	31.3	610
21. Society of Engineering Psychologists	482	95.4	23	4.6	505
22. Rehabilitation Psychology	695	79.5	179	20.5	874
23. Consumer Psychology	310	93.1	23	6.9	333
24. Philosophical Psychology	443	87.5	63	12.5	506
25. Experimental Analysis of Behavior	1,383	85.8	229	14.2	1,612
26. History of Psychology	418	87.6	59	12.4	477
27. Community Psychology	1,052	82.7	220	17.3	1,272
28. Psychopharmacology	913	86.5	143	13.5	1,056
29. Psychotherapy	2,576	76.8	780	23.2	3,356
30. Psychological Hypnosis	430	91.1	42	8.9	472
31. State Psychological Affairs	740	80.2	183	19.8	923
32. Humanistic Psychology	876	76.2	274	23.8	1,150
33. Mental Retardation	728	72.1	281	27.9	1,009
34. Population and Environmental Psychology	248	72.5	94	27.5	342
35. Psychology of Women	106	7.5	1,301	92.5	1,407
36. PIRI	450	72.7	169	27.3	619
No Divisional Affiliation	12,444	68.9	5,617	31.1	18,061
Total	50,335	75.0	16,786	25.0	67,121

9.6 percent of the 510 total number of members in Division 6 (Physiological and Comparative) were women, contrasted to 35.9 percent of the 843 Division 7 (Developmental) membership. By 1977 the number of members and the number of women in these divisions changed, but the relative percentage increase of women in these divisions was insignificant.

Participatory Activities in APA

Women are at last approaching parity in APA convention participation and in governance, relative to their proportion of APA membership. The percentage of women participating in the annual APA convention has increased from 14 percent in 1946 to 28 percent in 1977 (See Table 3). The jump from 15.3 percent in 1970 to 23 percent in 1974 can in part be explained by the fact that 1974 was the first year Division 35 (The Psychology of Women) was given program hours.

The percentage of women participating on APA boards and committees increased from 9.7 percent in 1946 to 23.8 percent in 1976 (See Table 4). Table 4 also indicates that on the APA Council of Representatives women's participation increased from 9 percent in 1969 to 20.2 percent in 1977.

Some of this increase is undoubtedly due to the impact and influence of the APA Committee on Women in Psychology, first established as an ad hoc Task Force on the Status of Women in Psychology in January, 1970, and finally regularized in 1972 as a continuing committee reporting to the Board of Social and Ethical Responsibility. The Association for

Table 3

Women's Participation in Annual Convention Program*

Year	Women	Total	Percentage
1946	37	265	14.0
1956	124	1,146	10.8
1966	229	1,648	13.9
1970	345	2,260	15.3
1974	842	3,600	23.0
1975	902	3,750	24.0
1977	1,169	4,143	28.0

* Source: Index of Programs. Percentage of women in APA now 27 percent.

TABLE 4
PARTICIPATION IN THE AMERICAN PSYCHOLOGICAL ASSOCIATION*

Year	Council of Representatives			Boards and Committees		
	Women	Total	Percentage	Women	Total	Percentage
1946				15	155	9.7
1956				31	365	9.5
1966				36	463	7.8
1970	9	135	6	55	526	10.5
1971	7	131	5	42	485	12.2
1972	10	133	8	51	442	14.9
1973	17	106	16	65	450	18.4
1974	20	121	16.4	56	316	17.7
1975	25	122	20.5	85	385	22.1
1976	26	118	22.0	85	357	23.8
1977	24	119	20.2			

*Data obtained from report on APA ad hoc committee on women (1972), Human Resources Office, and APA Monitor.

Women in Psychology (AWP), an organization formed in 1969, which operates outside the APA structure but includes many APA members, has also had an impact on promoting both women's issues and women in APA governance. In fact, by demonstrating and attacking unfair employment practices at the 1969 APA Convention, the Association for Women in Psychology was largely responsible for convincing APA's Council of Representatives to create the ad hoc Task Force to examine the status of women in psychology. The Task Force in its 1973 report[5] documented both overt and subtle forms of discrimination against women in the discipline.

Division 35 (The Psychology of Women), through its three council representatives, organized a Women's Caucus of the APA Council which works together on many social issues. The Caucus was instrumental in having the Council vote in 1977 not to hold annual conventions in states that have not ratified the Equal Rights Amendment. As more and, hopefully, still more women become part of the decision-making body of our organization, they are able to play a legitimate role in influencing the actions taken by this group.

The editorial staff of professional journals also showed gender shifts over the last decade. Many more women were designated as editors or appointed to editorial boards or were asked to serve as editorial consultants. TABLE 5 indicates changes in editorial staff that occurred during a ten-year period from 1965 to 1975 in many traditional APA journals. Thus, for example, the percentage of female editorial staff increased from 1.6 percent in 1965 to 11.7 percent in 1975 on the *Psychology Review*, from 3.7 percent to 5.7 percent on the *Journal of Comparative and Physiological Psychology*, and from 21.4 percent in 1969 to 50 percent in 1975 on *Developmental Psychology*. Through the efforts of the APA Committee on Women there are now guidelines for nonsexist language in APA journals.

Unfortunately, even in 1978 the vast majority of women psychologists noted above who participate in governance and on editorial staffs are still members of the white majority.

Largely through the efforts of the APA Committee on Women, a Women's Program Office was established by the APA in August of 1977, reflecting the acknowledged importance of devoting specific attention to

TABLE 5

SHIFTS IN EDITORIAL* STAFF IN TRADITIONAL JOURNALS

Journal	Year	Total	No. Women	% Women
Psychological Review	1965	124	2	1.6
	1975	162	19	11.7
J. of Comparative Physiological Psychology	1965	27	1	3.7
	1975	35	2	5.7
Psychological Bulletin	1965	23	1	4.3
	1975	224	18	8.0
J. of Counseling Psychology	1965	14	2	14.3
	1975	30	5	16.7
J. of Consulting Psychology	1965	34	0	0
J. of Clinical & Consulting Psychology‡	1975	55	12	21.8
Developmental Psychology†	1969	14	3	21.4
	1975	36	18	50.0
J. of Personality & Social Psychology	1965	37	1	2.7
	1975	51	4	7.8

* Editorial staff includes editors, editorial boards, editorial consultants.
† *Developmental Psychology* was first published in 1969, so shift is over six years.
‡ *Journal of Consulting Psychology* changed its name during the ten-year interval.

the needs of women. This office has a dual mission. It is responsible for developing programs to advance the status of women in psychology and also seeks to facilitate the use of psychology and psychologists to advance the public interest of women. Nancy Felipe Russo currently serves as the administrative officer for this office.

EMPLOYMENT

In 1976 a human resources program survey was conducted by APA which was answered by 30,332 respondents, including 8,328 women. Respondents ranged from 20 to more than 70 years of age. The data appeared in a report by Sharon Dyer, entitled, "An Overview of the Employment of Psychologists."[6] As seen in TABLE 6, a much greater percentage of men at all educational levels in psychology were employed full-time than were women (e.g., 91.8 percent of the doctorates for men compared to 77.1 percent for women, and 84.8 percent of the masters level for men compared to 59.7 percent for women). Conversely, more women were employed part-time than men at all educational levels. For all respondents with more than a baccalaureate degree, a higher percentage of women were unemployed. For those who reported their field was physiological psychology, all of the 277 men reported full-time employment. Only 16 of the 35 female respondents were employed full-time, four reported part-time employment, and 12 were unemployed. Six of the 554 male developmental psychologists were employed part-time and none were unemployed. In contrast, 40 of the 459 female develpmental psychologists had part-time employment and 29 were unemployed. The largest number of both male and female psychologists were in clinical psychology. No gender difference was apparent in amount of unemployment here. However, the general pattern of greater under- and unemployment for females was evident for most subfields of psychology. It should be noted that some part-time employment is by choice and some unemployed psychologists are not seeking employment. Even taking such factors into consideration, however, gender differences still occur. Similar gender differences were found in the 1947 study by Bryan and Boring.[1]

Employment settings for psychologists encompass colleges and universities, other educational settings, human service settings including hospitals and counseling centers, business and industry, federal, state, or

TABLE 6
EMPLOYMENT STATUS BY DEGREE LEVEL AND GENDER

Degree Level	Full-Time	Part-Time	Unemployed and Seeking	Unemployed and Not Seeking	Retired	No Response	Raw Total
Men							
No Post Baccalaureate Degree	75.7	3.1	17.8	1.0	0.0	2.4	112
Master	84.8	6.8	2.0	2.6	3.5	0.4	2,783
Doctorate	91.8	3.6	1.1	0.4	2.6	0.6	18,438
Other Post Baccalaureate Degree	80.2	12.9	1.6	0.6	4.1	0.6	371
Weighted n	19,661	898	275	146	594	130	21,704
Women							
No Post Baccalaureate Degree	42.9	44.2	2.9	4.0	0.0	6.0	35
Master	59.7	20.3	5.5	7.7	5.6	1.3	2,137
Doctorate	77.1	13.9	2.6	1.6	3.7	1.1	5,975
Other Post Baccalaureate Degree	74.5	15.5	2.1	5.1	2.1	0.8	182
Weighted n	6,033	1,308	280	269	342	96	8,328
Both Sexes							
No Post Baccalaureate Degree	67.9	12.8	14.3	1.7	0.0	3.3	147
Master	73.9	12.7	3.5	4.8	4.4	0.8	4,919
Doctorate	88.2	6.1	1.4	0.7	2.9	0.7	24,413
Other Post Baccalaureate Degree	78.3	13.8	1.7	2.1	3.5	0.7	553
Weighted n	25,694	2,205	555	415	937	225	30,332

local independent research organizations, government, the criminal justice system, and the military.

Generally speaking, women spend more time teaching, less time in research and administration, and greater time providing service than do their male counterparts.

In spite of decreasing job opportunities for Ph.D. recipients generally, at least recent doctorates, both female and male, are still finding jobs in psychology. A follow-up survey of recent doctorates (carried out in early 1977 by APA) indicated that only 1.7 percent of 1976 doctorate recipients were unemployed at that time.[7] A higher proportion of women than men are getting academic positions, but more men are in administration. In general, decreasing proportions of both men and women are gaining employment in academic settings. Those psychologists with specialities in applied fields seem to be faring better than those more dependent on the academic market. However, despite a generally good employment picture, a higher percentage of these female 1976 Ph.D.s were employed part-time or were unemployed than was true of their male counterparts.

A comparison of distribution of faculty by rank and gender in departments of psychology with APA-approved programs was made for four years—from 1972-73 to 1975-76. As shown in TABLE 7, in each of these four years the highest concentration of women is at the lower ranks. The higher the rank, the fewer the women, even though the highest percentage of all faculty is at the full professor level. The mean percentage for women over all four years at the instructor level is 35 percent; at the full professor level this figure drops to a mean of 7.5 percent. The strongest

TABLE 7

DISTRIBUTION OF FACULTY BY RANK AND GENDER IN DEPARTMENTS OF PSYCHOLOGY WITH APA-APPROVED PROGRAMS FROM 1972-73 TO 1975-76

	1972-73 Women	1972-73 Men	1973-74 Women	1973-74 Men	1974-76 Women	1974-76 Men	1975-76 Women	1975-76 Men
Inst. Lect.	30.39	69.61	40.63	59.37	32.83	67.17	36.08	63.92
Asst. Prof.	16.50	83.50	23.76	76.24	23.66	76.34	27.19	72.81
Assoc. Prof.	11.15	88.85	18.03	81.97	12.69	87.31	12.24	87.76
Full Prof.	6.50	93.50	8.73	91.27	7.51	92.49	7.76	92.24

increase in the percentage of women faculty members occurred at the assistant professor level, changing from 16.5 percent in 1972–73 to 27.19 percent in 1975–76.

Salary

An analysis of the financial experience of 1975 doctoral recipients in psychology was prepared by Sharon Dyer, Research Associate of APA, in 1977.[8] Statistically significant differences were found for both median and mean salaries. This, for the nine-to-ten-month salaries, the mean salary for women was about 94 percent of the men's mean salaries; for the eleven-to-twelve-month salaries the mean for women was about 91 percent of the men's mean salaries. Similar findings were reported for 1976 doctoral recipients (TABLE 8).

At entry level, salary differences, although significant, are relatively small in practical terms. However, gender differences in salary are more readily apparent when considering *all* Ph.D. psychologists and not just recent ones. Women are more likely to be concentrated at lower levels of rank, and therefore receive lower salaries. Full-time salaries for women Ph.D.s are lower in every important setting.

The 1973 Profile of Doctoral Scientists and Engineers distributed by the National Academy of Sciences in 1974 indicated the median salary for full-time employed male psychologists to be $20,580, compared to a median of $18,120 for females.[9]

In a recent 1977 report prepared by Nancy Russo, differences between male psychologists and female psychologists were reported to range from a low of about $1,000 in university counseling centers to $15,500 in medical/psychological group practice settings.[10]

Women who were employed before the recent laws and raised consciousness about equal employment were more likely to be paid lower entering salaries than men, as compared to those women who started their employment more recently. In fact, the longer a woman psychologist has been employed, the greater the discrepancy between her salary and that of a man with a similar employment background.

External Barriers to Obtaining a Doctoral Degree

Proportionately more women compared to men have the M.A. degree, rather than the Ph.D. For example, 23.9 percent of the doctoral level health-service providers are women compared to 44.6 percent of the

TABLE 8*

MEDIAN SALARY LEVELS OF FULL-TIME EMPLOYED 1976 DOCTORATES
BY GENDER AND SUBFIELD GROUPING

Subfield Grouping	Men	Women	Total†
Nine to ten months			
Helping Specialities	14,550	14,442	14,504
	(60)	(39)	(100)
Biopsychology	13,050	13,050	13,075
	(42)	(18)	(61)
Engineering/Industrial	14,925	—	14,925
	(17)	(0)	(17)
Social/Personality/Developmental	13,585	13,675	13,659
	(49)	(32)	(81)
General/Systems/Methods	—	—	—
	(2)	(1)	(3)
Educational	—	—	14,050
	(13)	(8)	(20)
Other		—	
	(12)	(3)	(15)
Total	200	103	305
Eleven to twelve months			
Helping Specialities	17,858	16,758	17,630
	(237)	(81)	(320)
Biopsychology	16,883	—	17,550
	(44)	(10)	(54)
Engineering/Industrial	—	—	—
	(13)	(1)	(14)
Social/Personality/Developmental	17,737	16,425	17,050
	(35)	(23)	(58)
General/Systems/Methods	—	—	—
	(55)	(2)	(7)
Educational	17,175	—	17,300
	(19)	(14)	(34)
Other	17,925	—	17,925
	(17)	(8)	(25)
Unknown	—	—	—
	(1)	(0)	(1)
	381	144	527

* Table excludes 76 respondents who did not report their contract period and 11 respondents who held some type of multiple employment arrangement they considered equivalent to full-time employment or who incorrectly reported their salary basis as part-time. Medians were not computed for categories with fewer than 15 cases. The n's upon which the medians are based are reported in parentheses. The column totals report the total number of cases for each contract period.

† Includes respondents whose gender is unknown.

master's level providers. Yet psychology primarily requires a doctoral degree for entry into the profession; one must have a doctoral degree for full membership in APA.

Women tend to be older than men when they receive the Ph.D. The lack of adequate financial support is the main reason for this delay in obtaining the Ph.D. Women and minority groups most frequently find barriers in their way when they attempt entry into a doctoral program.

Many of these potential students will be working and thus interested in entering a part-time program. Other women will have the B.A. or M.A. and wish to pursue graduate work after some years of absence from formal education. Part-time education may be all they can afford in terms of time and money. By contrast, many graduate programs have biases against women and/or part-time students. The *proportion* of women recipients of master's and doctoral degrees declined substantially from 1930 to 1970, despite the proportionate increase of women earning baccalaureate degrees.[11]

Institutional barriers prevent women's entry into graduate study and thus contribute to an enormous waste of talent. Clear evidence of discrimination against women has been found in terms of admission to graduate study and also in obtaining financial aid.[12]

Yet, studies have shown that most women admitted to graduate schools do obtain their Ph.D.s, do stay in the field, do publish, and do contribute.[12] It is true that the student who runs in and takes one or two courses and then runs home is missing a great deal. She doesn't experience the peer and collegial relationships so necessary to the making of a psychologist. The talk sessions, the colloquia, and just hanging around the department or the clinic are all part of the experiences one should participate in in graduate school. However, this need not be done on a full five-day-a-week schedule. Viable part-time programs in which students make orderly intellectual progress can be worked out on a two- or three-day basis, or over several half days per week, which incorporate all the essential features of a full-time program, including immersion in the culture of psychology. Two students on part-time basis can be admitted as the equivalent of one full-time student. Financial aid, which we hope will be available, can be shared by the two students. Even assistantships and other forms of graduate work-related experiences could be shared. Too often the part-time student loses out in any form of financial assistance simply because she is part time. Barriers such as this must be eliminated.

In summary, the situation for women in psychology *may* be in a period of transition. There are more women in graduate school, more recent female Ph.D.s, and in both cases, a higher percentage of women relative to the total number of students and graduates than has been true in the past. Affirmative action and the availability of employment has served to block obvious discrimination in *new* hiring. More women are also involved in the governance of the APA.

It should be noted, however, that data still indicate that the longer women are employed the greater their disadvantage vis-a-vis men. Many recently hired women have not received tenure. Attempts to reduce existing discrimination, especially in academia, as well as to monitor the ongoing process, must be continued. Psychologists must have a commitment to change women's status in the field.

REFERENCES

1. BRYAN, A. I. & E. G. BORING. 1947. Women in academic psychology: Factors affecting their professional careers. Am. Psychol. 2:3-20.
2. BIOGRAPHICAL DIRECTORY OF THE AMERICAN PSYCHOLOGICAL ASSOCIATION. 1977. The William Byrd Press. Richmond, Va.
3. AMERICAN PSYCHOLOGICAL ASSOCIATION OFFICE OF MEMBERSHIP AND RECORDS (from data obtained from D. Palermo). 1977. APA membership data-psychology Ph.D.s 1972-1976.
4. DOUVAN, E. 1977. President's column. Division 35 Newsletter. 4:(1) 1.
5. TASK FORCE REPORT ON THE STATUS OF WOMEN IN PSYCHOLOGY. 1973. Am. Psychol. 28:611-616.
6. DYER, S. E. 1977. An overview of the employment of psychologists. Human Resources Commission of the American Psychological Association.
7. HORAI, J. 1977. Minutes of the October 1977 meeting of the American Psychological Association Policy and Planning Board. Section 3:2.
8. DYER, S. E. 1977. The early labor market experiences of 1975 doctoral recipients in psychology. The Office of Programs and Planning. American Psychological Association. Report No. 1:6.
9. NATIONAL ACADEMY OF SCIENCES U.S.A. 1974. Doctoral scientists and engineers in the United States: 1973 profile:27.
10. RUSSO, N. F. 1977. Women as providers and consumers of health services: Some preliminary data. Assembled for the sub-panel on Mental Health for Women, President's Commission on Mental Health, by the American Psychological Association's Women's Program Office.
11. GINZBERG, E. 1966. Life styles of educated women. Columbia Univ. Press. New York, N.Y.
12. EKSTROM, R. B. 1972. Barriers to women's participation in post-secondary education: A review of the literature. Paper presented at the American Psychological Association Convention, Honolulu, Hi.

The Peak of the Pyramid: Women in Dentistry, Medicine, and Veterinary Medicine

AMBER B. JONES
Association of American Medical Colleges
Washington, D.C. 20036

EILEEN C. SHAPIRO
School of Dental Medicine
School of Public Health
Harvard Medical School
Boston, Massachusetts 02115

THE HEALTH CARE INDUSTRY is generally viewed as a hierarchy supported by a broad base of semiskilled workers. This pyramidal structure is particularly dependent upon the availability of women laborers; in 1974, 75 percent of the health-care labor force was female.[1] During the past ten years, the number of women at the peak of the health-industry pyramid has increased dramatically. This increase has occurred at a time when health-care consumers, as well as allied health professionals and hospital workers, have emerged as powerful and effective interest groups, and at a time when the structures of health-care institutions are undergoing great change. This background provides the context for our paper.

As we discuss the women at the peak of the pyramid in dentistry, medicine, and veterinary medicine, we use as our points of reference two critical issues: first, that increases in the numbers of women dentists, physicians, and veterinarians do not guarantee these individuals either the authority or the power to influence the quality or the quantity of health-care delivery; and second, that there is the potential for a powerful alliance among the relatively small number of women at the top of the health-industry pyramid, the large number of women workers who form its base, and health-care consumers (the majority of whom are female), and there is also the potential for great conflict, particularly between the women health-care workers at the top and at the bottom of the pyramid.

This paradox encapsulates an important dilemma facing women health-care providers today.

We have structured this paper in two parts: In the first part, we document selected aspects of the current status of women at the top of the hierarchies in the three health professions of dentistry, medicine, and veterinary medicine. In the second part, we discuss some of the effects of the changing structure of the health-care system on the present and future roles of the women in each of these professions, particularly in terms of the increasing demand for managerial and administrative skills for health-care professionals.

Before we proceed to these three health professions, it is important to review some of the reasons why the backbone of the health-care industry is overwhelmingly female, particularly in the context of an issue clearly and succinctly expressed by Olesen; namely, that for women in leadership positions in health fields, most of the individuals in lower status positions over whom they will have authority and power are women.[2]

Why is there such a large numerical predominance of women among health workers? Brown offers the following explanations:

1. Women represent an inexpensive source of labor; a work force composed predominantly of women costs less than one compared primarily of men.
2. Because a much smaller percentage of women than men enter the labor force, women represent a major reservoir of available unemployed personnel. This competition for jobs keeps wages low.
3. As a group, women lack access to social power in the forms of capital, specialized education, freedom from day-to-day household responsibilities, and the respect of political leaders. Thus, women in the aggregate pose little or no threat to the power structure within the health industry.
4. For social and economic reasons, women have limited occupational choices.
5. Measured against the median income for women in all industries, pay in the health industry is still higher.[3]

With this in mind, we now briefly review several aspects of the status of women at the male-dominated pinnacle of a female-dominated structure, by looking at women in each of the three most visible health professions: dentistry, medicine, and veterinary medicine.

Women in Dentistry

Of the three health professions considered in this paper, dentistry is the one that has the smallest proportion of women in its membership. The most recent figures we have indicate that as of 1974, there were 102,220 practicing dentists, of whom 3.2 percent were women.[4] This statistic is surprising, particularly when the practice of dentistry is carefully inspected. In many countries, dentistry is considered a woman's profession. Even in this country, as Schoen[5] points out, women constitute a majority of dental personnel if one includes dental assistants, hygienists, and secretary-receptionists in the tally.

Women who enter dentistry and become practitioners appear to be significantly different than their male counterparts. Coombs'[6] 1975 research on factors associated with career choice among women dentists elucidates the disparities: Women pursue a dental career one or two years later than their male counterparts, frequently after having attended graduate school in the basic sciences or having worked in some scientific field. Two significant factors in their choice are peer approval and support from parents. More women dentists than male dentists had mothers who worked for a living; in addition, both parents of women dentists are likely to be more highly educated than those of male dentists. Many women dental students have had work-related experiences in the dental field. The women students tend to be unmarried and to have grown up in nonurban areas. Finally, women who are dentists have more professional education than their male counterparts.

It is ironic that, even though there are so few women dentists, there are those who argue that dentistry is, by definition, a particularly suitable profession for women. In a 1974 article in the *British Dental Journal*,[7] the practice of dentistry is presented as an occupation of choice for women with family responsibilities on the following bases: 1. the lucrative remuneration which allows the purchase of domestic services and labor-saving devices; 2. the degree to which competency in practice skills can be retained when used on a part-time basis; and 3. the flexibility of working hours allowed by the nonemergency nature of most dental care. In spite of these factors, there are proportionately fewer women in dentistry in the United States than in any other health care occupation; according to statistics from the U.S. Department of Labor,[8] in 1972, only three percent of all practicing dentists were female, as opposed to twelve percent of physicians and five percent of veterinarians.

Having made several observations about the suitability of dentistry as a profession for women, it is appropriate to consider some of the support systems that have facilitated the entry of women into this field. The results of Linn's[9] 1970 study, based on a questionnaire sent to all women dentists in the United States, are strikingly similar to Coombs' study of women dental students. Linn's work suggests that American women who become dentists have had significant exposure to the field before entry. In addition, those women who have graduated from American dental schools reported having received personal support and encouragement from many sources, including practicing professionals, relatives, and friends. Apparently, for those hardy souls who can withstand the significant forces that would exclude women from the profession, familiarity with the functions of dentistry and support from important persons constitute an effective arsenal.

WOMEN IN MEDICINE

Men who become physicians do so for reasons that are different from those given by women doctors. According to a 1976 study by Urban and Rural Systems Associates[10] (URSA), in San Francisco, Calif., male students identify financial security, a comfortable life-style, and the status of the profession as chief attractions. Female students, on the other hand, identify the independence and power of the role of physician, the image of humanitarianism, and the potential for challenging involvement as their motivators. The URSA Study goes on to report:

> No set of pathways is distinctive to men or women, but one general difference does seem to emerge: men's routes to professional choice are less complex and more direct than are women's. This seems to be due to one quite clear and nearly universal difference between the decision-making patterns of men and women: because social expectations of men are unambiguous in terms of their adult roles as bread-winners and full-time workers, men do not make the decision of whether or not to construct a career but assume it and choose among available options. Social expectations of women, on the other hand, are quite ambiguous in this regard, and they must discover that they *can* be professionals and decide whether or not they will define a large part of their adult identity in terms of their construction of a career.[11]

There has been a wealth of research focusing on each of the many aspects of the training and career development of women doctors.[12-31] Perhaps the most provocative among these is Walsh's[27] history of women who have pursued medical careers. Walsh demonstrates that antifeminism has constituted an overwhelming obstacle to the determined and talented women who have sought access to the medical profession. Although there are more women doctors than women dentists or women veterinarians, the net increase in the proportion of women physicians since the early 1900s has been extremely limited: in 1910, women represented six percent of the total number of physicians in this country. Nineteen seventy-six figures indicate that women comprise 8.6 percent of the total number of U.S. physicians, a gain of 2.6 percent in sixty-six years. With female students comprising 24.7 percent of the entering first-year medical school class in 1976-77,[32] it is clear that both the proportion and absolute numbers of women physicians are undergoing a significant increase. This increase in numbers of women doctors *could* have an important influence on the delivery of health care. Among the factors affecting whether these women will have such an influence are demand for services, sources of reimbursement, health care regulations, and the socialization process experienced by all medical students and house officers.

Women in Veterinary Medicine

Of the three professions addressed in this paper, veterinary medicine is the smallest. This is not surprising when numbers of training sites are considered. In the academic year 1973-74, there were 58 dental schools, 114 medical schools, and only 18 schools for veterinary medicine.[33] In addition to being the smallest in terms of numbers of practicing professionals, veterinary medicine is different from dentistry and from medicine in that its clientele is animal rather than human. Of particular importance to women in veterinary medicine, however, is the fact that the focus of this profession has been changing; the Urban and Rural Systems Associates Study notes that while veterinary medicine is "still predominately an integral part of the national food supply production system, the demand for health care for urban and suburban pets has been increasing dramatically. Thus, small animal specialists have become a very much more substantial part of the profession, and this is reflected in a shift in the public's view of the profession from that of a primarily agricultural function to a more humanitarian profession."[34]

The image of veterinarian as a masculine profession is comparable to that found in dentistry. This concept has been particularly true for the large-animal practices and because of the inspection functions traditionally filled by veterinarians. As a result, statistics indicating that veterinary medicine has experienced a more rapid rate of increase in the percentage of women enrolled in first-year classes between 1968-69 and 1974-75[35] rather than either dentistry or medicine are somewhat surprising. This growth in the number of women students may be in part a response to the demand for more veterinarians. However, it may also relate to the fact that improved technology in this field has reduced the need of practitioners to rely on brute strength in the rendering of treatment.

One of the characteristics of veterinary medicine that differentiates it from the other prestigious health professions is its limited reliance on individuals with training in allied health roles. The support staff systems found in general dental and medical settings do not exist in the practices of most veterinarians. In a way, this self-sufficiency makes veterinary medicine a more independent and entrepreneurial profession than its medical and dental counterparts; the pyramidal structure with professional decision-makers buttressed by a variety of technical and support staff has not been traditionally a part of veterinary medicine. Thus, the number of women in occupations directly connected to the practice of veterinary medicine has been limited. There is, however, some evidence that a system of support staff is beginning to develop in this field. If such a system should emerge, there is little if any reason to believe that the structure will differ from that found in dentistry or medicine. As a result, one can forecast increasing numbers of women selecting support roles in veterinary medicine.

Individuals who select medicine and dentistry as careers frequently come from families that already include physicians and dentists respectively. Veterinary medicine differs from this pattern. To quote again from the URSA Study, "Veterinary medicine is not one of those professions which is handed down from preceding generations. In this respect, veterinary medicine is the least family-oriented of all the following schools: medicine, osteopathic medicine, dentistry, veterinary medicine, optometry, podiatry, pharmacy and public health."[36] One can argue, therefore, that veterinary medicine provides an unusual opportunity for women: because there is no family tradition connected with the field, there is no heritage to suggest that only men should select this career option. As technical advances have been made and as the demand for veterinarians who favor small-animal practices has grown, the logical barriers to women who would enter this field have fallen. The sharp increase in the numbers of women entering veterinary training programs is undoubtedly a reflection of these factors.

One last contrast between medicine or dentistry and veterinary medicine should be noted. Both medicine and dentistry have specialty training programs which follow the period of formal undergraduate professional education. Veterinary medicine, on the other hand, has very little to offer its students in the way of postgraduate education. As a result, the total amount of preparation for practice is shorter in veterinary medicine, a factor that may have appeal for individuals who have obligations that make extended training impractical or impossible.

Comparisons Among Three Professions

We turn now to some of the common issues facing women who select any one of these three professions as a career. FIGURE 1 shows the number of practicing women dentists, physicians, and veterinarians as of 1970.

At that time there were 3,270 women dentists representing 3.2 percent of the active dentist population; 21,474 women physicians, representing 6.9 percent of the active physician population, and 1,320 women veterinarians, representing 5.1 percent of the active veterinarian population. Although these figures represent the actual numbers of practicing female professionals as of 1970, they distort the present reality and future projections by their retrospective nature. A more reliable sampling of statistics for discussions about the present and future status of women in dentistry, medicine, and veterinary medicine is drawn from class composition data from training institutions, reflected in FIGURE 2.

In 1974–75, there were 631 first-year women in dental schools, representing 11.2 percent of the entering class; 3,275 first-year women in medical schools, representing 22.2 percent of the entering class; and 407 first-year women in schools of veterinary medicine, representing 24.4 percent of the entering class. Comparable figures from five years earlier give some indication of the changing composition of entering classes by sex. In 1969–70 there were 58 first-year women in dental schools, representing 1.3 percent of the entering class; 948 first-year women in medical schools, representing 9.1 percent of the entering class; and 146 first-year women in schools of veterinary medicine representing 10.9 percent of the entering class. Thus, the number of professionals being trained in each field is rising, as is the proportion of the total number of trainees that are women.

In addition to increasing their numbers relative to the size of profes-

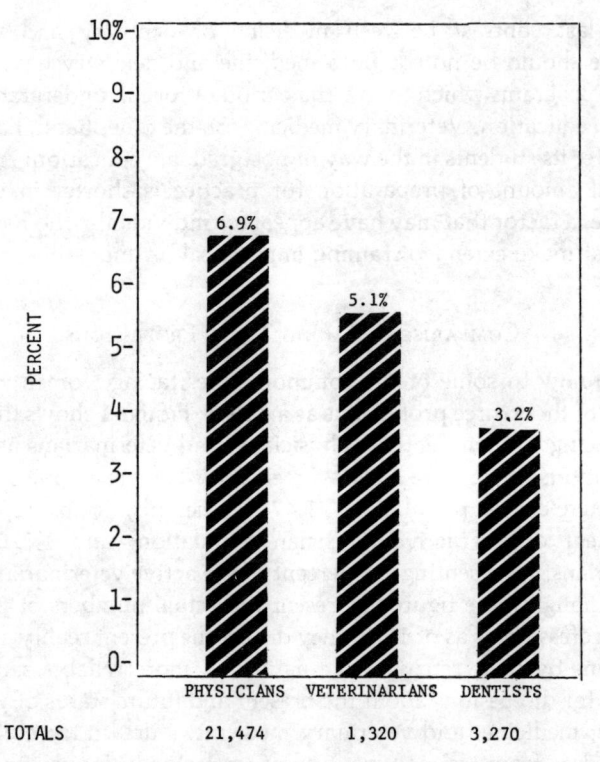

FIGURE 1. Women workers in selected health occupations. (From Division of Manpower Intelligence. 1974. 1970 Profiles and Projections to 1990. Department of Health, Education and Welfare, Washington, D.C.)

sions as a whole, women dentists, physicians, and veterinarians are now experiencing some common challenges. We choose as an example the fact that the entire structure of health-related professional educational programs is changing. Universities that have housed separate and, for all practical purposes, independent health-professions schools are now beginning to recognize the similarities of some aspects of the several educational efforts. As a result, some university administrators are restructuring their institutions so that all of their health-professions schools are conceptually unified within a "Health Sciences Center." This reorganization means that in those university settings that incorporate schools of dentistry, medicine, and veterinary medicine, there is the

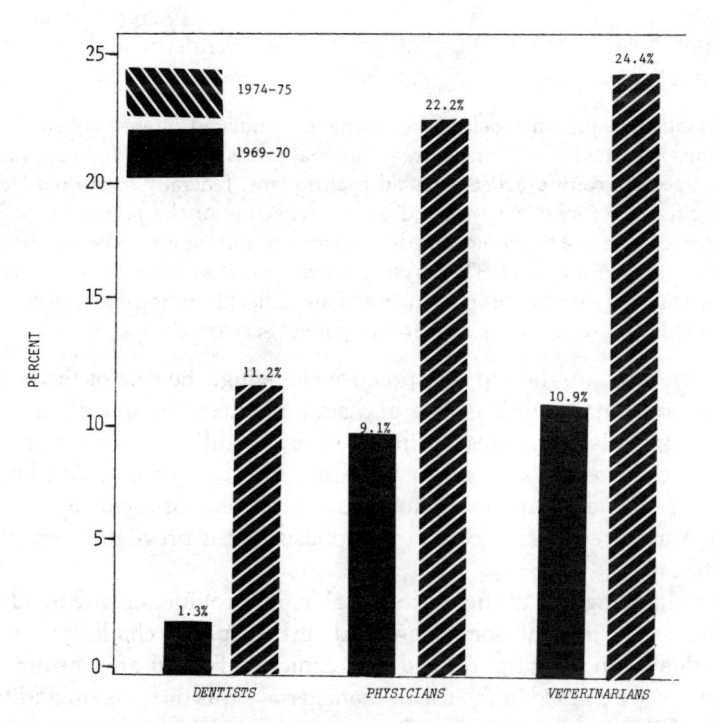

FIGURE 2. Numbers and percentages of women among first-year students in Schools of dentistry, medicine and veterinary medicine 1969–70, 1974–75. (From Department of Health, Education and Welfare, unpublished data from the American Veterinary Association, and reference 1)

potential for increased interaction among students and practicing professionals from the collective of institutions represented. Ideally, such a federation unites health professionals more closely through the sharing of training and facilities. Since schools of nursing and the allied health professions traditionally populated primarily by women are also included in the Health Sciences Center concept, it is possible that there will be an opportunity for an increased interchange among the women of the various schools.

A second structural change taking place within the health professions, particularly in dentistry, medicine, and veterinary medicine, is the way in which health services are delivered. Although the following quotation makes specific reference to physicians, similar statements are found in the literature describing current practices in dentistry and veterinary medicine:

> Mounting health care delivery costs have stimulated interest, research and some experimentation in new organizational forms of care including a variety of types of group practice, prepaid health plans, federally sponsored Health Maintenance Organizations, and others. The role of the physician in these forms of care is seen by most medical educators and experts to be significantly different than it is now. The physician is described as more an administrator and manager of other professionals and allied health professionals making up a health care team, less a deliverer of patient services.[37]

Thus not only are the types of practice changing, the role of the healthcare professional herself is also in a state of flux. The overall effect of these changes is at the present time unclear. Modification of the practice structure, however, appears to be in the direction of enabling healthcare professionals a more standard, less intensive, work schedule by providing for shared coverage and by emphasizing the preventive aspects of health care.

The changing role of the professional, from provider of care to administrator, may present some new and unanticipated challenges to the individual who has been trained as a clinician. Few, if any, health-care deliverers are trained in the use of managerial skills or tools. In addition, much of the current management theory is based on the experience of managers in for-profit industrial settings. As a result, only a limited amount of the management literature is of relevance for individuals with administrative responsibilities in health-care delivery settings. Men and women health professionals share the disadvantage of inadequate training in administration and decision-making, but the effect of such inadequacies are perceived as being different for women than for men. Estler makes the following argument:

> At higher levels, where policy is made, responsibilities cover a broader span and are less clearly defined. Such jobs often require response to a complex set of circumstances existing both within and outside the organization. In the absence of concrete, goal-related measures, readily observable factors such as race and sex may be used unconsciously as a proxy for assessing competence. In the face of uncertainty, familiar characteristics are reassuring to those who operate the filter points.[38]

If women in dentistry, medicine, and veterinary medicine are to occupy positions of leadership and authority, they must address and resolve conflicts at several levels. Not only are their male associates unlikely to perceive them as competent managers, other women within the health-care hierarchy may resist task delegation and/or supervision from other women in senior roles; as Olesen eloquently argues:

> The literature on women at work, as well as much of everyday life, makes it clear that both males and other females view women in leadership positions negatively. Repeated studies reveal that women prefer male supervisors to female supervisors, and even women leaders themselves . . . [have] stated that they would not feel comfortable working for a woman. These findings, coupled with the materials that show that some successful women discriminate against other females point to some of the difficulties which lie ahead for the woman who moves to a position where she supervises other women . . . Thus, discrepancies between the taken-for-granted order of male dominance and female submission in American society which exist in the presence of female supervisors exercising authority over other females, even when the supervisor also can claim professional dominance, as with a female doctor, are such that strains ensue for all concerned in health care settings where this is the case.[39]

Women who move into administrative positions in health-care institutions face what appears to be a paradoxical situation, again to quote Olesen:

> The interpersonal dynamics which produce the negotiated order also produce a role structure in which affect is distributed. These latter two orders may not be congruent with the formal structure of authority in the setting. The creation and dispersal of knowledge is crucial to action; hence, where it is held by persons other than those in leadership positions, the exercise in power becomes problematic. . . . It is crucial for women who aspire to and arrive in leadership positions to sense where knowledge is held, who generates it and to work with those lower status persons, mostly women, who have it. . . . This also means that the socialization of women for leadership in health settings is crucially in the hands of other women: the secretaries, aides, clerks and technicians who staff such a setting.[40]

Thus the acquisition of administrative skills is only one prerequisite for women professionals who aspire to positions of leadership and authority; a second and not inconsequential requirement is the development of the ability to identify and utilize sources of knowledge and information wherever they are found.

Summary

We have reviewed selected aspects of the status of women in dentistry, medicine, and veterinary medicine by focusing on the women in the peak of the health care pyramid within the context of the fact that the vast majority of women health-care laborers work in support capacities at the bottom of the hierarchy. Changes in the role of health-care professionals from providers of care to administrators and managers will have profound effects on the relationships among women of varying statuses within the health-care industry. Of even greater possible impact is the potential of women health-care providers at all levels in the hierarchy and women health-care consumers to determine the quality and quantity of health services to be rendered in the future. If this potential is to be fulfilled, those women aspiring to careers in dentistry, medicine, or veterinary medicine should carefully assess the education and training they will need to obtain. Further, they should be cognizant of the social and political forces that will affect their roles as administrators—i.e., as professionals who can mold the direction of health care delivery in the future.

Will women at the peak of the health care pyramid be able to garner the authority and power to influence the future directions of health-care delivery in this country? Will women at all levels in the health-care industry work together to form a new order, or will they identify on the basis of level in the hierarchy rather than sex? These are the questions of the next decade that feminists wishing to affect health care for women must face.

Acknowledgment

This paper was developed with the capable assistance of Janice Scarborough, Management Advancement Program, Association of American Medical Colleges.

References

1. PENNELL, M. & S. SHOWELL. 1975. Women in Health Careers. Chart Book for the International Conference on Women in Health: 8. American Public Health Association. Washington, D.C.

2. OLESEN, V. 1977. Reconceptualizing leadership: lower-status women and the exercise of power in health care settings. In Proceedings of the Conference on Women's Leadership and Authority in the Health Professions: 43-53. Department of Health, Education and Welfare. Washington, D.C.
3. BROWN, C.A. 1975. Women workers in the health services industry. Int. J. Health Services 5(2):173.
4. Division of Manpower Intelligence. 1974. The Supply of Health Manpower, 1970 Profiles and Projections to 1990. Department of Health, Education and Welfare. Washington, D.C.
5. SCHOEN, M. 1975. Women in dentistry—A view from Stony Brook. N.Y. J. Den. 45:307-308.
6. COOMBS, J.A. 1976. Factors associated with career choice among women dental students. J. Dent. Ed. 40:724-732.
7. REPORT. 1977. Part-time work for women dentists with family obligations. Br. Dent. J. 136.
8. WOMEN'S BUREAU. 1975. 1975 Handbook on Women Workers. Department of Labor. Washington, D.C.
9. LINN, E.L. 1970. Professional activities of women dentists. J. Am. Dent. Assoc. 81(6):1383-1387.
10. URBAN AND RURAL SYSTEMS ASSOCIATES. 1976. An Exploratory Study of Women in the Health Professions Schools II:56-57.
11. URBAN AND RURAL SYSTEMS ASSOCIATES. 1976. An Exploratory Study of Women in the Health Professions Schools II:58-59.
12. CHAFF, S.L., R. HAIMBACK, C. FENICHEL & N.B. WOODSIDE. 1977. Women in Medicine: A Bibliography of the Literature on Women Physicians. Scarecrow Press. Metuchen, N.J.
13. CARTWRIGHT, L.K. 1977. Continuity and noncontinuity in the careers of a sample of young women physicians. In Proceedings of the Conference on Women's Leadership and Authority in the Health Professions: 146-156. Department of Health, Education and Welfare. Washington, D.C.
14. HASELTINE, F. & Y. YAW. 1976. Woman Doctor. Houghton Mifflin Co. Boston, Mass.
15. HAUG, J.N. A review of women in surgery. Bull. Am. Coll. Surgeons 60:21-23.
16. HEINS, M., S. SMOCK, J. JACOBS & M. STEIN. 1976. Productivity of women physicians. J. Am. Med. Assoc. 236:1961-1964.
17. KILSON, M. 1976. Women physicians in modern American medicine. Paper presented at the Macy Conference on Women in Medicine.
18. LOPATE, C. 1968. Women in Medicine. Johns Hopkins Press. Baltimore, Md.
19. MCGRATH, E. & C.N. ZIMET. 1977. Female and male medical students: differences in specialty choice selection and personality. J. Med. Ed. 52(4):293-300.

20. MARKS, G. & W.K. BEATTY. 1972. Women in White. Charles Scribner's Sons Publishers. New York, N.Y.
21. BUREAU OF HEALTH RESOURCES DEVELOPMENT. 1974. Minorities and Women in the Health Fields. Department of Health, Education and Welfare. Washington, D.C.
22. NAVARRO, V. 1975. Women in health care. N. Engl. J. Med. 292:398-402.
23. PENNELL, M. & S. SHOWELL. 1972. Distribution of women physicians. J. Am. Med. Women's Assoc. 27:197-203.
24. PLATT, L.I. 1951. Women doctors in Washington today: a statistical survey. J. Am Med. Women's Assoc. 6:446-447.
25. POWERS, L., R. REXFORD & R.B. WIESENFELDER. 1969. Practice patterns of women and men physicians. J. Med. Ed. 44:481-491.
26. ROESKE, N.A. & K. LAKE. 1977. Role models for women medical students. J. Med. Ed. 52(6):459-466.
27. WALSH, M.R. 1977. Doctors Wanted: No Women Need apply. Yale University Press. New Haven, Conn.
28. WALSH, M.R. 1976. Feminism: A support system for women physicians. J. Am. Med. Women's Assoc. 31:247-250.
29. WICKNER, H. 1974. Chief residents: New role models for women. Stanford M.S.: Stanford Medical Alumni Association 13:22-24.
30. WICKLER, N.J. 1977. Coming in and moving up: Women in the health professions. *In* Proceedings of the Conference on Women's Leadership and Authority in the Health Professions: 10-22. Department of Health, Education and Welfare. Washington, D.C.
31. WOODSIDE, N.B. 1975. Women in health care decision making. Paper presented at the International Conference on Women in Health. Washington, D.C.
32. DUBÉ, W.F. 1977. Medical student enrollment, 1972-73 through 1976-77. J. Med. Ed. 52(2):165.
33. URBAN AND RURAL SYSTEMS ASSOCIATES. 1976. An Exploratory Study of Women in the Health Professions Schools 1:A165.
34. URBAN AND RURAL SYSTEMS ASSOCIATES. 1976. An Exploratory Study of Women in the Health Professions Schools 5:3.
35. URBAN AND RURAL SYSTEMS ASSOCIATES. 1976. An Exploratory Study of Women in the Health Professions Schools 5:4.
36. URBAN AND RURAL SYSTEMS ASSOCIATES. 1976. An Exploratory Study of Women in the Health Professions Schools 5:44.
37. BARCLAY, W.R. 1973. The future of medical education and women in medicine. J. Am. Med. Women's Assoc. 28:69-70.
38. ESTLER, S. 1977. Women in decision making. *In* Proceedings of the Conference on Women's Leadership and Authority in the Health Professions: 199. Department of Health, Education and Welfare. Washington, D.C.

39. OLESEN, V. 1977. Reconceptualizing leadership: lower-status women and the exercise of power in health care settings. *In* Proceedings of the Conference on Women's Leadership and Authority in the Health Professions :46.
40. OLESEN, V. 1977. Reconceptualizing leadership: lower-status women and the exercise of power in health care settings. *In* Proceedings of the Conference on Women's Leadership and Authority in the Health Professions :49-50.

Women in Engineering Revisited

NAOMI J. McAFEE

Westinghouse Electric Corporation
Baltimore, Maryland 21203

ONE OF THE MAJOR deterrents to women considering engineering as a career is the all-male image. This barrier is rapidly disappearing as the engineering image changes from that of a hard-hat roustabout at a construction site to that of a thoughtful, logical individual who is genuinely interested in solving the social and engineering problems which face us today. True, she may still show up at a construction site in her hard hat, but her time is more apt to be spent at a desk working on new solutions. A female engineer—unlikely? Not quite.

Although women make up an unimpressive 1 percent of the engineering population, their ranks have been growing. The latest Society of Women Engineers survey of schools accredited by the Engineering Council for Professional Development shows that female engineering enrollment increased from 1,035 during 1959-60 to 11,746 during the 1975-76 school year.[1] This increase may not be as large as it appears on the surface. Only 128 schools replied to the 1959-60 survey. But with the advent of the Civil Rights Act of 1964 and, more recently, the implementation of the federal affirmative action program, as well as an increased awareness on the part of the schools, 167 responded last year (FIGURE 1). However, since the number of female engineering students per school has increased, even as the number of males enrolled at these schools has decreased, there is little doubt that the percentage of women enrolled in engineering undergraduate programs is growing.

JOBS COME FAST, PROMOTIONS SLOWLY

What happens when the newly minted female engineer tries to enter the field? Initially, she is sought after by almost every employer in sight. Once she is on the job, however, things change. On the average, promotions do not come as rapidly for women as they do for men.

Discrimination can be a double-edged sword; however, unlike her male counterpart, the female engineer is highly visible, and if she does

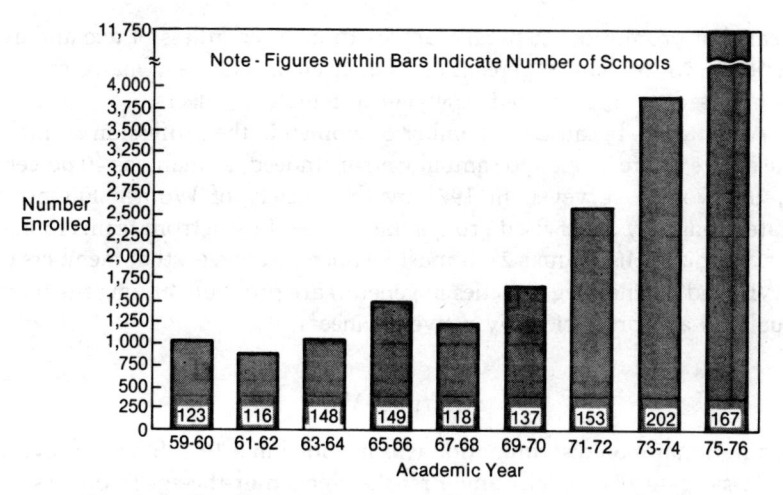

FIGURE 1. Enrollment of women in U.S. engineering schools.

an outstanding job, she may very well be rewarded faster than a man would be. If her performance is average or slightly below average, she may be judged in terms of a number of myths. Perhaps chief among them is the notion that men (and women) don't like to work for women. In my own experience, I have found that people who enjoy their work get it done without any thought of whether their supervisor is a man or a woman.

Some echoes of other misconceptions about women are still heard among engineers and undoubtedly contribute to the lag in promoting women to top management ranks. Examples of these myths are: A company's public image will suffer if a woman takes over a top management position, because men have traditionally been the corporate leaders; a woman won't travel on sales trips, to plant inspections, or to professional conferences; women don't want to accept responsibility; a woman's family will always take precedence over her career. (One must ask, why shouldn't it take precedence over a man's career as well?)

It has also been argued that promotion policies don't favor women because companies prefer long tenure for those elevated to executive positions, and they believe that turnover rates are greater for women. But not only do government figures[2-3] show that professional women have working careers comparable in length to those of men, it is also clear that promotions generally accrue to men regardless of age and experience. More than 20 percent of all male engineers are in management, as opposed to an estimated 2 percent of female engineers.

Admittedly, because the number of women in the profession is small, the above figure is open to sampling error. Indeed, as many as 40 percent of the women surveyed in 1974 by the Society of Women Engineers stated that they supervised groups that ranged in size from teams to major organizations (FIGURE 2). It must be noted, however, that members of SWE (and engineering societies in general) are probably among the more qualified and professionally active engineers.

ATTITUDES VARY

A questionaire on discrimination was included in a 1972 SWE survey. In a classic case of "which-came-first-the-chicken-or-the-egg?" the results showed that those women who were very successful in terms of salary, responsibility, and years of experience felt that they had not encountered

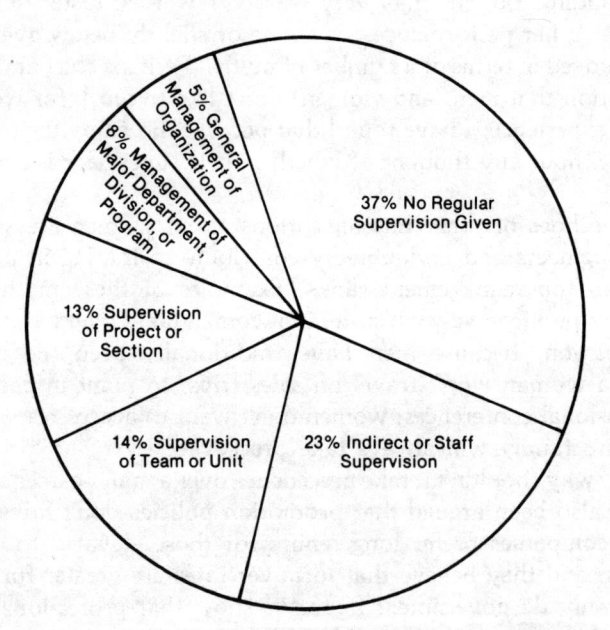

FIGURE 2. Supervisory responsibility of women engineers.

any discrimination. Those women who were moderately successful indicated that there was no discrimination encountered from their immediate superiors. They felt, however, that people in the upper levels of management hierarchy did discriminate and that there was some evidence of discrimination by coworkers.

Those women on the low side of the average in terms of salary and responsibility indicated that they had encountered discrimination at all levels. It can be argued that these women have less ability than their male cohorts and use "discrimination" as an excuse for their lack of advancement.

Salaries

All women encounter discrimination, perhaps not intentional or even conscious, from their male colleagues. This contention is borne out by the results of the SWE salary survey, compared with the results of the

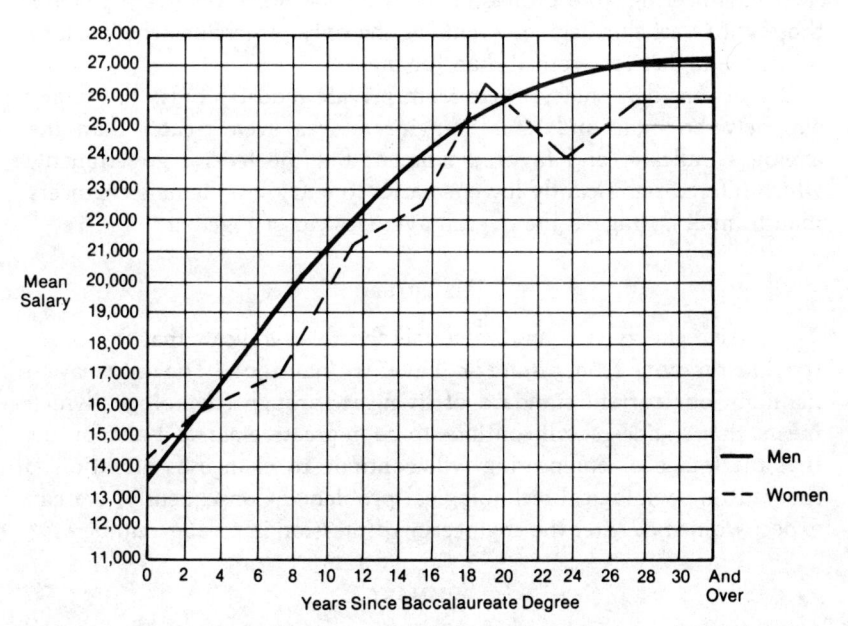

Figure 3. Comparison of median salaries for female engineers (SWE Survey) with those for all engineers (EJC Data).

survey of Engineers Joint Council for the profession as a whole. For engineers with 14 years' experience (the median for women), the median salary for female engineers is $19,675 per year, but that for all engineers with 14 years' is $23,715, according to the EJC (FIGURE 3) Both surveys were completed in 1977. The disparity may be even greater because, again, SWE members are more professionally active than all engineers taken as a group.[4]

Of course, the engineering profession is not alone in this disparity in salaries. In the federal civil service, men average $14,328 per year, and women only $8,578. This is not because there are separate pay scales for women, but rather because women employees are heavily concentrated in lower-grade jobs.

All is not bleak, however. In 1977, the average starting salary offered to women engineering graduates at the bachelor's degree level was $1150 per month, $43 a month more than the average for men, according to the College Placement Council. This represents a closing of the gap when compared with 1971, when women were offered $8 a month less than men. Engineering—the profession offering the highest starting pay for those with bachelor degrees—remains the only profession where salary offers are higher for women than for men.

If one considers salary offers from private industry only, the salary gap between male and female engineers was even greater than the averages indicate, and favored women. But the federal government, which offered significantly lower salaries to entry-level female engineers than to males, dragged the overall averages closer together.

THE FUTURE

The current energy crisis and materials shortages indicate that this country is fast moving from a state of "have" to "have not." The only way to maintain our current standard of living is through technology, which means that engineers will continue to be in great demand. It also means that the image of engineering will continue to change as attention is focused on sociological-technological problems. Consequently, we can expect women to enter the engineering profession in greater numbers.[5-6]

SUMMARY

Although women make up an unimpressive one percent of the engineering population, their ranks are growing. Undergraduate enrollment has

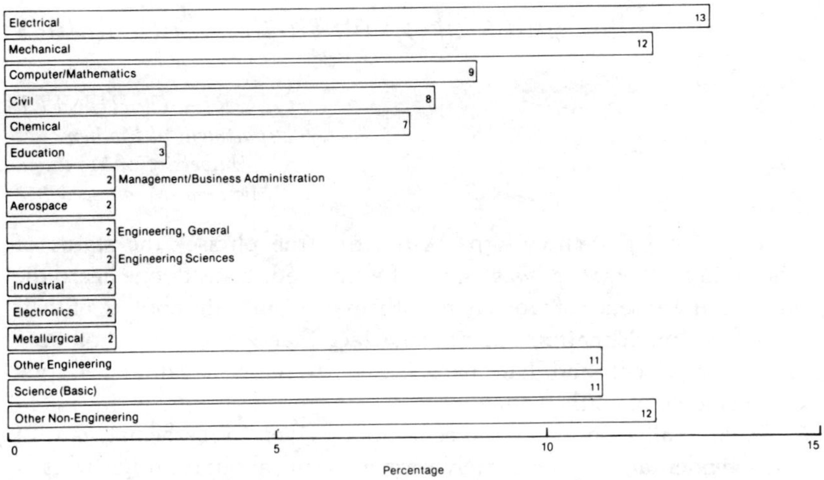

Field	Percentage
Electrical	13
Mechanical	12
Computer/Mathematics	9
Civil	8
Chemical	7
Education	3
Management/Business Administration	2
Aerospace	2
Engineering, General	2
Engineering Sciences	2
Industrial	2
Electronics	2
Metallurgical	2
Other Engineering	11
Science (Basic)	11
Other Non-Engineering	12

FIGURE 4. Distribution of female engineers by field of highest degree.

been increasing rapidly since 1970, and some universities today have women representing 10–15 percent of their engineering enrollment. Beginning salaries are higher for women than for men, but there is considerable controversy over what happens after the first job. Women initially have it better than men in engineering but the advantage disappears fast, and after the first five years the trend changes and the reverse is true.

REFERENCES

1. REPORT ON WOMEN UNDERGRADUATE ENGINEERING STUDENTS. Biennial Survey 1952–1976. Society of Women Engineers. New York, N.Y.
2. FACTS ABOUT WOMEN'S ABSENTEEISM AND LABOR TURNOVER. 1969. Women's Bureau, Wage and Labor Standards Administration. U.S. Dept. of Labor. Washington, D.C.
3. THE MYTH AND THE REALITY. 1971. Women's Bureau Report WB 71-113, Employment Standards and Administration. U.S. Department of Labor. Washington, D.C.
4. A PROFILE OF THE WOMAN ENGINEER. 1978. Society of Women Engineers. New York, N.Y.
5. WOMEN IN ENGINEERING. 1973. New Engineer.
6. BRIGHTER PROSPECTS FOR WOMEN IN ENGINEERING. 1974. Engineering Education.

The Status of Women in Mathematics

GLORIA C. HEWITT
Department of Mathematics
University of Montana,
Missoula, Montana 59812

LESS THAN A DECADE AGO, the phrase "the status of women in mathematics" was rarely, if ever, used. Instead, one heard the phrases "the absence of women in mathematics" and "the absence of their impact on mathematics," despite the fact that women had not been altogether absent and had participated in many great and lasting achievements in mathematics.

Traditionally, only casual recognition is given to mathematicians of either gender, and students rarely learn anything about the originators of mathematics unless they are in a history of mathematics course. However, the omission of the mention of women, even in history texts, is glaring. When many women mathematicians are mentioned at all, it is for their more secular activities, particularly when related to the lives of famous men.[1] This undoubtedly helps to perpetuate the myth that mathematics is a male domain. It is not clear how much the existence or nonexistence of role models inspires women to become mathematicians,[2] but surely the recognition that women have had an impact on mathematics cannot be hindrance. The writings of this decade that explore the role of various women in the history of mathematics, making this history available to a large audience, instill a mathematical pride which cannot be overlooked and which must be counted in a list of positive results of this decade.

Positive changes have occurred within the mathematical professional organizations. The Association for Women in Mathematics (AWM), formed about 1970 under the pioneering work of Mary Gray, has brought women mathematicians together in a sense of community and provided a medium through which their concerns and ideas could be discussed. Women now serve as editors, officers, and members of the Council, and are on various committees of the American Mathematical Society (AMS), the professional organization of research mathematicians. They also serve as editors, officers, and members of the Board of Governors and on various committees of the Mathematical Association of America (MAA). In fact, at present Dorothy Bernstein is president-elect of MAA and Julia Robinson is vice-president of AMS. The number of invited women speakers at annual, summer and regional meetings of both the AMS and MAA has increased greatly. To a large extent, I believe, these changes are the result of the efforts of AWM.

This has been a decade for efforts directed toward developing and utilizing the scientific and technical talents of women and ethnic minorities. A specific demand for women and minority women scientists resulted from the need of potential employers who receive federal funds to meet affirmative action requirements. The potential employer of a woman mathematician declares he would be happy to hire a well-qualified woman mathematician, but he can't find one. Yet, during the period 1966-70, women earned seven percent of the doctorates, 25 percent of the masters', and 36 percent of the bachelors' degrees awarded in mathematics.[3] Further, employment of mathematicians was enjoying one of the highest growth rates of any science.[4] It always amazes me when the request that "qualified" women not be overlooked gets interpreted as a request that "less qualified" women be chosen. It reminds me of a 1973 committee of the National Academy of Science where I sat listening to the complaint that they could not find "qualified" minorities for service on the various boards and committees. I was horrified (as were other members) when Percy Julian stated that he was not a member of the National Academy of Science (he was later elected to membership). Only one black person (a mathematician) had been found "qualified" for membership at that time. It was not until 1976 that a woman mathematician was elected to membership.

Once we set about the task of determining the actual availability of women mathematicians and how to increase that supply, we are forced to direct our efforts toward not only creating equal opportunities in employment, but toward eliminating the sexism which extends through all educational levels, as well as professional levels, and acts as a deterrent to women entering mathematics. The latter takes on added importance when we consider the higher attrition rate for women than for men at various levels of mathematical training[3-5], and that career options are severely limited by the avoidance of disciplines calling for the use of mathematics.

CAREERS AND EMPLOYMENT

Efforts directed toward developing the mathematical talents of women have yielded more fruit than efforts directed toward the utilization of these talents. Yet, the percentages of women mathematicians is not a true picture of their representation in the population, nor are the employment percentages an accurate indication of their representation among mathematicians. These should be our goals.

Actually, for as long a period as 1931 to 1970 only seven percent of the doctorates in mathematics were earned by women.[3] Further, during the period 1961-74, this percentage still obtained.[7] Since that time, we've seen an upswing in the percentage of Ph.D.s in mathematics earned by women: nine percent in 1973-74, 10 percent in 1974-75, 11 percent in 1975-76 and 13 percent in 1976-77.[8] Leo J. Eiden[9] and Betty M. Vetter[10] indicate that the percentage of degrees in mathematics earned by women has increased at all levels.

Minority women who hold doctorate degrees in mathematics are so few in number that they are practically invisible. The numbers of doctorates in mathematics awarded to minority women who are United States citizens were seven in 1974-75, three in 1975-76 and seven in 1976-77, of which 4, 0, and 0 were awarded to black women in each of the respective years.[8] McCarthy and Wolfe[11] report that only ten doctorates in mathematics were awarded to minority women during the period 1969-72 and nine during the period 1972-75. There is no upward trend, and these figures represent only a small percentage of the total doctorate recipients in mathematics. At this rate, many years will pass before we see any change in the development or utilization of talents of minority women mathematicians. Perhaps the entry of minority women into mathematics is now influenced by the same discouraging information the nonminorities are reading: the reduction in opportunities for employment, the reduction of financial support, and the reduction in graduate enrollment.

We might expect to find the percentage increase of women doctorates reflected in increased employment opportunities, but this does not seem the case. Each year approximately 80 percent of the new doctorate recipients in mathematics accept academic positions, overwhelmingly in doctorate-granting departments. Based on the nineteenth annual American Mathematical Society survey,[8] John Ernest[5] reports that for all doctorate-granting mathematics departments in the United States, in 1975-76 women comprised 4.8 percent of the regular faculty (with rank of assistant professor and above), up from 4.7 percent the previous year. For tenured faculty, the percentage is smaller: 4.5 percent of the tenured faculty were women, down from 4.6 percent the previous year. In actual numbers, there was an increase of 93 tenured faculty over the previous year and an increase of only one tenured woman faculty.

Based on the 21st annual AMS survey, in 1977-78 women comprise five percent (186 out of 3742) of the regular faculty, down from 5.1 percent (189 out of 3715) the previous year. For tenured faculty, the percentage stays at 4.7 percent in both years (138 out of 2936 in 1976-77, 139 out of 2974 in 1977-78). While the figures show a slight increase from 1975-76, there is no increase from 1976-77 of either women who are regular faculty or tenured faculty among the doctoral-granting departments.

If we restrict ourselves to the 27 most prestigious research departments, in 1975-76, three percent of the regular faculty were women, up from 2.2 percent the previous year (due to an increase in the number of women assistant professors). The percentage of women on the tenured faculty was 2 percent, down from 2.3 percent the previous year 1974-75.[5] Updating, we find that in 1977-78, 3.8 percent (31 out of 818) of the regular faculty are women, down from 4.2 percent (34 out of 811) in 1976-77. While for tenured faculty the percentage remains the same, 3.2 percent (21 out of 650 in 1976-77, 21 out of 661 in 1977-78) for both years.

It would appear that affirmative action requirements have had little effect on the doctorate-granting departments, especially when we consider that during the period 1961-74, 6.7 percent of Ph.D.s awarded by the 27 most prestigious departments and approximately seven percent of the Ph.D.s awarded by the top 65 departments were awarded to women. These percentages take on added significance when we realize that the top 65 departments awarded most of the Ph.D.s in mathematics. Despite declining graduate enrollment, since 1973 these departments have awarded 70 percent of the doctorates, with 43 percent awarded by the 27 most prestigious departments.[8] It is likely that the effect of affirmative action is most evident in the rank of assistant professor at which most new Ph.Ds enter mathematics faculties.

Even though, in doctorate-granting departments, there was an increase in the percentages of women among the doctorate-holding assistant professors, these percentages do not reflect the percentages of women earning doctorates. Again, based on the 21st annual AMS survey, in 1977-78, 8.4 percent (68 out of 804) of the doctorate-holding assistant professors in doctorate-granting departments are women, no percentage increase from the previous year. The percentages rose, however, from 5.5 percent in 1973–74 to 8.4 percent in 1976–77.[12-13]. At the 27 most prestigious departments, the percentages of women among the doctorate-holding assistant professors increased from three percent in 1974–75 to 10.2 percent in 1976–77, with a decrease to 8.6 percent for 1977–78.

The data[8] used above is by no means complete. It is compiled from responses of the various mathematics departments (the response rate was approximately two out of three). Further, because of the small numbers in some instances, a change of two or three women alters the percentages greatly. However, the percentages do give an indication of the employment picture for women mathematicians.

The statistics make us realize that we are not closer to achieving our goal. They refute the claims of some that women now have equal rights, that affirmative action has solved the problems. When employment in mathematics was plentiful, it was easy to find sympathizers. Now that employment has become a crisis, reverse discrimination becomes the cry, and it is time to rethink. Is it right to encourage women into mathematics when the employment situation is so bad? The freedom to become whatever we are capable of becoming, free from all sexual biases in education and employment, is the point. As Mary Gray[2] expressed so well, if we improve and encourage the mathematics education of women, if the attrition rate for women at each stage of their study of mathematics were the same as that for men (there will be more students to teach), and if we encourage students of both sexes to go on for advanced degrees only if they are committed to mathematics, the employment picture will ease.

It has long been the case that boys and men have been more career-minded than girls and women. Women and girls are becoming more and more career-minded,[14] but added encouragement is needed to reverse the trend of choosing careers of the traditional type[11,14] and to open doors to careers that have been closed because of mathematical prerequisites. In the study headed by John Ernest[5], even though the popularity of mathematics courses went down when mathematics became optional (in high school and college) for both sexes, there was no sex difference in mathematics preference through the grades. He conjectures that men take more mathematics courses, not because they like mathematics better, but because they realize such courses are critical to career options.

Much discussion has centered around the trend of adult women returning to college seeking to build careers and the condition of mathematical anxiety, a condition enhanced by inadequate training in basic mathematical skills. Several pilot programs have been instituted in mathematics to deal with the problems of mathematical anxiety. These programs are not yet widespread. In continuing education, many programs are designed for women, and women's studies programs are widespread. However, these do not have the necessary mathematical component. Perhaps the place to reach this large audience in need of mathematical training is through these established channels. Then, too, there is the bigger problem of educating the general public regarding the nature and purpose of a mathematics education.

Deterrents

Many articles have been written, many studies have been made, and many speculations have been made about the forces that affect the entrance and staying powers of women and girls in mathematics. They speak to the sex roles, the sexual stereotypes, the attitudes of parents, teachers, counselors, and classmates, the sexual biases to be found in mathematics texts, the ability of women and girls to do mathematics.

Many are suprised at the accusation that sexual biases exist in mathematics texts. Considerable sex bias in elementary mathematics texts have been uncovered as early as 1973.[15-17] This is one area where it is reasonable to expect early positive results. Helen Kuhnke,[18] upon examining two series of elementary mathematics texts (grades K-6) published in 1974, concluded that the publishers had responded positively to the critics of sex-role stereotyping, which indicated that the biases in text books can be eliminated when concerted effort is made. The two series were not identified, but I felt delighted that at last progress was being made and that perhaps other publishers would begin to follow suit. That elation was short-lived. Kepner and Koehn[19] thoroughly examined nine series of texts used in the elementary grades, chosen on the basis of recent publication dates and wide usage; they concluded that sexism was still very much in evidence in the eight popular series published in 1971 through 1975, even though there was little evidence of sexist language. Those published during the 1975-1977 period (two are revisions of the above and one new series) show some changes in sex roles. Females are assigned a greater variety of occupations and they appear more often in illustrations and problems. Even though females are now doctors and construction workers and typically playing baseball and basketball, there is little indication that male roles are changing.

The education of editors and publishers of more advanced

mathematics texts is apt to prove to be more difficult. Efforts at this level have been met with resistance (for example, see AWM Newsletters, September–October 1977, May–June 1976).

Fennema and Sherman[20] state that "if a person has confidence in his or her ability within a specific area, then that person is more apt to be motivated to achieve in that area." They conclude that "there is, then, an accumulation of evidence that points to the conclusion that sexual stereotyping of mathematics as a male domain operates through a myriad of subtle influences from peer to parent and within the girl herself to result eventually in the fulfillment of the stereotyped expection of a 'female head that's not much for figures.' It is in the operation of these subtly intertwined factors that one must look for the development of a course of remedial action."

It is interesting to note the parallels between the attitudes expressed by peer groups and the ways in which girls and young women view themselves. For example, in the study by Ernest,[5] out of a sample of 24 women and three men elementary and high school teachers, 41 percent felt boys did better in mathematics, whereas no one felt girls did better. In answer to why there are not more women mathematicians, Luchins[21] reports that responses from mathematicians included: 1) They do not think as well mathematically as men; and 2) it is not that women are not intelligent, but they have a different kind of intelligence.

How do the girls and young women view the situation? Levine[22] conducted a project that involved interviewing and administering questionnaires to students at grade levels 4, 9, 12, and sophomores. Some of the responses included: 1) Confidence, more than interest, influences one's choice of a career; 2) girls aren't as talented in mathematics as boys (they're conscientious but not talented); 3) top grades in mathematics imply intelligence (top grades in English Literature do not imply intelligence, but parents worry about whether a husband out there somewhere won't like me if I'm intelligent); and 4) college instructors of mathematics regard girls with humor (if they're there, the instructors will try to get them to pass the course, and if they're bright, the instructors are suprised).

The same attitudes are still at work for the graduate student and the university teacher. By now, we are just a little more confident. Only a few have chosen to continue; somewhere along the line somebody encouraged us to go on. Attitudes and remarks have become much more subtle. Those of us who are less aware can't figure out why we're upset, nor can we identify the drag we feel at times. We are pleased when the professor indicates that he is surprised at our cleverness, our brightness. We are flattered at his concern that family life is incompatible with good research (even though there are living examples to the contrary), flattered when he expresses a protective feeling towards us. Luchins[21] reports that family responsibility and child care were relatively more often cited by male than by female mathematicians as reasons for the small number of women in mathematics.

The situation which as troubled me most, I think, is baiting. In a social group, someone cites a study or an article, or makes a remark, which has a possible interpretation negative to women. It is hoped that I will respond. For many years I have fallen into the trap of engaging in the discussion, then not understanding why I went away feeling upset and totally occupied with it for several days. This could be dealt with more easily from a psychological standpoint if one could assume that this was a situation of blatant sexism or racism. The difficulty lies in not being sure and in feeling the continuing necessity of sorting out possible motives, intentions, and implications at each occurrence. The cumulative effect is to undermine one's confidence, and a great amount of energy is expended having to cope with perhaps unintended implications.

A very sensitive male mathematician once explained it to me this way. While there may not be much trouble speaking together on a one-to-one basis, there is always a group who must play the game "Get Someone." The victim is always either a woman, a member of an ethnic minority, or someone with enough sensitivity (usually because of personal involvement) to react to the game. Too often the game is not recognized, and the longer it is played, the more irrational the remarks become. To end the game, the victim is backed into a corner, and he/she becomes very upset. He recounted many, many instances of this game he had witnessed. This is a phenomenon I have witnessed time and time again in coffee rooms or at other social gatherings.

It is vital to recognize that these kinds of subtle games can sometimes be more damaging and more difficult to deal with than the struggles through school or the struggles to seek employment.

References

1. Osen, L. M. 1974. Women in Mathematics. The MIT Press. Cambridge, Mass.

2. GRAY, M. 1977. The mathematics education of women. MAA Monthly. 84(5):374–377.
3. LARNEY, V. H. 1973. Female mathematicians, where are you? MAA Monthly. 80(3):310–313.
4. LASALLE, J. P., C. R. RUSSELL & D. E. RICHMOND. 1970. Report on Aspects of Professional Work in the Mathematical Sciences 3. Conference Board of the Mathematical Sciences.
5. ERNEST, J. 1976. Mathematics and sex. MAA Monthly 83:595–614.
6. FENNEMA E. & J. A. SHERMAN. 1977. Sexual stereotyping and mathematics learning. Arithmetic Teacher 24(5):369–372.
7. HERSTEIN I. N. 1976. Graduate schools of origin of female Ph.D.s. Notices. AMS 23:166–171.
8. AMERICAN MATHEMATICAL SOCIETY. 1974. 18th annual AMS survey. Notices 21:255–259. 1975. 19th annual AMS survey. Notices 22:303–307. 1976. 20th annual AMS survey. Notices 23:313–320. 1977. 21st annual AMS survey. Notices 24:336–343.
9. EIDEN, L. J. 1977. Trends in female degree recipients. Project on the Status and Education of Women. Assoc. American Colleges; 1976. American Education 12(9).
10. VETTER, B. M. 1975. Women and minority scientists. Science. 189:751.
11. McCARTHY, J. L. & D. WOLFE. 1975. Doctorates granted to women and minority groups members. Science 189:856–859.
12. GRAY, M. & A. T. SCHAFER. 1976. Has affirmative action affected the composition of doctorate granting mathematics department faculties in the U.S.A.? Notices. AMS 23:353–356.
13. GREEN, J. 1976. Newsletter. Assoc. for Women in Mathematics.
14. PROJECT ON THE STATUS AND EDUCATION OF WOMEN. Assoc. American Colleges. 1977. Report of 1973–74 survey by the National Assessment of Educational Progress and a survey sponsored by the American Council on Education concerning career plans of young women. Oct. 1977. Recruiting women for traditionally "male" careers: programs and resources for getting women into the men's world.
15. MILNAR, J. 1973. Sex stereotypes in mathematics and science textbooks for elementary and junior high schools. Report on Sex Bias in the Public Schools. New York Chapter of National Organization for Women.
16. ROGERS, M. A. 1975. A different look at word problems: Even mathematics texts are sexist. Mathematics Teacher 68:305–307.
17. JAY, W. T. & C. W. SCHMINKE. 1975. Sex bias in elementary school mathematics texts. Arithmetic Teacher 22(3):242–246.
18. KUHNKE, H. F. 1977. Update on sex-role stereotyping in elementary mathematics textbooks. Arithmetic Teacher 24(5):373–376.
19. KEPNER, JR., H. S. & L. R. KOEHN. 1977. Sex roles in mathematics: a study of

the status of sex stereotypes in elementary mathematics texts. Arithmetic Teacher 24(5):379–385.
20. FENNEMA, E. & J. A. SHERMAN. 1977. Sexual stereotyping and mathematics learning. Arithmetic Teacher. 24(5):369–372.
21. LUCHINS, E. H. 1975. Why are there not more women mathematicians? AWM Newsletter 5.
22. LEVINE M. 1975. Reasons qualified women avoid mathematics: The role of the educator in developing mathematical confidence and interest. AWM Newsletter 5.

Women in the Biological Sciences

ELIZABETH M. O'HERN
National Institute of General Medical Sciences
National Institutes of Health
Bethesda, Maryland 20016

THIS IS AN OVERVIEW of the Biological Sciences, the numbers of women involved, and the opportunities available to them.

Women have been attracted to the Biological Sciences since the early days of women's college education more than a century ago. Some of the women in the Biological Sciences attained prominence, e.g. Nettie Stevens in Zoology whose work on the X and Y chromosomes was published in 1905,[1] Florence Sabin[2] in Anatomy, whose first paper on the lymphatics published in 1901 earned her a prize from the Naples Table Association in 1903.

Somewhat later, Alice Evans' critical research[3] and observations on *Brucella* launched her into a decade or more of dispute with the dairymen. If we count Jane Colden[1] (1724-1766), who learned botany as an apprentice to her father, then it can be said that in the United States there have been prominent women in the Biological Sciences for more than two centuries. The first three editions of American Men of Science (1906, 1910, and 1921) listed some 504 individual women of whom about 50 percent could be counted in Biological or Medical Sciences.[1]

Substantial numbers of women earned doctorates in the Biological Sciences during the 1920's, reaching approximately 20 percent of the total.[4] Although the numbers increased during the next three decades, the proportion decreased and it was not until the 1950s and 1960s that the percentage of doctorates awarded to women in the Biological Sciences showed an upward trend (FIGURE 1). The increase has been almost universal, in the totals for all fields, for the Life Sciences (which includes the Agricultural, Medical, and Biological Sciences). The ratio between degrees awarded to women and total number of degrees is narrowing in each category. The numbers involved are: from 9,734 total for all fields in 1960 to 32,923 in 1976, increasing from 10.7 percent women in 1960 to 23.3 percent in 1976; from 1,728 total in Life Sciences in 1960 to 4,971 in 1976, the percentage of women increasing from 8.9 percent to

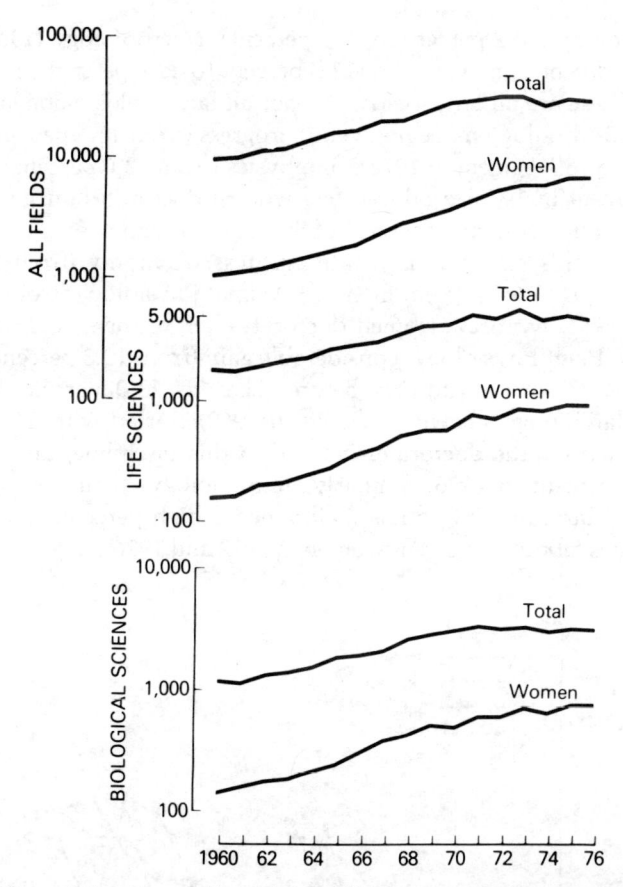

FIGURE 1. Earned doctorates, United States Universities, 1960–1976: All fields, life sciences, biological sciences. (From National Research Council Summary Reports: Doctorate Recipients from United States Universities.)

19.5 percent and 1,181 total in Biological Sciences in 1960 to 3,245 in 1976 with the percentage of women rising from 11.9 percent to 23.2 percent.

Progress has not been uniform among specific fields of the Biological Sciences, as is evident in FIGURE 2. The Biological Sciences, depicted as a solid line, show a steady rise (from 11.9 percent in 1960 to 23.2 percent in 1976). The fields of Biochemistry (from 14.3 percent to 22.9 percent), Botany (10.2 percent to 21.5 percent), Microbiology (13.6 percent to 25.9 percent), and Genetics (12.3 percent to 30.8 percent), made good gains. These are all large fields. But not all large fields made large gains (FIGURE 3). Zoology made no overall progress (from 15.4 percent women in 1960 to 16.7 percent in 1976). Biophysics (from 13.0 percent in 1960 to 16.3 percent in 1976) produced few women doctorates during much of the period, fewer than 10 percent of the total for many years.

Other fields reflected moderate progress: Anatomy (from 17.6 percent in 1960 to 26.3 percent in 1976); Animal Physiology (from 14.3 percent in 1962, with few women doctorates before then, to 18.6 percent in 1976); Plant Physiology, considerable gain (from 10.3 percent in 1962, with few women doctorates before then, to 23.0 percent in 1976). Molecular Biology, newly included in 1969, started with 21.1 percent women among the doctorates granted in this discipline, and increased to 29.1 percent in 1976. Similarly, Immunology, tabulated separately in 1972, started with and has maintained a high percentage of women doctorates (about 33 percent women in 1972 and 1976).

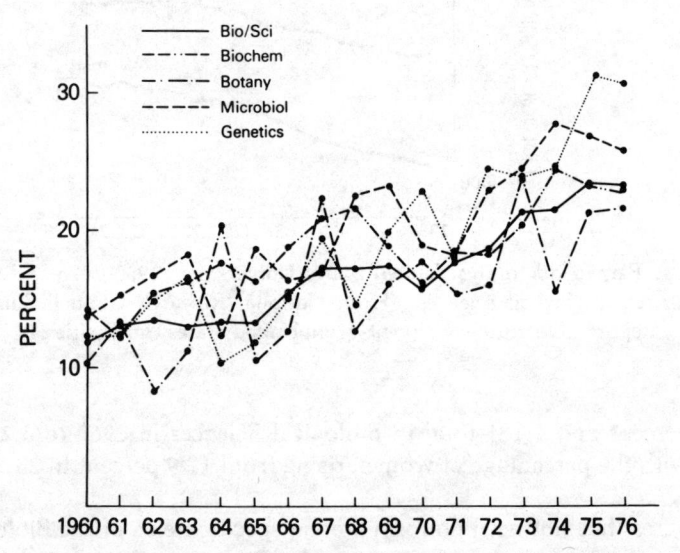

FIGURE 2. Percentage of earned doctorates to women in biological sciences. Selected fields (biochemistry, botany, microbiology, genetics) 1960–1976. (From National Research Council Summary Reports.)

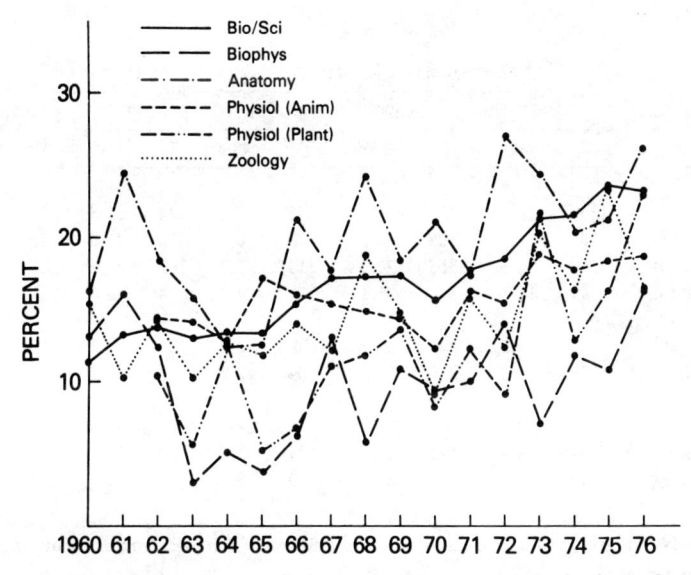

FIGURE 3. Percentage of earned doctorates to women in biological sciences. Selected fields (biophysics, anatomy, physiology, zoology) 1960–1976. (From National Research Council Summary Reports.)

Among graduate and postdoctoral students appointed to training grants supported by the National Institute of General Medical Sciences (NIGMS) from 1967 through 1975, the proportion of women appointed as predoctoral trainees has been equal to or greater than the proportion of all doctoral recipients who are women (TABLES 1 and 2). Among the postdoctoral trainees there has been an overall increase in percentage of women appointed and a generally increasing percentage among the individual fields, but the 1972 cutback and phaseout of some fields of training is particularly striking in the low numbers of postdoctoral appointments of 1973.

We do not yet have information on the numbers of appointed predoctoral trainees who completed this training and received doctorates. The data are available in the doctoral record file at the National Academy of Sciences. A number of concerned people at the National Institutes of Health (NIH), the National Science Foundation (NSF), and the National Research Council (NRC) are making a very careful and determined study

TABLE 1
NIGMS PREDOCTORAL TRAINING: NEW APPOINTMENTS

	1967		1969		1971		1973		1975	
	T	%W	T	%W	T	%W	T	%W	T	%W
Biological Sciences	1340	26.2	1223	27.9	1035	29.4	524	30.5	793	29.4
Anatomy	124	31.5	105	34.3	70	30.0	36	25.0	28	39.3
Biochemistry	369	24.1	388	24.2	313	24.3	162	27.2	155	32.9
Biophysics	141	11.3	134	26.1	111	24.3	54	13.0	52	25.0
Biomet/Epidem.	153	25.5	66	21.2	54	38.9	23	26.1	28	32.1
Genetics	143	35.0	107	32.7	109	42.2	57	47.4	81	48.1
Multidisc. Biology	122	30.3	165	33.9	144	29.2	43	48.8	78	37.2
Microbiol.	149	32.9	111	33.3	124	34.7	88	30.7	208	28.4
Physiology	139	23.0	147	23.1	110	25.5	61	31.1	48	31.3
Cell Biology									115	31.3

(From National Institute of General Medical Sciences: Office of Program Planning and Evaluation.)

TABLE 2
NIGMS POSTDOCTORAL TRAINING: NEW APPOINTMENTS*

	1967		1969		1971		1973		1975	
	T	%W	T	%W	T	%W	T	%W	T	%W
Biological Sciences	165	17.0	146	19.9	110	14.5	38	13.2	85	25.9
Anatomy	18	22.2	16	37.5	14	21.4	2	50.0	7	28.6
Biochemistry	33	21.2	17	5.9	12	25.0	1	0	8	37.5
Biophysics	25	12.0	18	22.2	17	11.8	2	0	10	10.0
Biomet/Epidem.	13	7.7	21	9.5	24	20.8	4	0	18	16.7
Genetics	27	18.5	30	30.0	22	9.1	14	28.6	25	28.0
Multidisc. Biology	20	15.0	11	27.3	5	0	4	0	3	66.6
Microbiol.	15	26.7	19	15.8	6	0	0	0	8	25.0
Physiology	14	7.1	14	7.1	10	10.0	1	0	2	0
Cell Biology									4	50.0

* (From National Institute of General Medical Sciences: Office of Program Planning and Evaluation.)

TABLE 3

FULL-TIME DOCTORATE FACULTY AND YOUNG DOCTORATE FACULTY IN SELECTED
SCIENCE FIELDS: 1975 AND 1980 (ESTIMATED)*

		December 1975			1980 Estimated		
	Number of	Total #	Young Faculty		Total #	Young Faculty	
Field	Departments	Faculty	#	% of T	Faculty	#	% of T
Biochemistry	72	1,005	224	22.3	1,121	279	24.9
Biology	67	1,740	502	28.9	1,930	504	26.1
Botany	32	507	127	25.0	539	120	22.3
Microbiology	70	822	224	27.3	971	270	27.8
Physiology	56	869	269	31.0	961	282	29.3
Zoology	32	688	197	28.6	735	177	24.1

* (From Atelsek, Frank J. & Gomberg, Irene L., Young Doctorate Faculty in Selected Science and Engineering Departments, 1975 to 1980, American Council on Education.)

of the legalities of getting at this sorely needed data under the restrictions of the Privacy Act.

To compare the number of doctorates and trainees with academic positions available, TABLE 3 presents data compiled by the American Council on Education pertaining to young faculty in a sample of departments within the Biological Sciences, with projections for 1980.[5] The data show that 30 percent or more of the present academic faculties are comprised of young faculty members (defined as having received their doctorates within the past seven years). Among the total faculty in the Biological Sciences there were, in 1975, approximately 225 positions in

TABLE 4

AMERICAN ASSOCIATION OF UNIVERSITY PROFESSORS DATA
ON STATUS OF THE PROFESSION*

	Percentage Who are Women			Percentage Difference Between Average Salaries		
	1974-75	1975-76	1976-77	1974-75	1975-76	1976-77
Professor	10.1	9.1	8.4	9.2	9.6	8.5
Assoc. Prof.	17.3	16.6	16.7	3.8	4.8	4.4
Asst. Prof.	27.9	27.9	29.7	3.8	4.3	4.5
Instructor	48.0	49.3	49.0	4.5	5.1	5.4
Lecturer	41.4	41.2	41.9	—	—	—
All Ranks	22.5	21.7	22.4	17.4	19.2	19.3

* (From Report on the Economic Status of the Profession, 1976-1977.)

Biochemistry and in Microbiology, 500 in Biology, 200 in Zoology, 275 in Physiology, and 125 in Botany. Only 25–30 percent of the positions are held by young—that is, new—faculty (both men and women), and the projections for 1980 are not much different.

TABLE 4 presents American Association of University Professors (AAUP)[5] data for 1974–75, 1975–76, and 1976–77 on proportions of women in the various academic ranks for all fields. Women comprise nearly 30 percent of the assistant professors, only about 18 percent of the associate professors, and about 10 percent of the full professors. The percentage of full professors who are women shows a decreasing trend. The discrepancy between men's and women's salaries increased from 1974 to 1976 at all ranks except full professor. The few women

TABLE 5
CELL BIOLOGY*—RANK VERSUS EXPERIENCE

	Total	Under 5 Years	5–9 Years	10–14 Years	15–19 Years	20–24 Years	>25 Years
Total							
Women	245	69	73	33	30	26	14
Men	881	151	258	181	109	100	82
Professor							
Women	43	1	1	9	8	15	9
% Women	17.6	1.4	1.4	27.3	26.7	57.7	64.3
Men	339	9	16	70	84	88	72
% Men	38.5	6.0	6.2	38.7	77.1	88.0	87.8
Associate Prof.							
Women	66	4	24	17	13	7	1
% Women	26.9	5.8	32.9	51.5	43.3	26.9	7.1
Men	262	9	121	97	18	12	5
% Men	29.7	6.0	46.9	53.6	16.5	12.0	6.1
Asst. Prof.							
Women	77	34	34	3	4	1	1
% Women	31.4	49.3	46.6	9.1	13.3	3.8	7.1
Men	209	94	103	8	2	—	2
% Men	23.7	62.3	39.9	4.4	1.8	—	2.4
Res. Assoc.							
Women	50	23	14	4	4	3	2
% Women	20.4	33.3	19.2	12.1	13.3	11.5	14.3
Men	61	30	17	6	5	—	3
% Men	6.9	19.9	6.6	3.3	4.6	—	3.7

* (From Clutter et. al.[6])

at this rank (8.4 percent) improved in salary status in 1976–77 (8.5 percent less than men's salaries) relative to 1974–75 (9.2 percent less).

To move to some specific examples within the Biological Sciences, TABLE 5 presents data from the American Society for Cell Biology (ASCB)[6] survey of 1976. There was a total of 1584 usable responses to the questionnaire, which represents 54 percent of the society membership. Because responses were anonymous, no followup was possible. Women represent 23 percent of the respondents and 21.7 percent of the academic cohort. The top row (TABLE 5) indicates the total number of respondents in each experience cohort. The first column shows the totals for each rank; not all ranks are included (lecturers were omitted). Among the total academic cohort, 17.6 percent of the women and 38.5 percent of the men are full professors. As we move across the chart (TABLE 5) from the less to the more experienced cohorts, the percentage who are full professors increases, as might be expected. Thus, 64.3 percent of the women and 87.8 percent of the men with 25 years of experience are full professors.

With respect to associate professors, 26.9 percent of the women and 29.7 percent of the men in the academic cohort are found in this rank. The highest percentage occurs at 10–14 years experience for both women and men. The numbers dwindle thereafter, but the percentage remains high for women but drops sharply for men, who presumably have moved on to be full professors.

With respect to assistant professors, 31.4 percent of the women and 23.7 percent of the men are found in this rank. Beyond ten years of experience the numbers and percentages decrease considerably for both women and men. Most have moved up or out.

With respect to research associates, 20.4 percent of the women and 6.9 percent of the men are found in this rank. A sizeable percentage of women, though a small number of respondents, remain in the research associate category at all experience levels.

TABLE 6 from the same ASCB Survey shows that nearly 22 percent of the respondents employed in professional schools of Medicine, Dentistry, or Veterinary Medicine are women (78 percent are therefore men). Small numbers of the respondents are employed in colleges; the largest numbers are in the professional schools and universities. In general (college and government excepted), the highest percentages of women are found in the first two experience cohorts, with less than ten years experience. This may be a reflection of the increasing pool size,

TABLE 6

STATUS OF THE PROFESSION: CELL BIOLOGY–TYPES OF EMPLOYERS*

	Total	Under 5	5–9	10–14	15–19	20–24	>25
Total							
Total	1455	340	402	260	184	152	117
Women	337	118	91	42	36	30	20
% Women	23.2	34.7	22.6	16.2	19.2	19.7	17.1
Avg. Salary W/M 75.8							
Med/Dent/Vet School							
Total	509	122	152	90	57	50	38
Women	111	38	38	14	9	9	3
% Women	21.8	31.1	25.0	15.6	15.8	18.0	7.9
Avg. Salary W/M 73.6							
College							
Total	64	13	19	16	9	1	6
Women	23	7	7	2	5	1	1
% Women	35.9	53.8	36.8	12.5	55.5	100.1	6.3
Avg. Salary W/M 87.7							
University							
Total	576	127	150	102	72	77	48
Women	132	50	29	16	13	16	8
% Women	22.9	39.4	19.3	15.7	18.1	20.8	16.7
Avg. Salary W/M 74.1							
Government							
Total	137	41	35	19	20	10	12
Women	41	16	10	3	4	2	6
% Women	29.9	39.0	28.6	15.8	20.0	20.0	5.0
Avg. Salary W/M 90.2							

* (From Clutter et. al.[6])

but one must keep in mind that ASCB is a young society organized in the early 1950s. With respect to salaries, women seem to fare best in government employment.

Another example comes from an unpublished 1976 survey made by the American Society for Microbiology (ASM). FIGURE 4 presents graphically the ratio of women to totals for the faculty, staff, graduates, and postdoctoral students. The survey format (a data-cell questionnaire for each category, at five-year intervals) was mailed to chairpersons of 322 departments. The response was about 45 percent. The data in

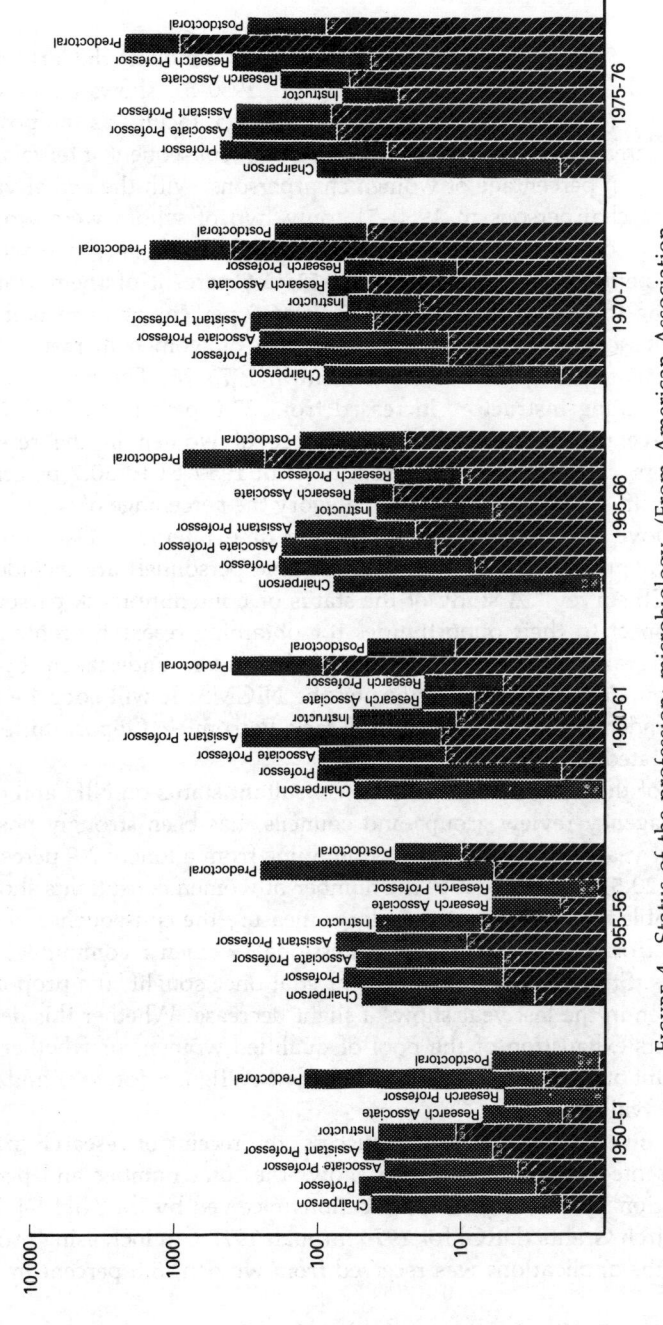

FIGURE 4. Status of the profession: microbiology. (From American Association for Microbiology, unpublished.)

FIGURE 4 are shown in logarithmic form to accommodate the large number of students. The first interval histogram, 1950-51, shows the expected rising percentage of women among tenure-track faculty as the position status decreases. There is greater variation in subsequent intervals, but a decrease in percentage of women chairpersons, with the actual values being: 42 chairpersons in 1950-51 (only two of whom were women) increasing to 143 chairpersons in 1976-77 (with still only two women among them); 50 professors in 1950-51 (5.8 percent of them women) increasing to 495 professors in 1975-76 (6.9 percent of them women). Among associate professors the percentage of women increased from 13.3 percent in 1950-51 to 17.6 percent in 1975-76. The percentage of women among instructors increased from 29.0 percent in 1950-51 to 39.7 percent in 1975-76. The percentage of women in the research professors' category increased from none in 1950-51 to 30.7 percent in 1975-76. In the research associate category the percentage of women has been above 30 percent for most of the time intervals. Data on this particular group (nontenure-track academic personnel) are included in the ASCB survey.[6] A study of the status of nontenure-track personnel, with respect to their opportunities for obtaining research grants independently, as principal investigators, has been undertaken by the American Council on Education for the NIGMS. It will soon be published under the title "Nontenure Track Personnel: Opportunities for Self-Initiated Research."[7]

One of the indicators of success, consultant status on NIH and other federal agency review groups and councils, has been strongly positive in recent years, as TABLE 7 depicts. Jumping from a lonely 2.9 percent in 1971 to 20.5 percent in 1976, the number of women consultants shows a remarkable increase, which is in large measure the consequence of concerted efforts on the part of professional women's committees and caucuses. Still short of the 30 percent goal once sought, the proportion of women in the last year shows a slight decrease. Whether this decline represents exhaustion of the pool of qualified women, or whether it is significant at all, can be evaluated better when figures for 1977 and 1978 become available.

Data on another indicator of success, the receipt of research grants, are presented in TABLE 8, which shows the total number and percent distribution by sex of grant applications received by the NIH Division of Research Grants (DRG) for 1974 through 1977. An increasing proportion of the applications was received from women, 8.3 percent in 1971 to 10.0 percent in 1977 (for many earlier years the percentage had hovered around 5 percent). The approval rate and award rate are largely in line with the application rate. Similarly, the percentage of applications recommended for approval tends to be nearly the same for women and men. The percentage of awards to women has improved from 1974 to 1977. The percentage of applications received that have been recommended and then awarded shows a similar pattern. The number of awards that can be made depends upon available funds, funds committed for ongoing grants, and the total number of applications received. In any event, women's applications were about as successful as those of men in 1977. These data refer to new applications of all kinds, including

TABLE 7

Women Members on NIH Public Advisory Committees*

Committee Function	Number Committees	Total Number Members	Number Women	% Women
Total	164	1,977	378	19.1
Policy and Program Advisory Councils and Boards	19	178	53	29.8
Initial Grant Review	77	1,045	184	17.6
Contract Review	27	342	58	17.0
Advisory Committees for Programs or Projects	13	126	23	18.3
Boards of Scientific Counselors	10	64	11	17.2
Initial Grant Review and Contract Review	18	222	49	22.1

Number and Percent of Women—1971-1977

	Total Members	Women Members	% Female Membership
July 1, 1971	1,632	48	2.9
July 1, 1972	1,753	213	12.1
June 15, 1973	1,819	261	14.3
January 1, 1974	1,523	274	18.0
January 1, 1975	1,583	327	20.6
January 1, 1976	2,008	411	20.5
January 1, 1977	2.069	389	18.8

* (From NIH Committee Management Office.)

TABLE 8
NIH COMPETING RESEARCH PROJECTS (RO1) APPLICATIONS RECEIVED, RECOMMENDED AND AWARDED 1974–1977*

	1974 F	1974 M	1975 F	1975 M	1976 F	1976 M	1977 F	1977 M
Received								
Total #	732	8060	722	8170	966	8584	1093	10888
Percent #	8.3	91.7	8.1	91.9	9.7	90.3	10.0	90.0
Percent $	7.7	92.3	7.2	92.8	8.6	91.4	9.2	90.8
Recommended								
Percent #	8.2	91.8	7.9	92.1	9.3	90.7	9.7	90.3
Percent $	7.3	92.7	7.4	92.6	8.4	91.6	9.0	91.0
Awarded								
Percent #	7.8	92.2	7.9	92.1	9.2	90.8	10.0	89.9
Percent $	6.9	93.1	7.3	92.7	8.3	91.7	9.1	90.9
Recommended/ Received								
Percent #	66.5	68.1	72.3	74.9	66.5	70.0	69.8	72.5
Awarded/ Recommended								
Percent #	57.7	60.8	67.0	66.7	55.7	56.3	48.0	46.0
Awarded/ Received								
Percent #	28.4	41.4	48.5	50.0	37.0	39.4	33.5	33.4

* (From NIH Division of Research Grants, Statistics and Analysis Branch.)

new research proposals from previous investigators. The percentage of women among successful first-time applicants has increased from 6.2 percent in 1966 to 11.7 percent in 1974 and 11.3 percent in 1975.

Women in the Biological Sciences have made certain gains: they are earning an increasing percentage of the doctorate degrees awarded in nearly all fields; substantial numbers of women are found in the lower ranks of the academic faculty; the percentage of women consultants on review committees and councils has increased significantly since 1971, and more women in Biological and Medical Sciences are applying for and receiving research grants. Women's salaries, however, still lag somewhat behind those of men, few women are found in top decision-making positions, and fewer still receive the accolades, honors, and awards of any kind.

To expand the role of women in the Biological Sciences, more factual information is needed to dispel the myths[8] about their exact status. Quite a number of the professional societies have recently elected women presidents (e.g., American Physiological Society, American Society for Biological Chemistry, American Society for Cell Biology, and the American Society for Microbiology), but few have surveyed their membership. Of those which have surveys in progress there is little or no information on the effect of discontinuities in employment, part-time employment, and immobility on productivity, salary differentials, and awards and honors. One need not ask the effect of unemployment on productivity and professional self-confidence, but we should have more precise data on the extent of unemployment among women and on how much of it is voluntary. The excellent registries such as those of American Society for Biological Chemistry and the Association for Women in Science are providing a great service for women but they need to be expanded. They also need feedback on the numbers of women actually offered positions, the numbers who have declined positions and why. In the face of retrenchment and contraction in numbers of academic positions, can we expect young women to continue to make the effort to get doctorate degrees in the Biological Sciences? Are they sufficiently motivated to face the half-open door of science? A strong support system among women scientists is needed to maintain the gains made and overcome the obstacles[9] that remain.

References

1. Rossiter, M. W. 1974. Women scientists in America before 1920. Am. Sci. 62(3):312–323.
2. Sabin, F. R. 1910-2. On the origin of the lymphatic system from the veins and the development of the lymph hearts and thoracic duct in the pig. Am. J. Anat. 1(1):367–389.
3. Evans, A. C. 1918. Further studies on *Bacterium abortus* and related bacteria. II. A comparison of *Bacterium abortus* and *Bacterium bronchisepticus* and with the organism which causes Malta fever. III. *Bacterium abortus* and related bacteria in cow's milk. J. Infect. Dis. 22:580–593; 23:354–372.
4. Vetter, B. M. & E. L. Babco. 1957-77. Professional women and minorities in the sciences. Scientific Manpower Commission. Washington, D. C.
5. American Association of University Professors. 1977. No progress this year: Report on the economic status of the profession, 1976–1977. AAUP Bulletin, August.
6. Clutter, M. E., B. Bowers, E. M. O'Hern, K. M. Baldwin & S. E. Baldwin. 1978. Profile of a professional society. In manuscript.

7. ATELSEK, F. & I. GOMBERG. 1978. Nontenure track personnel: Opportunities for independent research. Higher Education Panel Survey Report No. 39. American Council on Education. Washington, D. C.
8. ZUCKERMAN, H. & J. R. COLE. 1975. Women in American science. Minerva 13:82-102.
9. VETTER, B. M. 1976. Women in the natural sciences. Signs 1(3):713-720.
10. SHAPLEY, D. 1975. Obstacles to women in science. Impact of Science on Society 25(2):115-123.
11. CHASE, L. & C. PARR. 1977. Facts about women in higher education. Women's Equity Action League. Washington, D. C.
12. TRUMBALL, R. 1977. The biologist census. BioScience 27(3):192-195.

Scientific Sexism

LILLI S. HORNIG
Executive Director, Higher Education Resource Services
Wellesley, Massachusetts 02181

Introduction

THE TITLE OF THIS Conference, "Expanding the Role of Women in the Sciences," strongly suggests that all is not well in our various professions; were we not deeply concerned about issues of equity in educational experience, opportunity to apply our knowledge and training, and appropriate professional rewards, we would not be worried about expansion of our roles.

My purpose is neither to review the statistics of discrimination nor to attempt an assessment of the fairly substantial progress toward equality that we have indeed made; these issues have been very ably covered in other sessions. Instead, I should like to raise some questions about the nature of science and the structural framework within which we practice it, questions which in fact arise when we consider the role of women in science but that I believe have other implications as well. The ambiguity of my title is therefore no accident; the issue it poses is not only whether and to what extent sex discrimination exists in science, but also whether the conceptual and institutional settings of modern science are so constructed that they will almost certainly be discriminatory. The proposition we need to consider is whether some relatively simple adjustments in how scientific training and professional arrangements are organized and viewed might not make these disciplines both more attractive and more rewarding for women.

There seems to be little doubt that having more women scientists is a desirable goal. Top scientific talent has never been in oversupply, and we are currently utilizing little more than half of what we have.

We all know the easy explanation for that. It is because "young girls lose interest in mathematics and science at an early age because they don't want to compete with boys." Strangely, this unwillingness to compete doesn't seem to interfere at all with their performance in other academic fields, where they go right ahead doing better than boys. Could it be that they are even smarter than we think? Perhaps they have looked ahead and perceived the odd incongruity that bright girls become nurses and technicians while bright boys become doctors and scientists. There is little point in investing very much money and effort in a dead-end future.

It is worth remembering that as soon as "Equal Employment Opportunity" became a popular phrase, although one much more often honored in the breach than the observance, young women flocked into science and engineering courses. Many an engineering school would now have either underenrolled courses or less able students if there were not so many women in them. Similarly, medical schools would have lower standards if they had only male students.

The converse of this principle has been traditionally applied in raising the standards of stereotypically female occupations such as elementary teaching, librarianship, or, most recently, nursing. The statistical argument is equally valid in both cases: When the base from which candidates are drawn is expanded while the number selected remains essentially constant, selection will be more rigorous.

Bright young women, like their male counterparts, go where they find opportunities to use their talents. We are not yet providing those opportunities for fair competition in most scientific fields, simply because the most rewarding positions are seldom open to women.

It is more than mere coincidence that women in the scientific disciplines recognized their common interests so early and began to gather data to document their unequal status. The nature of scientific investigations to define the dimensions of a problem by its quantitative characteristics and then to use these to construct an explanatory hypothesis that can be tested against objective evidence. We all know, however, that there are pitfalls in this process and that elegant, precise, convincing demonstrations of the truth are rare. Most often, our results are ambiguous and open to more than one interpretation.

The problems of sex differences or discrimination in science are not exempt from such controversy. In its simplest form, our problem is to convince the scientific establishment that *in the absence of discrimination* we are as good or as bad as anybody else. To most of us, the evidence that discrimination against women exists in science is overwhelmingly convincing, but that interpretation is not widely shared by those who design and manage the structures, institutions, and even subject matter of science. "Those," of course, are virtually all male and white, and only a few of them so far have come to agree that there may in fact *be* a problem.

Let us look at some of the rules by which the game of science is played. It is taken as axiomatic that productive scientists are young, highly motivated, energetic, and dedicated. They had better be, because there is a long, tough trip ahead. They are expected to define their intellectual interests in early adolescence in order to have enough time to learn all they will need to master. (Perhaps we should reconsider the wisdom of life choices made at age thirteen or fourteen.) It is an arduous educational sequence, which ideally is completed in the early twenties, and its slightly monastic aura is carefully cultivated. By the time students obtain the doctorate, their mentors have made it clear to them that the only good life is the academic one and that theory is somehow a higher-order good than application. They are right about the academic life, of course. It is the only one I know of where, once on tenure, you can retire on full pay at any time.

It is a curious contradiction that disciplines dealing in exploring the physical world value most highly those activities which don't get your hands dirty. What follows from that, however, is that one advances even in purely experimental fields by getting progressively farther away from the actual work, becoming a producer of ideas and a manager of the many young and presumably willing heads and hands who test them. This leads quite naturally to helping to manage the institutions necessary for the conduct of most science and, if at all possible, to shaping them in one's own image.

None of this is necessarily bad, and if it were demonstrably the only or best way to do excellent work in science, one might accept it without further comment. I would suggest that we investigate other possible patterns.

For example, the team approach to research is almost certainly very productive. An understanding teacher should have no trouble integrating women fully into research groups, and it would be to the teacher's own advantage to do so. All too often this does not happen for women, and they are thereby excluded from a very valuable professional experience.

It is probably obvious, if only by association, that the abbreviated caricature I have drawn above depicts a man, and only one kind of man at that: the successful academic scientist who in his middle and later years will accumulate a few prizes and medals, help to determine the policies which ultimately govern the education and progress of more scientists, and probably advise our government at some level. He is not so much typical as exemplary—a model for the rest of us to emulate—and therein lies his importance to this discussion. You will note that his personal and physical characteristics have not been mentioned, but that omission was not accidental. They are not of great importance to his progress. Charm and good looks are an asset in any walk of life, but it is widely acknowledged that so long as he is a good scientist he will get along fine without them. Many of you will have shared my observation that prominent scientists are often short, fat, have had acne, wear thick glasses, are patchily bald or excessively hairy, or have as much personality as slugs. In fact, these traits follow a normal distribution curve among scientists, and are not thought to be related to intelligence. You will have observed further that none of these characteristics, singly or collectively, kept them out of Berkeley or Harvard either as students or faculty members, significantly diminished their eligibility for various honorary academies, or denied them access to the seats of professional power. Yet the Supreme Court has upheld the right of a medical school to dismiss a woman student in her last semester on grounds of an unattractive physical appearance and a less than gracious bedside manner.

Though even a successful scientist may worry about his looks at times, he is seldom troubled by the view, widely held by his colleagues in other disciplines, that he is cold, unfeeling, and inattentive to the needs of others, even sometimes described as an "emotional cripple." If he pays attention to this critique at all, it does not seem to bother him much, since he believes it to be clearly unrelated to his chief mission in life, the pursuit of objective truth. The discussion of whether *perception* of a phenomenon may also constitute objective truth is best left to the philosophers.

You may well be wondering by now what this cartoon character has to do with sexism in science, but he is not irrelevant. He and his colleagues have devised the courses, curricula, prerequisites, examinations, fellowships, postdoctoral arrangements, funding priorities, and other arcane rites of passage by which people become scientists. I have no special quarrel with most of these taken one at a time, but I question, for example, the selection rules which state that those who finish fastest are the most promising scientists. We all know of young geniuses whose discoveries have forever changed the shape of science, but we also know of others whose equally significant contributions were the mosaic of a lifetime of insights. No doubt we need both kinds, and I would suggest that a year or two, one way or the other, in a young scientist's life will not make much difference. In fact, it hasn't, if he happened to be drafted or went off to the Peace Corps. If she, however, chooses to spend it having a child, that raises very serious questions not only about her dedication but also about her intrinsic fitness for a scientific career. The difficulties she then encounters in finding an appropriate position may drive her out of science forever.

The age-old debate about women's fitness to be scholars and scientists at all, of course, underlies most of the problems we still encounter in pursuing professional careers. Aristotle's view that "we should look upon the female state as being as it were a deformity, though one which occurs in the ordinary course of nature"[1] has not gone out of fashion altogether. More than half of us are freaks, in other words. Skipping lightly over the intervening centuries, the familiar theories of Darwin and Freud and even Erikson's "inner space," we may note that *in 1969* philosopher Paul Weiss wrote, "A woman is less abstract than a man because her mind is persistently ordered toward bodily problems. Emotions, which are the mind and body interwoven intimately, are easily aroused in her as a consequence. There are times when she will give herself wholeheartedly to intellectual pursuits, and may then distinguish herself in competition with men. But easily, and not too reluctantly, she slips quite soon into a period when her mind functions on behalf of her body in somewhat the way in which a trained athlete's mind functions on behalf of his. . . . She, of course, has had her intellectual moments and has found them desirable, but they do not last as long nor come as frequently as his do."[2] It would be interesting to inquire of Professor Weiss what evidence he can adduce to support these speculations; perhaps they are simply his version of the revealed truth. But that version has appeal for many men. "People on the upper tiers of a hierarchy are more at ease if their inferiors seem inferior by nature. It is therefore not surprising that when scientists came to study the female of their own species, they should have looked at once for evidence of her inferiority."[3]

This persistent search for proof that the differential disposition of endocrine glands or muscular and adipose tissue profoundly affects intellectual function, one way or the other, has kept countless experimental and behavioral psychologists busy for a good many years. Maccoby and Jacklin, in their excellent and exhaustive review of this field,[4] have concluded that there is no significant difference in intellectual ability or function. One of the less fortunate consequences of Affirmative Action is the endless attempt to demonstrate, or if need be justify, small sex differences in test scores, grade-point averages, years to completion of the doctorate, or publication and citation counts. After spending a number of years following this literature in detail, I can conclude only that the differences (which go in both directions) are basically insignificant and clearly culturally conditioned and perpetuated. If women score slightly higher in verbal aptitude and men in mathematics, who is to say that science might not benefit, especially in its public and political relations, from a more felicitous form of expression than we commonly hear and read? If the average woman scientist takes a month or two *less* to earn her doctorate than the average man, what does it prove? Perhaps he is just overly conscientious; perhaps, as the data suggest, she has been more carefully selected, and is just a little smarter. If it is true that the average female scientist publishes a little less than the average male one, we need only remind ourselves that with the facilities and the students of the institutions in which she is commonly employed, the truly remarkable fact is that she is publishing at all. In short, the only thing wrong with women in science is that they don't have equal access to good jobs.

I have an uncomfortable feeling that the emphasis on speed, volume, and competition in science is not all to the good. This sort of suspicion is hard to document, of course; we all know, though, that in the rush to get there first a certain amount of garbage comes along too. Unfortunately, I have no sound prescription for keeping it from cluttering the pages of our journals, only a conviction that a little more time for reflection might often benefit our disciplines as well as us. I remember well an occasion when a professor put his entire research group on round-the-clock duty for several days to beat someone else in grinding out a quite insignificant result. This is not an uncommon practice, and I don't believe it should happen to students. It leaves their sense of values either permanently warped or so outraged that they develop a deep cynicism or contempt for their field. No one so handicapped will do her/his best. In any case, this emphasis on hurry does not fit a woman's normal life cycle very well, and if it does not do much for science in general, either, perhaps we should alter our lockstep approach.

A loaded question sometimes raised is whether the overall orientation of the sciences, the choices of fields and topics for investigation, might be different if scientists were equally distributed between the sexes. Presumably this arises from the well-known sex stereotyping of fields, which some people ascribe to free choice and others to the fact that women tend to enter those specialties where they feel least unwelcome. Nobody is likely to play well on the team that chooses him/her last. I have no certain way of predicting the outcome if all social, cultural, and educational sex barriers truly vanished. I am unlikely to live long enough to verify such a prediction if I were to make one. It seems reasonable to assume that in the very short term some sex stereotypes would persist. Perhaps women would, for a while, continue to prefer pediatrics to urology, or microbiology to astrophysics. Perhaps problems of environmental health, for example, would attract more of them than, say, hematology. Perhaps, if those choices were to represent what the majority of people consider important, they would not be inappropriate.

Occasionally the concern is voiced that women scientists will never take much interest in research problems related to defense and national security and that we might therefore run serious risks of becoming a second-rate power if half our scientists were women. Given the time-scale involved in that assumption, we could surely devise a way to interest them in military matters in the meantime. Equal pay and equal opportunity have been known to accomplish miracles. I can add only that the research I did during World War II at Los Alamos was as fascinating and intellectually absorbing as any other. Regrettably, when that war was over there were suddenly no more places for women in that field. On the whole, my guess is that our instinct for self-preservation is as well developed as those more commonly attributed to us.

Like everyone else, scientists do not work in an economic vacuum. Unlike scholars in many other fields, however, most of us cannot work at all without funds for facilities and equipment, and therefore funding priorities are of great importance to us. We must learn to make ourselves heard in this arena if we want to have adequate opportunities to work. The question is not only that of winning individual grants, but of learning the mechanisms by which policy decisions are influenced. If need be, we may also modify those mechanisms when there are enough of us.

Another economic aspect of life we cannot afford to ignore is the decreasing number of academic positions available. Although minor fluctuations of supply and demand may open up a slot here or there, the future for aspiring faculty members is not bright, for either sex. Nonetheless, men have continued to have the lion's share of the 35 percent increase in faculty positions since 1970. It is time for us to establish closer ties with industry. The usual explanation for the very low proportion of women scientists in industry is that women naturally gravitate to teaching, out of some need to gratify their maternal and nurturant instincts. I am uncomfortable with that, only in part because a houseful of teenagers at home provided me with quite adequate gratification. Teaching *per se* is neither highly regarded nor well paid, which is why those jobs have been more open to women. We should explore more carefully whether equal access to well-paid industrial careers might not lure about the same fraction of female and male scientists. We have directed our Affirmative Action efforts most explicitly toward the universities, because that is where most of us were and also because the places where people are educated are likely to be the most influential. In fact, sex stereotyping of jobs and careers is much more pervasive in industry, and it may well be time to turn more of our attention to what happens there.

We also need to be more vigilant about salary discrimination in general. With some minute exceptions, starting salaries in virtually all fields, at both baccalaureate and doctoral levels, are lower for women than for men. A difference of a few hundred dollars per year may not seem so significant at age twenty-five, but as time goes on the difference will grow. Equal percentage increases will produce a growing dollar gap; at some stage a manager, or a faculty review committee, will look at the actual salary figures and conclude that if that woman has been here for five years and is still only making $15,000, that's probably all she is worth.

Finally, let me share some observations regarding Affirmative Action itself. Most of us involved with it realized from the outset that the important problems were attitudinal more than procedural. No administrator has yet invented a procedure that a smart faculty couldn't evade if so inclined, and the instances of such evasions could fill many volumes. The body counts and regression analyses necessary to implement proper procedures are a burden and also a bore. The continuing collection and analysis of data on the availability and utilization of women and minorities have become a little tedious, the more so because they demonstrate that as the barriers to equal access in education have crumbled, the ones to equal employment opportunity have been lowered only very slightly. The data also demonstrate that educational institutions have a healthy sense of self-interest and were quick to note that as the outlook for enough students dimmed, women's money was just as good as what they had been used to—men's money.

Nonetheless, enforced changes in behavior produced by Affirmative

Action procedures have indeed begun to produce changes in attitudes. The horror stories, such as the one from a prominent woman administrator who was asked, during a job interview, to describe her preferred contraceptive method, are a little less frequent.

Affirmative Action continues to come under attack, however, although the sounds are now somewhat muted pending the outcome of the Bakke decision. It is likely that increasing economic pressure will raise the pitch of debate again. In such times it is well for women to be alert; the fact that they are supporting themselves, or are the sole supports of families, or work because they have a right to, is likely to get lost in the rhetoric. The early warning signals are already coming in: family values are currently high on the list of public policy priorities, funding for family studies is available if not abundant, and male scholars are writing definitive volumes on the history and sociology of the family. On another front, high-heeled sandals are in, and so are long, loose, flowing clothes, ill-adapted for working in a laboratory or almost anywhere else. It is all disturbingly reminiscent of the late 1940s. Some of you may remember what happened to us then: the New Look, Togetherness, and no more jobs. Get off the labor market, girls, and leave the work to those who need it to support you. Get back in the kitchen or up on the pedestal.

We cannot afford that cost in human capital another time, especially not in science where surely the best—female or male—is barely good enough.

References

1. ARISTOTLE. Generation of Animals.
2. WEISS, P. 1969. Women Athletes. From Sport: A Philosophical Inquiry. Southern Illinois Univ. Press. Carbondale, Ill.
3. O'FAOLEIN, J. & L. MARTINES, Eds. 1973. Not in God's Image. Harper & Row. New York, N.Y.
4. MACCOBY, E. E. & C. N. JACKLIN. 1974. The Psychology of Sex Differences. Stanford Univ. Press. Stanford, Cal.

PART III. Opportunities for Professional Advancement

Expanding the Role of Women in the Biomedical Sciences

ALEXANDER G. BEARN*
Stanton Griffis Disinguished Medical Professor
Cornell University Medical College
New York, N.Y. 10021

THE CHANGING ROLE OF WOMEN in our society is a matter of great contemporary interest. The roots for these changing patterns in the sexes are complex, largely biosocial and would require a mind far better trained than mine in the social sciences to unravel. There are, of course, many instances of outstanding women leaders in all areas of human endeavor. This is hardly surprising. Societal attitudes, however, have sharply limited women's potential for leadership, which, a priori is neither more nor less than the leadership potential of men. The reasons for social injustice are always complex and their correction slow. Rhetoric is more common than logic, and special pleading clouds the most well-argued positions.

I am a general physician interested in genetics, and so it has always been to me self-evident that, at least as a first approximation, the genetic contribution to intelligence, ability, and drive must be assumed to be randomly distributed between the two sexes. There are no cogent reasons to believe that the additional DNA possessed by women influences overall ability. Although ability may be distributed fairly, opportunity to use that ability is not.

Flexner's 1910 report came out loudly and clearly against special medical schools for women, but I went to a medical school where there were no women; no one thought it unfair. There was, after all, a special medical school for women; at that time only a few schools, Edinburgh was one, were integrated. When I graduated I worked for a person whom I regarded as one of the most talented of physicians. That physician was a woman; she is now a Professor of Medicine in England, a title that means more in the United Kingdom that it does here. However, it re-

* Since March, 1979, affiliated with Merck Sharp and Dohme International.

mains disturbing that in 1978 she is still the only woman Professor of Medicine.

In 1880 in the United States there were approximately 2,500 registered women doctors. In the 1890s, Johns Hopkins and my own school, Cornell, were the only two schools that admitted women. Hopkins was encouraged into becoming a coeducational school by an offer it could not refuse: an endowment of nearly $500,000 offered by Elizabeth Garrett Anderson if the school would waive all restriction on gender. By 1934, however, 28 percent of medical schools in the United States had never graduated a woman doctor, and in 1944, 9 percent were still restricting enrollment to men. In 1934, the year in which Jean Batten had flown from England to Australia in 14 days, 23 hours, and 40 minutes, 43 percent of all the hospitals in the country had never employed a woman doctor. The last stronghold of masculinity carried the name of Thomas Jefferson. In 1960, the walls of that Jericho in Philadelphia tumbled.

Historical Background

Until comparatively modern times, agricultural production accounted for a large share of all production and in countries such as India it still accounts for 70–80 percent of all output. Agricultural technology, such as it was, was stable. The economic stability required the provision of a large number of offspring, in the face of a high infant mortality rate. Women, in addition to performing local agricultural chores, were forced to oscillate between pregnancy and lactation in order to provide economic stability.

One of the paradoxes of the Industrial Revolution was that although it tended to diminish the need for manual labor and thus was a potential incentive to decrease childbearing, the development of technology required training of specialized manpower and the movement of people and capital funds to urban centers committed to production. The economic relationships of the family became altered as the men took jobs that did

TABLE 1
Live Births*

1960–1869	6.16
1900–1909	3.30
1935–1939	2.04

* (From Blake, 1974.)

TABLE 2

MEDIAN ANNUAL SALARIES IN THE 1970 TOTAL AND WOMEN'S SCIENCE/ENGINEERING LABOR FORCE: 1974

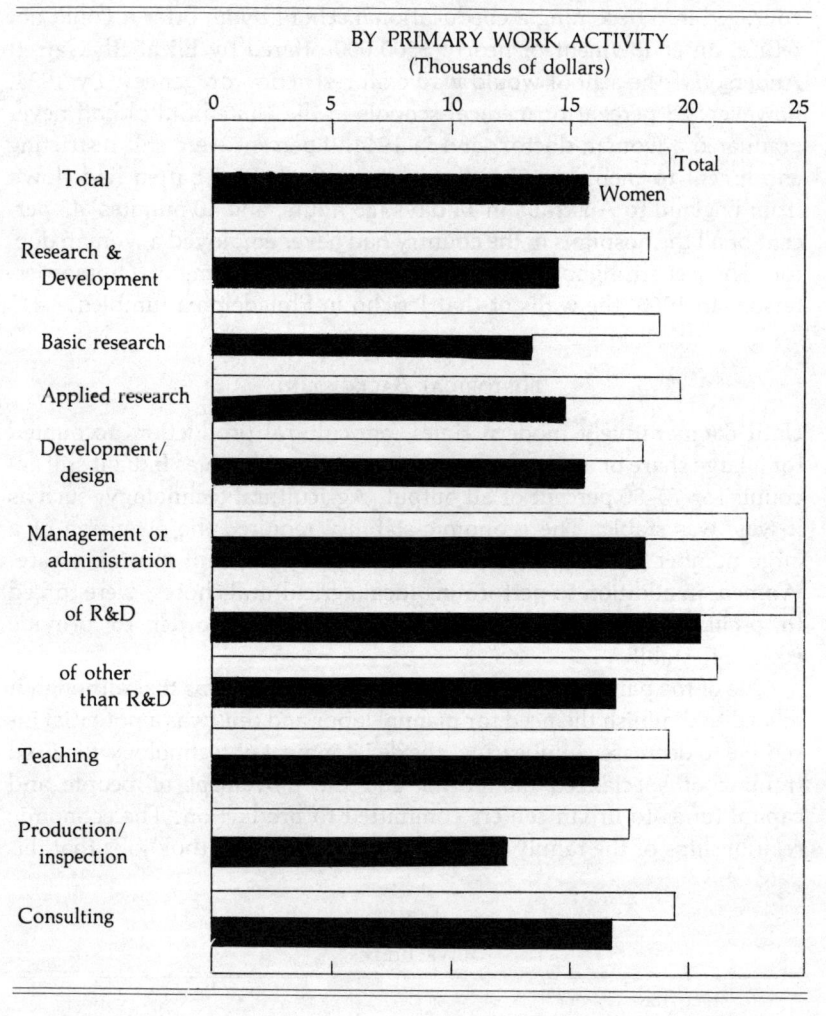

BY PRIMARY WORK ACTIVITY
(Thousands of dollars)

not include, as they had done so often in agricultural communities, participation by wives or offspring. Wives and children, as Judith Blake has pointed out, became "economic liabilities to the men." Except under the stress of dire necessity, few married women would have left their families to work long hours at the onerous, exhausting jobs that characterized the industrial enterprise. Thus the net effect of the Industrial Revolution was to ameliorate the economic conditions so that wives could remain at home. The status of women became skewed and diminished, at the same time that the economic need for children became less. Thus domestic encapsulation and isolation were paradoxically the consequence of an increased opportunity for women to fulfil their intellectual potential.

TABLE 1 illustrates the point that the actual number of live births has dropped dramatically. At the time of the Industrial Revolution the average number of live births per couple was over six, by 1939 it was 2.04, and is now much lower. In theory, anyway, women should have had more opportunity to spend their time working rather than in just raising children. In fact, for the reasons outlined, industrialization worked against them.

But time does not permit an analysis of the trends of the women's movements; they have been well-documented both for the scholar in learned tomes, and for the superficial television viewer with "Upstairs, Downstairs," which captured the Edwardian scene, at least in the United Kingdom.

A number of years ago I was invited to join the Commission on Human Resources. This commission is concerned with those activities of the National Research Council that contribute to the more effective development and utilization of the nation's human resources, giving emphasis to national programs and needs in education and employment. Its concerns extend to policies in both the public and private sectors that bear directly upon human-resource development, and to the collection, analysis, and reporting of data on scientists, engineers, and other highly educated personnel. The Commission's work also includes concern for the institutions and processes through which the country's human resources are deployed. As a consequence of that assignment and because through it I met such articulate, informed, and effective people as Estelle Ramey, I became interested in some of the quantitative aspects of women in the biological and engineering sciences.

It represented an opportunity for me to clothe my impressions with facts, and to substitute information for vague rhetoric. Perhaps my most powerful education on that commission has been the realization that in-

TABLE 3

MEDIAN ANNUAL SALARIES IN THE 1970 TOTAL AND WOMEN'S SCIENCE/
ENGINEERING LABOR FORCE: 1974*

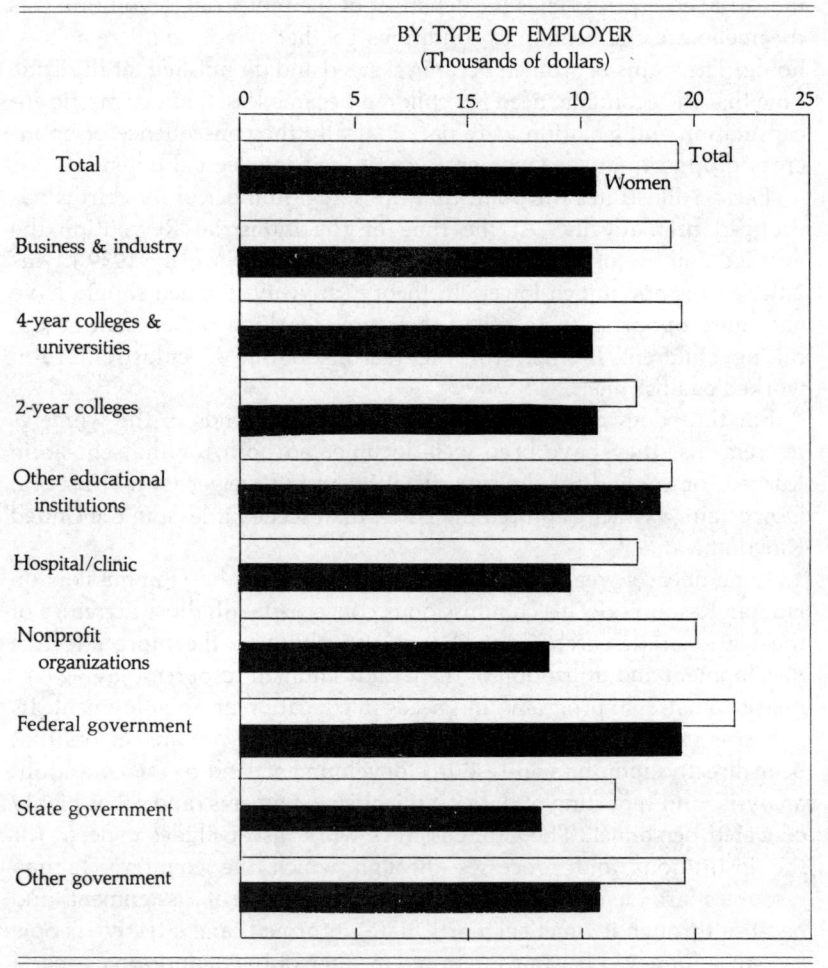

BY TYPE OF EMPLOYER
(Thousands of dollars)

* (From National Science Foundation, National Sample, 1974.)

TABLE 4
EMPLOYMENT STATUS 1971-1975*

	Males Married	Unmarried	Females Married	Unmarried
Postdoc.	15.6	28.0	26.4	27.3
F.T.	81.4	65.5	53.6	65.2
P.T.	0.6	1.6	6.8	2.2
Seek empl.	0.9	1.9	5.5	1.4
Other	1.5	3.0	7.7	3.9

* (From Commission on Human Resources, 1977.)

formation about many matters is woefully inadequate. My education in these matters has been greatly augmented by Estelle Ramey, and by Dorothy Gilford, who, as Director of Human Resource Studies of the Commission on Human Resources, has generously allowed me free access to the data at hand. Lilli Hornig, who heads the Committee on the Education and Employment of Women in Science and Engineering, has, since 1974, been examining the social, structural, and institutional constraints that limit the participation of women in science and engineering. She, not I, should be speaking, but perhaps she will allow me part of the action.

TABLE 2 illustrates the median annual salaries in the total labor force in 1974. It can be noted that at all levels women receive less money than men. In 1972, the average net income of 1,400 women was $27,558 compared to a salary of $47,945 in a sample of 7,000 men. The low income for women is only in part related to the fewer hours worked.

If you look at the situation from the point of view of the employer (TABLE 3), it appears that the nonprofit organizations show the largest dollar gap. The federal government approximates dollar equality, but even there women lag behind.

TABLE 5
MEDIAN ANNUAL SALARY DIFFERENTIAL, 1974*

Basic Research	$5,600
Development and Design	$2,500
Nonprofit Organizations	$6,600

* (From Characteristics of National Sample of Scientists and Engineers, 1974. Pt. 2 Employment, NSF 76-323.)

TABLE 6
SUMMARY DATA FOR 1973–1975*

1. Largest difference in percentage men and women employed is in Business and Industry
2. Women are not involved in administration
    Data   20.8% Men
           10.0% Women

* (From Gilford Snyder. 1977. Women and Minority Ph.D's in 1970s. A data book, NAS.)

TABLE 4 indicates that the number of married women seeking employment is very much greater than the number of married men seeking employment, although there is not as much difference between the unmarried men and unmarried women. Moreover, there are far more married men working full time than married women, although as far as part-time work is concerned there are more women in both the married and unmarried categories. Of course, one doesn't know whether those individuals prefer part-time work or whether they would have opted for full-time work if given the opportunity.

TABLE 5 reveals that the greatest median salary differential occurs in nonprofit organizations and then in basic research.

TABLE 7
SELECTED INSTITUTIONS THAT WERE ABOVE AVERAGE IN PROPORTION OF DOCTORATES GRANTED TO WOMEN, 1973–1976*

Rank	Institution	Women Doctorates	Total Doctorates	% Women
1	Texas Women's Univ.	148	150	98.7
2	Bryn Mawr	117	170	68.8
5	Cornell Univ. Med. Coll.	29	60	48.3
17	Columbia Univ.	683	2012	33.9
28	Emory	97	329	29.5
43	Howard	38	152	25.0
48	Harvard	581	2350	24.7
63	Yale	333	1391	23.9
79	Yeshva Univ. Einstein Med.	11	49	22.4
96	Univ. Chicago	377	1798	23.9

* (Source: Earned Doctorates, NRC, 1977.)

TABLE 8

INSTITUTIONS WITH HIGH PERCENTAGE OF FEMALE FACULTY, 1976*

	Female Faculty	Female Ph.Ds %
Texas Women's University	61	97
Bryn Mawr	37	77
Fordham	17	38
N.Y.U.	24	33
Rutgers	23	29
Univ. North Carolina	16	23

* (Source: Earned Doctorates NRC, 1977.)

The largest difference in the percentage of men and women employed is, interestingly enough, in business and industry (TABLE 6). But what I think is particularly noteworthy is that only half as many women as men hold high administrative posts. It is quite clear that if women are to have an increasing influence they must have an opportunity to rise to senior administrative positions.

It is interesting to compare the number of women granted the doctorate degree in different institutions (TABLE 7). Texas Women's University, not surprisingly, awarded nearly 99 percent of its doctorates to women. Cornell University Medical College, awarded 48.3 percent, but the total number of doctorates is small. (The figures would be different if one compared Cornell University.) Columbia is at about 34 percent, and Harvard, about 25 percent.

TABLE 9

U.S. DOCTORATES, 1966–1976*

Year	Total	% Women
1966	17,953	10.8
1973	32,727	18.0
1974	33,000	19.4
1975	32,913	21.9
1976	32,923	22.3 (40% doctorates by Black women)

* (Source: Based on Summary Report 1976. Doctorate Recipients. Commission on Human Resources, NRC.)

TABLE 8 shows the institutions with the highest percentage of female faculty and, particularly, the percentage of female Ph.Ds. Again, notice that 77 percent of the female faculty at Bryn Mawr have Ph.D. degrees and that the University of North Carolina has the smallest number, 23 percent with Ph.Ds, but, of course, the total female faculty is small.

TABLE 9 shows the very encouraging increase in the number of women among U.S. doctorates over the 10-year period 1966–1976. We have advanced from 11 percent to 22 percent over a 10-year period and, perhaps even more interestingly, despite the fact that since 1973 there really has been no increase in the total number of doctorates, the percentage of women among those doctorates has continued to increase. You will also notice that 40 percent of the doctorates were black women. The percentage of women doctorates in the life sciences over a three-year period is shown in TABLE 10.

TABLE 11 shows a profile of doctorates for fiscal year 1976. Note that 98 percent of the engineering doctorates were awarded to males with only 1.9 percent to females. By contrast, the percentage of women receiving Ph.Ds in the area of foreign language and literature reached 48.4 percent.

TABLE 12 shows the number of doctorate degrees granted to women between 1972 and 1977, a slow, steady increase.

Academic rank in U.S. medical schools is illustrated in TABLE 13. Note that although there are a substantial number of women in the younger age group, there are relatively few female professors and associate professors. I think this requires additional comment. First of all, it is only within the last four or five years that there has been a substantial increase in the number of women in the incoming class; the figure hovers around

TABLE 10

LIFE SCIENCES-PERCENTAGE OF WOMEN DOCTORATES FOR THREE RECENT YEARS

	%
1. Texas Women's University	100
3. Columbia University	50.8
5. Cornell Univ. Med. Coll.	48.3
6. N.Y.U.	44.8
10. City Univ. of New York	39.6
16. M.I.T.	32.8
25. University of Louisville	30.4

30 percent, in some schools a little lower, and in some a little higher. Many of those with the rank of associate professor may in fact be quite senior and have not been advanced. I think we will have to watch these figures closely over the next ten years, for there should be an increase in the number of female professors and associate professors with the increasing number of women coming into medical schools.

Behaviorial attitudes are inculcated early in life. How many boys are given Barbie dolls or girls mechanical toys at Christmas time?

Margaret Mead once said, "Our academic tradition was initially designed by and for the celibate, the monk, the occasional nun, a kind of sexless life in which activities of the intellect were joined with a disavowal of the flesh and a denial of the body. The academic world is fundamentally hostile, by tradition, to those acts of feminity which involve childbearing."

While overt hostility to childbearing may be decreasing, the financial burdens of raising a family while professionally employed has been acknowledged only recently. The President's Commission in 1963 recom-

TABLE 11
PROFILE OF DOCTORATES, FISCAL YEAR 1976

	1976 % Males		1976 % Females	% Married
Total (25,247)	76.7	Total (7676)	2.3	55.5
Physics & astronomy	95.6		4.4	51.9
Chemistry	88.4		11.6	55.6
Physical sciences	91.4		8.6	53.9
Mathematics	88.7		11.3	56.6
Engineering	98.1 ↑*		1.9 ↓	↑ 60.4
Basic medical sciences	76.3		23.7	53.5
Medical sciences	77.8		22.2	↓ 50.3
Life sciences	80.5		19.5	55.1
Psychology	67.1		32.9	54.8
Anthropology	67.3		32.7	57.6
English & American Language & Literature	58.2		41.8	57.7
Foreign Language and Literature	51.6 ↓		48.4 ↑	59.1

* Percentage numbers in boxes indicate high and lows (direction of arrows) for each column.

TABLE 12
DOCTORAL DEGREES GRANTED TO WOMEN*

Field	1972	1973	1974	1975	1976	1977
Physical Sciences	365	376	375	394	409	431
Engineering	21	45	34	50	53	74
Life Sciences	731	871	863	958	967	957
Social Sciences	1049	1243	1432	1599	1733	1830
Total	2166	2535	2704	3001	3162	3292

* (From National Research Council.)

mended that household workers be unionized and that facilities be established in child care. The present income tax law has been liberalized to give tax credit to a working woman who must employ household help to care for a dependent child under the age of 15. Such a credit sounds attractive because it reduces the tax that must be paid to the government, but the law limits the credit to a maximum of only $800. This credit is calculated by taking 20 percent of the expenses relating to household help, but the taxpayer is allowed a ceiling of $2,000 for tax purposes if there is one dependent and $4,000 if there are two or more dependents. Obviously, the cost of household help is not halved if there is only one child.

The tax credit may appear more generous than deductible business expenses, but such is not necessarily the case. If a working woman is taxed at a high rate, then she is clearly paying more tax under the present system. If her tax rate is the maximum 50 percent, and she pays $4,000

TABLE 13
ACADEMIC RANK U.S. MEDICAL SCHOOLS, 1970–1971*

Rank	% Total	% Male	% Female
Total faculty reporting 28,452			
Professors	23	96	4
Assoc. Prof.	23	91	9
Assist. Prof.	34	84	16
Instructor	14	69	31
Associate	3	68	32

* (From Women in Medicine, 1976. Josiah Macy Foundation.)

for household help, she is paying $1200 more in tax than she would if she could deduct this household help payment as a business expense. One wonders at the logic of making child-care provisions so restrictive.

In calculating the income tax credit, the actual income of the taxpayer is irrelevant. It is essential only that the expenses are for household services required to enable the taxpayer to be gainfully employed or to be a full-time student. There is no provision at all for household help, however unless there is a dependent child at home under the age of 15, or a disabled spouse, or a physically or mentally disabled dependent.

The present provision for income tax credit thus benefits primarily the younger professional women with school-age or younger children and should be made more generous if the tax law is to recognize, realistically, the need for women to be attracted to the professions.

I would like to close this brief and necessarily rather superficial review of a matter of large importance by quoting Eleanor Roosevelt, "It seems to me that we must have the courage to face ourselves in this crisis. We must regain a vision of ourselves as leaders of the world. We must join in an effort to use all knowledge for the good of *all* human beings. When we do that we shall have nothing to fear."

I submit that we will be able to reach this goal only if we construct a society so that everyone—all men and all women—have an opportunity to fulfill their potential and be rewarded accordingly.

Addendum

Since this lecture was delivered a number of additional surveys have been published. The most recent data (1977), as well as providing earlier references, can be found in Science, Engineering, and Humanities Doctorates in the United States, National Academy of Sciences, Washington, D.C., 1978. Further information can be obtained from Comprehensive Survey Project, Commission on Human Resources, National Research Council, 2101 Constitution Avenue, Washington, D.C. 20418.

An excellent survey can also be found in *Women in Medicine, 1976* published by Josiah Macy Foundation, 1977, and distributed by the Independent Publishers Group, 14 Vanderventer Avenue, Port Washington, New York 11050.

Changing Attitudes Toward Women in the Profession of Chemistry

ALAN C. NIXON*
2140 Shattuck Avenue
Berkeley, California 94704

INTRODUCTION

IN 1972 The New York Academy of Sciences sponsored a conference on Successful Women in Science: An Analysis of Determinants. The theme of the conference was expressed by Hilda Kahne: "Why should we be interested in stimulating women's interest in science and have a concern about increasing their opportunities in these fields? The answer lies partly in a desire to provide women, as for other groups, an opportunity to pursue educational work choice on an equal and competitive basis. Just as important, however, is the desire to provide all members of society an increased well-being that results from having the best possible fit between human resources available and the work that society needs done."[1]

I will not try to cover as broad a field as Dr. Kahne outlined. Rather, I will try to give you my assessment of the situation today in the field of chemistry as a profession for women and some thoughts about what might happen in the future and how we might influence what might happen in the most desirable way.

STATUS IN PROFESSIONAL SOCIETIES

There is no doubt that as far as the professional societies of chemistry are concerned, women have arrived. On the Board of Directors of the American Chemistry Society we now have a woman president, Anna Harrison, and a woman chairman, Mary Good, and 27 percent of the fifteen "man" board are women compared to 8 percent in the total society. We have numerous important offices being filled among the committees and in the local sections and divisions by females. Thirteen of the 175 chairpersons of the 175 local sections are women, nine are chairwomen-

---

* Past president, The American Chemical Society

elect, 32 are secretaries, and 18 are treasurers. Fifty (11 percent) of the 450 councilors of the Society are women. And we have Janet Berry, president-elect of the American Institute of Chemists. One of the most encouraging possibilities for improvement in the status of women arises from the fact that the American Chemical Society has a strong and vigorous Women Chemists Committee—originally organized for the purpose of administering the Garvan medal, funds for which were donated by Francis P. Garvan, president of the Chemical Foundation, to recognize the contribution of outstanding women chemists; but the committee has now branched out as an activist group to try to ensure that discrimination against women is diminished. Incidentally, I appointed the first man to the Women Chemists Committee.

According to Nina M. Roscher, Chairman of the ACS Women Chemists Committee and Associate Dean for Graduate Studies and Research at American University, Washington, D.C.: "Recent studies have indicated the outlook and opportunities for women chemists in the chemical profession have improved over the past 20 years. Greater interest by women in chemistry as a field of study coupled with changing social pressures and greater acceptance of women in the area where it counts most—salary—suggests a hopeful future.

The proportion of women receiving bachelor's degrees in chemistry has remained relatively constant, about one in five for the past 20 years. However, the proportion of women receiving master's degrees has changed from one in 10 in 1956 to one in five today. The proportion of women receiving doctor's degrees has similarly increased from one in 20 in 1956 to one in 10 today."[2]

She says, "In that context, you might say things have greatly improved."[3] But she also included an article written by one of her former students at Douglass College about her experiences as a recent graduate student at Stanford in California, and says, "This may give you some idea why I am less optimistic than I would really like to be."[3] The former student, Susan Groh, says, "I'd like to be able to tell you that the women's liberation movement has cleared the way for women who wish to pursue scientific careers, that prejudice and discrimination are practically nonexistent, that scientists are judged on the basis of their research and not their sex—but unfortunately it isn't so. Traditions die hard, and while the collective consciousness of society may have been joggled a little by the feminist movement, the battle has by no means been won. As a graduate student in chemistry, I've experienced some of the opposition women run into trying to establish a firm foothold in the 'masculine' realm of the physical sciences."[4] She goes on to say, "In my first week at Stanford it was made very clear to me—by too many people—that I was considered, more or less, as one of the three 'token' women in a class of 28."[4]

I also heard from Madeleine M. Joullie, Chairman of the Economic Status Committee of the American Chemical Society and Professor of Chemistry, University of Pennsylvania: "I am truly sorry to say this but I have seen very little change in attitude towards women. I could give you examples of the bad attitude that prevails *now* such as two truly outstanding women of international reputation being pushed out of the tenure track for some young man who has practically no publications, and others. . . . If you think attitudes have changed, I think you are kidding yourself, and possibly your audience."[5]

Here are the views of Susan Collier, late chairman of the Women Chemists Committee, member of the Committee on Committee of the ACS, and past chairman of the Rochester Section, ACS. Ms. Collier said that she has a somewhat negative attitude regarding whether any progress was being made or not. She did feel that full-time professional women chemists did have a somewhat better status than they had five years ago, which reflects changing attitudes among both men and women with respect to the role of working women. It is difficult, however, for the part-time, main-line professional to get a fair evaluation, although this is starting to get better in some quarters, perhaps more in the industrial world than in the academic. Opportunities for women to obtain part-time work are improving, although women with children still have a quite difficult situation and require extraordinary energy in order to be successful. She feels that many of the women who are now over forty have experienced considerable discrimination during the course of their employment and may be now in such a position that it will be difficult for them to extricate themselves. She feels that at present discrimination exists not so much in the hiring of women chemists but rather in the expectations that their employers have for them. In other words, a woman, to succeed to a certain degree, has to be better than a man of equivalent background and competence in the same sort of job.

A question on a questionnaire directed to members of the California and Santa Clara Valley Sections asked if the members thought that women chemists were getting a fair deal professionally. Twenty-eight percent thought they were, 42 percent said, no, they were not, but 30 percent didn't know whether they were or not. The response of the latter may have been due just to insensitivity and callousness or it may be that they had never encountered enough female chemists to know whether they were getting a square deal or not. It does show, however, that their curiosity and awareness were not at very high levels. It is not known how many of the respondents to the questionnaire were women, but it could not have been a very large number. However, the fact that 40 percent of those who had an opinion regarded the situation of women chemists as being fair and equitable indicates that there is a very large number of male chemists who are not aware of what the actual situation is in spite of the information that has been included in *Chemical and Engineering News*, in the public press, and other technical sources.

That the *C&EN* is not exactly falling over itself in reporting the plight of women in chemistry came to light recently when I received a note from Mathilde Kland of the California Section enclosing a letter she had sent to one of the writers on *C&EN* almost a year before, suggesting that *C&EN* do a story on discrimination against women in science, and the writer replied that both she and her "boss" were interested but they were very busy at that particular moment. On transmitting a copy of this letter on to the editor I received the assurance that they were indeed interested in the subject and were taking steps to prepare an article. It remains to be seen if they do indeed *take one giant step for womankind.**

Progress in the Academic World

The Women Chemists Committee of the ACS abstracted from the reports of the Committees on Professional Training and the Directory of Graduate Research information on the number of women on the staff of chemistry departments in this country offering doctoral studies in chemistry. The raw data implies some measure of discernible progress. Of the approximately 4000 full-time staff in these departments, in 1970-71 the percentage of women was 1.5; in 1972-73, 2.0; in 1974-75, 2.2. This, to save you the mathematics, comes out to a grand total of 88 in the whole country. At the same time, these departments were granting 181 doctorates a year to women in chemistry, 10.4 percent of the total. There are only *19 full-time women professors* in the whole country and only one in the entire University of California system, none in the New

---

* They did, c.f. *C&EN*, 1978, 56(37):26.

TABLE 1
STARTING YEARLY SALARIES OF INEXPERIENCED FULL-TIME CHEMISTS BY HIGHEST DEGREE EARNED AND EMPLOYER

Highest Degree Earned		Total Private Industry	Manufac- turing	Nonmanu- facturing	Employer College, University	High Sch Other Sch.	Federal Governmt	State, Locl. Gov.	Hospital Ind. Lab.	Nonprofit Res. Inst.	Row Total
Bachelor's	Median	12600.	13000.	12000.	8400.	9000.	9303.	8200.	9000.	10000.	11476
	Mean	12624.	12767.	11410.	8474.	9420.	8974.	8902.	9286.	10676.	
	Count	95	85	10	15	6	3	2	16	5	142
	Std Dev.	2085.	2049.	2099.	2003.	860.	570.	993.	1508.	2292.	2559.
Master's		14500.	14400.	15780.	9000.	9722.	11500.	10500.	10860.	15000.	13110.
		14736.	14678.	15780.	9465.	10356.	12333.	10500.	10860.	15000.	
		19	18	1	4	4	3	1	1	1	33
		2050.	2094.	0.	1190.	1875.	1443.	0.	0.	0.	2770
Ph.D.		20165.	20165.	0.	11000.	0.	0.	0.	12000.	0.	16786.
		20042.	20042.	0.	10580.	0.	0.	0.	12000.	0.	
		11	11	0	5	0	0	0	1	0	17
		1188.	1188.	0.	2003.	0.	0.	0.	0.	0.	4758.
Women Column	Mean	13598.	13771.	11807.	9078.	9794.	10654.	9435.	9524.	11397.	12227.
	Count	125	114	11	24	10	6	3	18	6	192
	Std Dev.	2938.	2936.	2388.	2020.	1347.	2085.	1159.	1589.	2705.	3228.

(CONT.)

Men

Highest Degree Earned		Total Private Industry	Manufacturing	Nonmanufacturing	College, University	High Sch. Other Sch.	Federal Gov. ernmt	State, Locl. Gov.	Hospital Ind. Lab.	Nonprofit. Res. Inst.	Other	Row Total
Bachelor's	Median	12500.	12480.	13000.	8300.	8500.	10000.	11139.	10000.	10800.	0.	11776.
	Mean	12396.	12320.	13170.	8743.	8755.	10964.	12510.	9698.	10835.	0.	
	Count	191	174	17	16	6	12	4	18	8	0	255
	Std Dev.	1977.	1967.	1966.	1539.	854.	1760.	2237.	1566.	2482.	0.	2250.
Master's		15500.	15500.	14825.	9000.	10500.	14097.	11000.	11000.	0.	0.	14103.
		15144.	15154.	15079.	8974.	12283.	12557.	12190.	12700.	0.	0.	
		52	45	7	6	3	3	4	4	0	0	72
		2508.	2506.	2724.	2633.	3220.	2756.	2340.	3092.	0.	0.	3118.
Ph.D.		20000.	20000.	20100.	12000.	11000.	17500.	0.	14300.	16800.	16000.	18313.
		20038.	19984.	20467.	12741.	11000.	18471.	0.	14300.	17400.	16000.	
		108	96	12	31	1	12	0	1	2	1	156
		1491.	1510.	1311.	2340.	0.	2383.	0.	0.	849.	0.	3432.
Column	Mean	15154.	15061.	15973.	11108.	10038.	14477.	12350.	10420.	12148.	16000.	14234.
	Count	351	315	36	53	10	27	8	23	10	1	483
	Std Dev.	3903.	3909.	3805.	2889.	2364.	4217	2126.	2292.	3540.	0.	4059.

York State system, none among the Big Ten schools, none in the Ivy League Schools (except The University of Pennsylvania). Practically none of the big research money schools have any women of any kind on their staffs, not Harvard, not Berkeley, not Stanford, not Yale, not Columbia, not Florida, not Michigan State, not North Carolina, not Northwestern, not Penn State, and not Washington. We must however, acknowledge that some of the big research schools do have some women on their staffs—Maryland has one, MIT has two, Michigan has one, Ohio State has one, Univ. of Pennsylvania has one, as do Princeton and Purdue and Texas A&M. But Texas Women's University has zero! So does Howard! The leading university is Rutgers (New Brunswick/ Douglass), which has six. Of course, Douglass is a women's university, or was. In second place is the University of Massachusetts (five associate colleges, including Amherst, Smith, and Mount Holyoke) with five and then American University, Washington, D.C., with four, Auburn, Ala., with three, and several twos—Brigham Young (Salt Lake City, Utah), UC San Diego, UC Santa Cruz, (both California), Missouri at St. Louis, New Mexico State, Polytech Brooklyn, Toledo (Ohio), and Wyoming. However, *half of the total* number of positions are as *assistant professor,* which we are learning is not always regarded as a continuing position. So much for statistics, which are not too encouraging.

Discrimination

The true attitude of the predominantly male scientific establishment toward females crops out most visibly in the courts, where laws prohibiting discrimination on the basis of sex have allowed courageous women to bring charges against their employers. One of the most dramatic and agonizing examples of this is the case of Sharon Johnson vs. the University of Pittsburgh, which was concluded last fall with a judgment by Judge Knox in which he stated, in effect, that, "Yes, the University did practice sex discrimination but not in this case," one of the more curious decisions in the history of American jurisprudence. I have written about this case over the years in *The Vortex,* the publication of the California Section of the ACS, and in my private newsletter, Nick Nacks, as follows:

June, 1973–"Two of the most interesting cases that the CPR (Committee on Professional Relations) (ACS) is dealing with at the present time, which can be discussed openly since they are in the public realm, involve Sharon Johnson who is alleging sex discrimination against the University of Pittsburgh for failure to grant tenure after her six years on the staff. (This, of course, is tantamount to firing.) Dr. Johnson has applied for injunctive relief. The case has been argued and is, at this time, awaiting a decision. ACS counsel has received the briefs of both sides in this proceeding and this information will be utilized to form the basis of an *amicus curiae* brief if the arguments of Dr. Johnson's lawyer are persuasive.

September, 1974-"Following the driving of the last nail by the Board of Directors at the June meeting on the Good Ship ACS Legal Aid Loan Fund, the craft has finally been launched by an application form and approval of a loan of $10,000 to Professor Sharon Johnson of the University of Pittsburgh who is engaged in a court dispute with the university alleging sex discrimination in their attempt to fire her just before she was about to achieve tenure. You will remember that Dr. Johnson, in a preliminary hearing, sought and won a preliminary injunction which restored her to her previous position with back pay. It will probably be some time next spring before the results of this case are known."[7]

June, 1976-"This is another report on the struggle that is going on between Professor Sharon Johnson and the University of Pittsburgh regarding their efforts to get her fired from her job as Assistant Professor of Biochemistry at the University. I went over to Pittsburgh after the national meeting in New York and appeared as an expert witness regarding the matter of discrimination against women in chemistry. I testified to this as a fact on the basis of my general knowledge of the situation and backed this up with information published over the years in *C&EN* regarding the comparative pay of men and women Ph.D. chemists (and/or biochemists) as well as their unemployment history. Over the years the statistics in both categories depict a dismal dissertation of discrimination. Since 1967 salaries of women compared to men range from 71 percent to 80 percent while the unemployment figures since 1971 (when they were first compiled) have been from two to three times as great. The opposing attorney, in an effort to discredit me, asked me if I belonged to any women's organizations so I replied, yes, that I was married. This seemed to shut off that line of questioning.

"The University of Pittsburgh obviously regards this as a very important case since they are spending a great deal of money fighting it. For instance, they had three attorneys in the court when I was there and at-

TABLE 2

SALARIES OF CHEMISTS (EXCLUDING TEACHERS AND SELF-EMPLOYED) BY DEGREE AND EXPERIENCE

Highest Degree Earned			1 or Less	2–4	5–9	10–14	15–19	20–24	25–29	30–34	35–39	40 or More	Row Total
Bachelor's	Percentile	10	8900.	10000.	10800.	12500.	15000.	15000.	14600.	11500.	15700.	15000.	
		25	9600.	11500.	12000.	14200.	16600.	18000.	15600.	17500.	17200.	15000.	
		50	11000.	13000.	13800.	16200.	19200.	20000.	19800.	22100.	17600.	15000.	
		75	12000.	14000.	15300.	18900.	22100.	27500.	22600.	24700.	19000.	27000.	
		90	13800.	14600.	17600.	20000.	25000.	33000.	26000.	31000.	19000.	27000.	
	Mean		10923.	12660.	14049.	16607.	19725.	22354.	20157.	22382.	18083.	21000.	16049.
	Count		22	77	47	41	28	26	21	11	6	2	281
	Std Dev.		1966.	1869.	2457.	3217.	4306.	6754.	5429.	6328.	1792.	8485.	5245.
Master's	Percentile	10	12500.	10300.	10000.	13800.	14500.	15000.	12500.	11300.	17300.	0.	
		25	12500.	11600.	13400.	15700.	17500.	16500.	13500.	19500.	17300.	0.	
		50	13500.	13000.	15700.	18000.	20000.	18500.	19800.	21000.	17300.	0.	
		75	13500.	15000.	18000.	20000.	21100.	19500.	21000.	23300.	17300.	0.	
		90	15000.	16800.	20000.	21300.	22000.	20000.	22800.	23300.	17300.	0.	
	Mean		13667.	13413.	15744.	18217.	19353.	18656.	19125.	21017.	17300.	0.	16711.
	Count		3.	31	34	24	17	9	8	6	1	0.	133
	Std Dev.		1258.	2353.	3458.	2958.	2701.	3015.	4108.	5659.	0.	0.	3888.
Doctor's	Percentile	10	11000.	11000.	14500.	12100.	14000.	20200.	18000.	17000.	13000.	34300.	
		25	11500.	16500.	17500.	16300.	19500.	21000.	20800.	27000.	13000.	34300.	
		50	17000.	19200.	19500.	22000.	23000.	21500.	26000.	28000.	21300.	34300.	
		75	18000.	20000.	20700.	26000.	24000.	26000.	29200.	32200.	22000.	34300.	
		90	18000.	23000.	22900.	28000.	26000.	29500.	32500.	32200.	30000.	34300.	
	Mean		15757.	18467.	19179.	22269.	22109.	24278.	25800.	28083.	21575.	34300.	21478.
	Count		7.	24	29	26	11	9	17	6	4	1	134
	Std Dev.		3398.	3687.	3084.	8573.	3719.	4494.	6063.	5907.	6947.	0.	6209.

Women

NIXON: PROFESSION OF CHEMISTRY

		1	2	3	4	5	6	7	8	9	10	11
Column	Mean	12238.	13892.	15925.	18649.	20080.	21991.	22063.	23513.	19282.	25423.	17537.
	Count	32	132	110	91	56	44	46	23	11	3	548
	Std Dev	3030.	3235.	3600.	5743.	3846.	5956.	6107.	6438.	4409.	9745.	5675.
Bachelor's	Percentile 10	8400.	9300.	11000.	12800.	14000.						
	25	10500.	11500.	13200.	15000.	16500.						
	50	12200.	14200.	16100.	18000.	20500.						
	75	15000.	17000.	19000.	22000.	24400.						
	90	18000.	21000.	26000.	32000.	41000.						
	Mean	11150.	13380.	16354.	19636.	29811.						
	Count	40	235	236	230	47						
	Std Dev	2386.	2433.	3217.	4544.	10998.						
Master's	Percentile 10	10200.	12000.	14400.	15800.	17500.						
	25	12000.	13500.	16500.	17700.	20000.						
	50	13000.	15000.	18000.	20100.	24000.						
	75	15000.	16400.	20500.	24000.	30400.						
	90	15800.	18000.	22000.	27500.	37000.						
Men	Mean	13364.	15021.	18357.	21209.	26506.						
	Count	22	123	175	169	104						
	Std Dev	2069.	2637.	2911.	5487.	7348.						
Doctor's	Percentile 10	11000.	14500.	17500.	20000.	24800.						
	25	16000.	17600.	20500.	23500.	28500.						
	50	17900.	19900.	23500.	26800.	35000.						
	75	19000.	21600.	26000.	30400.	41000.						
	90	19900.	23000.	29000.	34000.	50000.						
	Mean	16957.	19343.	23369.	27295.	38348.						
	Count	56	332	717	490	150						
	Std Dev	3452.	3363.	4587.	6268.	18894.						
Column	Mean	14319.	16542.	21124.	24157.	31480.						
	Count	118	690	1128	889	433						
	Std Dev	3899.	4034	5098.	6711.	14730.						

torneys don't work for chemist's wages. I think this is a very important case and I think Sharon should be helped financially. She has suffered with this situation for more than four years now; she has spent untold number of hours preparing statements and giving testimony; has turned the living room of her house into a command post as well as another room into a message center; at the same time has carried on her teaching and research at the University (thanks to a preliminary injunction). I think this case fits within the definition of a 'landmark' case. I recommend that the ACS undertake to underwrite a financial base of support so a decision is not arrived at by default. According to Sharon's attorney, Sylvia Roberts, a decision is expected by the end of this year and it is entirely possible that the University will appeal it."[8]

September, 1976-"The latest development in the Sharon Johnson case is, according to NOW's Legal Defense and Education Fund, harassment of Sylvia Roberts, SJ's attorney, by the lawyers for the University of Pittsburgh in an attempt to reduce the effectiveness of the plaintiff. The Pitt lawyers' charge is that Sylvia was guilty of unprofessional conduct in using the scenario of the SJ case in a money-raising letter which she wrote for NOW. The charge was kept concealed from Ms. Roberts for three months so, apparently, it could be sprung just as the SJ case was coming up to its final stages. Ms. Roberts was given ten days to answer the charges! While there is no doubt that the Pitt legal maneuvers will fail, the necessity of dealing with it will inevitably reduce Ms. Roberts effectiveness as Sharon's advocate."

"The lurking danger here is that if such tactics are condoned the route to relief against discrimination of all kinds, already fearfully expensive, will be effectively blocked to the ordinary citizen. As Dr. Johnson remarked, 'If these tactics were to become acceptable, only millionaires could afford to go to court'."[9]

October, 1977-"The number given above ($330,000) represents the number of dollars that I understand the University of Pittsburgh will seek in court costs against defendent Sharon Johnson as a result of a five year court battle which was resolved in the University's favor over Professor Johnson's allegation of sex discrimination. The suit came about as a result of the University's failure to rehire Johnson five years ago after six years of presumably satisfactory service, in order to avoid giving her tenure. The University's use of legal talent in the case was profligate. The day I testified there were three (3) Pitt attorneys in court (and attorneys don't work for chemists' wages).

"The judge's ruling on the case was peculiar. He said (in effect), Yes, Pitt has practiced sex discrimination over the years, but not in this case. He chose to believe the University's argument that her research was not relevant to the needs of the medical school (the Department of Biochemistry is in the med school at Pitt) and that her teaching ability was inadequate (the account of the Pitt students' reception of her teaching as reported in *C&EN* (Aug. 15/77 p 22) read like something put out by the Gestapo. If it is factual, then we have to conclude that Pitt students are a bunch of unmitigated boors; or that it occurred after the word had been put out that the administration wanted to get rid of Johnson). On the basis of my own discussions with her over the years, I refuse to believe that she is not a competent teacher. As for the relevancy of research, if we had to depend on the medical profession to direct biochemical research we would still be working on ways of improving the breeding habits of leeches.

"The Alice in Wonderland aspect of the case was further added to, according to the *New York Times*, by a warm statement of support from the dean of the medical school for Dr. Johnson as a faculty member. He pointed out that the events that the Court was judging had taken place five years before.

"Personally I have nothing but admiration for the way Sharon has battled for the principle of non-discrimination while enduring a very antagonistic environment meanwhile continuing to get grants, do her research, publishing, and doing her job as a wife and a mother holding her family together. It certainly shows that a woman has a difficult job getting a square deal whilst working in the male chauvinist higher educational system from the male chauvinist legal justice system in this country.

"It remains to be seen what the ACS will do. It did grant Dr. Johnson a loan under the legal aid loan program in '73 and stated that it was prepared to enter the case on appeal. However, I wouldn't blame Sharon if she decided to forego the agony of an appeal—after all one has only one life to lead and battling in the courts is a poor way to spend it."[10]

December, 1977—"*The Pitt News*, (Sept. 14, 1977) the student newspaper of the University of Pittsburgh furnished the details of an unpublicized pact that was entered into between the University and Sharon Johnson. This is the outcome of the five year legal battle stemming from the sex discrimination charge by Dr. Johnson against the University. The judge in the case, although admitting that the University had engaged in

TABLE 3
SALARIES OF CHEMISTS BY WORK SPECIALTY AND DEGREE

Work Speciality		Women Highest Degree Earned				Men Highest Degree Earned			
		Bachelor's	Master's	Doctor's	Row Total	Bachelor's	Master's	Doctor's	Row Total
Analytical	Median	14000.	17200.	18000.	17203.	18500.	20600.	22600.	21208.
	Mean	15945.	17174.	19947.		19378.	21757.	23361.	
	Count	69	35	32	136	588	313	420	1321
Inorganic		17600.	16000.	16000.	17567.	21000.	21300.	20500.	22468.
		18729.	17150.	17273.		22560.	22783.	22391.	
		7	4	22	33	75	41	257	373
Organic		14500.	14000.	18400.	16802.	21500.	22200.	23400.	24215.
		16250.	14943.	18346.		22986.	23631.	24615.	
		20	14	24	58	211	179	908	1298
Polymer, Macromol.		14500.	17600.	19700.	19100.	21800.	23400.	27000.	26772.
		16400.	18822.	22764.		23088.	25703.	28811.	
		14	9	11	34	286	189	616	1091
Physical, Theoret.		19000.	20300.	16800.	18175.	20600.	21500.	23000.	24298.
		18114.	20367	17736.		21945.	22824.	24561.	
		7	3	14	24	33	29	457	519

(CONT.)

Work Speciality	Women Highest Degree Earned			Row Total	Men Highest Degree Earned			Row Total
	Bachelor's	Master's	Doctor's		Bachelor's	Master's	Doctor's	
Biochemistry	12500. 13319. 27	16000. 15342. 19	20000. 19913. 46	17034. 92	17300. 19000. 39	17700. 21908. 48	25000. 25429. 568	24789. 655
Agriculture, Food	14200. 16195. 20	15000. 16813. 8	17600. 20400. 6	17082. 34	20800. 22340. 89	21000. 22830. 69	27000. 28577. 185	25803. 343
Pharmac., Medical, Clinical	14700. 15697. 31	16300. 16263. 19	19500. 19605. 21	17004. 71	19500. 21553. 132	20100. 23139. 93	27000. 29205. 336	26399. 561
Chemistry, General	13000. 14183. 24	13000. 14561. 36	16000. 15711. 19	14723. 79	21700. 23038. 200	19100. 20677. 179	23000. 26423. 275	23810. 654
Chemistry, Other	14000. 14982. 39	15000. 15374. 23	20800. 20756. 18	16394. 80	21000. 22569. 318	22000. 22876. 259	26000. 27008. 445	24841. 1022
Nonchemical	17700. 19267. 30	16200. 18025. 12	19700. 21343. 14	19520. 56	23000. 26049. 121	24000. 24146. 70	29000. 30363. 201	27921. 392
Column Mean Count	15922. 288	16146. 182	19288. 277	17076. 697	21881. 2092	22865. 1469	26154. 4668	24481. 8229

sex discrimination, says he could not find that it had in this particular case (an interesting bit of subtle sophistry). The News published the text of two letters giving the details of the agreement. The pact required a promise from Johnson not to appeal the case in return for the University agreeing not to sue her for the $300,000+ court costs and permitting her to continue her research until June 30, 1978 (on her NIH grant, of course) as a senior research associate. All parties agreed to remain silent except for a public relations announcement by the University. The News did not explain how it got copies of the letters except to say that they were not obtained from any of the obvious sources.

"It also stated that Johnson had applied to several hundred schools without being able to secure employment. I hope anyone who reads this who has any knowledge of a job possibly in biochemistry will let Dr. Johnson know of it.

"There is an ironic footnote to this affair. The News also reported on September 7 that Dr. Dorothy J. South, a research associate in the Pitt Biochemistry Department was found dead by suicide apparently by swallowing sodium cyanide five days before her NIH grant terminated. It was reported that she had submitted over 200 applications for employment without success."[11]

Also I quote from the reams of paper which accompanied this case the following paragraph written by E. R. Ramey, professor of physiology and biophysics at Georgetown University, Washington, D.C.:

"The procedures used by the Department of Biochemistry to deny Dr. Johnson tenure are in my experience without decency or precedence. She was not notified of the meeting which determined her fate. Nor was she asked to obtain an outside evaluation of her work. The accepted practice at my own medical school and at all the others with which I have been associated is to request a complete and current Curriculum Vitae together with letters from acknowledged outside experts in the scientist's field of research plus letters from students regarding the scientist's teaching ability. The Dean and then the Committee on Rank and Tenure may ask for additional data or may directly solicit further testimony from any source inside or outside the institution. Failing promotion or the award of tenure, the faculty member has the right to ask for the convening of a grievance committee made up of faculty representatives from the University Senate and the specific schools involved plus a faculty member appointed by the applicant. This is just a brief summary of the steps that are taken to assure each individual of a fair evaluation. These were not the procedures used to deny Dr. Johnson her promotion and tenure. The University of Pittsburgh has used techniques in this case which are unacceptable to all fine academic institutions. They are operating in the high-handed manner characteristic of another uglier time. If they succeed in this maneuver, all professional personnel at academic institutions will have been injured."[12]

And then we have the case of Molly Gleiser, to switch to the other side of the country, who had a case involving the Lawrence Berkeley Lab which is part of the University of California (but financed by the federal government). I quote from my column in *The Vortex* again as follows:

October, 1974-"This is the title (*An Obsolescent Life*) of a 'commentary' in the September '74 *Harper's* by Dr. Molly Gleiser of Berkeley, CA, who describes herself as a physical chemist, now 48 years old, and phased out of her job 3 years ago at UC Berkeley Rad Lab because of lack of funds. She describes all the various things she has done in trying to get a job, including more than 60 applications, many phone calls; and to live, as selling and making craft products and jewelry, writing articles, duty as a crossing guard, working in a 'boiler room,' etc. She says, 'I'm the author of four technical books and ten papers in my own field. I have worked for twenty years in my profession. At the end of this time I earned slightly less than a grade-school teacher, had three weeks vacation a year, could have been fired with two weeks notice, had no pension rights, and no Social Security.'

"I didn't know whether this was a put on or not so I got in touch with the author by phone. She assures me that the story is completely factual (but incomplete due to lack of space). She was formerly a member of the ACS but had dropped out. I encouraged her to use the California Section and National ACS Employment Services. Whether this will help or not I don't know. Certainly she falls in the age and sex category that seems to have the greatest difficulty in finding new jobs. However, it also happens to members of the 'stronger' sex and in other disciplines.

"Let's hope we can fashion a mechanism that will prevent such wastage of human resources."[13]

March 1978-"Discrimination—'Faculty of nicely distinguishing' (Webster's Collegiate Dictionary). That is not the definition that the word would call to mind in most peoples' minds nowadays: Read on—

'Lawrence Berkeley Laboratory has been found guilty of "violating Title VII of the Civil Rights Act, as amended, by refusing to rehire Charging Party in June 1975 and by failing to hire women with Ph.D.s in

TABLE 4
Salaries of Chemists by Work Function and Degree

Work Function		Women Highest Degree Earned				Men Highest Degree Earned			
		Bachelor's	Master's	Doctor's	Row Total	Bachelor's	Master's	Doctor's	Row Total
R & D, Mgmt., Adminis.	Median Mean Count	22000. 24338. 8	19000. 18440. 5	26000. 23300. 5	22411. 18	27000. 28721. 253	28000. 29272. 209	32500. 34137. 787	32226. 1249
Basic Research		13800. 13767. 42	14000. 14979. 33	19600. 20253. 53	16765. 128	18000. 17336. 92	17900. 19277. 101	24000. 25021. 693	23568. 886
Applied R & D Design		14800. 16273. 84	17300. 17587. 38	20200. 21318. 39	17805. 161	19400. 19828. 638	20800. 21436. 446	25000. 25484. 1160	23071. 2244
Gen Mgmt., Adminis		18600. 21971. 21	18800. 18750. 6	26000. 29117. 12	23674. 39	26300. 29255. 263	27000. 29156. 156	33500. 36883. 266	32195. 685
Teaching, Research.		10500. 10814. 7	13500. 14610. 49	15000. 15872. 92	15215. 148	11000. 13273. 26	16700. 16690. 164	19500. 20879. 1417	20329. 1607
Mkt., Sale, Pur., Teach.		15700. 16650. 12	17500. 19067. 6	19800. 18500. 5	17683. 23	23000. 23488. 223	24700. 26389. 97	28900. 30149. 88	25614. 408

(CONT.)

Work Function	Women Highest Degree Earned				Men Highest Degree Earned			
	Bachelor's	Master's	Doctor's	Row Total	Bachelor's	Master's	Doctor's	Row Total
Prd., Qual. Control	13200. 13748. 50	15000. 15617. 12	17200. 18400. 3	14308. 65	18000. 18551. 373	19000. 20513. 138	22500. 24441. 74	19759. 585
Forensic, Lab Anal.	13300. 14048. 29	14000. 14933. 12	19200. 22833. 6	15396. 47	15500. 16212. 119	16500. 17275. 65	20000. 20116. 51	17353. 235
Write, Abst., Library	18000. 18948. 21	17700. 18183. 18	19700. 19575. 8	18762. 47	20000. 20574. 19	19400. 19756. 27	22500. 24559. 34	21991. 80
Data Processing					22300. 21760. 5	17200. 18657. 7	20200. 19813. 15	19874. 27
Consulting	16200. 18420. 5	19000. 19000. 1	20800. 20800. 1	18843. 7	18000. 20416. 25	25000. 25444. 25	28000. 29036. 33	25358. 83
Other	11500. 13778. 9	13500. 14000. 2	24000. 28433. 3	16950. 14	18000. 20132. 56	20000. 25432. 34	26000. 26806. 50	23803. 140
Column Mean Count	15922. 288	16146. 182	19288. 227	17076. 697	21881. 2092	22865. 1469	26153. 4668	24480. 8229

chemistry." That is the nub of the determination issued in a case against Lawrence Berkeley Lab by the Equal Opportunity Employment Commission in San Francisco last August. The Charging Party in this case is Dr. Molly Gleiser, Ph.D. in physical chemistry and ACS member who was terminated in 1971. The determination refers to Section 706(b) of Title VII which establishes a conciliation process to which it "invites the parties to make a collective effort towards a just resolution of this matter." Presumably this would result in either rehiring of Dr. Gleiser or a monetary settlement but as of the end of January no action on this matter had been taken.

"The case is of interest because of the fact that it does indicate discrimination against women on the part of LBL and also because it indicates that one has to have a high degree of intestinal fortitude and persistence in order to get a satisfactory resolution under the process of the EEOC (the case was filed in 1974)."[14]

Progress in Industry

There are undoubtedly numerous other cases that could be cited but these are two very recent ones that I know about personally. As far as industry is concerned, by talking to women chemists in industry I gather that their circumstances are tolerable but they feel that they are not adequately compensated compared to men doing similar jobs, they are not given adequate consideration for advancement, particularly to management positions. From my own experience in industry, I know that it is difficult for a woman chemist to get the recognition and opportunities commensurate with her ability. One woman who worked with me for a number of years was an outstanding chemist but I was never successful in persuading higher management to recognize her abilities with either money or status.

Then we have a recent word from Nina Roscher:

"Some small progress is being made. Many of the industrial companies such as DuPont have been forced to hire a token number of women. It is hoped once they are on board that they will discover they are not only capable chemists, but also good administrators and ultimately their attitude will change."[15]

Susan Collier produced some pearls of wisdom regarding discrimination and affirmative action while she was chairman of the Women Chemists Committee, viz:

"What is discrimination today?

When you decide that a woman will spend less time in a given job than a man and you do not hire or promote her because of your assumption, you have just discriminated against her.

If you have a maternity leave policy that arbitrarily states that a woman must quit work when she is x months pregnant and cannot return to work until y months after her child is born regardless of the type of work she does and the advice of her personal physician; and you do not have such time restrictions for such things as heart attacks—you have just discriminated.

If you do not offer a job transfer to a woman because you are worried about what her husband will do in North Carolina, you have just made a discriminatory judgment.

Certainly if you do not invite a woman to be a participating member of her scientific peer group because you think she would be offended by the language and she doesn't drink beer, you are over 40 and discriminating.

To combat discrimination we have Affirmative Action. What Affirmative Action means depends on *Where* it is being practiced.

At one end of the scale Affirmative Action means that you hire a woman with Potential (translated—there are better men on the job market). To quote an anonymous administrator, 'I don't think she'll hurt the research program.'

I would like to insert a word of caution. Chemistry is a competitive profession and peer group interaction can be an important factor in achievement of success. If a chemist is not qualified to be a member of the peer group she becomes isolated from it and this can reinforce her lack of ability.

At the other end of the scale Affirmative Action means that you hire a woman only if she is about to win a Nobel Prize and there is no man qualified for the position available (this happened to Maria Goeppert-Mayer). This type of equal employment opportunity can most often be found in the academic community.

Somewhere in the middle lies hiring a woman when there are men of equal ability applying for the job.[16]

However, we should not lose sight of the fact that part of the reason for discrimination is not just male chauvinism but rather the hard facts of employment, now and in the future. Owing to overexpansion in the sixties, job opportunities in academia are very limited and will remain so into the eighties at least, due to falling enrollments and changing career perceptions of students. Similarly, the tendency in both industry and government seems to be to try to hold technical spending down to the same level in terms of constant dollars as it was in 1968-9. Thus, if both women and minorities were to achieve their reasonable goals of parity

TABLE 5
SALARIES OF CHEMISTS BY EMPLOYER AND DEGREE

Employer		Women Highest Degree Earned				Men Highest Degree Earned			
		Bachelor's	Master's	Doctor's	Row Total	Bachelor's	Master's	Doctor's	Row Total
Manufacturing	Median	14800.	17400.	20000.		21000.	23000.	27600.	
	Mean	16072.	17532.	22149.	17413.	22695.	24176.	29603.	26237.
	Count	165	69	45	279	1525	924	2170	4619
Nonmanufacturing		14000.	14500.	20000.		19000.	22000.	25000.	
		14521.	15533.	18471.	15770.	21052.	26371.	26569.	24514.
		14	6	7	27	126	80	140	346
College, University		12200.	13500.	15000.		11000.	17600.	20000.	
		12594.	14589.	16816.	15898.	12148.	17698.	21334.	20910.
		18	38	119	175	31	132	1643	1806
High Sch, Other Sch.		10000.	12500.	13300.		11000.	15000.	16000.	
		9800.	13387.	15650.	13216.	14028.	15452.	15700.	15219.
		4	23	4	31	18	61	15	94
Federal Government		20000.	18900.	23700.		22000.	23000.	28000.	
		20818.	18418.	24004.	21149.	22672.	22982.	28350.	25852.
		34	22	25	81	168	129	362	659

(CONT.)

Employer	Women Highest Degree Earned				Men Highest Degree Earned			
	Bachelor's	Master's	Doctor's	Row Total	Bachelor's	Master's	Doctor's	Row Total
State, Local, Gov.	14000. 14431. 16	14000. 14883. 6	19700. 20557. 7	16003. 29	16200. 16822. 93	18000. 18477. 53	21000. 21476. 58	18575.
Self-Employed	0. 0. 0	0. 0. 0	40000. 40000. 1	40000. 1	20000. 22650. 28	24000. 20965. 17	29000. 28680. 15	23680. 60
Hospital, Ind. Lab.	14100. 14586. 14	13500. 13800. 5	19100. 20760. 5	15708. 24	16000. 17087. 47	18000. 23521. 24	25000. 27254. 70	23230. 141
Nonprofit Research Inst.	13300. 13881. 21	15700. 16275. 12	20300. 20831. 13	16470. 46	18000. 19155. 47	19200. 20583. 46	24700. 25631. 190	23735. 283
Other	14000. 15000. 2	14500. 14500. 1	30000. 30000. 1	18625. 4	19500. 18756. 9	17300. 16433. 3	25000. 23300. 5	19682. 17
Column Mean Count	15922. 288	16146. 182	19288. 227	17076. 697	21879. 2092	22864. 1469	26152. 4668	24479. 8229

with white males the already gloomy prospects would be even more depressing. This is a reality that we will have to make plans to cope with.

The Bottom Line

The most recent surveys by the ACS continue to show that women suffer a considerable disadvantage in salary compared to men at all degree levels for most sorts of employment—manufacturing, nonmanufacturing, teaching, federal government, state government, hospitals and independent labs, and nonprofit research institutes. While the 1977 survey report shows that women have achieved parity as far as starting salaries are concerned for bachelor's degrees (11.5 K vs. 11.8 K) starting salaries for those with M.S. and Ph.D. degrees are still substantially less for women than for males (13.1 K vs. 14.1 K and 16.8 K vs. 18.3 K). This is shown in more detail in TABLE 1.[17] The most recent information where the data are broken down for men and women on the basis of experience comes from the 1976 report, and TABLE 2[18] from that report shows that the disparity between men and women starts in the very early years of experience and continues on as far as the data go. Thus, at two to four years the ratio is 1.19, 25–29 is 1.34, and 40+ is 1.24. Similar conditions prevail with respect to work specialty, TABLE 3;[19] by work function, TABLE 4;[20] and by employer, TABLE 5.[21] This type of information is shown in compact form in TABLE 6 from the 1974 report.[22] It would seem that as far as type of employment is concerned, as shown in TABLES 5 and 6, women are underrepresented in industry across the board but proportionately more women work in educational institutions, government facilities, and nonprofit organizations than do men. As far as work activity is concerned, they are very much underrepresented in management/administration and at the Ph.D. level in research and development. They are also much underrepresented in marketing, sales, production, and quality control. As far as fields of chemistry are concerned, a greater proportion, compared to men, are in the analytical field and a much greater proportion in biochemistry. They are greatly underrepresented in the polymer chemistry field.

There are some bright spots. One is in the increasing interest that women are taking in chemistry. The proportion of bachelor's degrees granted as a percentage of the total has risen from 18.5 to 22.5 in the last decade, master's degrees from 19.3 to 21.3, Ph.D.s from 6 to 12.1, while the ratio of women to men enrolled for advanced chemistry degrees has

TABLE 6
Comparison of Chemists' Salaries by Sex

	Bachelor's Men Salary	(%)	Bachelor's Women Salary	(%)	Master's Men Salary	(%)	Master's Women Salary	(%)	Doctor's Men Salary	(%)	Doctor's Women Salary	(%)	Overall Dist Men	Overall Dist Women
							Thousands of Dollars							
Employer														
Industry	$18.0	78.5	$13.2	56.4	$20.0	68.0	$14.4	43.5	$23.4	50.8	$21.0	18.7	61.4%	40.3%
Self-employed	15.1	1.6	na	1.2	22.0	1.2	na	0	25.0	0.6	na	0.9	0.9	0.7
Educational Inst.	11.5	2.7	9.0	10.0	14.0	13.6	11.0	32.7	17.5	34.8	15.0	53.4	22.4	31.0
Government	18.7	12.9	15.2	20.0	19.5	11.8	15.0	13.6	24.0	8.6	20.9	14.6	10.3	16.3
Non-profit†	15.8	3.0	11.0	10.4	16.3	3.8	12.1	8.9	21.0	4.3	17.0	11.4	3.8	10.2
Other	14.7	1.4	na	2.0	17.9	1.6	na	1.4	21.2	1.0	na	0.9	1.2	1.5
Work activity														
Management/admin.	22.7		15.0	10.6	24.1	30.5	18.0	9.7	27.0	28.6	23.0	14.4	29.4	11.6
Research/development	16.6	27.3	13.2	33.6	18.3	30.9	14.0	36.9	21.6	35.2	18.0	26.5	32.3	32.3
Teaching	11.0	1.6	na	4.3	14.0	11.6	11.2	25.7	17.0	28.1	14.5	45.1	18.0	24.4
Marketing/sales prod.	17.2	20.7	12.0	11.1	19.1	11.8	na	1.0	23.4	2.3	na	0.5	9.0	4.4
Other‡	16.0	20.3	12.8	40.4	17.0	15.2	12.8	26.7	21.0	5.7	18.4	13.5	11.3	27.3
Field														
Analytical§	16.0	32.6	14.1	40.9	18.3	22.5	14.2	22.3	20.0	10.5	14.1	10.2	18.5	25.0
Biochemistry§	16.0	4.9	10.5	15.7	16.5	6.6	12.0	18.4	22.0	18.2	17.4	37.2	12.5	23.6
Inorganic	19.2	5.3	na	2.6	17.0	8.5	12.0	10.2	19.0	6.6	13.5	11.2	6.6	7.8
Organic	19.0	12.1	12.7	8.5	18.6	15.9	12.5	15.0	21.2	24.4	16.8	14.9	19.6	12.7
Physical	18.2	3.5	na	2.6	18.5	5.6	na	5.3	21.2	14.9	15.6	9.8	10.2	5.8
Polymer	19.0	17.4	na	3.0	21.0	15.7	na	3.9	23.8	12.9	na	4.2	14.6	3.7
Other¶	20.0	24.3	13.3	26.8	20.3	25.3	13.8	24.8	24.7	12.6	18.0	12.6	18.0	21.5

*Percent in category. †Includes hospital and independent laboratory. ‡Includes technical services, laboratory analysis, writing, editing, abstracting, consulting. §Includes clinical and medicinal chemistry. ¶Includes literature, information science; na = not available.

TABLE 7
COMPARISONS BETWEEN THE SALARIES OF MEN AND WOMEN CHEMISTS

Sample Description	$	Women's Salaries as % of Men's
A. All Chemists		
Mean salary of men	22,720	100.0
Mean salary of women	16,291	71.7
Mean salary of women adjusted for		
degree level	16,996	74.8
years of experience	17,291	76.1
employer	16,633	73.2
work function	17,323	76.2
B. Chemists Engaged in Basic and Applied Research in Private Industry		
Mean salary of men	21,784	100.0
Mean salary of women	16,753	76.9
Mean salary of women adjusted for		
years of experience	19,164	88.0
years of experience and degree level	20,238	92.9

gone up from 0.12 to 0.19 during that same time. There is also a little brightness on the salary front. In the ACS publication "Professionals in Chemistry,"[23] 1975, an analysis of the information received in the 1974 salary survey indicates that womens' salaries are tending to approach those paid to males when adjusted for years of experience and degree level for those engaged in basic and applied research in private industry (TABLE 7). This figure stands at 92.9 percent for women compared to men. However, similar treatment for the data received from all women chemists compared to all male chemists made little difference in the comparison.

CONCLUSION AND RECOMMENDATIONS

Recognition for women in chemistry has improved markedly with respect to their acceptance in the major professional societies and in the public eye but only slightly with respect to employment and salaries. Discrimination has continued, and is difficult to combat. Neither men nor women chemists generally recognize sufficiently the lack of effective affirmative action, although measures to increase perception are being taken. This lack is probably only partly due to male chauvinism but rather largely reflects the difficulty of satisfying the aspirations of women and minorities in the face of the realities of an increasingly severe employment situation.

In order to improve the prospects for women chemists is achieve parity with men it is recommended that:

- The Women Chemists Committee of the ACS continue to expand its activities.
- A "war chest" be accumulated to support the legal opposition to discrimination.
- Funds be accumulated to support scholarships for promising young women in chemistry.
- Continuing efforts be made to nominate women for ACS and other awards and the NAS and the NSB.
- More publicity be obtained in C&EN News and other publications.
- The formation of Women Chemists Committees in ACS local sections and divisions and in other chemically oriented societies be promoted.
- Pressure be maintained on a number of the most prestigious universities and particularly industrial companies to hire more women chemists.
- More women chemists be encouraged to seek jobs in industry.
- Women be encouraged to enroll as graduate students at universities that have a very large proportion of foreign graduate students.
- Develop ways to increase the *total* number of chemically related jobs.
- Keep the faith!

REFERENCES

1. KAHNE, H. 1973. Ann. N.Y. Acad. Sci. **201**:143–153.
2. ROSCHER, N. M. 1977. Future looks brighter for women chemists, J. Commerce: 2A.
3. ROSCHER, N. M. 1978. Personal communication.
4. GROH, S. Susan Groh '74: graduate student. Douglass College publ. Brunswick, N.J.
5. JOULLIE, M. M. 1978. Personal communication.

6. NIXON, A. C. 1973. Nick Nacks. The Vortex. Am. Chem. Soc. California Section.
7. NIXON, A. C. 1974. Nick Nacks. The Vortex. Am. Chem. Soc. California Section.
8. NIXON, A. C. 1976. Nick Nacks. The Vortex. Am. Chem. Soc. California Section.
9. NIXON, A. C. 1976. Nick Nacks. The Vortex. Am. Chem. Soc. California Section.
10. NIXON, A. C. 1977. Nick Nacks. The Vortex. Am. Chem. Soc. California Section.
11. NIXON, A. C. 1977. Nick Nacks. The Vortex. Am. Chem. Soc. California Section.
12. RAMEY, E. R. 1975. Personal letter to Sylvia Roberts. Testimony in Johnson vs. U. Pitt. CA No. 73-120.
13. NIXON, A. C. 1974. Nick Nacks. The Vortex Am. Chem. Soc. California Section.
14. NIXON, A. C. 1978. Nick Nacks. The Vortex Am. Chem. Soc. California Section.
15. ROSCHER, N. M. 1978. Personal communication.
16. COLLIER, S. 1975. Excerpts from personal communication re Women Chemists Committee.
17. AMERICAN CHEMICAL SOCIETY. 1977 Survey Report. Starting Salaries and Employment Status of Chemistry and Chemical Engineering Graduates: 28-29.
18. AMERICAN CHEMICAL SOCIETY. 1976 Report of Chemists' Salaries and Employment Status: 53-54.
19. AMERICAN CHEMICAL SOCIETY. 1976 Report of Chemists' Salaries and Employment Status: 47-48.
20. AMERICAN CHEMICAL SOCIETY. 1976 Report of Chemists' Salaries and Employment Status: 42-43.
21. AMERICAN CHEMICAL SOCIETY. 1976 Report of Chemists' Salaries and Employment Status: 36-37.
22. AMERICAN CHEMICAL SOCIETY. 1974 Report of Chemists' Salaries and Employment Status: 19.
23. AMERICAN CHEMICAL SOCIETY. 1975. Professionals in Chemistry.

A Certain Restlessness

ESTHER A.H. HOPKINS
Polaroid Corporation
Cambridge, Massachusetts 02139

WE ARE COGNIZANT of the traditional areas into which women scientists go. They are, albeit with a bit more difficulty, the same areas in general into which men scientists go. When we consider expanding the role of women in the sciences, we should look not just at enlarging the number of women in conventional roles but also at expanding the scope of those things women do professionally that can be considered as within the province of science.

Scientists do not live isolated in a world called "Science." We live in society with others. Each group has a responsibility for contributing to the overall progress made by us all. We do not create in proud isolation. We are bound, interdependent.

There are numbers of places other than in laboratories and classrooms where science impacts society. Just so, there are numbers of persons whose habitat is not the laboratory nor the classroom but whose intellectual bent is toward the disciplined, cautiously reasoned approach that science uses for progress.

I'd like to discuss how we (and the "we" encompasses all those concerned about our society's direction and the contribution to a positive, value-full future to be made by our young people) can direct more young women into those parts of science not at first blush considered a part of Science.

I will focus on physical scientists and particularly on chemists. It is difficult enough to determine what women chemists are doing outside the laboratory or classroom without attempting to determine what women scientists in other areas are doing. About eight percent of the members of The American Chemical Society are women. There are no data to indicate that national figures, including nonmembers, would be in a different ratio. Most chemists are employed by academia, by industry, or by the government, chiefly to work in laboratories. The numbers approximate 30 percent academia, 60 percent industry, 6 percent government and "other." Expanding the role of women implies not only increas-

ing the number in the main categories but also increasing the number of people and the kinds of things that (chemists) do in the "other" category.
The original outline for this paper was as follows:
A. The kinds of things that can be done in science nontraditionally;
B. A broad-brush look at what some women were doing in these areas;
C. Details about a group of women in one specific area. (I had chosen women scientists professionally trained to the level of the doctorate who practice in the area of patent law);
D. Words urging the members of the conference to encourage young women into that area.

Then I discovered it was difficult to find enough women in a nontraditional area to be able to make statistically significant statements about what they are generally like and about the way in which they had, generally, achieved their positions. In fact, it was difficult to find women who were willing to say, "This, for me, *has* been a rewarding pursuit. *I* feel particularly happy about devoting my life to it. I feel successful. Tell others to try this." Instead, against a background of general satisfaction about their lives and careers, there seemed to be an implication that unalloyed success was further on, or perhaps, displaced a bit.

I further found that data are not easily available. Individual contacts showed numbers of women who themselves were doing the kinds of things I wished to talk about, but who could not direct me to a source for hard data about others such as themselves. "Gracious, I don't know," "You must be kidding," or "I haven't the foggiest" were typical of responses. These were understandable. For an example of attempting to track down some members, consider this. There are about 9,000 people in this country registered to practice before the Patent and Trademark Office. These people have scientific backgrounds sufficient to enable them to be of assistance to inventors in obtaining the limited monopolies the United States Government grants to first inventors of new, useful, and nonobvious products, processes, and improvements thereof. About 150 of the people are women, approximately half are lawyers and half nonlawyers. I sought a list of women lawyers who had science Ph.D.s who were registered to practice before the Patent and Trademark Office. I now that such people exist. I know four of them. I was, however, unable to get a list of those women from the office, Freedom of Information Act and office cooperation notwithstanding. I went looking for these women by cross-checking The Register against *Who's Who of*

American Women. I found only the ones I already knew. I cross-checked against *American Men and Women of Science.* No new leads. Certainly the four women I knew do not constitute a large enough sample from which to draw conclusions. Certainly their backgrounds, their life tracks, differ enough so that they don't collectively point to one well-marked path for an interested young woman.

I talked with women scientists in business, in marketing new products, in a very interesting liaison using a chemistry Ph.D., a J.D., and an M.B.A., in private consulting. I tracked down some life stories about women scientists in government, women in the administrative functions in academic institutions such as deanships. I tried to trace women scientists in several areas of law and in writing—an illusive bunch. I was becoming distressed as the deadline approached, until one day it all clicked into place. I couldn't find the women to describe that path nor the groups of women who by their lives had made the path because there is no path. Women, men too, who choose the nontraditional, step into an area not generally charted and for which there is no common beginning.

Who are these people? What do they do? What are they like?

Who are they? They are women trained in science, often with doctorates, who use their science training in fields not usually recognized as pure science. Often they must defend their right to be called scientists.

What do they do? They administer schools and colleges as deans and presidents. A woman, former Dean of Science at a college in New York, has been named president of Metropolitan State University in Minnesota.

They develop and manage new products in chemicals and pharmaceuticals. They correlate activities of industrial cost centers of departments concerned with marketing industrial hygiene and toxicology. They consult. They run governmental divisions. They write science and science fiction (even if under male pseudonymns). They are literature scientists and research administrators. They prosecute patents.

What are they like? They're like all the other women scientists you know, disciplined, trained, intelligent, thoughtful individuals *and* they add what one of my colleagues, who is very conventional, calls "a certain restlessness." Something pulls them out of the continuum that flows from the laboratory to the classroom and into a different dimension, neither above nor below, but orthogonal.

Although students often get their knowledge about the world of work from their teachers, I've found that numbers of people in the academic world do not know what it is that people outside the university walls do in the practice of their profession. Professors seem to think that industrial chemists are chained in some shabby basement laboratory using equipment thought of and developed by the academicians a generation ago, forced to crank out work by the clock on products conceived by marketing people solely to make money. Even fewer people know what patent attorneys do.

Let us look at patent law as one area in which one can have a nontraditional career in a science. If we accept the premise that at the forefront of progress is science, then it follows that scientists are *leaders* of the people. As leaders, scientists cannot abdicate their responsibilities to be dedicated, moral leaders. Science and scientists owe to the people full value. That sentence seems to say very lofty things. It sounds philosophical and just a bit removed from the bustle of the classroom or the laboratory. Yet, society has said some things about the importance it attaches to science. In the most important of the rules by which we as a people live, The Constitution, there is expressed a purpose of promoting the progress of science and useful arts and an indication of how our Congress should do that. The phrase is "by securing for limited times to authors and inventors the exclusive right to their respective writings and discoveries."

The nation, through the Founding Fathers, said, help science and, therefore, the nation advance by telling us what you've discovered, and we will give you protection from others making, using, or selling your invention for a definite period of time. That's what a patent does, and patent attorneys essentially present the case to the government to obtain this security.

That's what a patent attorney does. That is the role of the patent attorney in the progress of science. That is why what a patent attorney does should be of interest to some women.

Marcus Finnegan, well known and highly respected patent attorney, has described patent law in a chapter entitled, "Careers Combining Chemistry and The Law" in a book, *Legal Rights of Chemists*, published by The American Chemical Society. He says that "both chemistry and the law are founded on logical and symmetrical bases," that "records show that persons trained in science and engineering typically do exceptionally well in law school," that "for someone trained in the discipline of chemistry, patent law can be a fascinating career." Then he lists some skills required in the legal profession:

1. Correct use of language, especially the written language;
2. Speaking ability;
3. Personality factors: an ability to analyze and understand people, an instinctively curious mind and persistence.

All of these things are true but I'd describe the role a bit differently. My description is very personal and springs from the way I see my function, how I see my job.

The inventive concept springs from the mind of a person, not a machine. A chemist finds a new compound, a useful one that no one else has made previously and told the world about. As a parent does, the chemist would like to display this to the world, yet protect it. I mentioned earlier that the nation wants to encourage this disclosure; it sets certain requirements for it and gives certain rights in exchange for it. So the chemist must tell the world what the compound is, how to make it, and what its use is. Many chemists are adept with laboratory manipulations, are exceedingly elegant in their use of the scientific method, and yet are completely inarticulate when it comes to disclosing to an outsider exactly what it is that has been done. This is the initial place where a patent practitioner is of value. The patent attorney, agent, or liaison person must interrelate with this person who is the inventor to help bring forth the articulation of the central core of what the invention is. Understanding that, the patent attorney must express the idea and its reduction to practice, not in the patois of the laboratory but in language clear enough so that a person skilled in the art can reproduce the work. If science is to advance, people working in the area need to know what others are doing in order to avoid duplicating efforts and working and reworking ground that has yielded its riches. We progress by using our history and not repeating it again and again. This interrelation between inventor and patent attorney can be very satisfying, frustrating at times, admittedly, but generally very satisfying. The inventor explores in words her ideas, describes them, examines them, defends them. She tells them to a person who understands, who is not a competitor or a distractor, a person who recognizes the joy of discovery, the beauty of an elegant solution. The patent attorney writes this down in a form that is required to be logical, scientific, legal, and candid. The patent attorney has interacted personally with a unique mind operating at the forefront of science and has had an opportunity to withdraw from personal contacts to ponder the meanings and to write the words that flesh out the child.

Then, having written the document, the patent attorney presents the invention in the Patent and Trademark Office and acts as its advocate, pointing out where it comes within the requirements set out by society for the seventeen-year protection.

When prosecution is complete in the Office or in the courts, if necessary, and the patent has been awarded, the patent attorney shares with the inventor the pride in having created a piece of intellectual property that is valued and that pushes back the vast ocean of ignorance that surrounds us.

Why do I talk to you about a field practiced by just a few? A doubling of the numbers of women patent attorneys with and without science Ph.D.s would be unnoticed in the number of people practicing science in our nation. But each number is an individual, and each individual must make her place in the world. Some women make a conventional choice easily and naturally. Some women are unwilling to run with the herd. Some women opt out, citing a very cold, lonely way in a fraternity existing for the self-aggrandizement of its members. But for those with that certain restlessness who would stay, it helps to know not necessarily that there is a path laid out for you to follow, but that paths have been made, people have survived; you can, also, and there are people who are supportive.

I would urge the people at this conference who guide, direct, and train our scientists, our women scientists, to remember that each must do it alone, that it *is* possible to make an individual path that allows one person to adjust what she does to that which makes her most happy, that there is support and encouragement out there and that they should encourage their young people to grasp life and science with all its nettles with open, firm acceptance.

I have a quotation from a great woman scientist, Rosalyn Yalow, guest of honor at this conference. Those at the dinner heard it, but since everyone wasn't there, let me repeat some of it. She said that if women are to start moving toward a goal of full equality of opportunity, "we must believe in ourselves or no one else will believe in us; we must match our aspirations with the competence, courage and determination to succeed; and we must feel a personal responsibility to ease the path for those who come afterwards."

Careers in Industry for Scientifically Trained Women

IVY M. CELENDER
Vice-president and Director of Nutrition
General Mills, Inc.
Minneapolis, Minnesota 55440

WOMEN HAVE contributed their time and talents to the advancement of science for years. From Elizabeth Blackwell, who became the first woman in the United States to obtain a medical degree, to Rosalyn Yalow, who recently received the Nobel Prize, women have been intimately connected with the sciences. Through the years, their main work has been in research, teaching, dietetics, medicine, and government agencies.[1]

Only 5.5 percent of employed women hold managerial or administrative positions of any kind.[2] It is only fairly recently that women scientists have begun to aspire to management positions and to be considered by industry leaders for such jobs. In 1965, only one percent of management trainees were women. Max Ulrich, president of a New York-based executive recruiting firm was quoted in *Business Week* as saying, "In most industries, women are just beginning to come into the pipeline. But they are coming in fast."[3] This is the dawning of a new era of upward mobility for women.

Industry presents an entirely new spectrum of job opportunities for women and advancement opportunities completely different from the traditional academic or research setting. I am firmly convinced that the greatest opportunities for advancement are in management as companies meet their affirmative action guidelines. However, a 1974 survey of managers in the top 500 industries and the fifty largest banks, utilities, transportation, merchandising, and insurance companies indicates that there are still strong biases against women. This study showed that men have more bias and negative attitudes toward women than toward nonwhites, 74 percent admitted bias against women, 53 percent admitted bias against nonwhites for management positions.[4]

Another recent survey of women officers in industry reported that "discrimination against women" was cited by 48.5 percent of the women officers as the single factor that had impeded their progress the most. A distant second was "lack of education," mentioned by only 13.8 percent.[5]

Income levels are generally lower for women scientists with bachelor's, master's and doctorate degrees.[6] Newer women managers are more likely to be on an equal pay scale with men; a recent article in *Business Week* claims older women managers often receive 24 percent less pay than men in comparable positions.[7]

In spite of some bias and the pay discrepancy noted above, management careers hold much promise for women with scientific backgrounds. Therefore, I would like to ask three questions:

1. What are the characterisics of a good manager?
2. What are the reasons for lack of success for women in business today?
3. What can women with scientific training do to advance in corporate positions?

There are three characteristics of a good manager that are particularly critical, according to a leading firm of industrial psychologists: professional excellence, team work, and dynamic leadership. A woman scientist has the same professional competence as her male peers, but it is my belief that she must be better, brighter, and more able to apply that professional training than men in order to be considered at least equal. And it helps not to be attractive, because men assume an attractive woman cannot possibly be professionally competent. (After all, didn't our creator give women a choice of being dumb and beautiful or bright and homely?)

Teamwork is the second key attribute needed by an executive. Here women are at a distinct disadvantage because, based on my observation, most men have two training programs that teach teamwork that most women don't have: the military and team sports. These teach offensive and defensive strategies as well as subordinate one's own ego for the team effort; they provide a common denominator of behavior which is the underpinning of how any male-dominated organization works. And women must learn to play by men's rules if they want to work in an environment with a predominantly male hierarchy.

The third characteristic of a good manager identified by the industrial psychologists is dynamic leadership. Here again, team sports and military experience provide training, role models, and an expected "norm" for leadership. The coach, the sergeant, the sports idol all provide role models. My idols were Amelia Earhart, the aviatrix, and Anna Pavlova, the Russian prima ballerina, neither of whom was a teamworker or a leader of people.

There are other qualifications which are essential. The human relations skills of managers are extremely important since management is "making things happen through people." Teamwork and dynamic leadership are both dependent on a highly developed understanding of people and on the ability to work with individuals of varying backgrounds and behavioral styles at various organizational levels. This is one area in which the scientifically trained person is often weak.

We scientists are trained to be data or task-oriented rather than people-oriented. We measure our success by our personal accomplishments, number of papers published, experimental results, tasks completed, rather than by group achievements.

A good manager in business has learned to solve problems and to make decisions in a highly complex environment involving numerous alternatives, each of which has varying degrees of risk. Just a few of the environmental factors affecting decisions include: numerous state and Federal regulations, corporate policies, technical data and constraints, needs and wants of the end user of a product or service, potential hazards, responsibility to stockholders (e.g. profit and/or growth), responsibility to employees (e.g. avoiding layoffs), and social responsibility/morality. The good manager is able to analyze, evaluate, and resolve problems quickly and effectively. Her judgement must result in a high percentage of "right" decisions and in appropriate actions that contribute to overall operations.

I have observed that top-level managers are as highly motivated and disciplined to achieve their goals as Olympic athletes. Their motivation or drive is generally for power, money, or status. They have the intellectual discipline to work on the important problems, rather than on the interesting or easy ones. They discipline themselves to work long hours and to deny pleasures for accomplishments. They define short- and long-term objectives and persistently focus their energies and resources on them.

A manager must be tenacious and committed to career goals in order to actualize them. Any woman aspiring to management or to other high goals, must recognize that for everything she gains in terms of prestige and success, she must be willing to give up something. She must realize that loneliness and social isolation from coworkers and friends will occur the higher she goes up the ladder.

Hard work, long hours, and fat briefcases on weekends are the price for reaching high goals. Dr. Yalow, the Nobel laureate, said in a recent television interview that she works 60 to 100 hours per week.[8] A recent survey showed that women in business earning more than $40,000 average 57 hours of work per week, while women with lower incomes work less. "Hard work" was cited by 48 percent of women officers as the single factor contributing most to their success.[5] Hard work and discipline go along with commitment and tenacity in attaining high goals. But a manager also must know when to delegate responsibilities and when to take care of something herself.

Another important characteristic of a good manager is having long-range career plans. If long-range planning is ignored, a woman may unknowingly choose a career or job in which there is no upward mobility. One recent study showed 46 percent of women officers in industry have followed a career plan.[5] I looked at the field of nutrition almost 20 years ago, decided that some day human nutrition would be as important as animal nutrition, found a school willing to modify its biochemistry-oriented curriculum to give me a human nutrition degree, sought out a food company that had a long-term stake in human nutrition, convinced them that they needed me, and went to work developing the first human nutrition program in the food industry. Seven years after I started, nutrition came into national focus and the faith my company had put in me paid off. Other women with scientific backgrounds have the same opportunity to look ahead, pick a horse that's likely to win, and then work hard to make the investment pay off. In a recent article on the top 100 corporate women, quite a number had carved out their careers by spotting corporate needs and developing the knowledge to fill those needs.[9] Long-range planning does pay off.

A good manager is well organized and knows how to set priorities effectively. Her home and office life is simplified and organized so that she can get the job done. She must know how to manage time effectively. Mary Wells Lawrence, head of a major advertising agency and one of the highest paid women in the United States, says she has learned to allocate her time very, very carefully. Everything in her life is written down and planned in advance. She runs her life like a business, leaving nothing to chance. And she enforces this plan with enormous self-discipline.[10]

Highly developed oral and written communication skills are areas in which the manager also excels. She is able to express ideas, concepts, and data in varying ways to meet the needs of the listener or reader. When I discuss nutrition with the scientists in our research facility, I can use technical jargon, but when I talk with general managers, my language must be nontechnical and my concepts presented in the context of "risk-benefit," "the bottom line" (profit), or "control systems." When I speak with professionals in the health area, nutrition is communicated in terms of the "health delivery system," and when I talk to consumers, nutrition is often presented in the context of food.

Self-confidence, self-esteem and positive self-image are other characteristics I have observed in most managers. These characteristics are perhaps related to another important personal factor—courage. A manager has to take risks and often needs to have courage to act. I believe any woman who breaks with the traditional role of women in society, such as continuing her education to a doctorate, is willing to take some risks. When recruiting new staff, I always consider the extracurricular activities in which a person participates, and I find that women who pursue nontraditional extracurricular activities tend to have the courage to be individuals and to break out of the stereotyped female mold.

Last, but not least, a good manager needs good mental and physical health. Mary Wells Lawrence says she "happens to be as strong as a horse" and has enormous energy.[10] Success requires hard work, being on the job, and being able to cope with stress. A regular exercise program not only helps one's overall physical health and fitness, but also helps decrease stress and increases emotional well-being. Persons with poor mental or physical health are not likely to be successful.

This brings me to some reasons for women's lack of success. A major reason for lack of success seems to be women's own passivity. According to a recent article in *Business Horizons*, the majority of women are not committed to activities that would help them pursue their career goals.[11] Women are programmed early for female stereotypes. They are socialized not to achieve.[12]

Parents, and especially fathers, are a critical factor in a woman's success. I was fortunate to have scientifically trained parents who encouraged development and achievement. My favorite definition of love is "caring enough about people to give them room to grow." My parents gave me room to grow. But some parents unwittingly "program" girls to be nonachievers and to avoid competition. They don't give them room to grow, and even if parents do not "program" daughters to underachieve, girls often find when they enter high school that boys don't date girls with "brains." So, unconsciously, they stop trying to achieve.

Another barrier to success may be a woman's husband. It is my observation that a woman can rise only as high as her husband's ego will let her. Rosalyn Yalow was encouraged and supported by her husband in her work leading to the Nobel Prize.[8] Some women, however, unconsciously or consciously limit their own growth to appease their husbands' egos or because of direct pressure from them.

Another reason for women's slow success is a lack of academic leadership. Women are not encouraged, even in college, to pursue lifelong careers and to go into nontraditional fields for women, like business.

Another barrier to women's success is their own psyche. Women often limit their expectations; they are satisfied with far less than they need to be. They have accepted intrinsic rather than extrinsic rewards for their efforts. Women have been satisfied with receiving attention from a boss as a reward, rather than seeking additional money, status, or power.[12] One study done in 1970 by Horner has shown that many women are motivated to avoid success; over 88 percent of the women were found to actually fear success.[13-14] Interestingly, those studied were all white women. Black women participating in recent studies were found to have only 29 percent incidence of fear of success.[15-16]

Perhaps the problem for women is not so much fear of success as conflicting definitions or poor definitions of success. Success by the male definition is measured by power, money, status; success by society's definition is being a good wife and mother. Men's socialization is conducive to success; women's is not.[12]

Another possible explanation for fear or lack of success is that new career paths in male-dominated fields require a woman to survive without an emotional support system and in an environment where the "ground rules" are unknown. This is very different from success in attaining a doctorate, for example, where a woman has a support system of other students and where the procedures and ground rules for success are well established.

Lack of success may be due to lack of a "mentor." Men often have bosses or other influential superiors who help them through the process of advancement within the company, who give them information about important events and people in the system, and who help them avoid the pitfalls in the organization. Women rarely enjoy this type of attention.

Most top managers in industry, as in academia and government, are men, and it is my observation that men often consciously or unconsciously fear becoming a true "mentor" for women. There are a number of legitimate reasons for their fear. First, they might be accused by their wives or peers of intimacy with the women they are trying to help. Second, most men really do not know how to deal with women as professionals; they are used to dealing with subservient wives and secretaries who bring them their pipe, slippers, coffee, or morning mail. Many men also seem very afraid a woman will cry, and they just cannot deal with tears as well as they can with the fist-pounding anger of men. Third, most men are not used to competing with women and may unconsciously feel threatened by helping a competent woman grow for fear that they will have to compete with her.

This brings me to another general observation: A woman (or man) can rise only as high in any organization as the egos of her boss and his peers will let her. If a woman's superiors feel threatened, her growth will be limited.

In addition to a "mentor," many women do not have a good "role model," especially if they are entering a field which is predominantly male. Women seem to have different management styles than do men, and their way of operating may be criticized or unappreciated because it differs from the male style. Interpersonal behavior patterns of women may also differ from those of men, and, without role models, women may have to develop their own criteria for appropriate behavior.

Another reason for women's lack of success may be that they lack the built-in rapport which men possess. As one of two women participating in a three-month management course at Harvard University in 1974, I was able to make several observations about the men attending the course. I found that men integrate into any system by the two common denominators that I mentioned earlier: team sports and the military. From team sports they learn fair play and common norms for behavior; from the military they learn the ability to establish a rapport and to work by an unspoken set of rules.

The 162 men at the management course developed friendships and working relationships very soon because they had these common denominators. Even though they came from different countries and occupations, they could strike up a conversation about team sports or about their time in the military and immediately develop a rapport. I found it much harder to relate to them, and they also appeared to be uncomfortable in starting a conversation with me because they did not know what to talk about. In general, women have not been in management long enough for men to develop a sense of rapport with them.

There is hope, however. Joan Ganz Cooney, President of Children's Television Workshop, said in a recent issue of *Harvard Business Review* that she has proved herself as "one of the team" to members of the board of directors of Xerox as well as other companies.[17]

She keeps up with the issues on each board of which she is a member, and she does not mind receiving help to keep the pace. The rapport developed may have started with the men appointing her to the board of directors, but once they decided, she said, they were more than willing to help her succeed. I was pleased to read this statement from a woman who has moved high in the corporate world.

Lack of success may also be due to organizational barriers to advancement. Disparity between wages for men and women for the same job has been mentioned earlier. Women may be excluded from the promotional stream or from "fast track" training programs. They may be considered only for jobs traditionally held by women; for example, a woman with a master's degree in economics may be a secretary but may never be considered for a position in the finance department. Exclusion from men's informal network of communication, or physical isolation of women in one section of the building, are subtle barriers to advancement.

Another subtle barrier involves the organization of the company in which a woman wishes to advance. In companies with relatively static organizational charts, e.g. a family-owned business, or one with a slow growth rate, people 40-50 years old are often in key spots and plan to stay for many years. There is little or no room for advancement in such a structure, sometimes even in the lower echelons of management. This is a key factor for a woman to consider before making a career change. A rapidly growing company is much more likely to promote able persons to fill growth needs, hire younger men who are more likely to accept women as equals, and have a fluid organizational structure, permitting faster movement up the managerial ladder.

In some organizations, another barrier to entry may be lack of knowledge about job openings. The skills needed for higher level positions may also be unknown. An obvious solution to this problem would be open internal posting of information on available positions.

Women with scientific training are certainly as competent technically as their male counterparts. But sometimes women do not receive the diversity and depth of on-the-job training as men, or do not have access to management training programs. Building interpersonal skills relevant to management should be a high priority for any woman wishing to succeed. I encourage my professional staff to participate in courses and work experiences which will help them build management and technical skills; this helps prepare them for the next upward step.

What can a woman do to advance in corporate positions? First of all, she must obtain the best possible education and on-the-job training. This is especially true in a situation where a scientist moves up to head a department or company. She must have the technical background and academic degrees to be effective and to deal with the subject area. This is especially true if she is changing careers or jobs. Generally, she must learn new management and interpersonal skills. It is also helpful, and in some cases essential, to have formal training in business, economics, and/or law.

She also needs strong motivation, commitment, discipline, hard work, long-range goals, power-orientation, and a supportive family—all the attributes of a manager and lack of those factors which inhibit success.

Assuming she has the technical and management ability and potential, she must have the desire to advance. It is important that she make her skills and career aspirations known to the person above her in the firm, the personnel department, or others who can legitimately help her. Most companies today are looking for women with the ability and desire to advance, but women must verbalize these characteristics more effectively. Excellent training and hard work will not be automatically rewarded; the best people do not always rise to the top.

To advance in corporate positions, a woman must develop a strong sense of realism and the needs of her business environment. She must escape the image of the detail-conscious specialist she had as a researcher. She should read widely in the general business magazines and newspapers. As she moves into middle management, the demands change. She must learn to be a generalist and to think in terms of the company's overall goals and profit objectives.

In organizations managed predominantly by men, women must also learn to work within the system and by its rules. (This is the best way to effect change.) If women fight the system, they will create a barrier to further advancement for themselves.

Another key is to develop a socialized power motivation rather than a need for personal power. Successful managers build up rather than threaten others in order to move themselves up within the system. They are less authoritarian and more skilled in interpersonal relations than nonmanagers.[18]

Since women in management in industry are still rare, they are carefully and continuously scrutinized by everybody as they move higher in a corporate structure, and they must answer to more people in the process. Women lose much of their freedom to act spontaneously. But for women committed to management careers, the inconveniences are definitely worthwhile.

Last, a woman must anticipate being challenged, criticized, and condemned. When faced with a situation like this, she may think men are criticizing her because they do not want women in management positions. She must remember that men challenge, criticize, and condemn other men in managerial positions constantly. Many men feel uncomfortable when challenging women in a way similar to the way they would challenge men, but the successful women learns to accept criticism and grow from it. Finally, women must learn to compromise.

In summary, too many women and men believe the myth that women cannot be good managers and instead accept society's stereotypes of women. Women must employ long-term career strategies, discipline, and newly learned skills in order to advance in business. They must expect problems. They must learn to take the chaff with the wheat; but with proper training and hard work, they can expect to obtain their highest goals.

Mary Wells Lawrence, who has been called one of the most powerful women in the country, summarized my thoughts well when she said: "I think anything one wants, one can have. Absolutely, presuming you're born in a capitalist society, preferably the United States; that you're in good health; that you're reasonably intelligent; and that you keep your goal in sight at all times. You cannot miss."[10]

Acknowledgment

With acknowledgment to Beverly H. Tanis, Nutrition Communicator, General Mills, Inc., for substantial contributions to background research and preparation of this paper.

References

1. TODHUNTER, E.N. 1977. Women in nutrition. Professional Nutritionist. 9(4):12–14.
2. U.S. DEPARTMENT OF LABOR, BUREAU OF LABOR STATISTICS. 1976. *In* World Almanac & Book of Facts 1978: 88. Newspaper Enterprise Assoc. Inc., New York, N.Y.
3. BUSINESS WEEK. 1975. Up the ladder, finally. No. 2408: 58–68.
4. ORC PUBLIC OPINION INDEX REPORT TO MANAGEMENT. 1974. Bias at the top: Attitudes of the nation's executives toward the management potential of women and minorities. 32(13, 14). Opinion Research Corp. Princeton, N.J.
5. Profile of a woman officer. 1977. Findings of a study of executives in America's 1300 largest companies. Heidrick and Struggles, Inc. Chicago, Ill.
6. SCIENTIFIC ENGINEERING TECHNICAL, MANPOWER COMMENTS. 1976. 1975 Mean salaries of men and women chemists by degree level and years of experience. 13(6):12.
7. BUSINESS WEEK. 1977. A double standard for women managers' pay. 2511:61, 65.
8. NBC. Jan. 27, 1978. The Today Show.
9. BUSINESS WEEK. 1976. 100 top corporate women.2437:56–66.
10. GROSS, E.L. 1978. The all-out, attractive style of Mary Wells Lawrence. Vogue 168(2): 200–01, 205, 243–44.
11. BURKE, R.J. & T. WEIR. 1977. Readying the sexes for women in management. Business Horizons 20(3):30–35.
12. FAUNCE, P.S. 1977. Psychological barriers to occupational success for women. J. Nat. Assoc. Women Deans, Administrators, and Counselors 40(4):140–44.
13. HORNER, M.S. 1972. Toward an understanding of achievement related conflicts in women. J. Social Issues 28(2):157–175.
14. HORNER, M.S. 1973. Toward an understanding of achievement related conflicts in women. Ann. N.Y. Acad. Sci. 208:126–127.
15. FLEMING, J. & M.S. HORNER. 1971. Sex and race differences in fear of success imagery. Harvard University. Cambridge, Mass. Unpublished.
16. FLEMING, J. & M.S. HORNER. 1973. Sex and race differences in fear of success imagery. Ann. N.Y. Acad. Sci. 208:128.
17. HARVARD BUSINESS REVIEW. 1978. A woman in the boardroom. 56(1):77–86.
18. ARONSON, S.G. 1973. Marriage with a successful woman: a personal viewpoint. Ann. N.Y. Acad. Sci. 208:218–26.

PART IV. Altering Attitudes: Strategies for Change

Implications of Equality

ANNA J. HARRISON
Department of Chemistry
Mount Holyoke College
South Hadley, Massachusetts 01075

AN INTRODUCTION may create a gulf between the audience and the person being introduced. Consequently, I will give you a bit of personal background, not because it has any significance whatsoever, but because it may give some insight into what I say later.

I graduated from college in 1933. That was during a real depression. There were practically no employment opportunities for anyone, particularly not for chemists, particularly not for young chemists, particularly not for young women chemists. I did however, get a job. It led to two years that made a very great contribution to my development. During those two years I taught in a one-room rural school. The one-room building was set in the corner of a cornfield at an intersection of two dirt roads in the middle of the state of Missouri, my home state. If you got yourself into trouble, you got yourself out of trouble. During those two years I taught first, second, third, fourth, fifth, sixth, seventh, and ninth grades, everything including how to tell the age of a horse by its teeth. There are certain problems associated with that, one of which is that you have to hold the nag's mouth open while the children look in. Identifying the age of a horse depends upon the degree to which the crowns of the teeth have been worn down. Presumably, horses eat about the same things, so the teeth wear down at a characteristic rate. After a time, the pattern in the teeth is obliterated, leading to what is known as a smooth-mouth horse; hence the expression, "don't look a gift horse in the mouth".

The salary in this rural school was $60 a month for an eight-month term. I went back to the University of Missouri as a graduate teaching assistant at an income of $550 for the total academic year. This was perhaps my first encounter with reverse discrimination. The young men who were also teaching assistants received $500. This, I think, was the consequence of the chairman of the department having two daughters. He thought it cost more for a girl to live than it did for a boy; consequently, the extra $50. This I only learned about years later, I might add.

At the time I grew up you didn't plan a career in science. You did whatever was available to you and hoped something would turn up that was constructive. At the time I finished the Ph.D., a multiplicity of contacts scattered over the country turned up just exactly two opportunities for employment in which they would even look at the credentials of a woman Ph.D. in physical chemistry. I had been advised not to go into physical chemistry because the employment opportunities were less, that it would be better to go into organic chemistry or biochemistry. But my interests were in physical chemistry and my decision, with the support from several physical chemists, was to go ahead and do what I wanted to do with the hope that something constructive would turn up in the end. Of the two positions we did turn up where my credentials would be looked at, I got one of them. I was at last launched upon a professional career.

You might be interested to know that among the large number of letters I sent out and the replies that came back it was not uncommon to get a letter which said that they had no opening, but they would not consider me if they did, as they did not hire women. I still have that file of letters, and some day it will be interesting to see from whom these letters came. At the time, I didn't particularly question this one way or the other. It was a part of the society. This was just the way the game was played.

I want to talk with you a little about being able to respond to opportunities when they arise. You must be able to make up your mind yes or no, and you have to be able to do it quickly. About ten years ago, I had a call from the Washington office of the Association of American Colleges and Universities asking if I would testify before the Boland Committee in Congress in behalf of the education part of the National Science Foundation budget. Two days isn't a long time to prepare, and my full contact with Congressional hearings had been what I had read in the newspaper or what I had seen on television. The decision had to be reached within the length of the telephone call, either yes, or no. The answer I gave was yes, and I hung up the phone wondering what the devil I could do. Many of the things that have followed have pivoted exactly from that answer. In the process of testifying quite regularly for the Association of American Colleges and Universities for several years, I became visible, and was later appointed to the National Science Board. Professionally, sooner or later, frequently quite early in our careers, each of us is presented with an opportunity. You have to be able to recognize it as an opportunity that is right for you and go with it. Or, you have to be able to recognize it as an opportunity that would be wrong for you and turn it down. We must be prepared psychologically do this. My preparation for this started some years earlier at a conference on women's education. A representative from industry spoke quite eloquently at that conference on the importance of teaching young women to accept opportunities when they are offered. He pointed out that the first reaction of a woman seemed to be, "I am not prepared." His point was that the young men were not prepared either, and the offer was being made with the expectation that they would learn. Being asked is a vote of confidence in the abilities of the individual to develop. In my own career, this has been perhaps the most significant bit of advice that I ever received.

The appointment to the National Science Board was made by a telephone call to ask if I would accept, if appointed. I knew that I was being considered for that appointment, or at least that I had been nominated for it. What I did not know then was that by the time the telephone call came, the decision to appoint me had been made.

In responding to an opportunity, you should, I have learned, express a definite, positive interest, and then follow quickly with questions to determine what is involved. If you don't make the positive response, you are shooting yourself down. If you don't ask the questions, you are shooting yourself down. Express the interest and then ask what's involved, what are the obligations. You have to assess whether, in fact, you can, or are willing, to live up to those obligations.

Turning to the name of the conference, Expanding the Role of Women in Sciences, I want to place an emphasis on that which focuses not so much on expanding the opportunity to get hired by organizations that are involved in scientific matters, but on that which focuses upon the nature of that participation. This was considered by the last two speakers this morning, and in many senses what I say will overlap.

I hope what I have to say applies to the young scientist regardless of whether the degree is bachelor, master, or Ph.D. It is important that we not focus specifically on the Ph.D. The problems are different, but not all that different, and I am convinced that there are fantastic opportunities for young women, for young people in general, to come into the profession at the bachelors' level. There are different opportunities, but in comparison to the other opportunities at the bachelors' level, the opportunities may be very good.

Each of us must learn to distinguish between speaking as a member of a class and speaking as an individual. In other words, when do you speak as a woman dealing with the problems of women, and when do you speak as an individual without any regard to sex? Much of this conference is focused upon speaking in terms of women as a class. Eventually, in our involvement in any professional organization, we are going to be there as individuals. What we say and how we say it as individuals is quite different. It doesn't mean that one negates the other, but the manner in which you think and act is different.

I shall run through a list of questions that I think anyone entering the scientific professions should ask themselves. It does not matter whether it is a young man or a young woman. These are questions that the individual ought to face.

First, what investment are you willing to make? What investment are you willing to make in time, in education, and in the development of skills. It is essential that you be honest in going into a profession. In some cases, the question may be what investment can you make? You may have other responsibilities that will limit the investment you can make. It is essential that you be honest in this, because what you then plan in relationship to the profession is very closely related to the investment you are willing to make.

What sacrifices are you prepared to make? We all have a limited amount of time, and a limited amount of energy. If that energy and time go to one place, they cannot go to another. When you decide to do something, you are consciously or unconsciously operating within a priority system that has excluded or modified something else.

What is your capacity to endure? And you do have to endure. There are long periods in any profession when things don't go well. What is your capacity to hang in there during those periods and to ride it out?

Can you recognize an opportunity when it's presented to you? I have already touched upon this. Are you prepared to respond definitely to opportunities when they arise? It may be to respond affirmatively, or it may be to respond negatively.

What is the breadth of your concept of the profession? Do you see the scientific profession purely as research in an academic institution, or do you see great ramifications of it? The manner in which you perceive your profession will make tremendous differences in the way you view potential opportunities when they arise. Many are initially attracted to the sciences by their intellectual content. As careers develop, a number recognize that research in itself will not be rewarding to them personally. In an academic institution where there is great prestige placed on research involvement, you may find yourself in the position of really requiring a certain degree of moral courage to take the stand that research is not for you. This topic was beautifully treated here.

I would like to see more of our chemistry majors go to law school. Some of them are doing so. We need more lawyers who have a background of scientific knowledge. I am convinced that lawyers and scientists think differently. This is not to say that one way is better than the other. They are different professions with different orientations. I am also delighted that some of our majors now take masters degrees in business and public administration, and that some go directly from the undergraduate degree to positions in sales with industrial companies.

I did prepare a brief statement, which follows:

IMPLICATIONS OF EQUALITY

The title, "Implications of Equality," is ambiguous. There are many implications of equality. It is my intent to focus on one: the responsibility of the individual to participate as an individual in the formulation of goals and in the development of mechanisms to achieve those goals. This is one important implication of equality. It has nothing to do with sex or race or ethnic origin; it has nothing to do with social or economic or political background. Within the group, the individual has the responsibility to participate as an individual.

The manner in which an individual participates as an individual in any endeavor does depend upon the know-how and the value system of the individual. The know-how, the skills and technical knowledge, of the individual is characteristic of the individual and is dependent upon the prior experience of the individual. The value system of the individual is characteristic of the individual and is very closely related to the social, economic, and political background of the individual.

Without equality, the participation of the individual may be restricted by the group. Without a sense of equality, the participation of the individual may also be limited or modified by self-imposed restrictions of the individual. I have had some experience with tokenism. To impose restrictions upon yourself, I understand. You participate but you learn to select very carefully the windmills you tilt. You learn to conserve your resources.

It is my observation that as a class of individuals approaches equality of opportunity to be admitted to a group—to be employed, to be hired, to be elected—the individual so admitted is frequently granted full equality to participate within the group. It is important that any class of individuals, who have traditionally been excluded, recognize this difference between equality of opportunity to be admitted to the group and the equality of opportunity to participate within the group. It is the implications of this equality within the group that I seek to discuss.

For the first time, I shall now limit the discussion to women. Employment problems there have been; employment problems there undoubtedly are. Once employed, many women have encountered inequality of opportunity; many women will continue to encounter some degree of inequality of opportunity. These are serious problems. We must not compound them by our own expectations and the manner in which we seek to participate within the group once we are a part of that group.

Each individual brings to the group know-how, a capacity to perceive, and a value system. Frequently, the level of know-how is a necessary condition for admission to the group. Women understand this requirement. As a class, we expect to meet and to bring to an endeavor a more than adequate level of technical competence. As a class, we expect to use and do use effectively our technical competencies as participants within the group. We enter the profession fully expecting to achieve technical competence and to participate fully from a technical point of view in achieving the goals of the group. I have no misgivings on this score.

I am not as confident that we understand that full participation within the group also includes equal involvement in the evolution of the goals of the group and in the development of mechanisms to achieve those goals. This type of participation uses the individual's capacity to perceive the many things that might be achieved by the group and requires that the individual be willing to assign priorities to all options in terms of a personal value system. To be effective, the individual must participate in the articulation of the options and in the value judgments made by the group.

I first consciously focused on this element of participation when asked by a political scientist if research results in my field could be dependent upon whether the research was carried out by a man or by a woman. As a physical chemist, I have no doubt that the answer if definitely negative. I cannot see that gender could be a factor in the measurements made or the calculations carried out or the interpretation of the results. The answer would not be as simple for some other disciplines, and the question deserves careful consideration.

I suspect that sex could be a significant factor, even in the physical sciences, in influencing the direction of research. The priorities could be different and the distribution of the total research effort could be different.

In any case, goals and mechanisms of achieving them do change within the total society and within each subunit. Some changes are externally imposed. Many arise within the group as a consequence of the perceptions of individuals and the value judgments of the individuals. Women may have a unique role in the identification of alternatives to currently accepted goals and mechanisms, many of which have become stereotyped.

Within the group, each individual, male or female, has the responsibility to participate as an individual—to rely upon personal technical competence, personal capacity to perceive, and personal values. Recognizing this enables the individual to utilize his or her full potential, to make the maximum contribution to the endeavors of the group, and to make the maximum contribution to our total society.

Redress of Grievances

HELEN C. DAVIES AND
ROBERT E. DAVIES
Department of Microbiology, School of Medicine
Department of Animal Biology, School of Veterinary Medicine
The University of Pennsylvania
Philadelphia, Pennsylvania 19104

WE WERE ASKED to present this paper because for many years we have both been involved with helping other people in their grievances in various universities and Federal courts. Between us we have variously served as trustee of a major state university, on the trustees' committees on Affirmative Action, on educational planning and on finance; chaired a large department, chaired the Faculty Senate Committee on Academic Freedom and Responsibility, and the Faculty Grievance Commission; served on the Steering Committee of the University Council, on the Senate Advisory Committee and on the Executive Committee of four different Schools of the University of Pennsylvania. We have had a wide involvement with the governance of five different schools in our University, including committees on appointments and promotions, and admissions committees of undergraduate, graduate, and professional schools.

We will start with a brief look at how women have fared in academe. At the turn of the century women represented 8 percent of the full professors at the University of Chicago, whereas in 1968-69 only 2 percent of the full professors were women.[1] The records of the mathematics department of the University of California at Berkeley[2] show that in 1928 women held 20 percent of the tenured or tenure-accruing positions; in 1938 the figure was down to 11 percent; in 1948 it was seven percent; in 1958 it was three percent and in 1969 it was zero. During the period 1920-29, 10 percent of the doctorates in mathematics awarded by the department were received by women, and between 1960-68 it was 6 percent.

A major problem has been the long history of actions that have been perceived differently by most males and most females or have been embedded in generally accepted societal values. Thus, many engineers, chemists, veterinarians, and mathematicians were convinced beyond rational argument that theirs was a male profession and only the most unusual women could enter and be successful. The existence of "old boy's networks," the ready assumption that a search committee should find the best man for a position, and the myths that women were incompetent, not serious about careers, that they should remain homemakers, all helped perpetuate the present discriminatory situation.

The beginning of the turnabout for women came at the time the Federal law protecting them against sex discrimination was passed in 1964. Howard W. Smith, Chairman of the Rules Committee of the United States House of Representatives added the word "sex" to Title VII of the Civil Rights Act. Although widely accepted as a joke and as a device to divide the liberals and prevent the passage of the bill, Title VII became law.[3] The Federal laws and regulations concerning sex discrimination in educational institutions are Executive Order 11246 as amended by 11375, Title VII of the Civil Rights Act, the Equal Pay Act of 1963, Title IX of the Education Amendments of 1972 (Higher Education Act), and Titles VII and VIII of the Public Health Service Act. A chart of these laws prepared and updated (June 1977) by the Project on the Status and Education of Women of the Association of American Colleges is available from the Department of Health, Education and Welfare (DHEW).[4] A very fine discussion of the laws has been prepared by Bernice Sandler.[5] Under Executive Order 11246 as amended by 11375, Affirmative Action Plans including "numerical goals and timetables are required of all contractors with contracts of more than $50,000 or 50 or more employees."

Previously, it was virtually impossible to obtain redress of grievances brought on the grounds of discrimination because of sex, since nobody had the right to an appointment, promotion, or tenure. Today, at least when appointments and promotions are made, the law requires that they should not be discriminatory with regard to sex, race, and creed. This also applies to salary levels.

In order to substantiate a claim of sex discrimination a first step is to look for evidence that women are discriminated against at the hiring level in the institution concerned. There is empirical verification of sex discrimination in hiring practices in the scientific academic community. In the field of psychology, for instance, Fidell[6] has shown that academic departments of psychology in 1970 discriminated on the basis of sex. In this study, either of two forms, A or B, was sent to the chairmen of each 228 colleges and universities. Each form described the professional history of hypothetical psychologists, and the chairmen were asked to judge the candidate's chances of getting a position. Forms A and B differed in that some of the candidates who were women in one form were described as men in the other and *vice versa*. The chairmen's responses were such that the modal level of potential offers of positions for the women was assistant professor, while for the men it was associate professor. Only the men would have been offered full professorships.

In another study Simpson[7] submitted pairs of resumés to administrators with the descriptive material held constant and the names and photographs of women and men alternated on the two forms. He reported that deans, chairmen, and faculty in selected academic fields at six institutions in Pennsylvania rated the men higher than the women.

Lewin and Duchan[8] did a similar study of chairmen of graduate departments of a physical science discipline in institutions of higher education. The chairmen preferred an average male over an average female, but did recognize a clearly superior woman candidate. A significant number of unsolicited comments were returned with the questionnaires accompanying the resumés of the women. The chairmen expressed concern with the fate of the applicant's husband and children. They were also concerned with her compatibility with their department members, leading the authors to state that women faculty in the physical sciences may be evaluated on the basis of different criteria than are men when they compete for academic positions.

Marcus[9] holds that despite the recent widespread use of advertisements for academic positions the network approach is still the most important recruitment means in academe. Since the network among senior faculty is predominantly white male, the persistence of this approach as a major technique for identifying promising candidates inevitably leads to a disproportional hiring of protégés who are also white and male.

To substantiate further the claim of sex discrimination, it is recommended that evidence be obtained that the number of women hired and promoted at particular levels in a given department is not proportional to the number of women with advanced degrees and appropriate experience in that field. The basic source of our faculty is the pool of scholars who have earned doctorates in the United States. There is ample statistical information on this pool.[10-16] An example of the use of availability figures follows: Data produced in a study of the coeducational University of Pennsylvania by a Committee on the Status of Women in 1971[17] showed that in the College there were 164 male full professors and no women full professors. Of 88 departments, 48 had not one woman. Using the information about the number of doctorates earned in the respective fields of study for the appropriate years as an estimate of the proportion of qualified women in each discipline, a comparison was made with the proportion of faculty women found in departments at the University of Pennsylvania. From 33 departments for which this comparison could be made, 26 departments had less than the expected figure. Even ignoring the fact that most of these departments had no women *at all*, the probability of this distribution occurring by chance is 6.6×10^{-7}.

Of course, it is helpful in substantiating a claim of job discrimination because of sex if the woman is, in effect, a superwoman with an outstanding publication list in first-rate refereed journals, either as first or sole author, and has been extensively cited as well as widely recognized. Winning a job is harder for merely excellent or competent women scholars when compared with the equivalent men candidates. The present professoriate, chairpersons, and external referees, the promotions committees, deans, and provosts' staffs are overwhelmingly male. Although they now usually deny any sex bias, the results of their actions do not satisfy most women in academe. It is relevant that a committee of the Women's Faculty Club at the University of Pennsylvania examined virtually all the possible ways of determining excellence or quality of job performance in academe and found that nearly all of the ways had a strong built-in sex bias.

Filing an internal grievance or going to Federal court is a very serious matter. Such procedures are usually extremely wearing, oppressive, and expensive in terms of money, peace of mind, and friendships. Every effort should be made to resolve the problems informally, with a little bit of help or a lot of it from your friends and colleagues.

The most satisfactory way to redress a grievance may well be to do it privately and internally, but this rarely works. The presence of powerful friends, people who care about justice and are not afraid to speak up and act, and a local and national network of women, is often crucial.

After exhausting the normal channels of appeal to the chair of the department and the dean of the school, the office of the ombudsman, if it exists, may be helpful. The University of Pennsylvania has had such an office since 1971 and in the first five years of its operation more than 1300 members of the University community: students, staff, administrators, and faculty members have sought help from the Ombudsman.[18] This onerous yet important position has now been filled serially by three white male professors. About ten percent of the complaints were from faculty members and of these about ten cases which reached the Faculty Grievance Commission could not be resolved by informal negotiations.

One of us (R.E.D.) was a member of all the various committees and subcommittees that wrote the Faculty Grievance Procedure of the University of Pennsylvania and helped steer it through the Faculty Senate and University Council. It became operative in May, 1974, and R.E.D. served as Chairperson of the Faculty Grievance Commission for the first two years and as an ordinary member since then. He is currently chairperson of the subcommittee to recommend changes in the procedure.

The Faculty Grievance Procedure[19] describes formal mechanisms that make possible an investigation of claims that "action has been taken which affects the faculty member's personnel status or terms or conditions of his/her employment and which is: (1) arbitrary and capricious; (2) discriminatory with regard to race, sex, creed or national origin; or (3) not in compliance with University procedures or regulations."

The Faculty Grievance Commission is composed of at least sixteen persons from the University faculty. They include women, members of minority groups, and partially affiliated faculty but exclude department chairpersons and members of the administration. They are selected by the Senate Advisory Committee (an elected body of professorial faculty). The members of the Commission normally serve for three-year terms and, in a nonpublicized, random order, serve as the chairperson of a three-person inquiry panel. They are subject to challenge. Two other members of the panel are selected by the chairperson of the Commission from two lists of three members of the University community eligible to serve on the Commission, and selected respectively by the grievant and by the representative of the parties who made the decision that resulted in the grievance. This representative is designated by the Provost. In unusual circumstances, an additional two individuals from the Commission may be asked to serve on a five-person inquiry panel.

Informal discussions occur first to try to resolve the matter and to determine that the case is appropriate for the Commission rather than a School Committee on Academic Freedom and Responsibility. In the next step the grievant sends a formal written complaint to the Dean. If there is no reply, or it is unsatisfactory to the grievant, the chair of the Commission appoints an inquiry panel.

There are formal procedures concerning the right to be present, to provide evidence, and to call and cross-examine witnesses. The Panel has "access to all documentary evidence relevant to the grievance that was available to the parties who made the decision," and is "authorized to obtain additional documentary evidence and oral testimony on its own initiative such as the dossiers of other members of the same department who recently or currently are alleged to have received more favorable treatment." There are safeguards to maintain confidentiality. The grievant "may be accompanied by a University colleague when appearing at Panel meetings, who may speak on behalf of the grievant," and, if necessary, may have access to confidential information.

The findings of the panel are based solely on evidence provided according to the procedures and are sent to the grievant and to the Provost with recommendations. These "recommendations are to be accorded great weight," but are advisory to and not binding upon, the Provost.

In cases that involve reappointment, promotion, or tenure, and in which the Provost has declined or failed to implement such recommendations to the satisfaction of the grievant, the grievant may obtain a hearing before the Senate Committee on Academic Freedom and Responsibility on the actions of the Provost. The Senate Committee shall then promptly report its findings and recommendations to the President with copies to the Provost, to the chairpersons of the Grievance Commission, to the Inquiry Panel, to the grievant and the person acting on behalf of the parties making the decision. A copy shall also be given to the editor of the Almanac of the University.

Grievance procedures at other universities vary enormously. Most universities allow grievances to be initiated, based on claims of discrimination on account of race, sex, creed, or national origin. Some include grievances based on political conviction, a handicap, age, or even membership in, for example, the American Association of University Professors (AAUP). The AAUP itself has one of the most inclusive lists. The Association's Council approved the following in October 1976:[20] "The Association is committed to use its procedures and to take measures including censure against colleges and universities practicing illegal or unconstitutional discrimination on a basis not demonstrably related to the job function involved, including but not limited to age, sex, physical handicap, race, religion, national origin, marital status or sexual or affectional preference."

The mechanisms for investigation vary widely, are frequently vague, and are usually heavily weighted toward the administration. In some cases, the president, provost, or dean determines the composition of the investigating committee, fixes the rules of procedure, and can accept or reject the conclusions. In others, the committee is selected from past members of the Faculty Council by the Committee on Academic Freedom, or by the faculty of the university or school. The people who compose bodies are overwhelmingly white males, some of whom may not be sensitive to the special problems of women and minority groups.

In a few cases the grievant may have a right of selection of at least one member of the investigating committee, although the selection may be from present and past members of the Faculty Council, and only rarely from the whole university faculty. Most schools have no provision for peremptory challenge of the members or even for challenge for cause.

The rules of procedure are often vague and inadequate and rarely allow the grievant to be present during the investigation, hear evidence, call witnesses, cross-examine opposing witnesses, and either directly, or indirectly, through an advisor or colleague, have access to the relevant documents and files.

In some cases grievants remain alone, in others they may have a university colleague or counsel present who may speak for them. In some the right to counsel applies to witnesses, too, and occasionally to the Provost or Dean or whoever is defending the case for the administration.

In nearly all cases the report goes to the Dean, Provost, or President, who then decides what to do. Few institutions allow further appeals to the President, the Trustees, or the Committee on Academic Freedom in the event that the university official rejects the decisions or recommendations of the investigating committee.

It is sadly clear that what passes for "due process" at many academic institutions is extremely unsatisfactory, unfair, and heavily weighted in favor of the *status quo* and the administration. Where the Provost or the Dean is also the Affirmative Action officer, the chance of significant conflicts of interest may well be high.

In some universities, the faculty has designated the Association of University Professors, the National Educational Association, or some other body as the exclusive collective-bargaining agent. The agreements usually include many internal processes, but may also lead to binding arbitration. This, like a court decision, can compel the administration to act. However, it remains to be seen whether arbitrators who, like

Federal judges, are predominantly older white males, will act in cases involving claims of discrimination with respect to sex, in ways perceived to be fair by members of the various organizations of professional women.

So far the procedures have not generally been perceived by women as resulting in equitable treatment. Women who protest, file grievances, or go to court are almost uniformly disappointed, bitter, and in financial and personal distress. They become known as "trouble makers," are blacklisted, and frequently have the greatest difficulty or even find it impossible to remain active in their chosen profession.[21]

Despite help from the Association for Women in Science (AWIS), the National Organization for Women (NOW) and its legal defense fund, Women's Equity Action League (WEAL), various State Human Relations Commissions, the Equal Employment Opportunity Commission (EEOC), and the Department of Health Education and Welfare (HEW) of the Federal Government, trials in Federal courts can easily take years to resolve, cost many hundreds of hours of administrators' and faculty members' time, and cost hundreds of thousands of dollars. They can also result in much unfavorable publicity to all concerned. Much of the profit, if any, seems to go to some of the attorneys.

Although some institutions have gone through this whole process and have usually won the legal battle, several have chosen to settle out of court by negotiation. These include most of the cases that have come to a reasonably satisfactory conclusion. In our view, it is clearly necessary to improve procedures and morality and thus heighten the chance of justice being done.

From a direct knowledge of many grievance cases in many parts of the United States, some internal to the educational institutions and some that have reached the courts, we are distressed at the behavior of some professors, chairmen, deans, provosts, presidents, and trustees in the last few years. This behavior has included failure to operate and abide by the grievance procedures, attacks on the integrity of members of hearing committees, broken promises, lies, and deception. More specifically, this behavior has included severe harassment, deliberate solicitation of favorable letters for men and unfavorable ones for women, alteration of letters of recommendation (positively for men and negatively for women), the suppression of unfavorable letters and student comments for men, the suppression of favorable letters and student comments for women, the use of tailor-made advertisements for positions so that only some specific male candidate fits it completely, the falsification of curriculum vitae, the suppression of the results of departmental and promotion committee votes, the publication by men of professional women's research work without acknowledgement or joint authorship, and the denigration of a woman's research with the claim that it did not fit into the mission of the department or school, even though that identical line of research was accepted for the initial appointment and was being pursued in many other equivalent institutions.

If a grievance gets to court the problems multiply, and there are publications advising administrators on how to win cases and make it as difficult as possible for the plaintiff. For example, Stitt and Limitone[22] published a paper discussing the strategies and tactics that they have found useful in defending institutions in litigation against claims of sex discrimination. It is worth examining the techniques that at least some institutions find acceptable.

Stitt and Limitone[22] say that often the person against whom the complaint is being made (the respondent) and the concerned government official may be known to each other through acquaintance at religious, community, or other activities. Based on this acquaintance, the government offical may ask for an "off-the-record meeting" without lawyers about the complaint. The authors state: "Indeed, we have yet to be embarrassed by such informal approaches which often result in resolving immediately unjustified complaints."

Concerning the demand for university records, the authors say that these demands are always subject to discussion and negotiation. With regard to conciliation efforts, Stitt and Limitone[22] note that conciliation is a ". . . convenient and appropriate means of gaining time. . . ." Since, they say, HEW compliance review teams do not tend to become involved during the conciliation stage, more time can be gained.

They recommend pleading, as a defense by a university, that the complainant has failed to exhaust a union contract or an intrauniversity grievance procedure. It is clear that one of their important defenses is to demonstrate that universities are unique institutions and that complaints against them should be handled differently from the way complaints are handled against business corporations. They discuss the way to prevent the complainant from using a hearing for the discovery of necessary data required by the complainant.

Among the other tactics employed by Stitt and Limitone[22] are: challenging any agency's jurisdiction if the complainant has communicated about the grievance with another Federal or state agency, and suggesting that the second agency contact the other (here the authors note that they ". . . have never had any difficulty with EEOC in this area.").

Sometimes a complainant seeks an injunction to prevent the university from terminating her employment, since she maintains that she will probably prevail on the merits of the case and the injunction will prevent irreparable injury. Stitt and Limitone[22] here advise the University to answer by demonstrating that the termination was due to: financial stresses, departmental reorganization, insubordination, or a more qualified applicant. The university should also, according to these authors, direct the court's attention to the complainant's right to termination benefits and unemployment insurance. They even state that the court should be reminded that if the complainant is successful she can be awarded back pay with no loss of seniority. This last is, of course, unreasonable for any academic person, but particularly when the complainant is a scientist who is operating a research project, since termination can clearly cause irreparable injury in the laboratory and in obtaining and continuing her funding from outside agencies.

We hope that universities will change the direction in which their lawyers have been taking them. Universities' attorneys too often act like most other attorneys in that they do everything necessary to win the case for their clients, and they perceive their clients to be administrators rather than a community of scholars. It is surely the job of the faculty and staff to remind lawyers who their clients really are, and to prevent members of the administration from acting in an inhumane fashion. One of the signs of a great university may well be the resources it places at the service of women and minorities.

What is the current situation in academe as it bears on the future of academic women? In the courts the recent case of Sweeney v. the Board of Trustees of Keene State College in New Hampshire, was heard by the U. S. Court of Appeals, First Circuit, Boston. Dr. Christine Sweeney won her case in the U. S. District Court for N.H. and the judgment was affirmed on appeal on January 4, 1978. The district court had found that Dr. Sweeney had been a victim of sex discrimination in her second effort to gain promotion and ordered her promotion backdated to 1975 with the appropriate back pay. Senior Circuit Judge Tuttle said that the judges were rejecting an effort by the defendents ". . . to elevate the quantum of proof [of discriminatory motivation] to such a level that a litigant is necessarily doomed to failure." The judges voiced misgivings over ". . . the notion that the courts should keep 'hands off' the salary, promotion, and hiring decisions of colleges and universities." Citing their awareness that Congress has evidenced a concern for the status of women in academia they cautioned ". . . against permitting judicial deference to result in judicial abdication of a responsibility entrusted to the courts by Congress."

Of great interest is the judges'[23] acceptance of statistical evidence that a double standard was applied in promotion decisions. An important part of the case was the evidence ". . . that the person who nominally served as affirmative action coordinator did virtually nothing to advance the rights of women on the Keene campus." Many academic women will find that this statement has an all too familiar ring. Another hopeful sign is the recent out-of-court settlement in the case of Lamphere v. Brown University et al.[24]

Universities are still concerned about the possibility that HEW will withhold, terminate, deny, or suspend their Federal contracts. This can be done by HEW's Office for Civil Rights, which can refuse to certify the university as a responsible contractor if there are allegations that there has been substantial deviation from a university's approved affirmative action plan. It is very interesting to see how the Carter Administration is acting in this regard to fulfill its obligations to women scientists. Colleges and universities who do not submit Title IX forms assuring HEW that their institutions are in compliance with the ban on sex discrimination in federally aided programs will face possible withdrawal of federal funds, according to Secretary of HEW, Joseph Califano.[25]

At the end of February, 1978, President Carter sent to Congress a plan to consolidate Federal programs to combat job discrimination.[26] Enforcement powers are expected to be concentrated in the Equal Employment Opportunity Commission (EEOC), which has received a 35 percent increase in its enforcement budget. The EEOC would have the responsibility of developing standards applicable to the entire Federal Government as well as developing government-wide complaint and compliance review methods.

The Department of Health, Education and Welfare (DHEW) has established a system to expand and broaden its present requirements for the appraisal of Public Health Service (PHS) supervisors in meeting their Equal Employment Opportunity (EEO) responsibilities.[27] Since the memorandum states that it is the responsibility of supervisors to take actions clearly demonstrating that the principles of EEO are incorporated into the activities of the PHS and since supervisors will be evaluated on how they meet these responsibilities, academic institutions may well expect a more rigorous appraisal from DHEW. A more rigorous concern for fair employment practices is long overdue.

As Dr. Yalow said during her recent visit to Stockholm, "What women need is the equal opportunity they have not yet achieved."[28]

REFERENCES

1. GRAHAM, P. A. 1970. Women in Academe. Science 169:1284-1290.
2. SCIENCE AND GOVERNMENT REPORT. 1971. 1:1.
3. BIRD, C. 1971. Born Female. Pocket Books. Simon & Schuster, New York, N.Y.
4. FEDERAL LAWS AND REGULATIONS CONCERNING SEX DISCRIMINATION IN EDUCATIONAL INSTITUTIONS. 1977. Office for Civil Rights. Department of Health, Education and Welfare.
5. SANDLER, B. 1973. A little help from our government: WEAL and contract compliance. In Academic Women on the Move. A.S. Rossi & A. Calderwood, Eds.: 439-504. Russell Sage Foundation. New York, N. Y.
6. FIDELL, L. S. 1970. Empirical verification of sex discrimination in hiring practices in psychology. Am. Psychol. 25:1094-1098.
7. SIMPSON, L. 1968. A Study of Employing Agents' Attitudes toward Academic Women in Higher Education. Ph.D. dissertation. Pennsylvania State Univ. University Park, Pa.
8. LEWIN, A. Y. & L. DUCHAN. 1971. Women in Academia. Science 173:892-895.
9. MARCUS, L. R. 1976. Has advertising produced results in faculty hiring? Educational Record 57:4.
10. ASTIN, H. S. 1973. Career profiles of women doctorates. In Academic Women on the Move. A. S. Rossi & A. Calderwood, Eds.: 139-179. Russell Sage Foundation. New York, N. Y.
11. MINORITIES AND WOMEN IN THE HEALTH FIELDS. 1975. Department of Health, Education and Welfare. Publication (HRA) 76-22. Public Health Service. Department of Health, Education and Welfare. Bethesda, Md.
12. BURNETT, E. 1975. Doctors Degrees Conferred by all U. S. Institutions: By State, Academic Field, Sex, and Institution 1964-65 through 1973-74. Office of Education. Department of Health, Education and Welfare, Bethesda, Md.
13. MANUAL FOR DETERMINING THE LABOR MARKET AVAILABILITY OF WOMEN AND MINORITIES. 1974. Office of the Secretary, Department of Health, Education and Welfare, Office for Civil Rights. Bethesda, Md.

14. MANPOWER RESOURCES FOR SCIENTIFIC ACTIVITIES AT UNIVERSITIES AND COLLEGES. 1975. National Science Foundation. Washington, D.C.
15. VETTER, B. M. 1977. Supply and demand for scientists and engineers: A review of selected studies. Scientific Manpower Commission. Washington, D.C.
16. DOCTORAL SCIENTISTS AND ENGINEERS IN THE UNITED STATES 1975 Profile. 1975. National Research Council, Nat. Acad. Sci. USA. Washington, D.C.
17. REPORT OF THE COMMITTEE ON THE STATUS OF WOMEN, WOMEN FACULTY IN THE UNIVERSITY OF PENNSYLVANIA. Parts 1, 2, 3. 1971. Almanac. Univ. Pennsylvania. Philadelphia, Pa.
18. FREEDMAN, J. O. 1976. What purpose does an ombudsman serve? Almanac. Univ. Pennsylvania. Philadelphia, Pa.
19. FACULTY GRIEVANCE PROCEDURE. 1974. Obtainable from the Office of the Secretary, 112 College Hall, University of Pennsylvania, Philadelphia, Pa. 19104.
20. POLICY DOCUMENTS AND REPORTS. 1977. On Discrimination: Amer. Assoc. University Professors. Washington, D.C.
21. THEODORE, A. 1978. Academic Women in Protest. In preparation.
22. STITT, R. S. & A. P. LIMITONE, JR. 1973. University fair employment practices litigation strategy and tactics. J. Coll. Univ. Law:20–32.
23. SWEENEY V. BOARD OF TRUSTEES OF KEENE STATE COLLEGE. 1978. 16 FEP Cases: 378–387. Bureau of National Affairs.
24. GORTON, A. & A. F. WESSEN. 1977. The Lamphere settlement: a faculty view. Brown Alumni Monthly: 25–28, 37. Brown Univ. Providence, R.I.
25. SANDLER, B. 1977. On Campus with Women. Project on the Status and Education of Women. Assoc. Amer. Coll. **18**:2.
26. NEW YORK TIMES. 1978. Feb. 24. New York, N.Y.
27. RICHMOND, J. B. 1977. Memorandum on Appraisal of Supervisory Performance in EEO. Department of Health, Education and Welfare. Bethesda, Md.
28. JACOBY, S. 1977. The New York Times. Dec. 22. New York, N.Y.

The New Feminism and the Medical School Milieu

MARY C. HOWELL*
Medical Director, Charles Drew Family Life Center
Dorchester, Massachusetts 02121

I HAVE BEEN ASKED TO highlight for you what it is like, now, to be a woman and a medical student.

Women students in 1978 are increasingly differentiated, one from another, in their political positions. Fifteen or twenty years ago, in the 1950s and early 1960s, women students, for the most part, believed themselves to be apolitical; that is, they regarded themselves simply as women who happened to be attending medical school, or, more likely, as medical students who happened to be women. The latter stance was the more likely because then, as now, socialization as a physician was a very powerful, almost overwhelming experience. The culture of professional physicians is very distinct. Arrogance, interpersonal distancing, elitism, and the right to control others, among other values, attitudes, and behaviors, are taught by precept and example in an environment intensely designed to mold the student/trainee. Until recently there scarcely was a recognizable culture of women to identify with, to cling to as a touchstone through the experience of professional socialization.

I say that women used to *consider themselves* to be apolitical. Since politics is the playing out of power relationships, such students certainly did hold a political position, which was that they would go along with, and ultimately become a part of, the power elite of professional medical experts that they were learning about.

By contrast, today a small subgroup of women arrive as medical students with a well-thought-out political understanding of themselves as women and their place in the world, and of their mentors as professionals and medical experts and *their* place in the world. They understand, for instance that:

* Former Associate Dean, Harvard Medical School.

- few women physicians ever truly enter that realm of power, except as ineffectual token figures;
- those who do enter must, on the whole, act like "honorary men" and can neither create new and womanly models of professionalism nor work on behalf of women, from their positions of power and influence;
- the "elevation" of a few women into those realms of power does little to improve the lives of most women in this society.

These students, whose politics are radical and feminist, might be considered "new" feminists. By contrast, other women students are pressed to think through and to voice their own political positions with regard to women's place. It is now remarked that most of the women in entering classes declare themselves to be feminist, but that that identification often means only that they acknowledge the changes of recent years that benefit them, and since their lives (which have, for most of them, always been relatively easy) now seem to be better, they regard the battle for equal rights to be nearly won. Most are vaguely "for women," enjoy women's music and art and poetry, but also foresee, for their own lives, roles in work and in personal relations that are not very different from those of their elders. And, of course, there are some women students who declare themselves to be staunchly antifeminist, who are quite content with women's place in the *status quo*.

Those traditional roles are what students see most senior women with whom they might find identification—faculty, practicing physicians, and career investigators—as fulfilling. Some senior women propound that they have never had children because they believe those investments in personal intimacy to be incompatible, for a woman, with a professional career. Others, married and parenting, juggle almost full responsibility for household and marriage maintenance and childrearing, with busy work lives. All work in a world where women's jobs are mostly of lesser status and lower pay than those of men; many accept their career limitations as expected or even deserved. Almost none can find a way to work on behalf of women's interests. A few are feminist, but for many senior physicians the contradictions between feminism and professionalism and the established world of medical experts are so severe, so disorienting, and so cognitively dissonant that a feminist position is hardly tenable.

For the new feminist students, then—and there are more of them, more sophisticated in their politics, each year—there is a tremendous sense of loneliness, even emnity, in the world of medical school. One student spoke of knowing only a dozen people in the entire school with whom she felt comfortable for casual conversation. Virtually all seek to enlarge and maintain contacts with people outside the medical school, even though this endeavor can be difficult because medical schools are traditionally isolated, both geographically and socially, from the rest of the world. Maintaining contacts with nonmedical women is also difficult because many feminists are justifiably suspicious of the overpowering process by which ordinary people are transformed into physicians; on the basis of experience, they doubt that one can be both a feminist and a professional medical expert.

At the same time, the medical school climate is becoming increasingly conservative. There is a certain public approval now for antifeminist bias, much stronger and more open than the faint and mostly covert approval of expressions of bias against ethnic minorities. It is as if the professionals and experts now in positions of power in our society have looked at the civil rights movement and the women's movement, recognized the significant changes in their own lives that would be brought if proposed social changes were to come about, shuddered at the thought, and agreed that they would dig in their heels. Sexist remarks demeaning to women used to be made by men in medical school classrooms, at least in many instances, from a position of unthinking and naive ignorance of the effect of such pejoratives on their targets. Now, more often, such comments are justified by disparaging remarks about the trouble-making personalities of those who would object.

The conservative faculty and administration have been successful, at many schools, in selecting cohorts of students who are, compared to the entire population of applicants, also quite conservative. That not all of the admitted students *are* conservative speaks not only to diverse voices on admissions committees but also to the well-known ability of student applicants, chameleonlike, to appear to be whatever admissions committees seem to want them to be.

If there is extreme conservatism in medical schools now, there is also a conservative and antifeminist backlash in the wider society. At one medical school, a coalition of women students and houseofficers has accomplished some rather wonderful things. At every point, however, they are running into strong, well-financed opposition. There is a women's resource room, with reference materials such as *Our Bodies, Ourselves*, housed in a medical school building and open not only to women associated with the school but also to women of the community. Imagine the difference of climate in a medical school when community layfolk have access to the school facilities and to its students. Conservative opposition to this project has threatened a legislative investigation for this state school, charging misuse of state funds. The students and houseofficers have organized and are teaching a seminar on sex education to youth leaders such as Boy Scout leaders; members of the same group are teaching a course about women's bodies and women's lives at the local YWCA. Both seminars have been invaded, and are being disrupted and threatened with closure, by conservative opposition. The opposition in this small town is the local arm of the well-funded anti-Equal Rights Amendment and compulsory pregnancy (so-called "Right-to-life") alliance.

I, for one, am enormously impressed with these young women medical students. They are remarkably sophisticated in their political analysis and understanding. They are bright, stong, active, and intent. They intend to shape their work lives to turn their knowledge and skills on behalf of women. I believe that many of them will be successful, many more than have succeeded in this vision in years past.

Some will chose to work alone, as solo practitioners, understanding that this is one way to invent procedures for serving patients in a manner that strives to be compassionate and responsive. Whether or not they confine their practice exclusively to women patients, they will reserve a special attention and empathy to the health problems of concern to women.

Others will work with separatist feminist groups such as those now inventing women's health clinics. There they will struggle to learn to work collectively with other women and to create methods of health care responsive to the needs of laywomen for consultation with experts in a manner that enables a self-determined promotion of health.

Most, however, will work in established medical-care agencies: hospitals, clinics, and neighborhood health centers. They will join there with the feminist nurses and technicians who are already working quiet transformations in some small corners of the provision of medical/health care for women. There have been, until now, few physicians to join in that effort. In a few years, I am convinced, there will be increasing numbers of feminists who are also physicians.

I am very hopeful for this cohort of women medical students. I believe they will persevere, survive their training, and become astonishingly good doctors, both competent and compassionate. I am impressed with the strength of their feminism. I feel confident that they will help each other to sustain their feminist values throughout the process of socialization as physicians.

If they do so, it will be in part because they are aware of how much they need the support of each other. At this year's meeting of the American Medical Student Association, that liberal organization saw the coming together of a radical women's caucus. There were eight sessions of feminist-oriented meetings, including a presentation by the local Feminist Women's Health Center on self-help and self-examination. There was a resolution before the entire assembly to condemn states that have not passed the Equal Rights Amendment and to refuse to hold later conventions in any state that continues not to ratify the Amendment.

Do these feminist medical students indeed represent a "new" feminism? In one sense I think not, for part of their strength is their solid grounding in women's history, both old and recent. They are aware of and share with other women who are not medical students an interest in women's literature, art, music, and feminist theory. Most importantly, they are learning (though it be extraordinarily difficult while in medical school) to relax, to escape from the world of struggle, to laugh, and to regather their strength.

What is becoming new is the nature of the interaction between the medical schools and other agents of the established medical-care community, and these students. They are learning to be increasingly skillful in the public actions through which they press for change. At the same time, they are much stronger, I believe, than their predecessors in their private convictions. This is "new" feminism in the sense of the continual rebirth of a social movement that now has impetus to sustain a long struggle toward a better world for women, which will be a better world for us all.

Development of Feminist Networks In the Professions

ARLENE KAPLAN DANIELS
Department of Sociology – Program on Women
Northwestern University
Evanston, Illinois 60201

Introduction

THROUGH COMMON SENSE we know the importance of informal networks within any institutional system or any community. Put most cynically, we say "it's not *what* you know but *who* you know." Even recognizing the importance of real ability, we do not deny the help contacts provide. In academia and other professions, personal recommendations can be crucial, either when finding a job or when locating suitable candidates for a specialized task under deadline pressures. Quick information—the best scholarly references, access to agencies or key informants in preparing a grant proposal, the crucial areas to find in technical reports when building a documented case about something—may make the difference between success and failure on an important project. Informal networks also help when one needs information on strategies for an administrative or political action. How should one approach a strange agency on a difficult mission? Where should one first go for help in a bureaucratic agency when ignoring the informal gatekeeper can be ruinous? Knowing the right people can bring "tips" on how to manage these delicate matters.

These uses of networks should not be seen as in themselves somehow immoral or illegal; they are often necessary even to move the cumbersome machinery of an insider's own bureaucratic administration.[1] The links in the system combine personal friendships and/or respect for judgment between parties. If you trust and like them, you expect friends and acquaintances to make judgments in their own territories like those you would make if you were there to see for youself. The effectiveness of these systems, whether they are informal channels inside an organization or more widespread networks in other organizations or regions, reinforces and sustains their future use.

These guides are used by "old boys' " networks, in secret societies and fraternal orders.[2,3] Since these groups are commonly associated with exclusionary or discriminatory treatment of nonmembers, it is common for those outside to regard the whole pattern negatively. But the desire to break down this particular pattern in order to open the system of advantages and upward mobility to all ignores the usefulness of the pattern itself. The value of egalitarianism should not lead us to overlook the value of establishing additional networks. The positive social-psychological importance of informal networks for the individual participant are invaluable even in a democratic society: they facilitate a sense of mastery and a sense of self-worth. The first is provided in at least two ways. The knowledge of how to proceed through informal channels provides a feeling of efficiency and a sense of success, when it produces better results than ordinary, formal procedures. The reputation one gains from good results leads others to show respect and to request information.

Our self-image is affected by the willingness of others to accept us into a network, for it shows one is a person worth helping. The respect of others and their requests for help reinforce a sense of self-worth. Thus, the more important one's place within a network, the greater the opportunities for mastery and self-esteem.

DEVELOPMENT OF FEMINIST NETWORKS

As women develop an understanding of how the social-psychological benefits of networking may be especially useful to those whose position in a sex-stratified system encourages little positive or unambivalent sense of self-worth, they perceive that informal "old boy" or "old girl" networks are not intrinsically bad. It is particularly easy for those disadvantaged in or marginal to the formal hierarchy to see how the formal communications networks are often too cumbersome, outdated, or inaccessible to meet their needs, for bureaucratic machinery often suffers from the problems of "institutional" racism or sexism. With the best will in the world, the established authorities and elites may operate in a system that seems fair but that nevertheless excludes women or minorities from full opportunities. Understanding the importance of networks is born out of experience and necessity.[4] Women will not be recommended for good positions, much less supported through preliminary screening reviews, unless they are alerted to openings in time and can marshal powerful or influential references.[4A] To provide these opportunities, networks provided by the women themselves are arising to parallel the existing old-boy networks. These new channels make explicit what both formal and informal structures in education, business, and the professions have often left implicit: how to manage the flow of information through which professional reputations develop.

SOCIALIZATION

These bits of information about career development are usually acquired during professional training. Yet educational institutions often leave unspecified and unformalized these important lessons.[5-7] Some students who do well are specially favored by mentors. Others are both sharp and lucky enough to be in the inner circle of students who learn from one another and also exchange information learned from those above them in the hierarchy. Still others, though apparently able from admissions and early performance criteria, drop further and further behind. Proponents for affirmative action have long pointed to the disproportionate number of women and minorities in this last group; these proponents argue that the process of discrimination begins early in education and also affects entrants into professional schools who have survived the early barriers.

Women have some advantage over other minorities in overcoming discrimination because the privileged, white women among them have had more opportunities to learn the implicit messages from their earlier education and sponsorship. For example, women with helpful husbands and/or partisan fathers have always received some extra assistance and instruction. In consequence, sufficient numbers already exist, at least in some areas, to provide role-models and mentors, and to help socialize new entrants. The awakening realization of how important networks can be in this process has helped formalize this area of otherwise informal socialization and has provided justification for developing and strengthening such networks. Older women thus come to see part of their personal and professional obligation as offering general advice and specific information to the new recruit. Younger or less experienced women are encouraged to ask for help and guidance without diffidence or fear of rebuff. They now know it is legitimate to do so, just as it is legitimate for them to work together in peer groups of women, one helping the other.

Pooling Resources

Since resources, for informal socialization or anything else concerning the well-being of women, are still in short supply, feminist networks are used to fill gaps in information through pooling resources. Advice or teaching or informal socialization practicies (how to manage a job interview, how to speak to a superior, how to manage home and career, where to get advice for filing a grievance against one's school or employer) can be communicated through sessions at national and regional meetings or professional associations and through their newsletters, as well as through local channels. In addition, specialists in one area become known for their expertise and are contacted from distant cities. They can pool their knowledge and work as an advisory or consultant board for many women. As each learns about the others, an internal referral system develops. Other resources are also pooled. Long-distance calls and messages can be funneled through women with special phone privileges; some women may have secretarial and xerox facilities for mailing and duplication. Organizations can cooperate in pooling mailing lists as well as nonprofit franking privileges and legislative information vital for social action.

Networks with Outposts in Traditional-Elitist and Nonelitist Camps

The development of a feminist ideology provides the basis for appeals to common interest across occupational hierarchies. Women in the high-status occupations take an interest in issues and problems affecting women in clerical and other lower-status work. Their sense of identity is enhanced by the feminist ideology that women are oppressed as a class whatever the distinctions or other privileges some may have. Professional women are thus sensitized to the need to fight for promotions and other benefits, including better on-the-job treatment for female subordinates. When women share this ideology across class lines, subordinates (secretaries, receptionists, clerks) may leak information not otherwise accessible to superordinate professionals (lawyers, academicians, lobbyists, and legislators). "Old boy" bosses may then be astonished by the mysterious omniscience shown by those pressing for changes in the system. Female secretaries and research assistants who are "invisible" to their bosses may watch for pieces of information, unwittingly revealed, to relay to feminists on the outside. Advocates of affirmative action or other feminist causes may then embarrass The Establishment or gnaw away at its bastions with their knowledge of inside practices or foreknowledge of strategies planned to thwart reforms.

In any or all of the ways suggested above, feminist networks can supply the professional and personal support structure to dilute or negate the indifference or hostility many women face when operating in a man's world. For these networks also supply the recognition that is one of the benefits of any insider's network: reassurance, praise, and recognition to shore up a sense of well-worth. Equally important, success in these networks can develop skills and information necessary for successful entry into larger, heterogeneous networks of men and women. In addition, existence of these networks shows the visibility of a constituency as well as a leadership. This constituency makes the leaders difficult to ignore as individuals. Thus they gain the resources for infiltrating— or even crashing—the most recalcitrant and impervious old boy establishments and their networks.

Feminist Networks in Professions and Business Worlds

The opportunity to develop skills useful in infiltration or integration are particularly relevant to business and professional women; they must both accommodate to and change these virtually exclusive male territories. Some networks devoted to women's interests can exist and flourish with minimal attention to and from the male power structure. Nursery and child-care cooperatives, consciousness-raising groups for singles, divorced people, elderly citizens, or lesbian women are often (though not always) in this category. Other networks can develop quite well independently, but ultimately must contact (and sometimes combat) the male establishment. Pregnancy, self-help, and general medical counseling are clearly in this category, as are networks offering information about divorce, credit, and career counseling.

Women interested in succeeding within the traditional male-dominated world of high-status professions know from the start what they face. They will need networks that are both separatist (so the benefits of a woman-organized network can be gained) and assimilationist (so that opportunities to infiltrate the male hierarchy will arise). Two contexts are offered as examples of areas where women can benefit from feminist networks in infiltrating the professional networks now dominated by men: the professional convention and access to job openings in the academy.

The World of Professional Conventions

While the real professional importance of convention-going and paper-giving in any academic discipline or professional world is ambiguous, it is clear that there are some general benefits, particularly in the early stages of a career. It is then that new entrants and junior practitioners have an opportunity to make contacts, gain visibility, and, if they are lucky, "learn the ropes" in the informal socialization process. Peers can pool knowledge, elders may be met in a friendly, relaxed semisociable setting sometimes arising within the otherwise hectic and even alienating crush of a large meeting. In chance moments, then, friendships, tutoring, or collegiality may be offered. Occasionally as well, the avowed purpose of such meetings—the exchange of ideas in the forefront of research and the chance to exchange ideas with others of similar interest—may also be realized. Another avowed purpose of such meetings is to offer an opportunity for job-seekers and recruiters to meet.

Unfortunately, the larger the convention, the more difficult it is to assure these opportunities for any new entrant. Established professionals have many duties to perform for their association and must spend much time out of sight in committee rooms. In addition, they wish to meet old friends, enjoy the convention city, negotiate their own deals with editors and publishers, and make their own contacts for research, academic, or publishing interests. These interests divert attention from the juniors who see their elders as potentially helpful informants several steps above. In consequence of these diverging interests, new recruits, both male and female, report that they find professional meetings profoundly alienating: they are often treated cursorily, indifferently, or even rudely, with the net result that little seems gained by attending. If one is fortunate enough to be in a profession that contains minority, women's, gay, or radical caucuses, the separate activities (or miniconventions) provided by these groups can offer enough functions and interchanges to mitigate the loneliness and unpleasantness of the major gathering. In many women's caucuses within academic disciplines, a systematic effort is also made to provide useful information about "learning the ropes." (In sociology, the Sociologists for Women in Society provided a number of "how to" sessions over the past five years to discuss such issues as writing papers, getting grants, establishing women's research projects, preparing articles for publication, managing the hurdles of graduate school, and first jobs. These sessions were so successful and so well attended by women *and* men that a similar program has since been offered by the American Sociological Association. Currently similar sessions are also offered in cooperation between the Society for the Study of Social Problems and Sociologists for Women in Society.)

These adaptations highlighted the fact that many new recruits of *both* sexes found professional initiation painful. A few of the favored might arrive with mentors and sponsors who helped ease the way. But most entrants were not so lucky, and neither institutional supports nor supportive social contexts had developed to help them weather the period of initiation.

Initiation problems are faced by both men and women, but it is clear that the consequences of naiveté fall harder on more women than men.[10-11] Since women must surmount the barriers of sex discrimination, they need special assistance. It is easy, otherwise, for even very bright and talented women to become discouraged in the face of conflicting pressures and demands involved in meeting professional and family demands.

The importance of networks is seen in the steps women have taken to overcome the cumulative effects of all these barriers. In the professional associations, entry participation is mainly in the hands of convention organizers. Once women press for and win a significant number of the professional offices controlling access to the naming of panel organizers and session chairs, significantly larger numbers of women appear on the convention program.[12] A parallel increase appears in the number of papers in learned journals written by women when women assume key editorial management and advisory posts for these journals. Such victories offer women the visibility that also encourages invitations to conferences and conventions, furthering various informal opportunities for professional advancement.

My own experience as editor of *Social Problems* suggests the cumulative effect a woman editor can have upon the publication of articles by women. During my term (1974-78), the number of associate editors who are women more than doubled. Both the visibility of an editor known to be interested in encouraging women sociologists as well as the development of new research about women's issues encouraged a high rate of submissions from women. Although only a small number of articles ever received are appropriate for *Social Problems* (the journal only publishes about ten percent of all submissions), the high quality of some of the women's submissions and their eventual publication encouraged still other women to submit their material to us. The interest of editors and associate editors in discovering the best of the new research about women has also encouraged the development of this new area by showing the value this research can have for the growth of the discipline at large. The publication of new research in a learned journal serves both to encourage new research and to validate areas of interest primarily to women.

None of these approaches should suggest improper particularism or favoritism shown by women in their treatment of other women. Rather, the examples indicate both the difficulties and the importance of gaining attention in crowded, competitive worlds where even highly talented persons can go unnoticed without sponsorship or other advantages to spotlight their developing talents. Women are more likely to know other women, to encourage them, and be sought by them. Accordingly, women will often know more about the work of other women than their male colleagues. In consequence, knowledgeable women will also know when it would be appropriate to recommend women for appointments or their papers for publication. Such opportunities are *especially* important for women, who, by their personal or general socialization in this society, have to struggle against a sense of unworthiness for or marginality toward professional advancement in a man's world. But placement in a friendly network of women can go far in developing a sense of self-esteem and self-worth. A positive cycle of information feedback and professional rewards will encourage continued perseverence by women professionals, preventing discouragement and self-doubt in the face of other less heartening experiences that commonly occur, even in the lives of favored white males.

Job Information Networks

Although some might argue that the importance of participation in professional associations is overrated and that the advantages are dubious, everyone agrees that learning to behave as a professional has to occur somehow. A vital part of this socialization is learning how to get a job. Practically speaking, women need access to job information networks as much as they may need good references, a properly written curriculum vitae, and publication credits. If women have patrons, if they have attended a prestigious graduate school that their professors themselves have attended or if they have taught at such top schools and have wide contacts in the field, such students are a step ahead in collecting job information. If, as in the case of many women and minority members, students who have attended community and state colleges, worked or raised families, and then received a graduate education at a university of middling reputation, such students may have neither powerful nor well-known references. One consequence of limited connections may be lack of special knowledge of unforeseen openings and lack of an insider's track to a possible opening where, after judicious informal queries, the recruitment committee sometimes ends up writing job specifications just to fit a prospective applicant. In a tightening market where hundreds of applicants apply for every job, "ordinary" applicants are lost in the first published job advertisement. No friend of someone on the recruitment committee recommends them, no list of publications in prestige journals or tee recommends them, no list of publications in prestige journals or papers read at professional societies proclaims their professional caliber, even as a student. Without just one committee person sensitive to the particular career contingencies of women and minority students to plead for them, they never make it through the first round.[13] The advent of special networks in minority and women's caucuses within the professions has begun to provide alternative channels of information about such candidates.

The creation of a dual system of networks can be one way to bridge the gap between the desire of new groups to gain acceptance and the needs of the existing system to admit and promote recruits. Those women acceptable to (or already participants in) the established hierarchies have access to insider's information. Furthermore, the press to meet affirmative action legal requirements and the wish to abandon prior discriminatory practices make these women even more desirable as club members than they may have been previously. Now they are seen as necessary focal points for the gathering and dissemination of information about acceptable women recruits. It is expected that the older women, as already enrolled members of the establishment club, can be trusted to make judicious evaluations of these newcomers, telling the other "old boys" which applicant does and which does not meet the current standards of excellence. In this way they stand as "brothers" reporting on a foreign territory to colleagues at home, making decisions these colleagues might make if they knew that territory.

At the same time, these women, if they show some sympathy and interest, can stand as "sisters" to their junior women colleagues by encouraging their growth, helping feminist groups to achieve solidarity and develop mutual support systems, offering "tips" from the inside, charitable contributions to struggling caucuses, and by providing references, free long-distance telephone calls, and xerox privileges to the less affluent.

In this way dual systems or dual-purpose networks develop to promote solidarity within women's groups while showing the way to assimilation in predominantly male professional clubs. The task for senior women is , of course, difficult. They become doubly marginal and can provoke mistrust from both groups by showing sympathy and familiarity with the other. Nevertheless, the success of many women's caucuses in academic disciplines rests on the efforts of such diplomatic, senior women leaders as well as on the genuine talents, energy, creativity, and perseverance of those new entrants knocking on the doors of the gentlemen's clubs. The success of this venture is shown by how quickly a few have become elder stateswomen themselves in the past few years.

SPECIAL PROBLEMS FOR WOMEN IN THE PROFESSIONS

Despite some past successes, women's networks in the professions continue to face difficulties,[13A] which are compounded by the stratification of the occupational hierarchies. Professions hold themselves above other occupations, and, within the professions, the higher-status fields (as medicine, law) are esteemed above the "semiprofessions" (nursing, librarianship, social work, teaching). Such distinctions discourage the formation of alliances across specialities. And they highlight the difficulties of women in the higher-status (male-dominated) fields. The semiprofessions have traditionally been filled with women. But the high-status positions in these fields, as well as careers in such higher-status fields as medicine, law, and science are traditionally more open to men. The opportunities for women to develop a sense of solidarity and a practical system of network exchanges are correspondingly limited. Successful careers in the past were likely to depend on the ability to play handmaiden to male superiors.

Difficulties in Developing Feminist Networks Within Science, Medicine, and Business

The past scarcity of females and their continued scarcity in fields like engineering and physics has also encouraged the identification of those women who have succeeded with male authority figures. These women experience a status somewhat like honorary males if they survive the socialization process; and the philosophy of tokenism encourages them to see themselves as different and special, unlike other women. These processes encourage indifference to or even fear of the possibility that greater numbers of women can and should become professionals. If they consider experience in other countries, American women in these fields may be unfavorably impressed by the data showing how a great influx of women downgrades the status and economic rewards available. Finally, their own place within the top stratum (even if they are in the lower part of it) encourages them to overlook or ignore the issues affecting the "masses" below. Even when they do wish to be sisterly and helpful, there are too few women available to form a network of encouragement and support that could make such effort rewarding and effective. In consequence, there are not enough women with the ideology or energy to help young women professionals, much less the vast numbers of women in subordinate positions.

The Feminist Movement as Impetus for Change and Growth of Feminist Networks

On the other hand, the sense of working together as an embattled few can provide a sense of solidarity and an impulse to develop greater *esprit de corps*. Those women who see their numbers as too few for effective organization within a specialty may also be motivated to reach across traditional disciplinary boundaries in the formation of coalitions. Such organizations as AWIS (Association for Women in Science) are notable for their success in providing an umbrella organization for natural and physical scientists, where women are relatively scarce and in forming coalitions of "hard" and "soft" scientists as well. Today, the growing strength of the Federation of Organizations for Professional Women (FOPW) coalition suggests how networks may be formed across many of the traditional status as well as discipline barriers. This coalition includes feminist caucuses in the traditional professions, in welfare rights organizations, as well as in clerical and domestic workers unions. The common interests of such coalitions rest upon the common experience developed through individual interactions within a sex-stratified system. Such common experiences promote sympathy for and interest in the plight of other women, which can supersede some of the traditionally diverse interests of class and race as well as occupational specialty. It is possible that even the greatest barrier, that between professional and client, could be crossed, if, for instance, women should recognize their common interests and requirements in the field of health care and the unique problems of satisfying these concerns in a sex-stratified system.[14]

The feminist ideology provides a rationale for discussing such issues as the following: 1) How can we bridge the professional-nonprofessional gap to forge ties between higher-status professionals, business executives on one side of the gap and semiprofessionals, secretaries, technicians, aides, and custodial assistants on the other? 2) How shall we turn aside resentment of subordinate women when women join the superordinate male hierarchy? 3) What can encourage the development and proliferation of organizations or coalitions of organizations to consider common interests and problems in the areas of working conditions, salaries, and career opportunities?

The feminist ideology also suggests some of the immediate and personal benefits in the exhilaration provided by women working together. The literature on consciousness-raising groups in the women's movement[15-17] suggests that untapped energies and potentials are released when women confront common problems in a group. The realization that many problems are not necessarily signs of personal inadequacy but may well be indicators of both systematic and informal discrimination may first evoke great anger. Ultimately, according to the ideology of this movement, the relief of not having the guilt and sense of personal responsibility for earlier inability to achieve particular goals and general independence may release the energy for later success in these areas.

The potential of women's coalitions and networks, joined to work toward a common goal, has already been discussed. The victories are not yet overwhelming, as the delay in passage of the Equal Rights Amendment so clearly demonstrates. Nonetheless, the principles and practices of coalition formation (and the interconnection of a greater and greater number of networks) are accepted by more and more women's organizations. The recent growth of the Women's Action Alliance and the Women's Agenda give some indication of the potential power that such unlikely partners as the Association of Junior Leagues of America, the League of Women Voters, and gay rights organizations can bring to a group by giving their names as sponsors. If such diverse groups can see the potential in feminist networks, may we not hope for the same from women in the professions?

REFERENCES

1. BLAU, P. M. 1956. Bureaucracy in Modern Society. Random House. New York, N.Y.

2. DOMHOFF, G. W. 1974. The Bohemian Grove and Other Retreats. Harper & Row. New York, N.Y.
3. VER DER ZEE, J. 1974. The Greatest Men's Party on Earth: Inside the Bohemian Grove. Harcourt Brace Jovanovich. New York, N.Y.
4. SIMMEL, G. 1955. Conflict and the Web of Group Affiliations. Free Press. Glencoe, Ill.
4A. EPSTEIN, C.F. 1970. Encountering the male establishment: sex status limits on women's Careers in the professions. Am. J. Sociology 75:965–982.
5. BECKER, H. et. al. 1961. Boys in White. University of Chicago Press. Chicago, Ill.
6. BUCHER, R. & J. STELLING. 1977. Becoming Professional. Sage Inc. Beverly Hills, Calif.
7. KAHN-HUT, R. 1974. The Usefulness of Psychiatric Theory in Supporting the Mystique of Professionalism. Brandeis University. Doctoral dissertation. Waltham, Mass.
8. PASQUALE, T. & M. DUNKLE. 1976. Title IX: Upset victory for women. Women's Agenda 1(4):7, 10–11. Women's Action Alliance. New York, N.Y.
9. DANIELS, A. K. 1976. Local and Cosmopolitan Women's Networks in the U.S. Plenary Session. British Sociological Association. Manchester, England. Unpublished.
10. ROSSI, A. & A. CALDERWOOD. 1973. Academic Women on the Move. Russell Sage Foundation. New York, N.Y.
11. KUNDSIN, R.B., Ed. 1973. Successful Women in the Sciences: An Analysis of Determinants. Ann. N.Y. Acad. Sci. 208.
12. YOKOPENIC, P.A. et. al. 1975. Professional communication networks: A case study of women in the American Public Health Association. Social Problems 22(4):493–509.
13. DANIELS, A. K. 1974. The notion of appropriate professional conduct: an exercise in the sociology of sociology. Amer. Sociologist. 9:212–220.
13A. KAUFMAN, D. R. 1978. Associational ties in academe: some male and female differences. Sex Roles 4(1):9–21.
14. RUZEK, S. 1978. The Women's Health Movement. Special Studies. Praeger. New York, N.Y.
15. CARDEN, M.L. 1974. The New Feminist Movement. Russell Sage Foundation. New York, N.Y.
16. FREEMAN, J. 1975. The Politics of Women's Liberation. David McKay. New York, N.Y.
17. CASSELL, J. 1977. A Group Called Women. David McKay. New York, N.Y.

Strategies for Change: A Summary

JUDITH A. RAMALEY

Department of Physiology and Biophysics
University of Nebraska College of Medicine
Omaha, Nebraska 68105

You HAVE BEEN reading here a number of statistics interspersed with some personal experiences. From our formal discussions and some of our other exchanges, I should like to try to extract a list of suggestions for ways in which we can work to increase the entry of young women into scientific careers and to help them during their professional development once they are hired. Most of the points I am going to make can be read about in greater detail in several of the papers presented in 1977 at the Conference on Women's Leadership and Authority in the Health Professions sponsored by the Program for Women in Health Sciences, University of California, San Francisco,[1] and in the papers presented here.

As a way of ordering the various approaches that we have heard about, I should like to concentrate on issues affecting women as individuals ("The Self"), interactions with *other people*, and the nature of the *institutions* in which women will work. It is easiest to change oneself, less easy to change transactions with other people, and least easy to change the setting in which these transactions take place, namely, the institutions in which we work. For that reason, let's start at the most controllable point: ourselves.

THE SELF

There are several kinds of information that can be useful in helping women cope with the problems they encounter during the periods they are making decisions about careers, learning their professions, and, later, practicing their professions. For example, all of us are subjected to assumptions about which behavior is appropriate for the two sexes. There are a variety of ways in which we can deal with the conflicts set up by differences between societal expectations and our own wishes. It is useful to know, for example, that success in women is treated differently than is success in men. Irene Frieze[2] has documented what happens when a man or woman succeeds or fails. Success in a man is attributed to ability; failure is attributed to bad luck or circumstances beyond his control. Success in a woman is attributed to good luck and factors beyond her control, whereas failure is considered to be due to lack of ability. Many women internalize these ideas, accepting them as true, and then tend to discount themselves or accept discounting by others. It can be very liberating to become aware of this as sex-role stereotyping and to recognize that assumptions about behavior and values can change. Old messages about sex-appropriate behavior can be crippling.

OTHER PEOPLE
Handling Covert "Nonactionable" Discrimination

Last year at the annual meeting of the American Association for the Advancement of Sciences Meetings (AAAS), my organization (AWIS) organized a symposium on covert discrimination, those unconscious beliefs and behaviors that serve to put down women and minorities. A great deal of information can be found there.[3] There are many types of covert, often unintentional, discrimination, the cumulative effect of which can be debilitating. Women face discounting and condescension, hostility, sex-role stereotyping, sexual innuendos, or direct propositions, invisibility, and the rarer, but equally damaging, spotlighting.[4] All of these behaviors on the part of colleagues or supervisors can erode a woman's self-confidence because they act as false signals about a woman's performance and competence. To combat this, it is first necessary to recognize the forms that covert discrimination can take. It is then useful to determine how we respond to these assaults. Some women defend themselves by denying that such things happen, thus conserving the emotional energy that could otherwise be spent in endless contemplation of the array of daily incidents that serve to devalue women. Others become depressed or hold back their anger and frustration until the incident bursts forth as a major event, possibily leading to the charge of emotional instability.[5]

There are no easy solutions to the problem of how to handle discounting of any sort. It helps to act quickly, to respond calmly in an adult fashion to the insult or assault. This is not always either possible or wise, as leaders of assertive training point out.[6] It is useful to find a champion in a high-status position, either another woman who has power or a man who is a feminist. Through informal interventions by such people, the behavior of your adversaries can often be changed. It is also useful to be sure that the institution in which you work has adequate appeal and grievance procedures for professionals and staff, and in academia, for students. A good model to use for this is the procedure developed at the University of Pennsylvania, see article by Helen C. and Robert E. Davies (pages 200–202).

Support

To combat the frequently aversive messages from society, women need support networks of various sorts. These can be informal or formal ones.

Many people seek help from mental health workers for support and to help sort out their feelings and develop tools for dealing with problems. It is wise to keep in mind that not all mental health workers are feminists. To bolster this point, I would like to cite the study done by Broverman *et al.*[7] in 1970 in which 79 clinically trained psychologists, psychiatrists, and clinical social workers (46 men and 33 women) were asked to define the characteristics they would expect to find in a healthy adult person, a healthy man, and a healthy woman. They were provided with a list of 122 items that offered bipolar options such as not at all aggressive-aggressive, or very subjective-very objective. Both the male and female mental health workers defined the properties of a mentally healthy man differently from those of a mentally healthy woman; and both sexes agree on the features of a healthy person. The traits selected for healthy "adults" were very similar to those assigned to men, suggesting that women are not "people." To quote their discussion: "Acceptance . . . [of these norms] places women in the conflictual position of having to decide whether to exhibit those positive characteristics considered desirable for men and adults, and thus have their 'femininity' questioned, that is, be deviant in terms of being a woman; or to behave in the prescribed feminine manner, accept second-class adult status, and possibly live a lie to boot."[7]

It is also important to note that *both* men and women clinicians agreed on the traits of healthy men and women, showing how effective the socialization process had been during the training of both sexes in their profession. I would interpret this to mean that women clinicians learned to apply male standards to their own practices without questioning them.

Women also need mentors who will help them figure out how their professions and institutions work so that they can use this information to their advantages. Arlene Kaplan Daniels elaborates on this point eloquently (see page 217). Women can also form professional caucuses within their professional societies as a way of increasing the participation of women in the governance of their profession as members of editorial boards of journals, as speakers and chairpersons at meetings, as members of boards of directors and councilors, or as officers of societies. Finally, women can join together in larger umbrella organizations like the Association for Women in Science (AWIS) or the Federation of Organizations for Professional Women in order to work toward goals that will benefit all professional women and all women in the sciences.

Institutions

As Jewel Cobb has said at this Conference, there are filters that remove women from the professions at every level, from the nursery to graduate school and the workplace. The public needs to be educated about the appropriateness of women in scientific, managerial, and administrative roles. This must start very early, before a child's sexual identity is firmly established in its own mind. A child needs to be given options, and the artificial restraints set up by sex-role stereotyping need to be removed. This can be done by a variety of means, by showing women in professional roles on programs like "Sesame Street" or by having such materials in the preschool and kindergarten classrooms. Women can set up a speakers' bureau and visit elementary, junior, and senior high school classrooms.

Women must also become a visible, strong political group capable of putting pressure on legislators at local and national levels. This can be accomplished in a variety of ways. A number of professional organizations, for example, are joining a boycott against states that have failed to ratify the ERA and have agreed not to hold meetings or conferences in those states. Women also need to take steps to make themselves reliable, valuable sources of information for legislators and their aides. One way of doing this is through fellowship and internship programs that bring scientists to Washington for a year as consultants to individual members of Congress. An example of such a program is the AAAS Science Fellow Program.[8] Scientific organizations can also form affiliations with feminists in a broader context: for example, with The National Organization for Women (NOW) or the Women's Equity Action League (WEAL).

It is very important not to let up pressure on the entry points to a profession. Despite affirmative action efforts, we are not necessarily seeing a major influx of women into many scientific disciplines. Some areas are expanding, such as the petroleum industry (as told to us here by Dr. Schwarzer) but others haven't moved at all. Valuable material is now available to help employers find qualified women.[9]

Finally, conferences such as this one are extremely useful. Even if the older hands in the feminist movement have heard some of these statistics and solutions before, many younger women or women who have only recently become feminist may not have. Even if you have heard most of it before, you may make contacts with other women or feminist men that could be very valuable in setting up some of the solutions we have talked about here today. To sum it all up, there *are* things we can do. Go *do* them.

References

1. WOMEN'S LEADERSHIP AND AUTHORITY IN THE HEALTH PROFESSIONS. 1977. Proc. Conf. Univ. California, Santa Cruz, June 19-21. Program for Women in Health Sciences. University of California. San Francisco, Calif.
2. FRIEZE, I. H. 1978. Internal and External Psychological Barriers for Women in Science, *In* Covert Discrimination and Women in the Sciences, J.A. Ramaley, Ed. Westview Press. Boulder, Colo. In press.
3. RAMALEY, J.A. Ed. 1978. Covert Discrimination and Women in the Sciences. Westview Press. Boulder, Colo. In Press.
4. SHAPIRO, E. 1977. Some thoughts on counseling women who perceive themselves to be victims of nonactionable sex discrimination: a survival guide. *In* Women's Leadership and Authority in the Health Professions. Proc. Conference Univ. California, Santa Cruz, June 19-21. Program for Women in Health Sciences. Univ. California, San Francisco, Calif.
5. ROWE, M.P. 1977. The saturns ring phenomenon: micro-inequities and unequal opportunity in the American Economy. *In* Women's Leadership and Authority in the Health Professions. Proc. Conf. Univ. Calif. Santa Cruz, June 19-21. Program for Women in Health Sciences. University of California, San Francisco, Calif.
6. BLOOM, L.Z., K. COBURN & J. PERLMAN. 1975. The New Assertive Woman: 48-49. Dell Publishing. New York, N.Y.
7. BROVERMAN, I.K., D.M. BROVERMAN, F.E. CLARKSON, P.S. ROSENKRANTZ

& S.R. VOGEL. 1970. Sex-role stereotypes and clinical judgments of mental health. J. Consult. Clin. Psychol. **34**:1-7.
8. CONGRESSIONAL SCIENCE FELLOWSHIPS: For information, contact Dr. Richard A. Scribner. Congressional Science Fellow Program. American Association for the Advancement of Science. 1776 Massachusetts Avenue, N.W., Washington, D.C. 20036.
9. FOXLEY, C.H. 1976. Locating, Recruiting, and Employing Women: An Equal Opportunity Approach. Garrett Park Press. Garrett Park, Md.

PART V. Government and Academic Policy

Introduction to Part V

MARIE MULLANEY CASSIDY
George Washington University
Washington, D.C. 20037

WE HAVE BEEN HEARING HERE some rather devastating factual information on the current status of women in the sciences. In virtually all disciplines women scientists are neither being paid nor being promoted in a manner similar to their male cohorts. These observations continue to be made despite increasing enrollment of women in scientific educational programs. A curious anomaly, cited by several of our participants, is that the most prestigious academic institutions are, in fact, not hiring from the pool of women scientists which they themselves produce. Having attested to the competence of these women by awarding them doctorates, they are content to continue past inequitable hiring and promotional practices.

In particular, it appears that the least possible healthy environment for working scientists possessed of XX chromosomes is to be found in academia. This emergent perception is especially abhorrent to women scientists who have chosen or wish to choose the university setting as a place to nurture their own talents and those of others. Since the academy has been the major social institution that has probed underlying societal inequities, proposed solutions in many instances, and buttressed the arguments with much rhetoric, it is even more startling to discover the abysmal lack of progress within educational institutions themselves. Several hypotheses account for the data that have been put forward. These range from the intrinsic conservatism of isolated power structures to the laissez-faire attitudes of a legal jurisdiction system which presumes that the hallowed but ineluctable values of academe will be irreparably damaged by too deep an inquiry into associated practices and policies. It is difficult to believe that the essence of a university and the nature of its contribution to civilization is quite such a fragile flower!

This part deals with several aspects of the relationship between government and academic policy. In this context it is ironic to note that, in America today, an institution which considers its employees to be exempt from the legislation it ordains for others is the United States Congress itself. The dilemma of the female academician in a scientific discipline at this point in time might be epitomized by the canard: love it, leave it, or change it!

The topics chosen by our speakers will reflect their unique attempts to understand the nature of academia and their efforts to broaden and truly humanize the system. Jewel Cobb, from Rutgers University, will discuss the critical but covert filtering mechanisms that operate in the selection of future scientists. It has recently come to be recognized that scientific and technical facts cannot be isolated from their political and social settings. It should therefore follow, in a true Aristotelian sense, that scientific and technical discoveries cannot be separated from the political and social orders which gave them genesis. This is a concept that has been explored in the sciences by Ruth Hubbard of Harvard University, who will share with us her views on the impact of male exclusionary thinking on the very warp and weft of the scientific fabric of knowledge.

Ellen Weaver of San Jose State University in California has been a long-standing member of the faculty and also an administrator. She will discuss her observations of the differences to be expected in leadership style and professional interaction as women assume greater power in the academic milieu. It is a relatively short period of recorded history since dons at Oxford and Cambridge were forbidden to be married. It is still difficult, if not impossible, for a woman to obtain tenure if she decides to allot time to childbearing or child-rearing. In contrast, similar absences on the part of male professors for the purposes of war have traditionally been rewarded in the halls of academe. Diana Marinez from Michigan State University will discuss the conflicts and some innovative approaches to the problems of the professional decade in which the demands of confluent biological and professional creativity can be overwhelming. Our final speaker is James Rutherford of the National Science Foundation, Directorate of Science Education. This is the government agency which has been charged with the responsibility of improving the quantity and quality of women professionals active in science. A series of programs to achieve this goal has been devised which includes high school role-modeling for young women and opportunities for reeducation and reentry of women into scientific fields. James Rutherford will describe the thrust of these and other efforts and the successes recorded to the present time.

Filters for Women in Science

JEWEL PLUMMER COBB
*Dean, Douglass College, Rutgers University
New Brunswick, New Jersey 08903*

IN APRIL, 1977, the National Academy of Sciences, America's most prestigious body of science scholars, announced the election of sixty new members whose contributions to scientific research are outstanding. Only four of these were women. In fact, of the total membership of 1,208 of the National Academy of Sciences, only 28 are women.

Why are so few women elected to this prestigious academy? What are the reasons behind the fact that women, who constitute 52 percent of the population, make up only 10 percent of all scientists and engineers?[1] Women are 20 percent of the scientists but less than one percent of the engineers.

The paucity of women in science and technology points out, as does the minimal representation of minority scientists, a glaring deficiency in the health of America's scientific enterprise.

It is important to discover the reasons for this flaw and to correct it so that a population of women scientists can begin to contribute perspectives different from those of the male-dominated world of science. It is wasteful to neglect bright young female minds which have considerable contributions to make in every scientific field. It takes at least 20 years to produce a Ph.D. or an engineer. What happens to women during those years that prevents their final entry into science and engineering careers? That is the subject of this paper.

I have chosen the analogy of the filter. In the laboratory we recognize that the characteristics of the filtrate passing through a filter are determined by the size of the pores in the filter, and by the concentration and type of particles passing through. The pores of the filters passed through on the way to science careers are smaller for women than they are for men. As the filtrate (females in stages of development from birth to adulthood) is passed through successive filters, the pores become progressively smaller in real life.

We can describe essentially six important filters of science that are present in the life of a young woman scientist. These filters for men are either nonexistent or contain pores of larger size. The size of the pores of the filters are associated with mathematics.

The first filter is socialization in the preschool years. The socialization process begins at birth with pink blankets for female babies. The infant and preschool period is the first filter. Children learn behavior through contiguity. Sex-typed behavior is shaped very early in the home. A female child soon learns to act like her mother, usually through positive reinforcement.[2] She rapidly identifies her own sex. Verbal symbols from mother give very early instructions in sex-typed behavior. The appropriateness of certain sex-linked behavior is readily learned. As a female child enters the preschool period, she learns that dependency and passivity are generally acceptable, as are certain toys specifically designated for her sex. Physical aggression is not a behavior appropriate for female children, but it is applauded for boys. Stereotypes of female passivity for girls or masculine aggressiveness for boys develop not only from body concepts but by observation of highly visible differences in the people they see, both in the home and outside it.[3]

Almost twenty years ago, before the rebirth of the feminist movement, Evelyn Goodenough Pitcher, reported, without comment, on the difference in parental attitudes toward girl and boy children and how two- and three-year-old children conformed to their parents' expectations:[4] girls, the parents indicated, are interested in pretty clothes, domestic habit, families, and babies; boys are interested in bulldozers, trucks, cement mixers, and how things work. Even in the very subtle ways in which parents, particularly fathers, treat infants and young children—touch, tone of voice—girls and boys get different feedback from their parents.[5]

Parents who expect different interests and behaviors from their sons and daughters reinforce these expectations by the kinds of toys and games they purchase for them. Boys receive chemistry sets, erector sets, trucks, games geared to large-muscle development, sports equipment, and the like. Girls receive vanity sets, dolls, play ovens, carpet sweepers, games geared to small-muscle development, bead stringing and sewing cards.[6]

The second filter to science is the elementary school experience and its socialization effects. Mathematics, for example, is typed by our society as a "male" subject. Elementary school teachers, the majority of whom are women, are themselves rarely comfortable with math.[7] Between the initial, serious exposure to mathematics and the expectation of female behavior lie six years of classroom conditioning that reinforces attitudes at home or elsewhere. The female child tends to identify with like-sex figures[8] . . . including the female teacher who most typically, but not always, expresses math anxiety at some point. Such exposure shapes the female student's response and reinforces the self-image of passivity and dependency. Physically, aggressive behavior in boys is seen to be rewarded in our culture, as is female nonaggressive, doll-like behavior.[9] Feminine values develop out of the need to value things that are consistent with or like the self.[10]

Liking and excelling in numbers in grade school is not a performance pattern that has high priority for female children. Elizabeth Fennema and Julia Sherman, in a study of the effects of sexual stereotyping on attitudes toward mathematics, conclude that girls eventually develop the idea that a female head is not much good for figures.[11] In another study by Paul Torrance of fourth, fifth, and sixth graders showed girls unwilling to approach scientific toys, protesting that they were "not supposed to know anything about things like that."[12] Although there are no measurable differences between the sexes in the early years as far as mathematical skills are concerned, after elementary school, boys begin to excel girls. By the time they take the Scholastic Aptitude Tests in high school, boys score an average of 50 points higher than girls on the mathematical portion of the exam.[13] This fact is distressing but not altogether surprising. As girls and boys proceed through school, they are subject to pressures to conform to societal expectations of sex-appropriate behavior and interests. For, after all, society's institutions reflect the values of the society in which they operate. Most educators are dedicated people, people who believe that education should provide all students with the environment and skills necessary for the realization of their full potential. At the same time, however, educators perpetuate, consciously and unconsciously, their own attitudes with regard to sex-role socialization.

In a study by John Ernest of the Mathematics Department of The University of California at Santa Barbara,[14] a sample of elementary school teachers were questioned about their attitudes toward the teaching of mathematics. Although all the teachers questioned said they enjoyed teaching mathematics better than other subjects, 41 percent felt that boys did better in mathematics and none of the respondents felt girls did better. That teachers cling to this sex-stereotype is astonishing in light of the fact that no statistically significant sex differences in mathematical performance can be found in the testing of elementary school children.

The third filter is the junior high school experience. Female students themselves develop lower opinions of their abilities during these years. As girls and boys progress through school, their opinions of boys grow increasingly more positive and their opinions of girls increasingly more negative. Girls are more likely than boys to attribute poor performance on math tests to their own personal characteristics and habits.[15] They are less likely than male peers to be optimistic about grades they will receive.[16] Girls often suffer a loss of occupational potential. Girls' visions of occupations open to them are likely to be limited to four: teacher, nurse, secretary, or mother. Boys of the same age respond with a surprising range of things they can do when they grow up.

The loss of academic potential with particular regard to the fields of science and engineering has its basis in the differences in mathematical education offered. The study by John Ernest of USCB reveals the extent to which girls, directly and indirectly, are educated out of the math curriculum.[17] Examining elementary school and high school students' attitudes about arithmetic and mathematics, he found that preference for math as a favorite subject in the lower grades was identical for girls and boys; however, its popularity declined for both sexes in high school. Nevertheless, when mathematics becomes optional in high school, far fewer girls take it, it was discovered. Ernest concludes that boys take more math than girls because, like it or not, they are aware that such courses are necessary prerequisites to the kinds of future occupations—in medicine, technology, or science—that they envision for themselves.

Studies of differences in mathematical ability have yielded contradictory results, some showing no differences, some showing that boys do better, and some showing that girls do better. What *is* clear is that there is no consensus as to what constitutes mathematical ability. For some researchers it has meant computational proficiency, for others, geometric and algebraic aptitude, and for still others, some specific intellectual function. Boys seem to do better overall, but only slightly better, it should be pointed out, in certain spatial visualization tasks such as field independence. Field independence is the ability to perceptually separate items from their backgrounds, to overcome the influence of embedding contexts. Whether this is genetic or conditioned is not known, but it seems to me that erector sets and other construction-type toys give children practice in developing field independence and, as we've noted earlier, it is boys, not girls, for whom those kinds of toys are bought.

This fourth and most critical filter, the high school years, results in a decline of interest in mathematics and a decline, therefore, in enrollment in mathematic courses. Three or four years of high school mathematics are required in most colleges for a major in science. College-level mathematics is a prerequisite for math, science, and engineering majors. Women students are not encouraged by family and society to "stick it out" with mathematics; men are, because certain careers they want will require mathematics backgrounds for college courses. In high school, both boys and girls show some clear evidence of sex-stereotyped attitudes regarding mathematics: According to the Ernest study,[18] 45 percent of fifth-grade students go to their mothers for help with math homework, 18 percent consult their fathers. By high school the picture is reversed, with 50 percent of both boys and girls requesting help from their fathers and 12 percent requesting help from their mothers. Clearly, by high school, both boys and girls have decided that math is a male subject.

Inadequate secondary school math preparation is the chief deterrent for women who might otherwise choose to major in one of the sciences in college, and, for that matter, in many other subjects judging from a study done by sociologist Lucy Sells, at Berkeley.[19] In a systematic sample of freshmen admitted to Berkeley in the fall of 1972, 57 percent of the male students had taken four full years of mathematics, including the trigonometry/solid geometry sequence, compared with 8 percent of the female students. The four-year mathematics sequence is required for admission to Mathematics IA, which in turn is required for majoring in every field at Berkeley except the traditionally female fields of humanities, social sciences, librarianship, social welfare, and education.

Teachers, guidance counselors, as well as parents, must reevaluate their own attitudes and prejudices about math being a "male" subject in order to more positively influence girl students. This kind of change is not likely to occur in the short run.

The fifth filter, college, is a critical period for women. It is here that pressures from the external campus and peer pressures, can be even greater than in high school. There is a lack of encouragement for most college girls who have the ability and interest to major in science. This lack of encouragement for a science career on the part of an adviser in the early college years is partly due to a realization that the employment opportunities open to woman scientists are more restricted than those open to men. The disappointing female enrollment in college mathematic courses is exacerbated by the higher attrition rate for females. As the level of difficulty increases and more time and effort is invested in course preparation, it seems reasonable to assume that college women, like their grade school sisters, are likely to conclude that a poor grade is due to a lack of math ability rather than to the lack of effort, and, accordingly, may drop the course. And so as women proceed through life and through our educational systems, the filters get finer and finer, until few manage to move through them at all.

Academic advisers play a large role in determining how many women will continue to maintain an interest in science in the high school years. Unfortunately, these advisers often labor under misconceptions regarding the nature of work in scientific fields, believing it to be more demanding of time and commitment than jobs in other fields. Such ideas, however, fail to take into account the changes that have occurred in scientific fields. Doctors, for example, may work fewer than five days a week and for relatively short hours each day, making medicine an ideal vocation to combine with the tasks of mother and homemaker. Women in science professions consistently earn less than men.[20] This may also contribute to the tendency on the part of the advisers to steer women away from careers in science.

Given the real discouragement directed at potential female science majors and the dedication and extraordinary singleness of purpose necessary for a woman to pursue a science career, such careers are seen as impossible for all but a few women. A female MIT student majoring in aeronautical engineering recounted that she had to fight all her life to retain her interest in aeronautics; her friends thought she was crazy, her mother told her she'd never find a husband, and her teachers warned her she'd never find a job. How many men would be aeronautical engineers in the face of such contrary pressure?

Colleges, also, must take into account that women generally make their career decisions later than men, and therefore must be counseled to keep as many options open as possible. Although the same number of girls and boys graduate from high school, fewer girls enroll in four-year colleges. When they do and major in the sciences, they are exceptional. Many female freshmen have eliminated science as an option because of math anxiety (filter-block) and earlier inadequate prerequisite math preparation. Lack of female professors as role-models, especially as scientists, is clearly a problem in the majority of American colleges and universities. The sciences and engineering are considered male territories, and as such do not present congenial environments for female students who are always in the minority except at women's colleges. Even in the latter, there are usually more male professors in the chemistry and physics departments.

The decision to be a science major in college requires strong motivation and independence,[21] characteristics expected and developed in precollege years in males. Because of this, the college filter sorts out as survivors only the best and the strongest female students. It appears that this is valid, and it is evident in a study of female engineering students at Cornell.[22] These students demonstrated a very strong attraction to academic achievement, and a very strong record of successful achievement in secondary school.

The sixth filter is graduate school. Even though, according to the data from the National Center for Education Statistics, the National Science Foundation, and the Census Bureau, the number of women earning science doctorates increased by 59 percent between 1970-71 and 1974-75, women still lag far behind men in terms of the total number granted. In the fall of 1975, half of the first-year graduate students were women. By the end of the second year only a third were women. The pressures to drop out are enormous. For those who remain, however, the time for completion is shorter for women than for men. The female graduate student is seldom encouraged or sponsored by a graduate faculty member to begin research and to become part of a research laboratory team early on. In the past, women were not generally expected to complete the doctorate and enter a full-time research career. Hence, in a period of scarce research funds, time and effort is more often invested in the male student, who, it is calculated, will not "marry and leave science." The personal/tutorial/apprenticeship system of advanced science education takes place in a subjective male/male environment. Therefore, high attrition rates by women in graduate science programs are quite understandable.

The senior science researcher or mentor plays a pivotal role in the postdoctorate placement of a budding scientist. Encouragement is personal, subjective, and highly variable. Professor X may see women postdoctorates as scientists permanently in the marketplace and worthy of an endorsement to critical colleagues. Others, as documented from individual case histories, give little or no help to women in first-entry career placement because they simply don't believe women should, or will, remain permanently in the laboratory rather than at home. A 1973 survey by the National Research Council showed that 2.6 percent of women with science doctorates received between 1960 and 1969 were still working in postdoctorate positions at the time of the survey, while only 0.9 percent of the men were in the same position. Clearly, then, the sixth filter is the senior scientist/adviser who controls the development of the dissertation, its ultimate acceptance and publication; controls referrals, postdoctorate job placement, and career development.

The fully mature woman scientist emerges as a productive human being capable of taking her place at the laboratory research bench in creative work. Because of the special filtering system for women in science, she is, as a type, likely to be a superior scholar, independent and tenacious, and somewhat hardened by her experiences on her way through "the system." However, she will still not move as easily as her male peers to tenured positions at top universities where the big science action takes place; nor will she find government jobs as easily, and when she does find such jobs she will most probably receive lower pay than her male colleagues.[23] Women scientists are represented out of proportion to their total numbers in teaching positions at two-year and four-year nonresearch-oriented institutions, and they are completely underrepresented in the high-paying jobs in industry.[24]

We need to formulate new activities to change attitudes of the intra- and extra-campus population to understand the importance of eliminating certain female behavior patterns, most importantly, math anxiety. This affliction among elementary school and high school teachers, college students, and young mothers is widespread. Fundamental to encouraging more women to consider careers in the sciences is the eradication of the notion that proficiency in mathematics is a gender-linked characteristic.

The first step is to call attention to the sex-role biases of parents of young children. Then we must sensitize teachers in junior and senior high schools to the need for the special supports girls need to foster and sustain an interest in science. At the college level, programs in remediation and special counseling are essential to retain the small, but increasing, numbers of girls who have made it through the first several filters but remain especially prone to drop out when the going gets rough. If we take steps now, the next decade should see a change in the depressing underrepresentation of women in the community of science and technology.

To deal with one of the early filters excluding girls from the sciences it has been suggested that a series of films should be made and distributed to be viewed by girls from grades 9-11. Films describing positive career options for women in science could be used as a jumping-off point for discussion and follow-up in conjunction with ancillary materials which are, also, available. An excellent film on women in engineering, done at Massachusetts Institute of Technology, was partially funded by the National Science Foundation. Additionally, there should be a national program for high school girls with demonstrated aptitude and interest in math and science. Early orientation and recruitment would tag these girls before college and carry them into college as special science designates. Such an honor would help to overcome the negative social impact that tends to downgrade the very bright female student at the critical dating age. Girls' organizations such as YWCAs and the Girl Scouts should be encouraged to develop and promote programs for girls in science. For example, such programs might involve the awarding of merit badges for projects in electrical engineering and study projects in various scientific fields.

Neena B. Schwartz has made a suggestion to stimulate undergraduate college women in science. Teams consisting of prominent women scientists and senior women graduate students should be sent to spend 48 hours with beginning women graduate and undergraduate students in science departments. This visit would include informal discussions, scientific seminars, and opportunities for informal discussions in which successful women scientists could explain personally how they reached points of success in scientific careers.

To assist women students at the graduate level, it has been suggested that there be established a data bank of responses of women graduate students are asked to record what happens in the science department in the early professional socialization. The material, gathered in the form of a questionnaire, would be extremely valuable. It has also been suggested that there be developed and funded a series of short or year-long refresher courses, research internships, and/or combinations of these for women scientists who want to reenter their professional fields. The model of the NSF Summer Institute could be used, except that the students would be the reentry women. This last suggestion was made by Lili Hornig.

Another suggestion is that there be developed a special subset of graduate fellowships for women with emphasis on the first year of study in science areas where women are underrepresented. This first-year support often allows excellent women students without the necessary background, such as undergraduate majors in a tangential field, to compete successfully for a teaching or research assistantship the next year. This suggestion was offered by Vera Kistiakowsky. These fellowships would, in general, permit the women to attend higher quality schools where they might not have been successful in the competition for teaching assistantships and research assistantships, therefore providing a psychological boost. There might also be fellowships to cover the first two graduate years, but before that period is over the students should join a research group and hence be more likely to get research support. Building a mentor relationship into this program, the availability of an individual at the university with whom the student could discuss her progress and who would look out for her would probably increase the percentages of successful degree completion by women.

A number of suggestions have also been made with regard to women at teaching levels in the science disciplines. Patricia Albjerg Graham has suggested a two-year fellowship for the nontenured woman science professor in a four-year undergraduate college to facilitate research that will enhance her opportunity for tenure. This fellowship might allow her to work with a research team full time or to complete the writing of a science book. Such a fellowship at the nontenured level can be justified as "remedial" until women are at as significant a portion of senior tenured faculty at major institutions as they are of the Ph.D. pool, small though this group is. Mildred S. Dresselhaus has suggested the adoption of a faculty-development program to increase the faculty ranks in engineering at the major universities. Women with the potential to contribute in this area would be provided with partial support for a three-year period at top-ranked institutions where they would be able to acquire the kind of background that would be of value in moving ahead rapidly in their professions. The other partial support should be provided by the institutions as proof of commitment. Some preference should be given to institutions where the women grantees will have access to mentors who can be useful in support roles and in providing training in the nontechnical issues which are so important for the success of women professionals. In most cases, the grantee will move on to a permanent position elsewhere, and, in this way, can contribute in a supportive capacity to the training of another crop of woman professionals.

A number of other suggestions are directed at the specific difficulties that women encounter in entering job markets. Part-time support has been suggested for junior faculty women. This would not increase the overall numbers of women in the field but would certainly increase the numbers who are upwardly mobile. This sort of program could actually be a four-faceted one: (1) Offering seed money to start research programs; (2) permitting young mothers to remain active in research by paying part of their salary and thus reducing their teaching commitments or permitting them to work part time; (3) permitting women in nonresearch-oriented institutions the released time and financial support to set up programs of their own or to work with groups in other institutions; (4) offering re-entry support to women who have temporarily withdrawn from professional life. It has also been suggested that the NSF, for example, could also establish a special category of grants to individuals who move with their families. Such persons are usually women and need time to establish an institutional affiliation. This grant would be conditional on their being able to make a suitable institutional connection, if they have their own money because of the grant. Applications in this category, of course, would be prescreened under the usual procedures and then subjected to the existing review-processing. The reviewer would also receive a statement of the personal circumstances that may make this kind of application necessary. This suggestion was made by Lili Hornig.

A further recommendation was to fund a program that would conduct extensive training programs in math for volunteer mothers in elementary schools. This program could also send women who are math professionals into the schools to work an hour or two a week with students, especially with students who show an aptitude for arithmetic. This suggestion was made by Mary Gray, Department of Mathematics, Statistics, and Computer Science, The American University, Washington, D.C.

A career development award specifically aimed at young Ph.D. women has also been suggested. Such an award would give full salary and prestige, and give a university a free slot for five years. This suggestion follows the NIH model.

The need for a full spectrum of programs directed at increasing the proportion of women in science careers is painfully obvious. The time for putting such programs into action is long past due. The actions that must be taken range from the subtle socialization processes to specific programs for funding women in scientific research. It is only through such wholesale effort that we can begin to eliminate the system of filters that operate to keep women out of careers in science.

REFERENCES

1. U.S. SCIENTISTS AND ENGINEERS. 1974. 76-329. The National Science Foundation. Washington, D.C.
2. MACCOBY E.E. & C.N. JACKLIN. 1974. The Psychology of Sex Differences (8). Stanford University Press. Stanford, Calif.
3. MACCOBY E.E. & C.N. JACKLIN. 1974. The Psychology of Sex Differences (9). Stanford University Press. Stanford, Calif.
4. PITCHER, E.G. 1963. Male and female: excerpts from children's stories: an analysis of fantasy. Atlantic 211:87-91.
5. MACCOBY E.E. & C.N. JACKLIN. 1974. The Psychology of Sex Differences 309-312. Stanford University Press. Stanford, Calif.
6. MACCOBY E.E. & C.N. JACKLIN. 1974. The Psychology of Sex Differences 278-279. Stanford University Press. Stanford, Calif.
7. ERNEST J. 1976. Mathematics and Sex: 8. Mathematics Department. University of California at Santa Barbara.
8. MACCOBY E.E. & C.N. JACKLIN. 1974. The Psychology of Sex Differences (8). Stanford University Press. Stanford, Calif.
9. MACCOBY E.E. & C.N. JACKLIN. 1974. The Psychology of Sex Differences (7). Stanford University Press. Stanford, Calif.
10. MACCOBY E.E. & C.N. JACKLIN. 1974. The Psychology of Sex Differences (150). Stanford University Press. Stanford, Calif.
11. FENNEMA, E. & J.A. SHERMAN. 1977. Sexual stereotyping and mathematics learning. The Arithmetic Teacher 24:369-372.
12. TORRANCE, E.P. 1960. Changing reactions of preadolescent girls to tasks requiring creature scientific thinking during a thirteen-month period. New Educational Ideas. Proceedings of the Third Minnesota Conference on Gifted Children.
13. ROSSI, A.S. 1965. Barriers to the Career Choice of Engineering, Medicine or Science Among American Women. *In* Women and the Scientific Professions: The M.I.T. Symposium on American Women in Science and Engineering. J.A. Mattfield & C.G. Van Aken, Eds. The M.I.T. Press, Cambridge, Mass.
14. ERNEST, J. 1976. Mathematics and Sex: 6. Mathematics Department. University of California at Santa Barbara.
15. ERNEST, J. 1976. Mathematics and Sex: 6. Mathematics Department. University of California at Santa Barbara.
16. MACCOBY E.E. & C.N. JACKLIN. 1974. The Psychology of Sex Differences (154). Stanford University Press. Stanford, Calif.

17. ERNEST J. 1976. Mathematics and Sex: 4. Mathematics Department. University of California at Santa Barbara.
18. ERNEST J. 1976. Mathematics and Sex: 4. Mathematics Department. University of California at Santa Barbara.
19. SELLS, L. 1973. High School Mathematics as the Critical Filter in the Job Market. Developing Opportunities for Minorities in Graduate Education. *In* Proceedings of the Conference on Minority Graduate Education. University of California Press. Berkeley, Calif.
20. ROSSI, A.S. 1965. Barriers to the Career Choice of Engineering, Medicine or Science Among American Women. *In* Women and the Scientific Professions: The M.I.T. Symposium on American Women in Science and Engineering. J.A. Mattfield & C.G. Van Aken, Eds. The M.I.T. Press, Cambridge, Mass. 67.
21. ROSSI, A.S. 1965. Barriers to the Career Choice of Engineering, Medicine or Science Among American Women. *In* Women and the Scientific Professions: The M.I.T. Symposium on American Women in Science and Engineering. J.A. Mattfield & C.G. Van Aken, Eds. The M.I.T. Press, Cambridge, Mass. 113.
22. GARDNER, R. E. 1975. Decision Making by Female Undergraduates in Engineering: Patterns, Problems, and Programs. *In* Conference Proceedings of 1975 Conference: Women in Engineering-Beyond Recruitment.
23. ROSSI, A.S. 1965. Barriers to the Career Choice of Engineering, Medicine or Science Among American Women. *In* Women and the Scientific Professions: The M.I.T. Symposium on American Women in Science and Engineering. J.A. Mattfield & C.G. Van Aken, Eds. The M.I.T. Press, Cambridge, Mass. 63-67.
24. FIELDS, C. M. 1977. Women in science; breaking the barriers. The Chronicle of Higher Education: 7.

Feminism in Academia:
Its Problematic and Problems

RUTH HUBBARD
Biological Laboratories
Harvard University
Cambridge, Massachusetts 02138

LOOKING AT MY TITLE—Feminism in Academia—many of you must feel, as I do, that it is a self-contradiction. The universities and their academic tradition are archetypal male institutions, if anything even more male than their clerical ancestors. (After all, nuns and abbesses held a great deal more power than female academics do to this day.) Even Mary Beard—who was a revisionist in her interpretation of women's roles in shaping Western history and culture, since she believed that women's parts in both were much more significant than is usually credited by traditional male historians or by their feminist critics—[1] when she came to write about the academic curriculum, called it "basically a sex education—masculine in design and spirit." And she continued: "Its tissue consists of threads instinctively selected from men's activities . . . woven together according to a pattern of male prowess and power as conceived in the mind of man. If the woman's culture comes into this pattern in any way, it is only as a blurring of the major concept."[2]

Feminists and perhaps also increasing numbers of traditional scholars are aware of the partial nature of standard scholarship in literature, history, anthropology, sociology and psychology, partial because of its limited perspective. However, the realization that our view of ourselves as biological and social *organisms* is also an exercise in sex education comes as a shock to many people, and particularly to natural scientists. Yet it is crucial that we recognize that our view of the human organism as it has evolved and as it now exists and walks and talks and reproduces is a male view in which the female is a variant on "mankind's" basic plan.

One reason why this is so is that the outlines of our biological self-concept were sketched about a hundred years ago. Now, the nineteenth century is fascinating in many ways, and one of them is that it fathered the social and natural scientists or philosophers—call them what you will—who produced much of our present political and scientific ideologies. With regard to Feminism in Academia, the point is that the revolutionary doctrines of Liberty, Equality, and *Fraternity* and of the Rights of *Man* were not intended to apply equally to women. (The notion that "man" is a generic term is the result of a later need for male self-justification.) Indeed, that is what aroused Mary Wollstonecraft to write a *Vindication of the Rights of Woman* (1792). Nor, indeed, were these doctrines meant to equalize or level the developing class structure of the growing industrial capitalism that had spawned these movements for equality.

Much of the social and scientific thinking of the late eighteenth and the nineteenth centuries, starting with Malthus, therefore had to go into explaining why and how women, poor people, and non-Europeans (and by "Europeans" I mean, of course, also the immigrants who settled the American continent)—indeed, all the disenfranchised or, perhaps better, unenfranchised—were by nature unfit to profit from the new opportunities offered by the bourgeois revolutions and their peaceful correlates in the British Isles. In fact, one of the socially significant accomplishments of nineteenth century science was to replace the waning ideological power of the church by bolstering, replacing, or rephrasing God's Laws by Laws of Nature.

Let me not suggest for a moment that the scholars and scientists conspired to defraud the public. I am saying something more interesting: Namely, that the fact that these scholars and scientists were male and almost exclusively scions of the ruling classes led them to interpret the world so as to explain with minimal risk to their positions in society why they and their like were privy to education and power, whereas diverse other kinds of people were not.* A book such as Francis Galton's *Hereditary Genius* is only a blatant example of a subtler and more pervasive ideology. Furthermore, since their power was under attack from the "shrill" voices of feminists and their male supporters, such as John Stuart Mill, and since traditional ideological means for stilling such protests were being eroded by the egalitarian spirit of the age, it is not sur-

---

*Needless to say, severe limitations are imposed not only by sex, but by the class and racial biases that arise from the fact that scholars have largely been upper-middle and upper-class, and white, as well as male. The argument I present here therefore must be broadened before it can be taken as a comprehensive critique of the standard textbook description of the world.

prising that Victorian gentlemen like Darwin, Spencer, Huxley, or Galton should have come up with ways of interpreting biological and social relationships that would not necessitate a drastic reduction in their accustomed powers and privileges.

Nineteenth century scientists "proved" the inferior size and capacities of women's brains (as well as of those of "natives"), but this kind of shoddy research was relatively easy to dismiss. More effective were the extensive treatises, replete with case histories, that "documented" the drain that menstruation and the maturation of the female reproductive system was said to put on women's biology and, more importantly, the stress that would fall on these vital capacities if women's intellects were taxed by education. Scholars and their medical colleagues argued vehemently and extensively that women's uteruses would wither and the race die out if girls were educated like their brothers. One of the most widely read books of this sort was Edward H. Clarke's *Sex in Education*, published in 1873, which went through seventeen editions in the next thirteen years. Clarke, a former professor at Harvard Medical School and a Fellow of the American Academy of Arts and Sciences, details the histories of many girls whose health, he assures us, was severely damaged by education, and then conservatively summarizes his position:

> (I)t is not asserted here, that improper methods of study and a disregard of the reproductive apparatus and its function, during the educational life of girls, are the *sole* cause of female diseases; neither is it asserted that *all* the female graduates of our schools and colleges are pathological specimens. But it is asserted that the number of these graduates who have been permanently disabled to a greater or less degree, or fatally injured, by these causes, is such as to excite the *gravest alarm* . . .[3] (original emphasis)

And the warning was worded strongly enough to worry those who would educate women. "(W)e did not know when we began whether women's health could stand the strains of education," wrote M. Carey Thomas, first president of Bryn Mawr College. "We were haunted in those days by the clanging chains of that gloomy little specter, Dr. Edward H. Clarke's *Sex in Education*.[4A]

Another physician-scientist, blending medical and Darwinian evolutionary views, derived from biology the Victorian model of the appropriate relationship between the sexes. He concludes:

> . . . The female organism has always been merely the vehicle for the maturation of the ovum, and for the reception of the fertilizing influence of the

male; being, in fact, what we may call the passive factor in the reproductive act. . .

For the male, on the contrary, a constant tendency to aggression is necessary that he may be in readyness at the time required. Further, the struggle for the survival of the fittest has constantly been carried out in its chiefest severity amongst the males of all animals, and only partially amongst the females, so that it has come to be that the physically fittest has necessarily been also the sexually most powerful. *It ought to be, therefore, no matter of surprise that in the human race the sexual instinct is very powerful in man, and comparatively weak in woman*[5] [my emphasis].

A pointedly explicit warning was sounded in an address to his fellow-members by a Dr. Withers Moore, president of the British Medical Association, who proclaimed that allowing women access to higher education "will hinder those who would have been the best mothers from being mothers at all, or, if it does not hinder them, more or less it will spoil them, and no training *will enable themselves to do what their sons might have done"* [my emphasis]. Citing Herbert Spencer to confirm that mental labor produces infertility he continues, "Unsexed it might be wrong to call her, but she will be more or less sexless." (Note the scientific restraint of all these quotes, full of "more or less"es and other weakening qualifiers.) He continues: "And the human race will have lost those who should have been her sons. Bacon, for want of a mother, will not be born . . . (W)omen are made and meant to be, not men, but mothers of men . . ."

As though this were not enough, the account of this speech ends:

Dr. N.G. Davis (Chicago) in proposing a vote of thanks to the President for his able and interesting address, said that he cordially sympathized with its sentiments. There could be no room for doubt as to the truth of the statement it contained, and in America they had abundant evidence of it; *when the laws of nature are set at defiance* a fatal blow is struck at the welfare of the race.[6] (my emphasis)

Don't think that I am drawing my examples from the last century because male bias has ceased to govern what we learn and "know." Quite the contrary. I and others have written similar analyses of contemporary biology and medicine.† The reason for citing examples from the nine-

---

†For example, see *Women Look at Biology Looking at Women: A Collection of Feminist Critiques*, Ref. 4A. This collection contains articles on various topics as well as an extensive bibliography.

teenth century is that many of the roots of our present-day biological self-concepts lie in that period. Also, the ideological bias is more obvious, since we no longer share precisely the same ideology, or at least not in the same form.

And don't misunderstand me: I am not reciting a litany of disadvantage and self-pity. Quite the contrary, I want you to realize that not only our history and psychology are male constructs, but that our biology also was created not by God the Father, but by His scientific and medical sons. When they came to study woman's biology and noted quite accurately that there are ways in which it differs from their own, they interpreted these so as to disqualify us on *scientific* grounds from participation in their world. But more than that, women's physiology thereby came to be judged as abnormal, and our life cycle was classified into five debilities: menstruation, pregnancy, childbirth, lactation, and menopause; to which more recently has been added a sixth: fecundity. Two medical specialties, obstetrics and gynecology, were constituted, and in the name of cures for our "diseases" came a series of assaults on women's normal physiology that began with the inventions of medicalized childbirth and gynecological surgery (in a time when surgery almost inevitably induced infection), and led in our own day to the wide-spread hormonal interventions in fecundity, pregnancy, childbirth, lactation, and menopause.

What I am saying, then, is that feminists in academia must have as our program nothing less than the reexamination and reevaluation of everything we have been taught about ourselves and the world. Recently at a conference on the future I heard Wilma Scott Heide, former President of the National Organization for Women, say "All knowledge is suspect," and quite rightly, too. This statement is not antiintellectual, but the very opposite. It simply is the consequence of understanding that most of what we "know" has been certified by a male power elite who, of course, defined female experience as trivial and marginal to the mainstream of human thought and action. We need to pick up each piece of knowledge and look it over carefully and, equally important, look carefully at how it relates to all the other pieces and to the whole picture. Nor need we take it for granted that it is right or needful to divide up knowledge into the traditional slices by using the standard procedures that create fragments of expertise that do not enrich us, but in fact *decrease* our understanding and autonomy.

The agenda, the problematic, for feminists therefore is vast. Among other things, it requires us to reevaluate the divisions of our daily lives into productive versus reproductive labor, into public versus private spheres, into work versus leisure time: divisions that make little or no sense in the lives of most women, in the lives of most people. Further, we must inquire into how the knowledge we generate is communicated, into who has access to it and who makes decisions regarding its use.

I think that all these questions are part of our agenda. They are some of the questions that are usually deemed irrelevant by traditional patriarchal research, and I would suggest, precisely because their answers direct attention to the unequal distributions of power and privilege that underlie the scholarly/academic establishment as much as the business/entrepreneurial one.

Let me move on and talk about our problems. I don't know whether it is because women's lives are punctuated by obvious physiological transitions that make individual variations and experiential varieties obvious, or because we have traditionally lived within relationships that unfold organically, or perhaps for other reasons, but I have no doubt that academic life, and its artificial rites of passage between hierarchically arranged positions that must occur in proper sequence and at appointed times, are particularly offensive to women, though of course they are uncongenial to everyone.

It is important to understand that during the past hundred years scholarly labor has moved away from the feudal model and has become alienated, like the rest of work under industrial capitalism.‡ This means that the most valued rewards of one's achievements lie not in the intellectual and aesthetic satisfactions one derives from them, but in the cash and power and prestige they bring. The fact that scholarly work has been turned into wage labor means that it cannot be guided by an internal rhythm and dynamic based on curiosity, insight, perhaps even inspiration. It must produce marketable results. This, in turn, means that the questions that are asked must be readily and reliably answerable, hence narrow in their focus and definition.

Moreover, the capitalist mode of production in the academy is particularly inconvenient to women's lives because it generates maximum stresses at the time when, if we choose to have children, our reproductive lives also are most demanding: during the decade from, say, 25 to 35.

‡I am using the term *alienation* in the Marxist, economic sense, not in the popular, psychological one. With reference to labor it means simply that you work not to have the *products* of your labor, but for the cash you can acquire from *selling* your labor.

Clearly some of the problems that I am outlining arise for all academics who come to scholarly and scientific work with the illusion that their productivity will be allowed to unfold organically and unencumbered by market pressures. But the difficulties are more serious for many women because of the synchrony of market demands with the demands of our reproductive lives which, even in this society, are still lived in precapitalist terms to the extent that they depend on unpredictabilities of personal relationships and body rhythms. I suggest that these are among the stresses that led feminists like Shulamith Firestone to ask for the transformation of reproduction into a technology that makes it, too, alienable, and hence more consonant with our workaday lives.§

What I am saying, then, is that the practical problems of women in academia, feminists or not, are similar to men's problems in kind, but exaggerated because of the dissonances between production and reproduction.¶

So much for the practical contradictions. But there are also the theoretical ones I referred to before, which derive from the fact that the content of scholarship is a man's eye view and that makes it necessary for us to reexamine and reevaluate everything we know and believe in order to stop it from being "sex education."

The obvious problem here is that power over our jobs and over their definition rests firmly in the hands of men who feel threatened even by women who conform to the traditional patriarchal definitions of what is real and true. After all, as Virginia Woolf says, men "had thought that nature had meant women to be wives, mothers, housemaids, parlormaids and cooks. Suddenly [they] discover that nature . . . had made them also doctors, civil servants, meteorologists, dental surgeons, librarians, . . . and so on."[7]

The disaster is compounded when it comes to feminists, whose

---

§My thinking is this section has been influenced by two essays in the recently published collection edited by Hilary and Steven Rose. 1976. The Political Economy of Science. Macmillan, Ltd. London. They are: On the class character of science and scientists (59-71) by Andre Gorz, and Women's liberation: reproduction and the technological fix (142-160) by Hilary Rose and Jalna Hanmer.

¶Of course, this situation can be improved by good provisions for socialized child care and by egalitarian living arrangements in which domestic responsibilities are shared between partners. By not talking about these I don't want to imply that they are not laudable goals; merely that I don't know any academic woman who can allow the day-by-day care of her chldren—should she have them—to be as secondary a concern as can most men, while still feeling justifiably confident that they are well cared for physically and psychologically.

research questions and results may transgress boundaries of intellectual propriety or may threaten established power relationships. Again, quoting Virginia Woolf, it is not pleasant for a man who "has been out all day in the city earning his living, and he comes home at night expecting repose and comfort to find that his servants—the women servants—have taken possession of the house." It is even worse if they have started to put out the rugs and rearrange the furniture according to their own requirements and needs.

In summary then, for us feminists in academia the problematic is exciting and challenging; the problems are difficult and threaten to get worse as the market for scholars shrinks, a circumstance that always favors orthodoxy. I have no solutions other than to urge that we continue to foster networks that give us the courage and determination to continue to look hard, see clearly, and report honestly. And that is one of the important things a conference like this can help us do.

References

1. Beard, M.R. 1946. Woman as Force in History. Macmillan Company. New York, N.Y.
2. Lane, A.J. Ed. 1977. Mary Ritter Beard: A Sourcebook: 206–207. Schocken Books. New York, N.Y.
3. Clarke, E.H. 1874. Sex in Education; or, A Fair Chance for Girls: 117. James R. Osgood and Co. Boston, Mass.
4. Thomas, M.C. 1908. Present Tendencies in Women's College and University Education. Educ. Rev. 25:68.
4A. Walsh, M.R. 1979. In The Quirls of a Woman's Brain. R. Hubbard, M.S. Henifin and B. Fried, Eds. Women Look at Biology Looking at Women: A Collection of Feminist Critiques. Schenkman Publishing Co., Cambridge, Mass.
5. Austin, G.L. 1883. Perils of American Women, or, a Doctor's Talk with Maiden, Wife, and Mother. Lee and Shepard. Boston, Mass. In Root of Bitterness. 1972. Nancy F. Cott. Ed.: 298. E.P. Dutton and Co. New York, N.Y.
6. The Lancet. Aug. 14, 1886: 314–315.
7. Woolf, V. 1977. Speech of January 21, 1931. In The Pargiters. M.A. Leaska, Ed.:27–34. Harcourt Brace Jovanovich. New York, N.Y.

Implications of Giving Women a Greater Share of Academic Decision-Making

ELLEN C. WEAVER

Department of Biological Sciences
Executive Vice President, San Jose State University
San Jose, California 95192

WHAT are the implications? Will there be more women in academic positions where they can have some influence on the course of their institutions? Why should the universities and colleges be interested in women as administrators? Aren't they interested solely in quality, and isn't quality independent of gender? Do women administrators have anything special to offer to the institution, to the students, or to faculty or staff by virtue of being female? Are women being deprived because there are so few of them in the top positions, and isn't this perhaps not so much a consequence of prejudice but rather the way the women themselves want things? Do women administrators have any influence on the curriculum? Are women capable of making the hard decisions on budgets and personnel? Do women work as hard as men? Are their careers in administration as important to them? Is leadership a proper role for women? Where does power lie in the university, and can women utilize this power for the good of the institution?

These are some of the questions that occurred to me when I was asked to speak on this topic. I am a scientist by profession, a plant physiologist who is fascinated by the intricacies of the biophysics of light absorption and utilization in the process of photosynthesis. I have had many of the difficulties and frustrations that are experienced by women scientists in general. My career as a researcher was sidetracked five years ago when I took on the job of being the grantsperson at San Jose State University, seemingly the only professional route open to me at the time within reasonable distance from home. I reported to the graduate dean, a woman who was and is an excellent administrator; she is now president of this university and serves as an admirable example of what can be.

Subsequently, after a short stint at a full-time teaching assignment here, I am now serving as interim executive vice president. There are so few women in positions of real influence that each must more or less establish her own style. Thus I have carried out a preliminary probe by talking with a number of women, each of them quite remarkable, about the questions I raised in the previous paragraph. While some generalizations are inevitable, I cannot present them as research findings which will stand up under scrutiny. The women who spoke freely with me shall remain nameless for the most part, but they are presidents, former presidents, vice-presidents, deans, sociologists, anthropologists, and others, each in some way an expert on women in academe. They work for institutions in all parts of the country, public and private, large and small, women's colleges and large state universities.

First of all, there are very few women at the top. There are fewer than fifty women college presidents out of a total of over 3,000 such positions in this country.[1] The proportion is scarcely greater for the positions of executive or academic vice-presidents or academic deans. Furthermore, in the words of Patricia Albjerg Graham, "Discussions about the status of women in higher education have become as contagious as cholera and just about as popular with predominantly male faculties and administration."[2] Colleges and universities have not taken a leading role in changing this situation, at least not so you would notice it. In order to reach an average of thirty percent of administrative positions held by women by 1990, universities would have to maintain as a whole a proportion of one woman hired for every one man hired.[1] But the species *woman administrator* does exist. Let us assume that their proportion will increase through the efforts of the American Council of Education (ACE) National Identification Program, through the active efforts of women who *are* administrators, and, of course, through those men who can see past the cultural stereotypes to the abilities women possess.

At this point, I'd like to say that neither I nor any of the women with whom I conferred asserted that women have any physical or physiological characteristics that render them intrinsically superior to men as administrators. Nor is anyone forgetting that there *are* men with all the qualities that I propose are valuable in an administrator. However, the nurture of girl children is very different from that of boy children and results on the whole in rather different kinds of people. These differences can be of great value to the institution. Note that *administer* means "minister to" and has quite a different connotation from *manage*.[3]

Why should a college or university have any interest in increasing the number of women in academic administration? A call for equity is not particularly compelling in a time of declining college enrollments, decreasing school budgets, and demands from the Federal government for ever more numerous and more expensive reporting and compliance procedures for universities to follow. Universities are in trouble on many counts, and although there are many intelligent people in these institutions, those in the decision-making roles are almost all pale males who need some of the fresh ideas, energy, and creativity that women have. The men have been brought up in a remarkably uniform kind of culture, and they are in the same position as inbred crops (my biological parallel there): terrific producers when the climate is exactly right, but vulnerable when times are tough or changing. A decrease in the administrative homogeneity of the university will provide the hope of opening up alternative solutions. The universities need substantial infusions of people who are now just on the periphery of influence, and these include minorities as well as women. Bernice Sandler remarked that the Peter Principle doesn't apply to women because they haven't had a chance to rise to the level of their imcompetence,[4] so that at any given level of responsibility, while the men have risen to the level of their incompetence, the women haven't, even though the women seem to be far more capable. The men who were their equals in ability have long since been promoted upwards.

Most men have been brought up in a tradition of sports competition, of military games, and of the absolute necessity of winning (and the utter shame of losing). In some situations this background is no doubt very valuable, and it is carried through to adult life in many ways. On the other hand, women acquire special skills in interpersonal relationships and learn to achieve their ends by less direct means. They are sensitive to the emotional state of those with whom they deal. Women are trained as diplomats from the time of the cradle, and they also learn early to redefine issues so that the issues may be viewed from a fresh perspective, thus enabling differences to be resolved. If a defeat occurs, a woman is more able to accept it gracefully, often the most constructive action possible at the time. Of course, I am not describing every woman, but a rather special type of female who will be of great help to any institution struggling with common problems.

Women tend to simplify things. All institutions (not just those of higher education) are terribly bound up in bureaucracies and seemingly unavoidable convoluted procedures of Byzantine-like complexity. Not knowing that a given set of procedures is "the way it is done" (and therefore sacred), women can take a fresh look and suggest short cuts in many situations if they are given the authority to do so. Women in all types of jobs, even at the top professional levels, more often than not have responsibilities at home, too. They've learned to devise short cuts that work. Several of the women with whom I spoke recounted the difficulty of getting some segments of the institutions they had recently started to administer to adopt a more direct and simple way of dealing with recurring problems. Once accomplished, the improvement was obvious. In most of life's tasks, the process isn't particularly interesting, but the result is necessary or desirable: getting dinner ready every night is a case in point.

Women are also more willing to ask "dumb questions" and they sometimes find out that in a group of men, no one else knew the answer either, but no one was willing to reveal that he didn't know. The male ego makes it hard to admit ignorance.

Then there's the matter of "keeping cool." The professional woman, the woman administrator, simply must never lose her composure. No matter how emotional she might feel, she must contain herself. Yet a man can blow up, yell, range, march out of the room, and the next day everything is normal again. He seemingly doesn't lose respect or authority when this happens; it is just taken in stride as part of his style. No one ever says he's behaving just like a woman. Women *don't* behave like that, yet emotional behavior is attributed to them. It is really just the other way around. In the words of Patricia Albjerg Graham, "Men are permitted their idiosyncracies of whatever sort, but women are expected to maintain a much more precarious balance between conspicous confidence and tactful feminity."[2]

The ability to ask good, fresh questions and to seek answers to them through channels that are not used most commonly is part of what makes women so good on committees. A committee chaired by a woman of some skill and experience is likely to accomplish its task in an expeditious manner. Committee work consists of a series of compromises as the group moves toward its goal, and the skilled chairperson must keep the group moving with minimum abrasion, letting most members feel that their inputs have been an integral part of the group's accomplishment. Time and again I've watched a skilled, low-key woman make suggestions that were later taken up by others as their own and that proved to be the resolution of the problem. She has long since learned not to press for recognition in an egocentric way, but takes her satisfaction from the accomplishment of the group. Isn't this another womanly attribute? Women are *expected* to be this way. In an institution where a great deal of the work of running the place is done not by fiat or by the overt exercise of authority, but by a network of committees, aren't these among the skills the institution needs most? The characteristics that make us women are the characteristics that are the least valued by society, yet they might be those of most value to the institution.

Are women good at decision-making? Do they have a special style? Most of those with whom I spoke answered yes to both of these questions. In fact, they felt that women administrators are as good as the best men, and better than most. Since much decision-making rests on a prior agreement on goals, the skills of women about which I've been talking have great value here. As one president in a large state system wrote to me, "I have not had any problems with the decision-making process, but some of my male faculty members do have problems."

Women who have risen to positions of responsibility in academe are extraordinarily conscious of quality and excellence, and impatient with sloppiness, mediocrity, or drift. They tend to be more uncompromising, and intolerant of decisions made by default. The kind of decision that must be made at the top echelon is apt to be a difficult one, with no easy outs, and of the kind that is likely to leave all parties somewhat dissatisfied, or some parties even bitter. Although one woman president felt that there was no difference in the way men and women made the difficult decisions, such as those on budget or in personnel situations, most were emphatic in their belief that women were superior to many men administrators in dealing with them. At the same time, they were likely to be humane in rendering these decisions, helping as they could in sparing the feelings of those whose egos were involved, and careful that no lasting animosities were left.

There is a general opinion among the women administrators that women are on the whole harder working than men. Any person at the top has to have unusual reserves of energy, and a woman in high gear can be truly remarkable. It may be the result of the rather stringent selection that goes on: so few women get to the top that only the extraordinarily energetic one makes it there. Part of what drives her is a determination that no one will be able to say that she was too weak or frail for the job. In addition, women are brought up to handle a variety of jobs more or less simultaneously. Most administrators complain that it is difficult or impossible to put in sustained work on any one matter, since the nature of the job is to fragment effort. However, a woman who has made it into administration has learned to juggle a lot of different things and I think that here, again, a woman's lifelong skills stand her in good stead.

Let me now turn to the effect on the students of seeing a woman in a leadership position. Without any doubt, every woman in a visible spot has enormous effect on the aspirations of the young women in that institution, and in others, too. I remember how excited my daughter was when she found out that a *woman* was president of the coeducational state college she attended. I don't think anything I had said or done had nearly that impact on her. This president was not only intelligent and capable but approachable, and she had "class." Young women without role models in responsible positions can conceive of their futures only in terms of somewhat limited ambitions. In most institutions, it is the "work" of a few men (especially in the more scholarly and prestigious institutions) which becomes a sacred value in whose name numbers of women are expected to serve. As Adrienne Rich has pointed out, "the structure of the man-centered university constantly reaffirms the use of women as means to the end of male 'work,' meaning male careers and professional success."[5] Those women who do rise to the top seem to be able to get along with much less of a retinue.

It is in this connection that the woman's college is enormously valuable. These colleges have a greater number of women in administrative positions and on the faculty. Women students in particular need to see these role models. (The men have always had plenty of role models.) There are no subjects that are reserved for men, there are no functions in the academy that require that the person who does them be a man. Yet in the large coeducational college, a top woman administrator is viewed as an aberration. A markedly disproportionate number of the women in the top ranks of academe came up through a woman's college.[6] At these institutions, the faculties have, on the average, 45 percent women, whereas at coeducational institutions the average is around 20 percent, and at men's colleges eight percent or less. This means that the student at a woman's college has before her a wide range and substantial number of women role-models. The message is powerful; high achievement really is possible for women, and they *can* move up the career ladder. Moreover, women who teach in women's colleges rate themselves fairly high in self-esteem. Contrast this with the situation in the State University of New York, where 51 percent of the 375,000 students are women, but only three academic vice-presidents in 72 units happen to be women, and with one president. In the California State University and College system, which is almost as large, with 275,000 students, there is now one woman president and there is one woman vice-chancellor.

The value of mentors is generally recognized, and yet how hard it is for a woman to find a mentor in situations such as these. True, it is possible for a woman to have a man as mentor, but there are often problems in this kind of relationship, and it remains much more difficult for a woman than for a man to have this kind of help in entering realms of real responsibility.

It is not only valuable for women to see women achieving, it is important for men. Young men are rather used to having young women as their equals, but as they get older they move up a career ladder and eventually join their elders as equals. But the women lag behind, and the older woman generally remains in a subservient role. Her former buddies are now her bosses. A man who has experienced a competent woman in high position may have his whole perception of women altered, and for the better. He may be better able to think of his wife as a partner and his equal, and more tolerant of the aspirations that women are putting into effect in every area of American life today. Tidball puts it very well: "For women to develop non-biological competence, there must first be the expectation that such competency can exist." She goes on to write, ". . . true liberation requires a mutuality of respect, acceptance, and approbation in nonsexual terms, that is mutual interdependence."[7]

I think that we still have a long way to go before men are generally aware of the fact that women can function as administrators, or can exert any influence, for that matter. As an illustration, I am currently chairing a university committee to choose candidates for dean of the school of Engineering. We have just finished the preliminary screening of some 80 applicants, all men. (I'm sorry to say I was unable to persuade any of the qualified women I could find to apply!) These eighty presumably all want the job, and yet not a single one of them made *any* allusion to the possibility that women could become engineers, even though I think it might have occurred to a few of them that I (my name was on all the advertisements) might have had some interest in the cause of women engineers.

It seems obvious that universities and colleges will serve their own interests well by appointing women to top positions with greatest possible speed and in large numbers. Are there problems in doing so? The first problem is to find the women. There is no denying that the pool is small for many reasons, among them the Peter Principle I mentioned earlier. It probably isn't possible to find women have had just the right kind of experience not only in dealing with people, but in dealing with budgets, raising money, in understanding physical plants, and the rest of the nitty gritty of running the place. So the institutions must start immediately to *consciously* give women the opportunity to learn these things. Many men learn these things by doing them. I predict that there will be no dearth of women willing and anxious to gain the skills that lead to power. This will mean breaking down the sexual stereotyping which permeates every institution, especially the coeducational and men's schools. Internships and training programs are essential but expensive, and an on-the-job approach might go far provided there is a genuine interest on the part of men in getting women who really help run things. There must be a willingness to try to identify able, ambitious, and energetic women, to give them support on the job and enough security so that they are not washed up when they make the first mistake. There is a great tendency, apparently irresistible for many men, to watch and wait, after a woman has been given some responsibility, for her to make some sort of blooper, and then to say with great satisfaction, "Just like a woman!" So for a woman to succeed, those around her, both women and men, must want her to succeed, and make sure she gets the information she needs to do the job well. This type of woman might just be the one who makes a great contribution, because since she has not come up the traditional system she doesn't share the same values and perceptions. She can be innovative because she doesn't know any better. There aren't many real leaders in higher education because most administrators are not really able to see that there's another way of doing something.

What other tactics will work well in getting women into administration? Women who have top positions *must* take it as their special duty to bring other women in, which is not to exclude men from this responsibility. If women do not recruit other women, this lack provides men with an excuse for also not doing so. Women should be hired for acting positions, eventually to be in a good spot to win the permanent job. Women must be appointed to search committees and other personnel committees such as those involved with retention, promotion, and tenure in numbers enough to exercise influence and to make sure that qualified women are actively sought out.

What difficulties face women administrators because they are women?

Administrator Cynthia Fuchs Epstein has noted that decision-making in the top echelons is characterized as being highly informal, and that the presence of women disturbs that easy informality.[8] Dr. Epstein calls this the "locker-room problem" or the "men's room problem". Of course the men's room can be the golf course or lunch at the club. It is a frustrating situation, and is referred to by almost all the women administrators who operate in a largely male milieu. One's only defense is to insist on rather formal decison-making procedures, and to inform people that business is not going to be conducted in inaccessible places.

One of the results of having more women in higher education administration is the broadening of the base for women and a weakening of the old-boys' network. One concrete example of a *probable* effect of a woman at the top is cited by Mina Rees (President Emeritus of the Graduate School and University Center of the City University of New York, former President of the American Association for the Advancement of Science, and the recipient of seventeen honorary degrees) in a report to the American Council on Education. While she was president of the Graduate School, there was a significantly higher proportion of women admitted and women completing the Ph.D., both with greater success and greater speed than was typical of graduate students. While she points out that there were other factors that could have contributed to this result, such as the convenient location and the urbanity of New York, but it seems to me highly probable that in addition to these considerations, women realize that in an institution headed by a woman, they are very likely to get fair and unprejudiced treatment. Achieving a Ph.D. is sometimes a very personal procedure based on the "chemistry" between student and mentor, and there have been cases of "unfair" procedures on the part of an individual. Such practices were bound to be minimal at CUNY Graduate School under President Rees.

Another possible result of more women university administrators would be a shift in curriculum. The contributions of women might become truly integrated into the humanities courses, and those of science to a greater extent as women assume responsible roles.

Then there's the reality of power. One of my conversants cynically said that any role in society into which women were allowed to move had no power, no matter what the title might be. Several of the men presidents, chancellors, and deans I know complain that their positions don't hold any power, that they are just functionaries without any real influence despite the impressive titles and stately garb. Power in the universities is legally in the hands of the boards of trustees whence it flows to the top administrators, but a good administrator doesn't exercise that power. If he does, he'll have a mutiny. What he/she must do is to constantly delegate it, to work with groups who have appropriate responsibilities. Power is a matter of synthesizing on the highest level. Women must learn to understand the ways of power, which is diffuse, or distributive, in academe. Once they understand it, their talents for gaining personal support and for getting people to pull together should stand them in good stead. In a state system, it's the legislature that has the purse strings, and then the trustees of the state university. Women in those bodies can be a great help (and we must get them there!). The woman administrator must learn to cultivate women legislators and women trustees, work with them, and keep them aware of the important functions, missions, and problems of the universities. On the CSUC Board of Trustees, there are several women, and they display a genuine concern and regard for the faculty and students. Women board members bring a sense of human dignity, human rights, and a sense of humane concern to the whole enterprise.

What are the personal satisfactions and rewards for the woman administrator? I asked several women presidents if they enjoyed their jobs and they said they did. Several who were not yet presidents had plans for moving up. A fascinating study of men and women in graduate administration revealed that significantly more women than men felt that the rewards of the leadership role were the most important aspects of the administrative role: being able to influence policy decisions, the pleasure of being able to carry plans to fruition, and solving problems. Women gave responses indicating that they enjoyed the exercise of authority and the opportunity for leadership *significantly* (at the 99th percentile!) more often then men.[9]

I'm convinced that the more women administrators there are, the better will be the academy and the society it serves. The qualities that are intrinsic to women are the qualities that are most needed by our universities today. As we move toward a woman-centered university, the greatest beneficiary will be the university itself. The talents of distinguished women teachers and researchers will be fostered, the aspirations of women will be raised, and the vision of all will be broadened.

REFERENCES

1. GREBNER, M. 1977. University College Quarterly.
2. GRAHAM, P.A. 1972. Status transitions of women students, faculty and administrators. In Academic Women on the Move. Alice S. Rossi & Calderwood, Eds. Russell Sage Foundation. New York, N.Y.
3. WAGNER, M.D. 1977. Talk given at Berkeley, Calif. June.
4. SANDLER, B. 1975. Women in administration, seek and you shall find. In Women and Management in Higher Education. N.Y. State Department of Higher Education. Albany, N.Y.
5. RICH, A. 1975. Towards a woman-centered university. Chronicle of Higher Education.
6. TIDBALL, E. 1976. Of men and research. Journal of Higher Education.
7. TIDBALL, E. 1976. On liberation and competence. Educ. Records 57:101-110.
8. EPSTEIN, C.F. 1970. Woman's Place. Univ. California Press. Berkeley, Calif.
9. FULLERTON, G.P. & C. ELLNER. 1977. Unpublished data. Claremont Graduate School.

Innovative Approaches: Meeting the Needs of Women Faculty in the Eighties

DIANE IDA MARINEZ
Department of Natural Science
Michigan State University
East Lansing, Michigan 48823

LET US REVIEW the needs of academic women in the 1980s. What these needs are will depend upon whom you ask, as I discovered when I spoke with my colleagues and friends at Michigan State University. Surprisingly, many of my colleagues espoused traditional responses, such as "What more do you women want?" One older male colleague, though, hit it on the head when he said that men did not have what women thought they had, and maybe women didn't really want that at all. There is much truth to his statement, since it tells us that men recognize the restrictions imposed on women equally affect men and that men, too, could benefit from change. What follows is a synthesis of many conversations with women colleagues and friends.

Women in academia suffer from a lack of unity in articulating their needs, or, for that matter, accepting the system as it is. That this is particularly true for women in science is evident when one looks at the literature written on academic women. *Women on Campus, The Unfinished Liberation*,[4] from the editors of *Change*, illustrates that although much progress has been made, equality of opportunity on our campuses is far from a reality. An examination of the papers and authors in this work shows no treatment of women in science, although one of the authors is in the hard sciences. In addition, concerns of women in academia were not raised strongly at such meetings as the Michigan International Women's Year Conference (IWY),[2] nor at the National IWY Conference,[3] except for a resolution introduced by me at the Michigan IWY Conference workshop entitled "Full Partnership for the Homemaker." The problems of women in nontraditional fields was recognized in the report of the National Commission on the Observance of International Women's Year through reports submitted by the United States Interdepartmental Task force for IWY. It is apparent that even though women from academia were present at some of these gatherings, they were seen as having "made it." Therefore, their problems were not deemed, often by themselves as well as others, as significant.

Women in science have not been visible in the initiation of change, just as men in science have seldom left the labs to view the impact of their discoveries. I realize that the time-demands of the profession account for at least part of this lack of participation in initiating change, but it is now imperative that women in science join forces with other academic women in initiating change. Women in science or other nontraditional fields stand to gain the most.

Current trends in our society will directly affect women in academia, and women in science in particular. First, statistics have revealed that in 1977, women accounted for 93 percent of the enrollment gains at American colleges and universities, outnumbering eighteen and nineteen-year-olds on campuses and making up 49 percent of the total enrollment.[5] In addition, they comprise 53 percent of part-time students. This gain alone should probably provide an increased pool of women going into science or other nontraditional fields. That this conclusion is probably correct can be seen by the 34 percent increase in enrollment in colleges of agriculture and natural resources across the nation. At Michigan State University alone, more than 50 percent of the undergraduates in the departments of Animal Husbandry and Horticulture are women.

Second, there has been an increase of professional families or dual-career couples at our colleges and universities. A colleague in psychology told me that at the 1975 American Psychological Association convention a group of such couples made a plea to universities to facilitate their professional goals. This increase has a twofold effect: that of the necessity of two professionals acquiring employment in the same area or field or university, and that of increasing the number of child-bearing-age women in the university, a situation the university has not had to deal with in the past.

Third, programs and conferences such as this one, designed to break down barriers for women in science career fields and to make women more aware of their suitability and opportunities in science, will, if successful, increase the number of women choosing careers in science.

Fourth, an AAUP study has shown that the use of part-time faculty has dramatically increased to the point that part-time faculty now constitute one of every three full-time faculty at four-year colleges and universities, and they outnumber full-time faculty at two-year colleges.[6] With tenure rates high and budgets low, colleges and universities have found the use of part-time faculty a way to save money and avoid long-term commitments.

While the study does not reflect which percentage of part-time faculty are women, or if the use of part-time faculty is the same for men as for women, it does state that when compared with full-time faculty, part-time faculty tend to be more closely tied to their communities and are more likely to accept whatever the local colleges and universities will pay.

Women readily fall into this category, and regardless of competence, these professional women find themselves not only relegated to part-time status, but unable to increase their career potential. In hiring part-time faculty, the study cites that colleges and universities accepted applicants with lesser qualifications, offering few if any nonteaching services such as advising students or serving on committees. There is less likelihood of such applicants' engaging in research and in publishing papers. Therefore, they are less likely to contribute to the prestige of the institution than their full-time colleagues. In addition, the use of part-time faculty is an expedient way of complying with affirmative action.

These trends, coupled with the economics of higher education and a declining enrollment have raised anew some of the traditional issues of higher education policy. We must reexamine the current values implicit in the practices of granting tenure or promotion, rigid scheduling, salary determination, protection against "inbreeding," hiring part-time or temporary faculty, granting benefit packages, evaluating productivity, and determining the role of women.

The university must first recognize that women provide an element that is necessary to the institution and that they can give tremendous vitality to the profession of higher education and to the people within it. Concurrently, women must come to view themselves as providing an asset to the university rather than the university providing them merely with employment. If this is not reason enough, then one can use, in support, the economic argument of the underutilization of women. The amount of money spent on the education of women does not equal the utilization or return for the money spent. There are, of course, many benefits gained from educating women that cannot be measured directly but our society is geared to think in economic terms. Today, however, the climate is ripe for women to participate in a more direct way.

The unidimensional approach to situations needs to be explored. This approach is based on the unexamined assumption that everyone must fit into one model or way of doing things. There must be flexibility in order to provide a range of options for academics. Innovative approaches must be instituted.

Our traditional ways of doing things have been based on a unidimensional approach. This, in turn, is based on separate roles for the sexes. Innovative changes producing transformations from within, with little overt change in outward organization, are needed for the greater potential for success. The success factor is the greater acceptance and accessibility to resources and budgetary stability. In the short run, this is less painful. But transformations from within have a history of allowing programs to make dents but then springing back to their original forms, because while allowing the program to exist, no real change in attitude and philosophy occurs. What it boils down to is that it is time to deinstitutionalize some of our traditional ways.

That our institutions reflect the importance of the family in our society needs to be examined before changes can be made. If the structure of our institutions is based on separate sex roles, then they do reflect the importance of the male providing only the material neccessities, but not of his role as a parent. Indeed, our institutions do a poor job of reflecting our commitment to the importance of the family, for both men and women. I find it very difficult to separate the needs of women from those of men, even though at this time many men are not aware of their needs. Although my topic is academic women, changes for women alone will not succeed unless equivalent changes occur for men.

Women in science have been forced to make choices when it comes down to marriage and family. A look at the statistics compiled by the Carnegie-American Council on Education survey of colleges and universities and used by Hamovitch and Morgenstern[7] reveals these choices. The sample from the major disciplines included Ph.Ds under forty, of which 8,538 were men and 596 were women. Women accounted for seven percent of the total Ph.D. pool under forty; 42 percent of the women were single, compared with only ten percent of the men; the average number of children of married women was 1.13 compared with 1.89 for married men.

Productivity needs to be redefined. Productivity is synonomous with publications; I feel that we have lost sight of our true mission in the universities: teaching, research, and community service. It was not until I started teaching undergraduates that I discovered that it really was research and filling administrative positions that were held in highest regard by most ambitious academicians. It took me even longer to be convinced that this should not be so. I had been well indoctrinated into the system. Again we see an example of the unidimensional approach. In Hamovitch and Morgenstern's study, 49 percent of all women taught only undergraduates, compared with 29 percent of all men, and the average number of articles published by men was 7.26 compared with 3.46 by women. Teaching undergraduates provides flexibility and therefore forces women to opt for teaching rather than research just because of their biological make-up. Other reasons why women may choose teaching have to do with the myths surrounding the predisposition of women to nurture: the idea that women want only to get married and have children; that women are less productive; and that women are more emotional and therefore unsuitable for science. The universities therefore need to provide more than lip service to undergraduate education and to consider teaching a measurement of productivity by including it in the reward system.

To dispel the myth surrounding women and productivity, Hamovitch and Morgenstern, while not questioning the validity of using publications as a measure of productivity, do point out which variables affect productivity. For instance, there is no evidence of lessened academic productivity associated with the presence of children in the household. The results of this study run contrary to the results of other researchers and to what is generally accepted as true in the academic community. It is probably a more accurate assessment of the situation, because the sample studies were women doctorates under forty in the labor force, rather than all women doctorates. A sample of all women doctorates would stack the cards toward finding a fertility-productivity relationship.

Factors positively correlated with publication for both men and women include: number of years since earning the Ph.D.; whether the field is biology or the physical sciences; whether currently teaching at a university; and whether the first teaching job was at one of President Carter's list of the twelve leading universities. Factors negatively related to the number of articles published are: the number of weekly hours of teaching; teaching only undergraduates; if the field is in the humanities; if the authors are single; if the authors are female.

When the sample was restricted to women only, factors positively correlated to the number of articles published were the number of years since winning the Ph.D. and whether the researchers were teaching either biology or the physical sciences. Negatively related were the number of hours spent in teaching and whether this teaching was restricted to undergraduates. Neither marital status nor number of children were found to be significantly related to publication output.

The study did find that overall, women faculty do publish somewhat less than men. The bulk of the differences, i.e., 64 percent, could be explained by variables other than gender that were not amendable to measurement by this statistical analysis. These turned out to be psychological factors thought to stem from the attempt to reconcile dual careers, from discrimination by journals, and from the so-called lower average level of competitiveness and the drive of women. These factors allegedly had their seeds in their early upbringing and in societal expectations.

Changes in basic values, then, will bring out new systems to provide for acceptance and advancement of women in science. One of the most important benefits will be new attitudes toward part-time employment in academia.

The concept of part-time tenured faculty employment is not a new idea, but it can be considered innovative because it is a change in the way of doing things. It does not dramatically alter the present tenure system or question its validity, but instead, makes the tenure system more flexible. It extends the privileges and responsibilities of tenure to individuals who work only part-time. It also increases the number of individuals in the university system rather than increasing the total number of positions in the tenure system. Such opportunities are already in operation in half the universities of the Big Ten schools and in some fourteen others throughout the nation.

The first proposal regarding part-time tenure was introduced at Michigan State University as far back as 1973. A revised version is literally stuck in two committees of Academic Governance and has been accepted, at least in part, only for those professors approaching retirement and it will probably be approved for this group.[8] Women on campus have been primarily responsible for initiating this change, but they will still have to wait a number of years before this concept benefits them.

Besides increasing flexibility in the tenure system, other benefits stated by the Michigan State University proposal include: providing opportunities to increase possible affirmative-action appointments; opening up opportunities to professionally qualified individuals for whom full-time employment is not feasible. This would benefit: 1) women or men professionals with child-care responsibilities; 2) dual-career couples or academic families who share domestic involvement or who are willing to take part-time positions in order to have professional employment; 3) women or men of distinction who are available only on a part-time basis because of consulting, lecturing, writing, or other commitments; and 4) professionals with expertise in a specialized area that does not justify a full-time position within existing priorities but that expands the range of specialties represented in a unit.

With regard to providing opportunities for some currently full-time tenured faculty involved heavily in consulting, writing, or other activities, part-time tenure status would not only free a tenure slot but would provide a means of making honest people out of some allegedly full-time faculty whose consulting or other activities involve a high proportion of their time. A rethinking of the policies allowing teachers to supplement salaries with consulting fees is being forced on universities by legislators and public opinion.[9] It also exemplifies that the fears of abuse by men expressed by many women regarding part-time tenure already exist in the tenure system. This should not be used as a reason for rejecting the whole concept of part-time tenure.

Part-time tenure would also provide a transition to retirement for older faculty members, thus softening the hardship often encountered in our "cold turkey" approach to retirement.

A variation of part-time tenure not included in the part-time tenure proposal is the concept of job sharing. In this situation the responsibilities of one job would be shared by two qualified individuals. For academics in similar or related fields, it could provide a humanistic approach, especially if one of the individuals is a graduate of a particular department and fear of "inbreeding" is silently functioning to eliminate that individual from employment.

These programs will attract women into nontraditional fields and will provide opportunities for shared parenting and career development. While this paper has not made a comprehensive review of the needs of faculty women, it has discussed that what is primarily needed is a redefinition of our value system. This redefinition, in my view, is the responsibility of the academic community. We need to remake the pie and then divide it equally, rather than dividing the old pie equally.

REFERENCES

1. BERNARD, J. 1964. Academic Women. Pennsylvania State University Press. University Park, Pa. 1977.
2. FOCUS: MICHIGAN WOMEN. 1977. Michigan's International Women's Year Meeting. Final Report:46.
3. JUSTICE FOR AMERICAN WOMEN. 1976. Report of the National Commission on the Observance of International Women's Year: 322–325, 338.
4. WOMEN ON CAMPUS, THE UNFINISHED LIBERATION. 1975. Change Magazine.
5. MAGARRELL, J. 1978. Women account for 93 percent of enrollment gain. The Chronicle of Higher Education. January 9:1.
6. MAGARRELL, J. 1978. Part-time professors on the increase. The Chronicle of Higher Education. January 16:1.
7. HAMOVITCH, W. & R.D. MORGENSTERN. 1977. Children and the Productivity of Academic Women. Higher Educ. 48(6):633–645.
8. GULLAHORN, J. 1976. Proposal regarding tenure-line faculty employment. Michigan State University. Unpublished.
9. WATKINS, B.T. 1978. Outside income on university time: a conflict for professors? The Chronicle of Higher Education. February 21:1.

The Role of the National Science Foundation

F. JAMES RUTHERFORD
Directorate of Science Education
National Science Foundation
Washington, D.C. 20550

Introduction

WHAT SEEMS LIKE ONLY YESTERDAY, 1976 to be exact, Congress appropriated $1,000,000 with which the Education Directorate of the National Science Foundation was "to develop and test methods of increasing the flow of women into careers in science." This may appear to be a rather tardy response to the extremely gender-distorted career pattern characteristic of American science. Be that as it may, it represented an opportunity for the Foundation to get seriously to work to try to rectify a situation that was becoming less and less tolerable: less tolerable because it violated our gradually developing sense of equity, less tolerable because it condoned the underutilization of our most valuable natural resources—human intelligence, inventiveness, and wisdom. In the first part of this paper I will sketch, quickly and impressionistically, how the NSF has responded to that opportunity by describing the array of current activities in our Women in Science Program. In the second part, I will present some of the issues that have emerged as we plan for the future.

Current Activities

The language of Congress in establishing the program was not specific. Since it left open the question of how to go about getting more women into science, the Directorate staff worked with the National Science Board's Committee on Minorities and Women in Science to develop a specific program strategy, which was then approved by the full Board. Three approaches were established: 1) Science Career Workshops to give women students in college information and practical advice about science careers and how to prepare for them; 2) Science Career Facilitation Projects aimed at getting women who already had some college science either back into science careers or into higher degree programs, and then jobs; and 3) a Visiting Women Scientists Project, targeted at high school students to encourage them to consider science careers.

Science Career Workshops

The workshops consist of one- or two-day sessions conducted by science departments or other units such as women studies centers, usually on college campuses. They draw college students from about a 100-mile radius. At these workshop sessions, both on-the-scene and visiting scientists and job specialists from colleges, industry, and government, mostly women, discuss career options and existing opportunities in all fields of science supported by NSF. Workshops may be at any one of four levels: freshman-sophomore, junior-senior, graduate, or posteducation. The last type, which is new in 1978, will be for women who have at least a bachelor's degree in science, but who are presently neither in graduate school nor employed in scientific jobs commensurate with their training. Naturally, the type of information and motivation provided varies from one level to another.

All indications are that these multidisciplinary workshops—46 of which have now been held in 28 states and the District of Columbia—are doing what we had hoped they would do in helping women students define science-related career goals. And there have been unexpected byproducts: some apparent change in the attitudes of male faculty members who have participated, and new ties formed between women scientists in different science departments. We expect that the workshop experience will lead to some serious improvements at these colleges in the way of ongoing counseling regarding science careers.

Science Career Facilitation Projects

These projects go a step further. They are putting new polish on rusty degrees by helping women who have let their bachelor's or master's degrees in science lapse for from two to fifteen years update their knowledge and either return to graduate school or get right into jobs. Placement is a prominent feature of all the projects, placement in jobs or graduate school.

The Science Career Facilitation Projects (11 were funded in 1976 and 10 in 1977) provide training in a broad spectrum of the sciences. This year (1978), for example, three are in engineering, three in chemistry, two in interdisciplinary fields, and one each in life science and computer science. Within each general field, there is further variation. For example, Chatham College in Pittsburgh, Pa. is carrying out a project in industrial chemistry; Southern Illinois University in Carbondale is concentrating on food chemistry and environmental science; and the City University of New York is preparing 45 women to be systems analysts in areas related to their previous scientific training. The relatively large numbers of projects in engineering and chemistry reflect our emphasis on training in fields where there is now an unusual underrepresentation of women, and at the same time there are good job opportunities. The institutions receiving Facilitiation Project awards in 1977 are located in seven states and include three all-women's colleges and one minority institution. About 290 women are expected to participate in these 10 projects.

Some of these projects have been remarkably successful. At the University of Dayton, for example, there were only four dropouts from a group of 31 women—women with degrees in chemistry who were retraining for jobs in chemical engineering, and women with degrees in physics and math who were retraining to become electrical engineers. All 27 graduates had at least one job offer, and all but three are now working in the jobs for which they had been retrained. Two of the three who did not take jobs shortly after graduating did not do so because the jobs would have meant relocation. These results are not, we believe, unique. We are, however, having a third-party evaluation made of the Science Career Facilitation Projects to assess their impact carefully.

The Visiting Women Scientists Project

This Project, which is being carried out under contract by the Research Triangle Institute in North Carolina, is an experiment at the senior high school level. During the current academic year the Project is being carried out on a pilot basis with 30 women scientists visiting approximately 120 high schools throughout the United States. They will discuss the diversity of career opportunities and the variety of alternative life styles that are available to young women seeking careers in science and technology. In addition to making presentations to large groups, the women scientists will be available to visit classes and meet with interested students, teachers, and counselors on an individual or small-group basis. Students and school staff members will also be given assistance in obtaining additional resources including pamphlets, films, and bibliographies for further study.

We do not yet know how feasible or effective this project will be in encouraging girls to consider careers in science, but already we have learned one thing: There is no difficulty in getting women scientists to serve as visitors. Over 600 women volunteered for the 30 available slots. This is reassuring testimony to the willingness of women scientists in America to help the next generation make informed decisions about their careers.

Issues

We are now into our third year of the Women in Science Program. Our appropriation for this year is the same as for the two previous years, approximately one million dollars. We are continuing, with minor modifications, the kinds of activities originally approved by the National Science Board, but we are taking stock and we are looking to the future.

We believe our program is having some positive effects, and we know we are learning some things. However, as is the case for any kind of experiment, we are perhaps coming up with as many questions as answers. Let me briefly review some of the more important issues for the future as we see them.

What Kinds of Science Careers for Women?

As I look over the list of speakers at this Conference I note that most have the Ph.D. or M.D. degree. When we think about motivating young or not-so-young women to pursue careers in science, I suspect that many of us are thinking of ourselves as templates. This may be unwise for several reasons.

First, we can no longer argue that the doctoral degree is the best guarantee of employment. In all candor, I would have to tell the high school senior that today the woman with the new B.S. degree in engineering is far more employable than the new Ph.D in biology. But I would also tell her that if she truly wants to be a biologist and will settle for nothing less than a job in academia, she should get her undergraduate and graduate degrees in the best possible schools, get the best possible grades, do the best possible postdoctoral work, and then be prepared to take whatever academic job she can get.

Second, for persons with less than a doctoral degree, scientific and technical careers exist that can be rewarding for them and that can contribute significantly to society. A woman with a master's degree in physics teaching in a high school can serve as a magnet to girls who would ordinarily avoid a course in physics like the plague. A woman with a bachelor's degree in biology, some laboratory experience, and good writing skills can make a valuable contribution to a community by conducting environmental impact studies for a state government agency. These are only two examples of many that might be cited.

Third, many women—as well as men—with the intellectual ability to become Ph.D. scientists lack the incentive to do so. The high school sophomore whose parents' education ended with less than a high school diploma might be perfectly willing to contemplate six more years of formal education but would shrink in horror from the thought of ten or twelve more years.

In my view, raising the level of aspiration of such a young woman from obtaining a high school diploma to a B.S. degree in science should not be counted as a failure, particularly if that degree means a better life for her than her parents had. And especially if there are practical ways for her to continue her scientific education later on if a positive career experience should lead her to raise her horizons. Incidentally, the trend at the undergraduate level is reassuring. From 1965 to 1976 the proportion of bachelor's degrees earned by women in science and engineering went from 22 percent to 33 percent, a 50 percent increase. By comparison, for all fields combined the degrees awarded women went from 43 to 46 percent. As the undergraduate population approaches gender parity, the fraction electing science and engineering majors is escalating. The issue, then, is not whether, but how much NSF should depart in its efforts to increase the participation of women in science, from its traditional orientation to the Ph.D. degree, careers in research, and employment in academia.

The Rules of the Game

One of the reasons often given for the small number of women in science is that many women fear they will be labeled unfeminine if they study science or pursue careers in science or engineering. The currently accepted way to deal with this is to try to persuade young women to overcome such fear and to prepare themselves to compete with men on men's terms. It implicitly assumes that science, a game whose rules have been largely made by men, is necessarily "masculine."

But surely we ought at least to speculate on what might happen to those rules if science were to become less of a man's game. Would we have a different kind of science? Would research priorities, for example, be different? Would there be more concern with the social and economic consequences of science and technology? Would we find 60-hour weeks replaced by 30-hour weeks, as part-time employment became as attractive to male as well as to female scientists?

Would science, in short, become more humane? Would a humane science be less productive? Would a humane but less productive science be a better science?

I have no answers to these value-laden questions. I raise them only because we need to realize not only that science can do something for and to women, but women can do something for and to science.

Science Literacy

The final issue I wish to bring up has to do with a kind of participation in science different from the one we have been discussing. What I am referring to is an understanding on the part of all citizens, whether scientists or not, of what science and technology are, how they differ, what their relationships are to society, and what their potentials—and limitations— are for solving the world's problems. A not very satisfactory term often used for this understanding is "science literacy."

We do not need to rely on the findings of the National Assessment of Educational Progress to realize that science literacy for females is less than that of males. We know that they take fewer courses in science and mathematics, read fewer science-related books and magazines, and are less involved in amateur science activities. But we also know that their need for science literacy is just as great, perhaps even greater, for in a real sense I think we are dependent on women to *raise* the level of public decison-making in our society. All of the evidence indicates that from infancy onward females are more person-oriented than males, more inclined to caring, less to winning. These humane attributes are not, however, enough in a world based on science and driven by technology; scientific knowledge is also needed.

This is to say that for the sake of us all, it is urgent that the scientific literacy of all women be raised. And at the same time, a solid science education for women, irrespective of career preferences, can enhance their lives by helping them come to terms with the natural world, and as a bonus expand their career options. In this regard I note with despair that the parents and schools of America still do not "require" girls to take mathematics to the same extent that they do boys.

It is for this reason, among others, that we are planning a major thrust at the junior high school level across all the divisions within the Education Directorate of the National Science Foundation. We see this level of particular importance for minorities as well as for women. It is here that differences in mathematics performance by boys and girls appear for the first time, and it is here that irreversible decisions regarding science careers may be made if science and mathematics course sequences are not entered or continued. Good science materials taught expertly at the junior high level can, we believe, have profound effects on the science literacy and science career decisions of all students.

Acknowledgments

I would like to acknowledge the outstanding job being done by Joan Callanan in managing the Women in Science Program, and to thank her and Anne Woodward, Office of Government and Public Programs of the National Science Foundation, for their help in the preparation of this paper.

PART VI. Experiences in Achieving New Directions

How a Scientist Who Happens To Be Female Can Succeed in Academia

DIANE HADDOCK RUSSELL
Department of Pharmacology
University of Arizona Health Sciences Center
Tucson, Arizona 85724

Those qualities necessary for success in any profession do not differ for a male or female in our society. However, cultural mores have a direct effect upon the self-image, and the self-image is the foundation for the development of the individual. Given a positive and dynamic self-image, the other factors important in achievement are motivation and ambition, tenacity and determination, awareness and willingness to learn, training and professional contacts, and finally, flexibility and dedication. Females have an advantage in that society enhances their awareness and willingness to learn as part of the female role, whereas females are at a disadvantage since all the other traits are in direct contrast to cultural definition of femaleness. As more women assume positions of power and handle them effectively, the female self-image will be altered to allow for personal achievement. Respect for individual accomplishments and increasing numbers of female role models whose life styles encompass the above traits are the factors involved in the ability of more women to achieve and to be recognized as authorities in their fields.

There it is—the formula for success as perceived in 1978 by a female scientist whose peers in academia suggest she is "successful." The ways in which the various traits mentioned above are reinforced or suppressed in any individual are as varied as our perceptions of the attitudes and pressures which shape our lives. This paper will deal with those forces which have shaped my life, and with those decisions which were instrumental in my achievement of the proper title and job security (professor with tenure), with efforts to obtain independent grant support to develop my own scientific ideas and the freedom to train and inspire students, which is the only way to impact in a major and long-term manner on the scientific world.

Self-Image

My early perceptions are related to a small town in Idaho, a community so small that everyone was acquainted with and interested in the welfare of everyone else. Personal and geographical openness was the key there, with many exciting ponds and streams to be explored, interesting animalcules to be discovered, amidst an overall feeling of personal security.

There are two factors related to my background of key importance to my image of self. First intelligence and the pursuit of scholarly endeavors were held in high esteem by my parents. Second, I participated in competitive, individual sports events as early as age eleven. I can recall vividly the intense pleasure connected with "winning." It is important to stress that I excelled in individual, noncontact sports such as swimming and tennis.

I developed a keen sense of self-esteem based on my ability to be "Number One" in sports and academia. I remember being emotionally distraught when graduating from the eighth grade, having never received a grade other than A, and a boy (a friend of mine) who had As and Bs was named valedictorian. I was salutatorian, not valedictorian, because, as the principal explained to me, this honor would be more important to a boy in his later academic career. Although I did not overtly act out my frustration, I harbored a great deal of hostility toward the system and became extremely sensitive to my perceptions of discrimination.

I competed on a one-to-one basis with my brother who was two years my senior. It was not until I was twelve and my mother insisted I wear a shirt playing baseball that I got the impression there were glaring differences between boys and girls. Not that anatomical differences had escaped my attention, but the added restrictions for girls again left me angry and frustrated.

In spite of my achievements throughout high school (which in retrospect far outweighed those of my brother), my father and mother doted on his achievements, since he was the stereotype male: 6'4", athletic, and good-looking. I was *not* the female stereotype, being too aggressive, fun-loving, and athletic. I competed for their attention by achieving more and more, and only in later life have I realized that to them men are important as achievers and doers and women should give moral support to men. As a teenager I had continual verbal battles with my father, whom I perceived as wanting to control my life and my thought processes. From these conflicts emerged a desire to get so big that no one could tell me what to do.

This family situation was tempered by my attachment to my grandmother, who was my idol and role-model. I felt she could do everything well. She lived in a large house with acres of grass and instilled in me a great love of plants. As a young child I worked hand-in-hand with my grandmother, planting, weeding, and absorbing her strong sense of being in control. In return, she lavished her affection upon me and paid scant attention to my brothers. She treated me as a person, not as a child. More than anyone or anything else in my life, she gave me the sense of being bigger than life, so that anything and everything became possible.

Motivation and Ambition

The intensity of my motivation can be accounted for in large part by the secondary rewards associated with achievement as a tennis player, as a swimmer, as an editor of the high school paper, and as a student and scholar, while always feeling insecure constantly striving to be the best.

My ambition to become a research scientist is slightly more complicated. I wanted to attend college after high school, but the emphasis in our family was that my three brothers should be the ones to obtain a college education, that it was less important for a female. My mother was a reasonably strong woman who believed marriage and homemaking was the ultimate goal for a girl. My father was a schoolteacher and felt that education was important. Money, however, was certainly a problem; in fact, my meager college funds which I saved by raising calves on a small acreage for later sale were used to support my older brother in *his* first year of college. This was a devastating blow to my particular plans at the time, and because of the complexity of my conflicts with my parents, I chose early marriage, if not intentionally, at least subconsciously, picking a man who would allow for my intellectual development. It was always strong in my mind that, even though there might be some delay prior to my entering college (perhaps five years), this would eventually occur, and it did. I worked as a secretary and credit manager at a utility company while my husband attended college, majoring in psychology.

At the time I matriculated at Boise Junior College, I had three daughters, the youngest three months old. I assumed that the upper reaches of my career potential at that time would be as a secondary school teacher. However, I very rapidly found that I disliked the lack of content and uninteresting material present in most education courses, and was quickly drawn to natural and physical sciences such as zoology, chemistry, and physics. By the time I graduated from junior college, I decided my first love was science. I can recall that I had the highest passing grade average in the graduating class, and my psychology professor indicated to me at commencement that he thought I was an overachiever. At that time I perceived his statement as somewhat of a "putdown," since I had not really studied that diligently to get through junior college, for at the same time I was making all the arrangements necessary to keep three small children happy. This entailed many long searches for good babysitters, long hours away from home, and long hours of work at home. My husband was a guidance counselor in the school system, and the only four-year school available was approximately 40 miles away, which meant I would have to commute in order to finish my education. The College of Idaho was a small Presbyterian school with a student body of less than a thousand students. It has an excellent reputation in the premedical field, and such distinguished Idahonians as Senator Frank Church graduated from this college. Its strengths are related to the small class sizes and the ability of the faculty to allow students to develop at their own pace. I found that although the commuting was very difficult, the stimulation and teaching excellence was so high that, in spite of my duties at home, going to school was always pleasurable.

It was while I was working toward my bachelor's degree at the College of Idaho that I finally learned that my second daughter had a degenerative brain disease, etiology unknown, which was progressive. She started to have petit mal seizures at the age of two, and by age six was severely retarded. Throughout my college years, she became progressively more hyperactive and more retarded. I was fortunate to have a very dear German woman babysitting at that time who was very supportive, because she had a mildly retarded son who was thirty and still very dependent on her, although he could walk, talk, and function to some extent. Extensive neurological examinations of my daughter could point to no reason for her rapid degeneration, but this was of little satisfaction to me. I decided that I wanted to know enough about physiological and disease processes so that at some point in time I could contribute to the knowledge related to such processes and the control of diseases.

My first impetus in that direction was also my first research experience. As a senior at the College of Idaho, my honors paper in order to graduate *summa cum laude* related to studies of chromosome abnormalities in mongoloids. Mongoloids either have an exact copy of a small chromosome, chromosome 21, or they have part of chromosome 21 bridged to one of the longer chromosomes so that, in fact, they have an abnormal amount of genetic material from chromosome 21. In order to develop the chromosome techniques, I analyzed and cultured my own blood cells. I will never forget the Friday afternoon in the laboratory when I peered into the microscope and saw preparations of my own chromosomes obtained from my white blood cells. At that moment I was "hooked," and knew that what I most wanted to do in life was research.

I had a problem upon graduation from college because I wanted to go to graduate school. We had just built a large, expensive house which everyone told me I should just be happy to come home to and adore. Somehow, this particular rationale did not appeal to me, and I persisted in exploring places to attend graduate school. I was offered a rather substantial fellowship to work with Dr. Donald S. Farner, an esteemed ornithologist and physiologist at Washington State University. Fortuitously, my husband decided to attend graduate school at the University of Idaho. Although in different states, the two universities are only nine miles apart. So all roots were torn up; the house was rented; I moved in advance to the state of Washington since I had to take calculus during the summer session at the University to be allowed into the program; and on the side, I contemplated the kind of research I wanted to do. Because during the summer I worked on histochemical techniques to localize neural secretions in the hypothalamus of migratory birds, I was sure I wanted nothing to do with such tedious and laborious techniques. My professor was intensely interested in circadian rhythms related to seasonal gonadal growth and mating behavior of white-crowned sparrows. I was deeply impressed with the caliber of scientists, postdoctoral fellows, and visiting professors who worked in his laboratory and to whom I was exposed. His Germanic background resulted in a very disciplined approach to research. The early training with Dr. Farner added the discipline and the structure that I feel has been instrumental in developing my research capacity.

Against my major professor's advice, the second summer I was in graduate school I applied for a multidisciplinary behavioral genetics institute to be held at the University of California at Berkeley. He vehemently voiced the opinion that this would severely extend the length of my graduate program, but because of pressures at home and the pressures of graduate school, the thought of "escaping" to such an esteemed institute to deal only with intellectuals, all expenses paid, was too tempting to turn down. As it turned out, this again was a very decisive experience related to my intellectual development. The range and the depth of the interests of the people at the institute added a new dimension to my life and to my desire to become an intellectual and a scientist. Further, since starting college, it was my first opportunity to spend my entire energy and direction in academic pursuits. Fortuitously, I had decided prior to the trip to Berkeley that I wanted to work on some aspect of the regulation of gonadotropin release from the anterior pituitary and was contemplating the use of an enzyme, acetylcholinesterase, as a marker of alterations in activity of the hypothalamus-anterior pituitary axis. A group at Berkeley had developed an easy colorimetric assay to measure acetylcholinesterase activity in brain tissue. I took the opportunity to visit the laboratory and actually did assays with a scientist in the laboratory; this particular experience gave me the confidence and the skills to return to Washington State immediately and start collecting data related to my dissertation.

Tenacity and Determination

In graduate school, as I was working on my Ph.D. degree in Physiology, the scuttlebutt among graduate students was that endurance, not I.Q., was the most important quality. My retrospectroscope tells me this was a subtle way used by less successful students to justify their lack of performance or their desire to remove themselves from a highly competitive program. One of my professors at Washington State University put a Ph.D. degree in perspective for me by his statement that the degree was only a "gondola" (the lower part of a lighter-than-air balloon) or a license to practice, and that the later practice (the ascent) was really the measure of the person rather than the degree.

Because I was awarded a three-year National Defense Education Act Fellowship to obtain my degree, I simply assumed that I would finish the program in three years. Although I fulfilled essentially all the requirements in three years, and my research was finished, the department insisted that I have some training as a teacher prior to leaving graduate school. Therefore, I applied for a National Institutes of Health (NIH) predoctoral fellowship for the fourth year of my program and received it. I taught human physiology to physical education majors and home economics majors who used that particular course for their science requirement. I was appalled at the casual attitudes these students displayed toward learning and toward science and do not have fond memories of that particular experience. At the same time, however, I was a teaching assistant in the upper-division physiology course, which comprised mainly premedical students and graduate students. This was a very rewarding experience, since everyone in the class appeared to be there to learn to develop skills in laboratory sciences. To this day I am very uncomfortable as a teacher, probably because of my basic insecurity and the need to excel. My tendency is therefore, to cover too much material and go instantly to a scientific depth not related to the student's experience. Proselyting about my research, however, to a group of peers is a very rewarding experience for me, probably because I feel more secure as an expert in my field; therefore I can lecture and discuss my research with a great deal of confidence and poise.

My ability to be tenacious and determined regarding my long-term goals has been important in my rapid rise in academic circles. It was apparent to me that a Ph.D. degree in itself was not enough to gain entry into the hallowed circle of scientists who are allowed to do nearly full-time research. The jobs I was offered based on a Ph.D. degree in Physiology and no further experience were as a full-time teacher at various small, nonprestigious colleges, usually to teach a wide variety of courses ranging from electron microscopy (which I knew nothing about) to comparative anatomy. I could see that taking a job as a full-time teacher and trying to do research on the side, as was suggested, would be a death toll to my ambitions to become a research scientist. Further, being from the west, it had been adequately illustrated to me through the backgrounds of my major professors and my contacts at Berkeley that those who attained academic excellence and acceptance had usually graduated from prestigious universities and were postdoctoral fellows with very powerful major professors, most of whom were in northeastern prestigious universities. I therefore decided that I probably should do a postdoctoral fellowship on the east coast, preferably with a well-established, well-esteemed professor. I applied as a postdoctoral fellow to the Johns Hopkins School of Medicine in Baltimore, Md., wishing to work with a very renowned endocrinologist-biochemist. However, he did not have room in his laboratory but did recommend me as a "pair of hands" to a young assistant professor who already had a fairly impressive reputation in neuropharmacology. During the time of this negotiation my husband received an Office of Education fellowship in Washington, D.C., so it seemed that my best bet would be to accept the postdoctoral fellowship at Hopkins, cross my fingers, and hope for the best.

This was perhaps one of the more fortuitous happenings in my continual development as a research scientist. Solomon Snyder, with whom I worked, is indeed a research giant and a very creative scientist. He has been responsible in large part for much of the development related to the discovery and substantiation of the opiate receptor and endogenous substrates for the opiate receptor. He is also very well known for his work on catecholamine metabolism. He taught me how to read critically, assessing whether the author of a scientific paper has interpreted the data correctly and drawn the right conclusions. He also emphasized the importance of taking into account physiological parameters and working within the right physiological system. It was in his laboratory that I became deeply interested in polyamines and started to delineate the concept that polyamines were important in all cells as growth regulatory molecules. This has been my major field of investigation for nearly ten years, starting in Dr. Snyder's laboratory and continuing to the present time.

As a woman, I felt very little discrimination academically at the undergraduate and graduate levels. I assume this is because students, whether male or female, are not job threats to their teachers or professors at that point in time. Therefore, a great deal of benevolence and rapport can be established and maintained. However, of the many female graduate students that entered the physiology Ph.D. program at Washington State, I was the first female to complete the program. It was as a postdoctoral fellow that I became aware of the intense competition for ideas, important papers, and recognition. Starting at the postdoctoral level, a female does indeed have to prove that she is more intelligent, more dedicated, more creative, and more productive than any given man in order to achieve a position that allows the monetary support necessary to do scientific research. So that is what I did. Even with an outstanding bibliography and having worked with an outstanding scientist, it was difficult to find a position that would allow me independence.

After being offered continuing postdoctoral fellowships ad nauseum, I did finally succeed in obtaining a position with the glorified title of "Staff Fellow" (really a postdoctoral fellowship), but in reality the job offered me my own laboratory, funds to do research, and the assurance that I could do my own research. That turned out to be the case, and I worked happily for four years establishing the importance of polyamines in growth regulation in mammalian systems.

Here is the critical step where most women limit themselves. They do research at a postdoctoral or research associate level and publish with an established male scientist, and as such, never reap all of the rewards that should be related to the input they have into the research. Many of them choose this solution because of their lack of flexibility, usually related to family obligations in which the husband's career comes first.

What key decisions established my reputation as an authority in my field? Firstly, after leaving Dr. Snyder's laboratory, I continued to publish in the field and he published very few papers related to polyamines, since his main interests were catecholamines and neurotransmitter receptors. Rule 1: Run with the ball once you are independent, then you become the expert. One of the first independent actions after leaving Hopkins to work at the National Cancer Institute was the decision to publish a review in The New York Academy of Sciences on polyamines* separately from a review which Dr. Snyder was writing. We had informally determined that we would publish a joint review, but in reading the final efforts, it appeared that most of the work I had finished post-Johns Hopkins was incorporated as Dr. Snyder's and not Dr. Russell's. This, again, is a psychological point related to the way the world perceives you, and, more importantly, to how you perceive yourself in competition with other scientists, both male and female. It was an extremely difficult decision to make because of personal reticence and my respect for Dr. Snyder, but I decided on a review of current research and appealed as an independent speaker. I was the last speaker on the program and my review was placed under "Discussion."

The second major decision related to the publication of a symposium that I organized under the auspices of the National Cancer Institute related to polyamines in normal and neoplastic growth. At the time I organized the symposium, I was a Senior Staff Fellow and had been recommended for promotion to Civil Service status (which would have given me job security), but had been caught in the first freeze of promotions that President Nixon instigated. I organized the symposium with the support of my immediate superior at that time and, shortly after

*RUSSELL, D.H. 1970. Discussion: putrescine and spermidine biosynthesis in growth and development. Ann. N.Y. Acad. Sci. **171**(3):772.

finishing the organizational tasks, left for a workshop on molecular aspects of development being held at the University of California at San Diego. This was a six-week workshop to familiarize scientists with the latest molecular techniques that could be used to study developmental systems. I had been at the workshop approximately four weeks when I received a carbon copy of a letter suggesting that I was no longer the chairman of the symposium and that my "boss" was now the chairman. I talked to him on the phone and he said we would settle it when I arrived back in the laboratory, so I tried to put it out of my mind. It was, however, one of the few times in my life when I was livid for a long length of time. The rationale was that since I was still a Senior Staff Fellow, I did not have enough seniority to run an international symposium and to edit the book that was to be published from the symposium proceedings. I countered this with: I organized the symposium; no one else at the institute would have been able to organize the symposium; I already had a contract to have the book published; and it would be highly unjust were I not allowed to finish this endeavor and actually be credited with its organization. The administration did back down, and although initially I had intended to give my immediate superior coauthorship of the volume as a gracious gesture, I decided against such generosity. Rule two: Sometimes in building your own reputation you should not act the instinctively feminine way; i.e., being overly generous. Once established, you can afford to be generous, but not before. The rule I was learning was that a male with a more powerful position who coauthors a paper with a female will be credited as the creative scientist, the one responsible for the ideas. The same would hold true for the female in a more powerful position and a more prestigious title, but this occurs less often because of the limited number of women with professional independence.

Flexibility and Dedication

The assertion of my authority related to the NCI polyamine symposium brought me into disharmony with the power structure. Suddenly, no one was any longer pushing for my promotion, and all kinds of restrictions regarding meetings that I could attend and equipment and supplies that I could purchase began to appear. I felt the greatest hostility related to my achievement from women, usually secretaries. My interpretation is that many of them were bright, older women locked into jobs in which there was never going to be either high monetary rewards or increased professional esteem. The positive assertiveness I demonstrated in order to build my own professional reputation was not in line with their interpretation of femininity and was interpreted negatively as aggressiveness. The same behavior exhibited by males would be interpreted by them as positive assertiveness or justifiable aggressiveness. I believe one of the major obstacles to the upward mobility of woman professionals is their inability to be assertive at the proper times. Women feel they should strive to be popular, and although assertiveness may bring respect, it rarely brings popularity.

My position was the following: I was not going to be promoted because I had become "too big for my britches." The administration had assessed my position and felt that it was improbable for me to obtain a better position without moving out of town or out of state. Because of my marital status, this was unlikely. During this point in my professional career, I withdrew further into my work, made it a point to publish all of the outstanding data, and looked for alternative ways to further my career. What I wanted to do was find a tenure-tract position in a medical school. I had been fortunate in being able to work with work-study students from Johns Hopkins University while at the National Cancer Institute, since this portion of the National Cancer Institute was affiliated with the USPHS Hospital on the edge of Johns Hopkins' campus. I had been privileged to work with several very bright premedical students from Hopkins' campus and served as a major professor for a graduate student who obtained a Ph.D. degree from the University of Maine. I really wanted a position in academia and had exhausted all of the possibilities in the Baltimore area.

This was a time of soul-searching regarding my future goals and trying to put my personal life in perspective. My children were teenagers at this time, and my child who was retarded and who had been institutionalized for approximately eight years suddenly died. I flew home for her burial alone, because my husband did not wish to accompany me. This was a very traumatic time, and a time that accentuated the fact that for ten years of our marriage we had been going in different directions and had come to the point where we had different life styles.

At Johns Hopkins University School of Medicine I was a postdoctoral fellow in the Department of Pharmacology, and at the Baltimore Cancer

Research Center, a division of the National Cancer Institute, I was affiliated with the Laboratory of Pharmacology. In *Science,* the University of Arizona Medical School advertised for an assistant or associate professor of pharmacology. I applied for the job, gave a seminar, and found that I could carry on some of my clinical work at the University of Arizona because of their emphasis on biochemical markers of cancer, but I was reticent to take this position, since I did not know whether I could get independent grant funds and I did not know if my husband would like to relocate. We discussed it at home and decided that if I were able to get a grant, I should probably take the job, even if it meant we would be separated. The next grant deadline was approximately one month away, so I drove to the National Institutes of Health to obtain grant forms, wrote the grant, sent it to the University of Arizona to go through the hierarchy of necessary signatures, since it would be awarded through the University of Arizona, got the grant back, and hand-carried it to the National Institutes of Health to be evaluated. I was ambivalent about what I wanted the outcome to be. I knew that it would be professionally to my advantage and that I needed a stronger power base, but I instinctively had the feeling it would be the death blow to my marriage.

The grant came through; we both moved to Arizona; and it was the death blow to my marriage, but it did provide me with the power base to operate as a progressive scientist, to be assertive without major retaliation. The professional jealousies are still there and are always there for anyone who is successful in terms of money, power, and/or prestige.

In summary, women can and do achieve in academia. Those who do must push their own little red wagons and also must make the right professional contacts. Dr. Snyder has been extremely generous in his continual support of my research efforts, and Bernard Brodie, a well-known pharmacologist at the University of Arizona when I first arrived, has helped enormously in making available to me the many international contacts so important to the dissemination of scientific ideas. Dr. Brodie is also one of my role-models in terms of his influence on pharmacology. He trained many who are today the heads of major pharmacology departments and he instilled in me a sense of the necessity of impacting on science not only through your own efforts but through your ability to train and excite students to want to know and achieve.

Women scientists will continue to pay untoward personal prices for the right to achieve. More and more they will probably choose between a normal family life with children and a research career. Perhaps the options will be more rational if the choices are out in the open and made early in life as distinct alternatives. There is a tremendous excitement coupled with asking questions about tissues and their functions and getting answers. These "highs" far outweigh the problems of scientific research. It is indeed a privilege to be allowed to do research.

From Clerk-Typist to Research Physicist

SHIRLEY A. JACKSON
Bell Laboratories
Murray Hill, New Jersey 07974

I WILL NOT CITE statistics or give scientific case studies. Instead, I should like to personalize the histories of women in achieving new directions by focusing on some experiences of three Black women (myself included) who are now physicists—two working and one in graduate school. Actually, I was not a clerk-typist, although I did study typing in summer school. The title of my paper refers to the evolution of self-aspiration as a result of expanding opportunities and awareness, and refers to the fact that the careers I and the other Black women have achieved are still running counter to prevailing expectations.

I'd like to discuss this evolution of aspiration by considering several elements of the picture: 1) the historical milieu from which the three of us came, i.e., family, community, and school encouragement as sources of continued motivation to pursue *something*, and the fact that there were no sexual distinctions of roles, although there were no direct female role-models; 2) the fact that for each there was no focused career in mind at the time of college entrance, but that an inclination toward science had been established earlier, and 3) that problems we have encountered are a result of ambition, awareness, sensitivity, and direct treatment, which became most apparent in college, graduate school, and on the job.

The schools (public) that I attended were initially legally segregated, then integrated by law, then *de facto* resegregated. A tracking system was introduced when the schools were integrated and seven Black girls ended up in the so-called Honors track. Except for one of us, our parents had little formal education. Our mathematics, Latin, social studies and English teachers were Black women. We were pushed to compete with students from suburban and other city schools in various programs (including It's Academic) and the George Washington University English grammar and composition examination. Our performances raised our expectations of what we could do. We learned that we could aspire to something more than the usual, and having Black female teachers encouraging us helped, although our Black male assistant principal and

Black male guidance counselor also were very helpful. Half of us attended predominantly Black colleges, half attended predominantly White colleges. The career results were: a physicist, a statistician, a business woman (who owns her own business), an artist, a lawyer, a psychiatric counselor (working on a Ph.D in psychology), and a high school counselor.

Another of the three Black women physicists grew up in one of the major metropolitan areas, and her family was not particularly well off. Her parents were not college graduates. Nevertheless, she attended one of the Seven Sisters colleges and now has a Ph.D. in physics. Her sister, an engineer by training, is now high up in the hierarchy of one of the major U.S. companies. In the case of this young physicist, her parents were a strong influence. They felt she could be anything she wanted to be and were willing to go along with what she chose, to see how it would develop. There was a strong motivation to go to college, win a scholarship, and get a job (which was what college was considered useful for). In her community, being Black and going to college was important enough; what she studied was irrelevant as far as her neighbors were concerned.

The third young woman grew up in a well-traveled military family. She lived in Europe while growing up, which heightened her awareness of the world and what she might accomplish in it. She attended one of the major U.S. universities and is now a graduate student at another such university.

In all cases, our parents encouraged us to get ahead in *whatever* field we chose. Working women were not an aberration in our lives, even with marriage and a family (perhaps because of having a family to help support). Many people in our communities and schools wanted to see one of "theirs" make it. It did not matter if one was male or female—if one had talent and ambition, one was pushed. In two instances, the church and community organizations encouraged excellence, and in one case the church contributed directly to college expenses, and in another, a Black lodge contributed tuition money. Although there were no direct role models in the sense of the existence of someone pursuing a career that one wanted to pursue, indirect role models were very important such as mothers, high school teachers, and prominent women in the spotlight.

We responded to expanding opportunities and were aware that college was essential. So when the opportunity arose, we eagerly sought a higher education and, not surprisingly, all of us made our career decisions while in college. We were fortunate to have had the prerequisite backgrounds to pursue what we wanted in college. None of us had a focused idea of a specific career until well into college (perhaps later), but a leaning toward science and mathematics was established early.

In my own case, as a hobby, I collected live bumble bees and did behavioral and environmental experiments with them. I did nutrition experiments with mice, studied molds and bacteria. You may ask why I am not involved in biological science—I also constructed a slide rule based on Boolean algebra.

Another of us was a musician who used to play in various jazz clubs around the city while in high school (accompanied by her father), and also played in her church. She was fascinated by the structure of music and studied it because it was mathematical. The third young woman always liked mathematics and science and, indeed, considered them to be recreational activities, since she enjoyed them so much.

The fun began after high school when we were no longer in the supportive environment of home and community. The problems we encountered sound very much like the litany we have heard here, i.e., the low level of expectations of some with respect to our desires and abilities to pursue certain paths (one of us was told by a professor that "colored" girls should learn a trade; in this case physics was studied probably out of determination and pique). We had our problems to work out, such as being left out of discussions, study and work groups, and other networks in and out of school, e.g., getting one's fellow students to discuss homework problems, or being privy to the "in" developments in one's field. The last is more of a problem on the job than in school. However, one coped with it in school by ignoring it since one was oriented to "getting the degree" (one student, however, was extraordinarily bothered by this). These problems have, on occasion, been compounded by the unfriendliness of White females who did the same thing to Black women which others had done to them. I'll come back to this.

One Black woman felt that her actual socioeconomic background, or her perceived (by others) socioeconomic background made a difference in how she was treated. She felt that people assumed a different background for her because she is a Black woman, hence with different interests, and didn't bother to include her in things, and so she was left out of situations involving science. Another has experienced actual resistance to scientific discussions by male colleagues and to her ideas, the usual "woman" problems.

What can be gleaned from this exposition? There are several things, I think. Scientific and mathematical talent must be identified early and nurtured. The development of the requisite background and of heightened awareness is important, so that young women will be in a position to respond to challenges and opportunities as they arise. Community and family support is crucial, and indirect role-models are useful in helping a young woman to understand and face the problems she will encounter later. In school it may be possible, to some extent, to ignore lack of acceptance because worrying about it can be destructive and one has a specific goal to focus on: the degree. However, this lack of acceptance can be harmful because it may be the beginning (if it hasn't started earlier) of a continuing pattern. It becomes more serious when a young woman is out of school, since such rejection impinges directly on career progress by leaving her out of networks and by perpetuating the resistances to successful collaboration and interaction which *define* a successful research career. This is where the experiences of all women scientists touch base with each other. It is important, however, to remember the double bind which operates against Black and other minority women scientists. Insensitivity to them by majority women is not helpful, and this should be borne in mind and dealt with as we all work for our rightful place in the scientific sun.

So what about us here together today, and how should we proceed? I can't speak for all women scientists, not even for those I've discussed, but what I've tried to do is become more forthright and confident. I discuss *science* with male scientists and I try to avoid discussing women's or Black issues with male scientists who want to discuss *only* these issues. I try to focus on physics. I feel that I've gained the respect of many of my colleagues, but the struggle continues.

Academics, Bluestockings, and Biologists: Women at the University of Chicago, 1892–1932

DIANA LONG HALL
Departments of Biology and History
Boston University
Boston, Massachusetts 02215

INTRODUCTION

THIS PAPER ON the experiences of academic women as scientists and as women in twentieth century America has two sections. It begins with an abbreviated but substantial discussion of the development of the biological sciences at the University of Chicago from 1890 to 1930, indicating the importance there of ecology and sex biology. The second section is a brief statistical and historical analysis of the careers of the 138 women who took Ph.D.s in the natural history and biomedical disciplines at that University from its inception in 1892 until 1932, one year after the University was reorganized into four divisions which included the Biological Sciences headed by Frank R. Lillie, a University of Chicago graduate and Zoology Department Chairman. Lillie's characteristics as a scientist and as an authoritative figure in the University clearly affected the lives of the women as scientists. Their image of themselves as privileged women, by contrast, came at least in part from the Dean of Women, Marion Talbot, a dedicated and ambitious career woman who played a watchdog role to prevent backsliding into female stereotyping by either the University faculty, students, or her charges. I have designated the mandate to her women as "bluestocking"* to indicate both its perfectionist and puritanical character and its resourcefulness.

The women who chose the competitive and elitist careers open to

---

*The term "bluestocking" (Oxford English Dictionary) has had an adverse connotation of unwarranted female pretense to literary scholarship. This paper denies the pretense of female competence, but does retain the scholarly and puritanical connotation of the term.

Ph.D.s in the first four decades of the University of Chicago needed strength and creativity. I will present evidence of their successful survival as academics in the face of a system that discriminated against them as women to a degree that made the professional career patterns of their male mentors at the University almost inaccessible to them. The creativity of these women in surviving and even outflanking the obstacles suggests not only their inner resources, but some peculiar features of early twentieth century academic science. In spite of the professional limitations on women, the biological sciences were sufficiently diverse and flexible to provide unusual opportunities for individuals who were conscious of what was happening to professional life, to the biological sciences, to traditional disciplines such as zoology, and to women.

THE BIOLOGICAL SCIENCES AT THE UNIVERSITY OF CHICAGO

The peculiarities and changes of the biological sciences at the University of Chicago in its first four decades affected both men and women. I shall first discuss the sciences as part of the University of Chicago, a self-consciously modern and growing university, before the Depression of the 1930s; then I shall summarize the peculiar fascination of its biological departments with organismic and medical studies, using the Zoology Department as the major focus. From this we can see that the changes in zoology, and in the natural history and medical sciences as a whole, were distinct though not separable from those of the University, a distinction that will be even clearer as we turn to the women doctorate candidates for our examples.

The new University of Chicago, "Harper's University,"[1] might also be described as the "Athens of land-grant country." Students and faculty at that University were remarkably attached to their alma mater even as they were led away from it in two directions: to the ideal of the university created to rival the elitist men's universities of the Eastern Seaboard, and to the fact of Chicago, the economic and cultural center of the Midwest. Harvard and Yale actually sent a few students to the University of Chicago, eleven and seven, respectively, in the 1920s, while 227 of the 1397 graduate students of that decade came from the University of Chicago itself, followed by Oberlin College in Ohio, and the Canadian McMaster University.[2] The University of Chicago graduate school was also the source of the majority of the faculty: 408 out of the 784 members in 1930, 31 percent of whom had a second degree from the University of

Chicago.[3] This would seem to indicate an exceptional self-confidence on the part of those hiring new faculty and a reluctance on the part of graduate students to leave. When they did leave, graduate students continued to measure their academic experience by the excellence of Chicago, with the letters back from the rapidly changing state universities to the biological mentors at Chicago complaining that it was "difficult for them to keep abreast."[4]

The ideal of the new University of Chicago was to be ahead, not abreast, and to excel in the biological sciences as in all fields. Jacques Loeb, the outstanding German experimental biologist, was the first chairman of the department that combined physiology, physiological chemistry and experimental therapeutics at the University of Chicago. Before leaving for Berkeley in 1902 (and later for the Rockefeller Institute in New York), Loeb shocked the popular and scientific world with his demonstration of chemical parthenogenesis in sea urchins as well as with his assertion that "General physiology is identical with an energetics of vital phenomena."[5]

No less impressive experimentally was C.O. Whitman, the first director of the Woods Hole Marine Biological Laboratory, at which Loeb performed this wonder, and the first chairman of the Zoology Department at the University of Chicago. Whitman, like Loeb—and like Loeb's fictional counterpart in *Arrowsmith* (published in 1925) by Sinclair Lewis[6]—was interested only in research aided by graduate students. The University of Chicago Zoology Department was, therefore, nationally prominent in research while handicapped as a teacher facility. Here, Whitman sought in vertebrate embryology the proof that evolution was orthogenetic, or directed to preformed ends. He brought with him briefly to Chicago W.H. Wheeler, who, in a 1910 lecture at Woods Hole, expanded this teleological viewpoint, which described populations as "organisms," as wise and integrated in their function as the developing pigeon's eggs on which Whitman did his research.[7]

Over the years, both the philosophy and research fields of the Zoology Department changed. A glance at the students of Loeb and Whitman and at the development of their departments indicates a reduced preoccupation with vertebrate research in response to scientific changes and administrative needs. Over the first four decades, the dissertations in biological science became more practical.[8] In botany, many of the men and women wrote on topics closely related to urgent demands for fertilizers and unspoiled vegetables, a realistic recognition that their contributions could be in agriculture and other applied sciences. In zoology and the medical sciences, deficiency diseases and other health concerns appeared in the dissertation lists in significant numbers. After 1918, professional education, combining the basic sciences with traditional concerns of business, agriculture, and medicine, grew more rapidly at the University of Chicago in terms of new resources than did the Graduate School of Arts and Sciences.[9] Loeb and the scientists of the Rockefeller Institution who symbolized these changes for Sinclair Lewis, and the Rockefeller Foundation, which supported the University of Chicago, were committed to the creation of medicine as applied natural science.

At the University of Chicago, the actual history of medical education was far from that of a simple creation and enlargement of a medical school of the Johns Hopkins type. Conflicts between the University (which endorsed Rush Medical College) and the Rockefeller Foundation resulted in the creation of two medical schools and the delay of graduate status for medical education at that University until 1924. Only under Lillie's guidance as head of the Division of Biological Science in the 1930s were the different groups reconciled to a smooth pattern of professional growth.[10]

Lillie is also the key figure in the relationship between the different biological sciences, especially between Physiological Chemistry and his Department of Zoology. Loeb had been intolerant of any but reductionist biological science. In particular, he had a grievance with Lillie, who challenged Loeb's theory of fertilization with biological criticism and with his own biological model. In 1921 Loeb sent a friend a scornful characterization of Lillie as a mystic and a vitalist.[11] Lillie, in turn, wrote Loeb's obituary notice in 1924 in the respectful terms of the man who has had the last word.[12] Lillie also had the last word at the Marine Biological Laboratories, of which he was the director in 1910, and in University of Chicago biology after Loeb left in 1902.

The administrative style at the University of Chicago was the style of F.R. Lillie, Chicago Ph.D. in 1894, Zoology Department Chairman in 1910, and head of the Division of Biological Sciences in 1931.[13] The character of Lillie's leadership deserves attention. Starting out as a researcher in vertebrate embryology under Whitman, Lillie became a superb teacher, and ended up as "a captain of science . . . who holds down two jobs either of which might easily floor many a man who patronizes professors."[14] The industrial image is appropriate to the University of Chicago described in its ten-volume *Survey* of 1933.

These volumes on the state of the University reveal a university self-conscious of its emergence from the scholarly enclave of excellence in the days of Harper, Loeb, and Whitman to the large, professional enterprise that made possible hundreds of academic careers for "keen young men" in the humanities, social sciences, biological sciences, and physical sciences—the four divisions in the reorganization of arts and sciences in 1931. *Trends in Growth*, the title of one of the volumes, could stand for the whole series. In this volume, one learns that the size of the faculty and of the student body doubled from 1913 to 1930, with the number of graduate students tripling, 1908-1930, from 1400 to 4200. The number of graduate students peaked, in fact, in 1928 at 4600, and the number of professional students in 1921 at 4200; by 1931 it was down to 3000.[15]

The faculty at the University of Chicago was a publishing faculty and, taking the division between Instructor-Assistant Professor and Associate-Full Professor as that of Junior and Senior faculty, evenly distributed between the two halves. Seventy percent of the faculty of 1924-1929 published. The scientists were notably productive: all of the Zoology faculty, for example, published during this period an average of 11.1 items.[16] They were duly rewarded. Forty percent of the full professors and 12 percent of the Assistant Professors were listed in *American Men of Science* of 1927.[17] All seven of the zoology faculty were listed, 75 percent of the botanists, but only 30-60 percent of the medical scientists. Success, meaning recognition of one's research as well as professional advancement, was the expectation in the biological sciences at the University of Chicago.

The biological sciences were of differing popularity with the students. The departments of Physiology and Zoology offered a large number of courses, perhaps because of their medical connections. (One University of Chicago undergraduate from this period recalls that she and all of her upper level embryology course classmates under Lillie went on to medical school.) Ninety-five percent of the botany courses, on the other hand, had less than ten students. Only 48 percent of the physiology courses were that small.[18] The biological sciences were second only to the social sciences in the increase of student majors from 1909 to 1928, in spite of the fact that tuition for them was much higher than for courses in other divisions. At the Master's level, biological sciences courses cost twice those of the average graduate or professional courses.[19]

The cost of the University became much more of an issue after 1929, when the Depression made the administration, the Rockefeller Foundation (which financed the University), and the parents of students unable to pay for further *Trends in Growth*. This change appeared only slowly in the statistics, which show the assets of the University rising from about $10 million in 1900 to about $110 million in 1931. Endowments counted for about two-thirds of these figures.[20]

The increase in size of the University, now with ample facilities and rewards for research, teaching, and service, offered a variety of opportunities for its students and for those who returned as faculty.

Lillie's career development, eight years from Ph.D. to Associate Professor at the University of Chicago, plus four years with higher rank at Michigan and Vassar, was a rapid version of the career pattern emerging for men during this period.[21] In 1894 C.M. Child graduated at age 25 with Lillie with a specialty in Zoology; he taught at the University of Chicago and he required 22 years to become a full professor.

In general, faculty who stayed took longer to be promoted. H.H. Newman went away. A full professor at the University of Texas six years after his Ph.D. in 1910, Newman became an Associate Professor at the University of Chicago that same year, and Full Professor in 1917, twelve years after his Ph.D. George Bartelmez, who stayed at the University after his Ph.D. in 1910, took only nine years to become an Associate Professor, but nineteen years to earn Full Professor. W.C. Allee left the University of Chicago and became a tenured Professor at Lake Forest College before returning in 1921 to the University as an Assistant Professor in 1927, ten and fifteen years after his Ph.D. A final example of this younger generation on the University of Chicago Zoology faculty was not a University of Chicago Ph.D. at all. Sewall Wright needed nine years from his D.Sc. to become Associate Professor in 1924, and thirteen to become Full Professor in 1928. These men, in short, regularly ascended the ladder at the University of Chicago, averaging 8½ years to tenure, and 15½ to full professor. One example each from the Pathology and Physiological Chemistry Departments suggest that promotions in the medical sciences were at least as rapid. It took F.C. Koch seven years after his Ph.D. in 1912 to become Associate Professor and Chairman in 1919, and eleven years more to become Full Professor at age 47. Esmund R. Long, with his Ph.D. in 1919, was Associate Professor in only four years and a Full Professor five years later.†

---

†All data on the scientific careers of the men and women, unless otherwise noted, are from *American Men of Science: a Biographical Dictionary*. 1906-1938. James McKeen Cat-

The standardization and growth of the academic industry at the University of Chicago in its first four decades should be kept distinct from the quantitative and qualitative changes in the sciences if we are to understand the diverse needs and achievements of the scientists. The two, however, were associated in the minds of the new generation of young men and women eager to take advantage of the new opportunities, which were associated in the minds of the University administrators, too. All were aware of the industrialists who might "patronize professors" for their scholarly ideals while insisting on their productivity of knowledge that could eventually be used for the social good as advances in medicine and technology. In general, these were not new American educational ideals; they had been supported federally as well as philanthropically since the Land Grant Act of 1862. In the 1920s, however, the notion of pure science as a basic science, as the foundation on which useful technologies and future economic development would depend, was prominent. Lillie received a lengthy plea from the Dean of the Graduate School at the University of Missouri to support such a federal program of scientific research in 1930.‡

Although he was sensitive to his role as "captain of scientific industry" and familiar with the real business world through his wife, Frances Crane, and his connections with the meat packing and dairy industries that helped scientific research, Lillie did not join in this particular move to a closer integration of the universities, the federal government, and business.§

Lillie did develop, however, a Zoology Department in which diverse scientific interests wre integrated and expanded beyond the limits set by C.O. Whitman and C.M. Child. As chairman, Lillie insisted on the importance of undergraduate teaching,[22] as well as of graduate research.

---

tell, Ed.: 1–6. This measure of scientific importance was used by the University of Chicago Survey in the works I have been discussing; also, by Margaret W. Rossiter, in her important study of "Women Scientists in America before 1920" 1974. *American Scientist*. 62:312–323. Rossiter is completing a monograph on the subject of women in American science from the colonial period to the present.

‡William J. Robbins and Charles W. Greene sent to F.R. Lillie, (December 23, 1930, Lillie Papers, Box I, file "A.A.A.S.") a long argument that "it would appear inconsistent to subsidize the superstructure, as has been done in the acts above referred to, without giving attention to the foundations as well."

§By no means do I intend to imply that either the interests of industry or the industrial model were irrelevant either to Lillie or to the development of science at the University of Chicago.

Given the opportunity for new appointments in the 1920s, he brought in men capable of teaching the new genetics and biochemistry without giving over the department entirely to any particular form of biological analysis. By 1919, the senior faculty was Lillie, Child, and H.H. Newman, an authority on evolution and eugenics. The junior faculty, by contrast, consisted of three experts in reproductive biology (Carl Moore, A.W. Bellamy, B.H. Willier) along with the ecologist W.C. Allee. Ten years later, the junior faculty was senior, and Sewell Wright had been added to teach genetics.[23] The return of Allee, a former student, to teach ecology made it clear that Lillie did not include the modern ecologists in his list of those naturalists who had "outlived their major usefulness to the growth of scientific knowledge."¶

Ecology was a joint concern of the Departments of Botany and of Zoology. The first chairman of the Botany Department, John Merle Coulter, established that tradition from the beginning. A student of Asa Gray and the evolution controversy at Harvard, Coulter was also a part of the new generation impressed with the physiological studies of the Germans, and was able to spread their gospel to the American Midwest.[24] Coulter was soon able to make Botany the largest department of the biological sciences,¶¶ and was able to establish a distinctive research tradition, too. His student and colleague, Henry C. Cowles, called Coulter's dynamic ecology "physio-graphy," and made the first effective study of a biological community based on its principles in 1899. This work, in turn, inspired the fundamental ecological studies of his students, including C.C. Adams, Paul Sears, and William Cooper and also inspired the zoologist who had studied under Whitman, and, in turn trained W.C. Allee, V.E. Shelford.** Botany and zoology were closely

¶F.R. Lillie to L.J. Cole, May 22, 1921, in reply to Cole's suggestion that the Society of Naturalists become a new Genetics society. Lillie believed that out of deference to the older naturalists their society should be allowed to die quietly rather than be transformed into a new entity.

¶¶By the biological sciences, I mean the Departments of Anatomy, Bacteriology-hygiene, and Pathology, which I will refer to collectively as "Pathology," the departments of Physiology and Physiological Chemistry/Pharmacology, which I will refer to as "Physiological Chemistry" and the natural history fields of botany and zoology. These departments were all part of the Division of Biological Sciences in 1931, along with Physical Culture, Home Economics and Psychology. Initially, there had been a separate Department of Neurology while Physiological Chemistry was part of Physiology and Pathology was joined with Bacteriology. *Survey.* 5: *Admission and Retention of Students* 15.

**See Henry C. Cowles, "The ecological relations of the vegetation on the sand dunes of Lake Michigan. 1899. *In* The Botanical Gazette 27:95-175. Reprinted *In* Readings in integrated in the study of ecology, and it is not surprising that six of the 32 doctorates in science in the years 1902-1904 were jointly in the two departments.

Twenty years later, the closest ties of the Zoology Department were with physiological chemistry. These ties were cemented by a common interest in reproductive physiology, and a Rockefeller-supported grant from the National Research Council (NRC).[25] Lillie won approximately $143,000 over the eleven years from 1922-1933 by virtue of his own research linking hormones to the development of sex characters, and by virtue of the cooperative studies by biologists and biochemists that he could promise at Chicago. Lillie's skill as a vertebrate zoologist allowed him to answer the riddle of the freemartin, an embryological puzzle of some standing concerning cattle twins, the one male and the other of uncertain sex. Lillie showed, by painstaking morphological and statistical study, that the cotwin must be a female masculinized *in utero* by a blood-born substance from her brother.[26] Lillie thus enhanced his prominence as an embryologist, while giving a decisive turn to the science of endocrinology, which then included the study of blood-born chemical messengers producing changes in the form, function, and behavior of organisms.[27] The correlation of chemical parts in the determination of sex became the concern of his student and colleague, Carl Moore, who joined the faculty in 1919, and devoted his research entirely to the elucidation of the causal factors of sex characteristics. Moore's success in this new subject led to his national prominence as a biologist and to the chairmanship of the Chicago Zoology Department when Lillie left for a higher academic post in 1931. That research was supported by the NRC grant. B. H. Willier and A.W. Bellamy also joined this broad research venture, the first as an embryologist, the other as a cytologist. In all, Lillie trained and supported on the research grant a large number of the prominent researchers in this field for the next generation.[28]

These cooperative studies between zoology and botany, and between zoology and physiological chemistry were intended to be a balance and challenge "against the extreme Mendelian school and also the extreme mechanistic school of thought in biology," as Lillie put it in a letter to the

---

Ecology. 1965. Edward J. Kormondy, Ed.: 129-133. Widely divergent interpretations of this holistic ecology which emphasize the social and moral issues at stake are Nature's Economy by Don Wooster. 1977. Sierra Club Books. San Francisco, Calif., and The Economy of Nature and the Evolution of Sex by Michael Ghiselin. 1974, University of California Press: Berkeley, Calif.

Rockefeller Foundation.[29] Sex researchers at the University of Chicago were responsible for the development of important bioassays and chemical analyses of the hormones involved in reproductive control. Carl Moore and Dorothy Price in 1930 developed a new model of reproductive control by "negative feedback" between gonad and pituitary, a development of enduring significance. Finally, the Chicago group—Lillie, Moore, Domm, and Mary Juhn—played the major role in creating the first textbook of sex endocrinology, *Sex and Internal Secretions* published in 1932 under the auspices of the NRC.[30]

These interdisciplinary studies were also of significance to the professional development of students at the University of Chicago. For the zoologists, they meant new opportunities at a time when "there seems to

TABLE 1

138 WOMEN EARNING PH.D.S IN NATURAL HISTORY AND BIOMEDICAL SCIENCES UNIVERSITY OF CHICAGO, 1892–1932

	1893–1902	1903–1912	1913–1922	1923–1932	Total
Natural History = 86					
Botany	1	15	17	33	66
Zoology	3	3	4	10	20
Total	4	18	21	43	86
Biomedical Sciences = 52					
"Pathology" Anatomy	0	1	2	1	4
Bacteriology/Hygiene	1	0	2	4	7
Hygiene Pathology	0	0	2	0	2
Subtotal	1	1	6	5	13
"Physiological Chemistry"*					
Physiology	2	1	3	9	15
P. Chemistry	0	0	0	6	6
P. Chem minor	0	0	4	7	11
Chemistry	1	5			6
Home Economics	0	1			1
Subtotal	3	7	7	22	39
Total	4	8	13	27	52
Total	8	26	34	70	138

* Physiological Chemistry separated from Physiology in 1916–1917. I have included data in the Chemistry, Home Economics, and Physiology women, before that change, as well as on the later Physiology women. The term "minor" is mine, indicating the second department listed in the *President's Report* on dissertations.

be more demand for physiology and pathology."[31] The man who wrote this to Lillie ended up as chairman of the medical department at the University of Texas; the following chart of the number of women in different fields at Chicago from 1893 to 1932, by decade, reinforces this view of the professional demand for medical scientists. The percentage of women in natural history fell from 69 to 61 from 1903-1933, whereas the percentage in "Pathology" peaked in the third decade at 17 percent, and the percentage in "Physiological Chemistry" in the fourth decade at 31 percent. The percentage of zoologists rose slightly to 14 percent.

ACADEMICS, BLUESTOCKINGS AND WOMEN: 1892-1932

While looking at the use that women made of the scientific and professional training available at the University of Chicago, I will introduce three overlapping interpretations of their experience to suggest the complexity of the demands on these scholars. The first is a model of opportunity, the second of discrimination, and the third of compromise. The first, that Chicago provided a rare opportunity for women to get a higher education equal to that of men, was the ideal of Harper's University, which produced a major share of all women Ph.D.'s in the United States in Harper's early years. The personal accounts of the women entering Chicago throughout this period reflect a sense of awareness of personal opportunity, despite gender, that was both unexpected and seen as "marvellous." Letters to Lillie from grateful graduates who describe themselves as happily situated in congenial teaching positions and continually inspired by the research ideals learned at the University of Chicago indicate the validity of this perception.††

The glitter, however, wore a little thin as the University of Chicago grew and diversified in the 1920s, and women came to realize that they were not successfully competing for fellowship money, for jobs at their Alma Mater, or for positions of authority. The situation at the University of Chicago was particularly discriminatory;‡‡ TABLE 2 shows that the small numbers of women make an absence of role models, and

††Margaret Murray was among those who wrote back fondly to the zoological "family" with gratitude for the opportunities Lillie opened up for her; Lillie Papers, Box 5, Folder 16. See also in that collection the correspondence with Ellinor Behre, Hazel Field, Marie Hinrichs, Libbie Hyman, Helen Ingraham, Alice MacDougall, M.S. MacDougall, Bertha Martin, Chi Che Wang, Alice Wilcox, and R. Arlena Young.

‡‡Compiled from the reports of the Dean of Women, Marion Talbot, *In* The President's Report, The University of Chicago Press, for the years given.

TABLE 2

WOMEN FACULTY MEMBERS, UNIVERSITY OF CHICAGO, 1892–1924

		Rank				
	No. Fac. Women	Arts Science	Profs.	Instr.	Other	Fellows
1892–1897	18	—	4	1	—	—
1903	52	17	3	14	—	14
1912	49	23	8	6	9	18
1913	51	25	8	7	10	19
1920	58	39	12	10	19	21
1921	56	31	12	17	2	21
1922	61	32	12	18	2	16
1923	78	33	12	20	1	26
1924	75	—	—	—	—	27

strengthens the message that women belong in the lower ranks and in particular subjects.

The story of the development of Home Economics as an alternative to careers in chemistry for women will not be told here. Instead, I will briefly describe the attempt to challenge the "feminine stereotype" of intellectual inferiority and disinterest with an inspiring vision of superiority and success, a "bluestocking" ideology appropriate to the early years at the University of Chicago. In conclusion, I will suggest some social influences on the career experience of the women, in addition to the experiences of professional discrimination and scientific opportunity.

Marion Talbot took seriously her mandate as Dean of Women at a University officially committed to equal opportunities for men and women when it opened its doors in 1892. Over 30 years of service, she worked to construct an environment in which women could work and live effectively by allowing them to make scholarly and social contributions in order to justify their existence and privileges. (This was the Chicago not only of the Home Economics Movement under Talbot and Sophonsiba Breckenridge but the Social Work Movement of Jane Addams and other social scientists and social activists.§§) At the University

§§Rosalind Resenberg describes the attack on the traditional feminine stereotypes by Chicago social scientists in The dissent from Darwin: the new view of woman among American social scientists. 1890–1915. *In* In Search of Woman's Nature, 1850–1920, *Feminist Studies*, 1975, **3**:141–154.

of Chicago, Talbot paid attention to the provision of resources for women's sports. Physical Culture was a department in the Biological Science division, and for uplifting recreation and guidance in the house system *in loco parentis* for these young ladies and scholars. Talbot fought for these resources on an equal footing with the men, and her efforts culminated with the building of Noyes Hall in 1913, a triumph she describes in her autobiography, *More Than Lore*.[32]

Talbot also describes her efforts to prevent the backsliding of the University on its commitment to nondiscrimination. This discrimination took two forms, the attempt in 1902 formally to segregate the women from competition with the men in separate sections of all their courses. This protection of the male ego failed, as Talbot tells it, because of the inability of the administration to make all departments conform, and because of the preference that males continued to show for integrated classrooms. By 1907, when some male students requested permission to use quarters designated "for women only," the whole scheme folded.[33]

Talbot found that the move to formal segregation was linked to the relative superiority of the women scholars, which she tried to document in her annual reports to the President. *Survey* statistics showed that the women's colleges sent Chicago its best graduate students.[34] At Chicago, Talbot showed that they won a superior share of undergraduate and graduate honors, and completed their courses with no more absence or tardiness than their male costudents They did differ in one respect, however. As students they were awarded less scholarship aid, three-fifths of the fellowship money their numbers deserved in 1902–04 and less than one half in 1922.[35]

Talbot also went to some pains to show that women were anxious to go on to graduate studies, and that the feminine stereotype of the "shrinking" (as well as intellectually inferior) girl student was false. In spite of the discriminatory fellowship situation in 1903, she found that in the first decade Chicago women had gone on to graduate studies in equal numbers with men. They still did so in 1920, when more took MAs, and fewer took Ph.Ds.

The fights that Talbot could not win against feminine stereotyping and against sex discrimination relate to another struggle, the one with which I began this section: equal career achievement for women at the University of Chicago. Only two women of the class of 1923 had been given faculty appointments as instructors at the University, whereas 15 men found places as associate professors, one as assistant professor, six as instructors and one as an assistant.[36] Only two women were full professors in the entire faculty. Talbot finally sent a modest and discreet list of grievances to the President in 1923 that scarcely mentioned promotions but the list did result in the appointment of three women to full professor in the next few years. By 1929, there were 34 women in professional positions on the University faculty, 18 of them in Chemistry and the Biological Sciences, exclusive of Home Economics. Meanwhile, feeling that "no great progress was made," Talbot resigned as Dean.[37]

With the departure of Talbot, the University set up a committee on women's affairs as part of "the present day tendency toward group study and control."[38] The tendency was away from the advocacy role of feminist bluestocking.

The bluestocking model failed to prevent academic discrimination against women, as Jessie Bernard had shown; it also failed to produce growth in the numbers of women entering careers rather than marriage after 1929. Bernard has been particularly sensitive to the sociology of women's assignment to marginal professional roles and to their exclusion from certain scientific fields.[39] This is true, but the experience of the women trained in Biology at the University of Chicago indicates a resourcefulness and tenacity on their part in their careers that should be included in a description of their academic behavior.

There were significant differences in the career experiences of the women trained before, and those trained after the first World War. Let us begin with the ten women botanists graduated in the seven years before and seven years after the war whose biographies are included in *American Men of Science*. These initial entries, in the first to sixth editions of 1906–1938, do not tell us the ultimate achievements of the women, only their status at the time of this professional recognition. The women in the first group averaged 22 years of age at the time of their B.A.s and 30 years of age at the time of their Ph.D.s. Three had prepared at the "Seven Sisters," the eastern elitist women's colleges, two had studied at the University of Chicago, two at State Universities, and two at small coeducational colleges. Five of the ten held fellowships at the University of Chicago, but all worked before and during their Ph.D. education. Their positions five years after graduation were comparable to those of the men who were advanced every four or five years at the University of Chicago. Two became instructors, three assistant professors, and two, full professors at small Midwestern colleges. The assistant professors were at state universities, and the instructors were at

Smith College and the University of Chicago. One woman was in business and two of the married women were unemployed.

The postwar group of eight were all employed; the five about whom I have data were in academic jobs, two at the "Seven Sisters" and three at small private colleges as assistant or associate professors. These women were clearly finding their niches in teaching natural history. Several made use of personal connections as 28 percent (5/18) returned to their undergraduate colleges to teach, (More than one held a position at Milwaukee-Downer College, the University of North Dakota, and Tulane University for reasons that are not clear.) Their entry in *American Men of Science* indicates thast they had national status and defined themselves as research scientists in a variety of botanical fields including the ecological studies suggested by their Chicago training. The most successful member of the group, however, was slow in advancing, since she stayed at the University of Chicago. Sophia Eckerson, a Ph.D. in 1911, left Chicago still an instructor in 1920; however, she found advancement in the U.S. Department of Agriculture, the University of Wisconsin, and the Boyce Thompson Institute. She was starred in the 1938 edition of *American Men of Science* for her research in plant Physiology and Microchemistry, a field not favored by her Alma Mater, but one in which she excelled.

A look at the zoology graduates from 1903–1932, fourteen years before and after the Great War, indicates a decline in the status of women during this period, and highlights the peculiar ways in which they found opportunities for rewarding scientific work. These women were as uniformly academic as the botanists, four of the twelve as assistant professors, three as instructors, and four as research aides to their departments. The one reproductive biology researcher, Mary Hardesty, was unemployed. The failure of Mary to "make it" in this important area of research was a continuation of her graduate experience. Twelve of the 13 zoology Ph.D.s in reproductive biology were men, as were seven of the eight graduate students supported with the funds from the Natural Research Council. The reason for this exclusion was professional competition, rather than scientific competence, as the two women who made major contributions to reproductive biology at Chicago discovered. They were both research assistants whose elucidation of the endocrine control of sex characteristics did not lead to advancement on the tenure track, a professional cost balanced by their scientific recognition and prestige.

Professional advancement in zoology was difficult. The women, like the men, found zoology positions harder to find than those in medicine. One postwar woman graduate, without an MD, was an instructor in surgery, and one of the two preeminent prewar zoology women graduate students, Maud Slye, was hired in 1911 without her Ph.D. at the Otho Sprague Memorial Institute of Pathology, an appointment that eventually took her up the ladder at the University of Chicago as far as associate professor. She was a scientist dedicated to a single and compelling hypothesis: the hereditary nature of cancer. The second zoology "great" of the prewar period was Libbie Hyman, Ph.D. in 1914-15 and research assistant and associate for C.M. Child until his retirement in 1934, after which she supported herself in the backrooms of the American Museum of Natural History by the proceeds of her textbooks in vertebrate zoology written for the University of Chicago courses which she, as a staff member, did not teach. Also ironic is the fact that Libbie Hyman's achievement as a scientist was a monumental study of the invertebrates, not in vertebrate zoology. Nor was she famous (starred in the third edition of *American Men of Science*) for a great discovery. Future study will help us understand how women made the psychological adjustments to their failure relative to the status of men, and to the demands of the bluestocking model. This study simply shows that a number of women saw in their disadvantaged position an opportunity to excel at what their mentors regarded as the margins of science and the byways of their profession.¶

Libbie Hyman succeeded by filling in an important but ignored niche in the traditional literature of her field. She made herself valuable as a research assistant to Child by virtue of her chemical ability, which compensated for the deliberate ignorance of chemistry on the part of the holistic morphologist. We have seen that Sophia Eckerson, trained in botany, also became expert in the new chemistry, as did, perforce, the women who went into the medical sciences. These women had the opportunity to develop with physiological chemistry from its status as a tool of medical research to that of revolutionary new science.

¶ All the biographical information on these women is from American Men of Science, Editions 1-6. Additional information about Libbie H. Hyman from American Women of Science, 1943, E. Yost, Ed.:122-138, J. B. Lippencott, New York, N.Y., and about Dorothea Rudnick (Zoology Ph.D. in 1931) from Women of Modern Science, 1960, E. Yost, Ed.:156-170, Dodd Mead & Co., New York, N.Y. I am grateful to Susan Ruane of Boston University for her help in compiling these data.

After an initial interest in physiology coincident with the establishment of the University of Chicago, there were no women Ph.D.s in the subject until the time of World War I. Clara Jacobsen took her Ph.D. in 1916 and her M.D. three years later. This was also the career path of Greisheimer in physiology who followed Jacobsen in 1918, then Tower in 1925, Smith in 1926, and Stewart in 1927. The two degrees allowed these women to make careers jointly in medical research and medical practice, while two other women (about whom I have information from *American Men of Science*) were able to carry on research in systems physiology. Four of the women held academic appointments in physiology five years after the Ph.D., as did Marie Hinrichs, Ph.D. in zoology in 1922. Lillie arranged an NRC fellowship for her that helped her move from her traditional study of the effects of caffeine on *Planaria* (under Child) to an expertise on the hereditability of induced light sensitivity. (Later Hinrichs took an M.D. at Chicago and moved into school and public health work in the Chicago area.)[40]

The physiological chemists also had the opportunity to move into clinical positions. Eloise Parsons took an M.D. and went into clinical work after a brief period on the Chicago faculty in 1923. Two others who were on the faculty and were married were outstandingly successful in scientific research: Ida Kraus (Ragina) and Elizabeth Miller (Koch). The latter was the wife of the acting chairman of the department, who was collaborating in sex research with F.R. Lillie. She was an autonomous worker with her own grant from Rockefeller Foundation in the 1930s, with an outstanding set of discoveries concerning vitamin D, and a discontinuous professional career.[ІІІ] Unlike, for example, Hathaway, who moved from Physiological Chemistry to Home Economics for her career after Chicago, Elizabeth Miller made her first career in Home Economics at Battle Creek College and a full professorship. She then transferred into Physiological Chemistry and then did her research at Chicago.

The women "pathologists," that is the graduates in anatomy, bacteriology and pathology, had the most success in finding jobs at Chicago. L. DeWitt, after a long and tortured career, became an associate professor on the faculty in 1918, the grade to which we have

---

[ІІІ]See the Rockefeller Foundation archives file on "University of Chicago, Spectroscopic Biology," *passim*. Note especially the favorable comments on Elizabeth Miller (Koch)'s work in Warren Weaver's diary entry for January 14, 1937.

seen that Maud Slye, the zoologist, was also able to rise. Florence Seibert attained a similar rank in 1928, when two recent graduates, Ada Verder and Gail Dack, were given junior positions. The two most famous of the group made their names elsewhere: Ida Bengtson, whose distinction was scientific and professional as the first woman appointed to the Federal Department of Agriculture in 1916, three years before her Ph.D., and Maud Menton, graduate in 1915-16, who made an academic career at the Rockefeller Institute, Western Reserve and the University of Pittsburgh. She, like Libbie Hyman, and Sophia Eckerson in the natural history departments, made good use of the chemical opportunities and competed at the center of the new biochemistry of enzyme kinetics.

CONCLUSION

This paper has outlined the constraints and opportunities faced by women in the biological sciences at the University of Chicago. The opportunities were inherent in an expanding university and a controversial, contradictory field; and the constraints were inherent in a society in which it was assumed that with men and women in competition, the woman must lose.*** I have described some of the responses to that constraint on the careers of the women that show us their ability to exploit exciting and well-funded field peculiarities: their advancement was slower, and their interest in social services greater than that of men. In spite of this, and in spite of the model of male advancement exemplified by their teachers, the women were surprisingly successful in surviving in a variety of roles in academic life developing en route alternative life styles from that of most women while overturning the traditional stereotype of females. Some women recognized that they could trade-in the status of "ladder" positions for the security and intellectual advantages of the research assistantships from which the most notable made their impact on science. They traded, in other words, professional marginality for scientific success, a trade that could work only for the unusual woman in an unusual field at a time when science was becoming increasingly dependent on organization and resources.

***This discouraging message was explicitly stated as reasonable in a career guide for women in 1927. O. Latham Hatcher, *Occupations for Women*, Southern Women's Educational Alliance: 24. Richmond, Va. An article by Jo Freeman in *Green Hearings*, 1969, 994-1003, describes the absence of "Women in the Social Science Faculty since 1892 at the University of Chicago."

Even this introductory picture of the conditions for success by women in American Science before World War II must at least mention the social position of these women in relation to marriage, class, and ethnic background. The barrier of marriage to a career was lowered for women in the 1920s, when some of the most successful combined that traditional feminine role with scientific research in the same field as that of their husbands. The dissertation lists for physiological chemistry, with pairs of names such as Still in 1928 and D'Amour, suggest that student as well as faculty women were successful in this social innovation.

The dissertation lists also tell us something of the class and ethnicity of the Biology women at Chicago. Students such as Harrison, Hardesty, and Vincent carried the names of successful scientists of the period. The names that *reappear* on the list are predominately the common English names Still, Gregory, Vincent, Roberts, Young, Smith, Evans, Johnson, and the old Yankee names of Clapp, Abbott, Fernald, Claypole, Hardesty. They are also Scottish, like Kyrk, Dutch, like DeWitt, Rudnick, and Behre; German, like Kuch and Pfeiffer; and French, like Blount and D'Amour.

The predominance of Yankee and northern European families in higher education at this time is not surprising. It was incorporated into the bluestocking model for academic success. Talbot firmly believed that the intellectual claims of women should be tied to their social behavior, just as she worked to form a congenial social environment in which they could work. She was not always successful in controlling that behavior, and, like most of the early feminists, she viewed the changes in social *mores* of the twenties with some alarm. That she found it necessary, even before World War I, to remind the women that "we are talking about American ladies, not German professors"[11] indicates the gap that existed between social expectations and behavior. It also reminds us that the bluestocking social model was competing with the intellectual claims of the University and of science. For the historian, all three must be included in an understanding of the changing role of women in American science.

Acknowledgments

I wish to thank Peter Buck and Gerald Geison for their helpful criticism of this paper.

References

1. STORR, R.J. 1966. Harper's University: The Beginnings. University of Chicago Press. Chicago, Ill.
2. REEVES, F.W. & JOHN DALE RUSSELL, EDS. 1933. University of Chicago Survey. Admission and Retention of University Students 5:142. University of Chicago Press. Chicago, Ill.
3. SURVEY. 3:25. University Faculty.
4. JOHNSON, G.E. to F.R. Lillie. 1922. Letter. Papers of F.R. Lillie. Box IV. Folder 18. University of Chicago. Chicago, Ill.
5. LILLIE, F.R. Typescript of obituary notice. F.R. Lillie papers. Box V. Folder 5 cites this passage from Arch. F.d. ges Physiol. 1897. 69:249. The best account of Loeb's mechanism is by Donald Fleming, Introduction to Jacques Loeb, The Mechanistic Conception of Life. Harvard University Press. Cambridge, Mass. 1964.
6. ROSENBERG, C. 1963. Martin Arrowsmith: the Scientist as Hero. American Quarterly 15:447-58.
7. LILLIE, F.R. 1911. Charles Otis Whitman. J. Morphol.: 22:xv-lxxvii; M.A. EVANS & H.E. EVANS. 1970. William Morton Wheeler. Harvard University Press. Cambridge, Mass.
8. UNIVERSITY OF CHICAGO. Abstract of Theses: Science 1922-1933. 10 vols. University of Chicago Press. Chicago, Ill.
9. SURVEY. Trends in Growth 10:130: Table 23.
10. WATTERSON, R.L. Frank Rattay Lillie, 1870-1958. Dictionary of Scientific Biography 8:354-60.
11. LOEB, J. to J. Pickering. Letter. Jacques Loeb papers. Library of Congress. Washington, D.C. My thanks to Donna Haraway for this reference.
12. LILLIE, F.R. Jacques Loeb's Work in General Biology.
13. WATTERSON, R.L. Frank Rattay Lillie.
14. Personalities in Science: Frank Rattray Lillie. 1937. Scientific American: 123.
15. SURVEY. Trends in Growth. 10:14.
16. SURVEY. University Faculty 3:296.
17. SURVEY. University Faculty:40.
18. SURVEY. Trends in Growth 10:63.
19. SURVEY. Class Size and University Costs, 11:136.
20. SURVEY. Trends in Growth. 10:167.
21. SURVEY. University Faculty, 3:64-65.
22. WATTERSON, R.L. Frank Rattray Lillie, 1870-1958. Dictionary of Scientific Biography 8:354-60.
23. NEWMAN, H.H. 1948. History of the Department of Zoology at the University of Chicago. Bios. 19:4.
24. DUPREE, A. HUNTER. 1968. Asa Gray: 384-409. Atheneum. New York, N.Y.

25. ABERLE, S., & G. CORNER. 1953. Twenty-five Years of Sex Research: History of the National Research Council Committee for Research in Problems of Sex 1922-1947. Saunders. Philadelphia, Pa.
26. LILLIE, F.R. 1917. The Free-martin: a Study of the Action of Sex Hormones in the Embryonic Life of Cattle. J. Exp. Zool. **23**:371.
27. HALL, D.L. 1976. Biology, Sex Hormones and Sexism in the 1920s. *In* Women and Philosophy. Carol Gould and Marx Wartofsky, Eds.: 81-96. Putnam. New York, N.Y.
28. WILLIER, B.H. 1947. Frank Rattray Lillie 1870-1947. Biog. Mem. Nat. Acad. Sc. **30**:179-283.
29. LILLIE, F.R. to Warren Weaver. 1933. *In* The F.R. Lillie Papers in Woods Hole, Garland Allen, Ed. (9):3. Massachusetts. The Mendel Newsletter. 1973.
30. ALLEN, E. Ed. 1932. Sex and Internal Secretions. Williams and Wilkins. Baltimore, MD.
31. SINCLAIR, J.G. to F.R. Lillie. Lillie papers. Box VI, Folder 10.
32. TALBOT, M. 1936. More than Lore: Reminiscences of Marion Talbot, Dean of Women, University of Chicago 1895-1925. University of Chicago Press. Chicago, Ill.
33. TALBOT, M. 1936. More than Lore: Reminiscences of Marion Talbot, Dean of Women, University of Chicago 1895-1925. University of Chicago Press. Chicago, Ill.:171 and The President's Report, 1907-08: 102.
34. SURVEY. Admission and Retention of University Students **5**:151.
35. THE PRESIDENT'S REPORT. 1902-04: 110; 1922-23: 33-34.
36. THE PRESIDENT'S REPORT. 1922-23: 34.
37. TALBOT, M. 1936. More than Lore:37-39.
38. THE PRESIDENT'S REPORT, 1925-26: 41.
39. BARNARD, J. 1964. Academic Women Penn. State Univ. Press. University Park, Pa.
40. **MARIE HINRICHS. American Men and Women of Science, 12th Edit.**
41. TALBOT, M. 1936. More than Lore: Reminiscenses of Marion Talbot, Dean of Women, University of Chicago 1895-1925. University of Chicago Press. Chicago, Ill: 67.

Psychological Challenges Confronting Women in The Sciences

RUTH MOULTON
William Alanson White Institute of Psychiatry
New York, New York 10024

THE EXTERNAL CHALLENGES that confront women in the sciences have changed dramatically in the last ten years. Many more career options are available, especially in the so-called "hard sciences" such as physics and mathematics, where the clear, precise, rational approach usually attributed to men was deemed most necessary. The intuitive, empathic approach attributed to women had earlier allowed them entrance into medicine, psychology, and social sciences. The male-oriented culture could accept women as healers and observers of social processes because these came closer to the accepted sex-role stereotypes. Having worked recently in therapy with women physicists, biologists, and biochemists, I have become aware of how much more prejudice women in these fields face than do women physicians, psychiatrists, and psychologists. The latter are now in more demand due partly to the effects of feminism. The biological basis for differences between the capacities and behavior of the two sexes has now been carefully studied by endocrinologists, neurophysiologists, psychologists, and others and it is now proven that innate differences vary more between individuals than between sexes, except for the differences between the sexual organs themselves.[3] It has also been shown statistically that small variations in activity patterns, in sensitivity to visual and auditory stimuli, in tendencies to cling or withdraw under stress—all the observable differences between newborns—are rapidly altered by child-rearing practices. Thus, the effect of the environment, of learning through parents who transmit the culture, is responsible for the vast majority of differences observed between adult men and women. Although there is more work to be done for further clarity, the constitutional basis for sex-role stereotypes has been greatly undermined. Prejudices remain, however, despite new evidence and increased social awareness.

Another positive advance has been the addition of new legal supports for women such as laws against sex discrimination in jobs, in pay, and in advancement into responsible jobs. There are new avenues for redress, such as grievance committees, mechanisms for affirmative action, and an increase in serious women's groups for mutual encouragement and support. Many of these avenues are not properly utilized and exist much more on paper than in fact. Too often the old prejudices have had to go underground, becoming more hidden, covert, and discreet, because of the new laws. Since it is harder to see the issues clearly, there is added confusion, self-doubt, and bewildered resentment among women. The problem of using "apparently" available new opportunities is further increased by the present economic situation, which has in general increased job competition.

Women scientists are seen as very real threats to male survival. These external problems are only too real and deserve all the public attention and political action possible. However, many women here know more about this aspect of the problem than I and are in a better position to fight the outside battle.

As a psychiatrist, my contribution is in a different sphere; namely, to point out the internal psychological challenges that threaten to undermine a woman's effectiveness to fight for her rights because of inner fears of which she may not be aware. Successful women scientists have been shown to be intellectually superior to their male counterparts in many instances.[1] This is not surprising, since the woman usually has to obtain better grades and work harder to advance in the man's world. These women often appear to be unusually independent, having gone against the mainstream rather than following the expected domestic, marital path. Thus they often appear more self-confident and stronger than they really are. When one looks at their inner psychic lives, their doubts and anxieties hidden even from themselves are evident to the psychiatrist, who discovers them in the process of therapy. Of course, there are many who could profit from psychotherapy who do not come because they feel it would an admission of weakness. But from those who do, we can make observations that apply to many others. One of the purposes of this paper is to spell out some of the hidden conflicts; increased awareness of them may be quite helpful to others who are faced with similar dilemmas.

The women scientists I have seen would not be considered "psychiatrically sick" but they did have character problems that interfered with their professional struggles. They also had enough knowledge of, or curiosity about psychotherapy to come to see if such treatment could help. They came once or twice a week, usually for a matter of months rather than years. Their central problems were very similar to those of women in other professions such as law, banking, and medicine. The differences were not in the basic psychodynamics but in the external specific issues. The most prominent intrapsychic conflicts will be discussed under the headings of 1) Hidden Dependency Needs, leading to fear of disapproval and separation anxiety; 2) Fear of Assertion, Aggression, and Anger; 3) Fear of Failure and/or Success, leading to performance anxiety; 4) Fear of being Unfeminine, sexually unattractive, unable to attract or hold on to a man; being childless, or a "bad" mother. These various problems may overlap and reinforce each other. They will be described briefly and then illustrated by specific case examples.

Hidden Dependency Needs

Competent women who are often financially independent, have authority over students and technicians and who are presumably in command of their own sphere of influence, are often unable to see their hidden areas of dependency. This inability may be seen in their sensitivity to disapproval and criticism by peers who may be competitive and jealous and whose comments may be undermining, self-serving, and lacking in scientific objectivity. Women are prepared for male hostility but expect support from female coworkers and are often surprised that other women can sometimes be their worst enemies.[1] Women, as underdogs, have too often vied with each other instead of fighting the common enemy, whether it be a man, a committee, or a federal agency. This fear of female disapproval may often be traced back to a submissive, housebound mother who tried to persuade her daughter not to go into a scientific field but to be more like "other women." The daughter may have resisted and seemed to have rebelled successfully, only to find that when the female head of her department or laboratory finds fault with her work or fails to give it appropriate credit, she begins to doubt the value of her own work and feels like a helpless, tearful child because her faith in herself has been shaken. She may feel too defeated to argue her own case. A hidden area of psychological vulnerability has been hit, immobilizing her. If exactly the same thing happened with a male authority, her years of competition during training would have prepared her. The wish to gain acceptance from mother-figures goes back to early childhood. A woman may, unknowingly, spend a large part of her life proving that her way, although quite different, was right after all. This shows that the separation from mother was never fully resolved; her autonomy rests on a shaky base.

Unresolved dependency on male authorities is also common. The majority of women scientists received their first intellectual encouragement from their fathers; these girls were often the oldest child, taking the place of the father's son.[5] If there was a son, the father may have been more critical and demanding of him and felt less need to compete with the girl. She may have enjoyed the role of father's favorite, enjoyed pleasing him, and became the typical "good" girl and good student that I have described before.[10] This pattern may work very well through graduate school and postdoctoral fellowships when the capacity to work well with men can be an asset, especially if she is pleasing, gracious, not overly competitive, able and willing to add a welcome "feminine" touch. This equilibrium tends to break down over a period of time as the struggle for advancement grows; there is competition to get on the tenure ladder, to get tenure, to be given increasing responsibility, earn a larger salary, and so on. Then the woman is apt to lose out if she continues to be placating or ingratiating, to be too tactful, to keep too low a profile. Those men who consider science to be their realm may accept her help or even copy or steal her ideas, but they may exclude her from informal conversations and other sources of peripheral data that are necessary to keep her oriented regarding the immediate political and current scientific situation. This was documented fifteen years ago by the sociologist Jessie Bernard in a study of laboratory bioscientists.[1] Laboratory policy showed no evidence of discrimination against women, but fewer women belonged to professional societies, went to professional meetings, visited other labs, were editors or members of professional panels or committees. They were more sedentary, more limited in face-to-face contacts with other bioscientists. They were as active as men with respect to communication by mail, sending reprints, and other activities that required less direct confrontation with male colleagues. It is hoped that, today there is less difference between the sexes on these points. Many women have learned to expose themselves publicly in a more assertive way. Others may expect men to reward them automatically for excellent work, long hours, and faithful attendance, as did father, teachers, thesis advisers, and other earlier male mentors. They are caught in the familiar female stereotype of facilitator who accommodates to man's needs and submerges her own.[2] If she does not learn how to deal with this kind of exclusion differently, she may go on slowly, discouraged with her work, resentful of the men who get ahead. She may lose much of her early enthusiasm and imagination, settle for low status, or even drop out of the field entirely. Or, she may become bitter and hostile, sabotaging her own work, being so unpleasant that she antagonizes people and decreases her opportunities for advancement. It is necessary and constructive, given the tenets of the particular situation, for her to find an appropriate and effective way of fighting.

Fear of Being Aggressive or Self-Assertive

Boys and men have been encouraged to learn to fight for themselves, to express their anger and use it as fuel for action. Girls and women have been discouraged from fighting because it is "unladylike." They are expected to repress anger even when it is justified. Thus most women have much less experience in fighting for their rights; are afraid of aggression as dangerous and "unfeminine." They are more apt to back away from a battle, resorting to anxiety, tears, or hysterical, inappropriate outbursts than confronting the issues directly, seeing them clearly as a matter of fact demanding appropriate action. It has been said that "the aggressive man commands our respect. He shows courage and strength" to stand up and fight for what he believes in or what he wants, even when it brings anger or disapproval from others.[8] The "aggressive woman," however, is seen as castrating, bitchy, even repulsive. The fear of being so labeled further handicaps women in their efforts toward healthy self-assertion.

Examples of this are seen in women who are so anxious about speaking in public that they become tremorous and inarticulate, and cannot make their point clear, or are so confused—even faint—that they have to leave a conference or remain silent. Childhood fears of ridicule return; memories of boys who taunted girls who talked up in class. Some women find it very difficult to handle scientific meetings attended mainly by men, combined with social situations, such as luncheons, dinners, cocktails. They find it very hard to make sudden transitions from social chat to serious discussion; these two levels of discourse were so separate for them originally that they find it hard to shift smoothly from one role to another. The problem of appropriate clothing can be torture; do they dress in a feminine or a professional style? Male clothing is more homogeneous, less revealing.

Some women are all too aware of how men dread female rage, fear female power,[12] and become protective of the man, using his fragile self-esteem as an excuse for their own inaction. This can often be traced back to a wish to protect father from mother's contempt or indifference. It can also reflect her need to protect the husband or male authority on whom she is dependent. She fears she will lose him if she speaks up, and she suffers from "separation anxiety." Previous unfortunate experiences with men who abandoned her may reinforce this. She than fails to discover that some men will respect her more and treat her better if she stands up for herself.

A good example of this fear of self-assertion is shown by a woman physicist who felt that she owed her early success to the tutelage of a brilliant but very chauvinistic man who had helped her get her Ph.D. but who had also exploited her both professionally and sexually. He was able to exclude her from presenting their findings at an important international meeting because she lacked funds. He failed to let her know that the Federal Government would give matching funds to equal those offered by the scientific society, and she did not even inquire about such a possibility but gave her share of the money to him. He then not only presented the paper on his own, omitting her name entirely, but used the extra money to take a trip around the world. She did not learn of this until several years later. It became useful data in therapy to illustrate her passive acquiescence. By then she was working on her own in a large, prestigious university. Supported by sound experimental work, she had made an observation that could have enormous, significant repercussions. In order to document this work further, however, she needed some expensive apparatus. She politely asked the head of the department for the equipment, only to be told that it was prohibitively expensive. She felt defeated and gave up. Later she overheard a younger male colleague making a similar request in such a more urgent and compelling way as to elicit immediate agreement from the same authority. She noted that he had presented his need for equipment with great self-assurance, explaining how essential the apparatus was. In essence, he *demanded* help; she had merely *requested* it in due humility, as she had been trained to do at home and under male tutelage. This episode made her examine her lack of an adequate professional stance and her tendency to understate her cause, presenting herself as a "nice girl" who was undemanding and almost apologetic. In a later episode, however, when the equipment was said to be defective and the cost of repairs prohibitive ($3,000 or more), she decided to explore the situation herself. Knowing the local technician to be inadequate, she brought in a technically-skilled friend to examine the equipment with the result that after they had done some really "dirty" work to clean it up, they found the equipment could be repaired for only $300. She thought the head of her department might be angry at her "going over his head" and making an independent investigation. Instead, she found he was delighted. He was a passive man who had not kept abreast of new technical advances and was only too glad to have her enthusiastic assistance in updating his department. He was especially grateful that she had done this tactfully, not to show him up, but merely because she was interested in the further development of new ideas. The background of this girl's failure of assertion will be given in a later case presentation.

Fear of Success and/or Failure

It has been observed that in the early grades girls often surpass boys not only in reading and writing skills but also in mathematics and science.[9] This early superiority steadily declines, so that, compared to males, female A-rated students in high school begin to lose ground in college. They may even fail or drop out in graduate school. Apparently the cultural pressure for women to have social success and find a suitable marriage partner who is brighter, more motivated, or less ambivalent about professional achievement than they are, finally overtakes them. The "fear of being over-educated" and thus unmarriageable still affects women today.[6] They fear rejection by their families, by their more domestic female peers who may be jealous and who cling together to make the professional female feel ostracized socially. They also fear being a threat to their lovers or husbands who still need male superiority, or so they may assume. It is hard for some of us to believe in the possibility of a man who is capable of being proud of a woman's success; who is strong enough not to compete with her but to enjoy his own ability. Often when a woman's success has been presented as the cause of marital stress, it evolves in therapy that what the man resents is not her success but her guilty irritability, her self-preoccupation in off-duty hours, or her anxiety about her position as a role-breaker that makes her psychologically inaccessible to him even when there is time for leisure.

Dual career marriages are certainly complicated, but not necessarily unmanageable. They have been studied recently by both sociologists and psychiatrists. Sociologists point out that role proliferation affects both men and women, but that women do have more difficulty in handling the complications.[7] Because they are not as much at ease in roles of authority and are thus more inclined to "do it themselves," women find it harder to delegate jobs to secretaries or younger coworkers. They are also more deeply concerned about child-care and family illnesses, which men usually assume are "women's work." Child-care help, substitute mothers, and housekeepers are more difficult to find in metropolitan areas. There is a movement beginning to upgrade the status and the pay of the housekeeper so that women of higher educational and social backgrounds will find more satisfaction in this type of work which is so necessary for the professional woman who has children. Many younger professional women delay having families or decide to remain childless, daring to put their professions first and rejecting the age-old assumption that woman's chief justification and value lie in raising children.[13] Zero Population Growth has helped promote childlessness but such an approach does not solve the anxiety of young women who fear to give up motherhood because of possible later regrets, loneliness, or failure of their professional lives to be as fully satisfying as anticipated. Such career women are often not aware that having children can also be disappointing and not fully satisfying. Certainly having children complicates the life of a scientist more than any one factor I can discern.

Fear of Being "Unfeminine"

If women are to enter a formerly male profession, if they are to have few or no children at all, how do they verify their sexual identity? One might ask why it is so necessary to do so, but it is clear that both sexes have a pressing need to feel they are sexually attractive as male and female. The answer probably has to do with the fact that the early sense of personal identity, "I am I, me, myself, a unique person," evolves around age two, when the difference between the sexes begins to be noticed and becomes increasingly important throughout growth until maturation. Anatomical differences between the sexes are the most obvious and unalterable ones and gain significance both as frightening and exciting. All other human skills, aptitudes, behavior characteristics are more amenable to training and conscious control. The preoccupation with one's sexuality may be partly because it is so unalterable, so resistant to conscious control. Is this the reason why so many people would give up academic or professional success if they could feel sexually proficient and satisfied? Both sexes feel this, but women are especially vulnerable because they have been judged for thousands of years mainly on the basis of their sexual, wifely, maternal, and domestic functions. The three factors discussed above—fear of dependency, fear of aggression, and fear of success—are all tied up with their fear of sexual failure. Some women scientists try to avoid the problem by appearing asexual, attracting as little attention to their bodies as possible. However, to be "mousey," poorly dressed, "dowdy," is now seen as evidence of low feminine self-esteem and attracts either indifference or contempt. If it is combined with overt hostility to men and/or women, it is even more of a deterrent to success.

At the opposite extreme, sex may be used inappropriately to strengthen the bond and to gain special support from a male coworker. This may not be a conscious maneuver but an inadvertent result of a desire to please, a fear of antagonizing the male by rejecting his sexual advances. Acquiescence may be seen as the price for acceptance and professional support. Sexual liaisons may also develop quite genuinely as the result of two people working together closely over a long period of time, sharing interests and solving problems together in a way that brings closeness that neither finds in marriage or in outside relationships.

The most typical example of this is seen in the young female graduate student, admiring an older male teacher or "mentor" on whom she feels increasingly dependent. If either or both of them lack a satisfying heterosexual relationship apart from the professional association, there is danger of their relationship's becoming sexual.[11] At first this may be stimulating, but the mixture of sex and/or love with scientific work can be confusing; an irrational element of deep yearning and dependency disrupts the rational perspective needed for good research. Jealousy, conflict of interests, and guilt can be destructive to a smoothly working relationship. One woman allowed her slightly older co-worker to take credit for all the work done because her sexual need for him and her awareness of his great ambitions immobilized her. She felt she "owed" him something special because he had satisfied her loneliness and sexual needs after her traumatic divorce. It did not occur to her until months of therapy that he had taken advantage of her vulnerability to get revenge on his wife and to get extra sexual gratification without endangering the security of his marriage as well as to bind her into professional acquiescence and exploit her fresh intellectual vitality. She decided that "love and work" do not mix and became increasingly suspicious of men picking her brains, taking possession of her mind as well as her body.

Case Illustrations

A young biologist, sexually attractive and lively, was happily married to a successful academic administrator. She had two attractive children, whereas the head of her department was unattractive, unmarried, and jealous of her. The young woman was a favorite teacher who was noted for spending time with students, acting as a good role-model. Having published little, she was pressured into writing a grant proposal, a job she detested. Also, in this instance, she did not even believe in the content of the research design, but being a compliant "good girl" she could not refuse the task. It was such a burden to her that she locked herself away from students in order to finish it. She then, for the first time, received poor student evaluations, since they missed her personal availability after classes. In order to spend a previously arranged vacation with her husband and children which was to start a week before summer session was over, she made special arrangements to cover this last week of a ten-week summer program. However, the department accused her of asking for too many special favors, although she had always tried to avoid just this type of accusation, since she believed it is so often leveled at a woman. Feeling desperate, her reaction was to take a leave of absence and turn to therapy to figure out her next move.

Enormous problems of lack of self-assertion were uncovered, with the surfacing of such symptoms as a fear of making phone calls, a fear of asking for anything, a fear of turning down a request or an invitation. She had been raised in a very proper academic environment in which her father had been head of a school department as well as a noted authority in his field. Her mother was a phobic recluse who never even entertained friends, relatives, or students. She was her father's favorite, and became determined to be like him. However, his intellectual goals for her were so high that she developed severe examination anxiety and work inhibitions. Good grades cost her enormous effort but advancement evolved as projected. While she was teaching college part-time and not on the tenure ladder she felt free, and therefore had little trouble. She devoted two thirds time for one third pay, and thus felt she owed the college nothing. However, when her own children started school she decided to become a full-time instructor, and the pressures mounted. She could no longer please everybody even when she agreed to all demands. Every class she taught became a test, and her performance anxiety skyrocketed.

In therapy she saw the results of her placating attitude, she learned how to speak up, to defend or explain herself, to say "no" at the appropriate times, and to experiment with self-assertiveness so that she would be prepared to reenter the teaching world, or find an alternate role to make valid use of herself. During the year's leave she "caught up" with many things, but discovered that being home full time did not make her happy. The mounting anxiety of the previous spring was linked to her fear that she was becoming "just like her mother," who had failed her father and herself. In this instance, short-term therapy was very useful in her self-reappraisal. After she overcame her panic, she was offered a choice of part-time teaching with her husband or returning to the tenure ladder at her former school. Her husband had been offered the presidency of a fine midwestern college, and she was glad to go with him into a less competitive, less political atmosphere, even though she had to face the unmerited suspicion of nepotism. She enjoyed returning to teaching a group of enthusiastic students who appreciated her interest in them, and the midwestern college felt fortunate to have her part-time staff contribution. This more relaxed atmosphere suited her immediate needs. She used her extra time to explore a new aspect of her field and looks forward to a major contribution later.

The "young physicist" mentioned above was actually ten years older than she appeared, being slender with a childlike face and soft voice that was anything but convincing. She was the last child of a European couple who had migrated during World War II to the United States, going from an industrial area into a rural part of America to find peace. The patient was to be the "quiet" child to grace their later years, to "make up" for the cruelty they had faced, to counteract the hostile quarreling of the older children who had felt displaced. The patient grew up in an idyllic setting knowing her role was to make her parents happy. She was kept in a state of innocence, protected from the competitiveness and political deviousness of the outer world. She received a good education and became a brilliant student, although she never quite believed it. Home began to seem confining and she married a serious, older, academic man while still quite young. He turned out to be cold, remote, and critical of her rather ineffectual efforts at housekeeping. She became bored with domestic life and returned to get a graduate degree, apparently with his support. However, he resented her being less accessible to him and withdrew from her sexually, and she felt isolated. This was the background for her affair with her thesis adviser who was not only bright but also warm and enthusiastic. They worked well together, and at first he taught her a great deal. Later, however, she found how dependent he was on her for research details as well as for restraining the violent temper outbursts that eventually cost him his job. They also had a passionate love affair which opened up new feelings in her and caused her to divorce her husband, who now seemed inert and unstimulating as well as an undermining person. Her "mentor" was married with children and temporarily separated from his wife but not willing to divorce her. Different job placements separated them. His jealousy and her sense of being deserted and betrayed made for great anguish. She finally broke the relationship and tried to work on her own, having won a postdoctoral scholarship at a large university. A self-effacing person accustomed to trusting others, she found it almost impossible to fight for her own rights and to get proper recognition of her own work.

These problems were presented and studied early in therapy. She recalled more examples of how she been taken advantage of, such as the time her name was omitted from a paper that included her work. She became dependent for companionship on an older, divorced man in her building, and although in some areas he supported and encouraged her, she found herself being exploited by him, too. With her meek facade and quiet ways she was not put on the tenure ladder, and so temporarily took a job in a woman's college as a teacher. Her teaching was appreciated by many, and she began to feel that she did not need a man to be "someone." The large university called her back repeatedly for advice on the use of special equipment, and she began to realize that older men were dependent on her specific skills but unwilling to acknowledge this, so that she felt "exploited." As she became more aware of being used, being called in to provide data for conferences she should have been conducting, she began to withhold valuable unpublished data so that it would not be stolen. When she saw senior scientists making errors, she matter-of-factly corrected them rather than remaining silent. She realized that her fear of showing anyone up or "hurting anyone's feelings" had made her seem ineffectual and uninformed. She finally began to protect herself, to push for acknowledgment, to get her basic material published quickly and under her own name. She was then in a better position to get a good research job for her own fulfillment rather than teaching undergraduates as a "service." Growth continued; healthy skepticism replaced blind faith, and healthy self-assertion let to more independent action.

These two younger scientists can be compared with two older ones in their forties who have gotten tenure and recognition after a long struggle that included psychotherapy. Both were lively, interesting teachers who felt unappreciated in this area while they were being faulted for not serving on multiple committees or not attending uninteresting evening school meetings. Both commuted from New York, both had children, and both needed to go home at the end of the working day. Both were zestful and energetic and not suited to a "low profile." They did not expect to have their popularity with students held against them. One was quite phobic of strangers and men but covered this with a formidable facade that drove people away. She was afraid of her competitiveness and hidden aggression and thought of herself as a castrating bitch. She got involved in petty political battles, after which she felt defeated. Gradually she was able to accept herself as an assertive, bright person with much to offer. She became disentangled from internecine rivalry and began to rely on her own abilities. The department began to acknowledge her real value. She acquired a reputation for being impartial, invulnerable, or refusing to get involved in the power game. She was rewarded with a prestigious fellowship, wrote a fine book, and was granted tenure.

The other successful woman was also a charismatic teacher who aroused jealousy because of her famous husband and her own brilliance and attractiveness. No one knew how anxious and uncertain she was. They interpreted her tense facial expression as one of rage, and her winning smile as seductive. In the beginning of therapy she had no awareness of what effect she had on people. She had written two books that received international attention and that had added prestige to her department at school. In spite of this, a young, unmarried man who had published nothing got tenure when she did not. At first she was devastated, paranoid, immobilized. She had not expected the typical prejudice against married women with children, who "don't need the money" and who miss time at work. The single male, mediocre but always present and compliant, got rewarded in this case.

It has been shown that woman's productivity and time spent in medical work is almost equal to that of a man.[4] This is also true in academia; some women teachers put in much time, but prejudices remain.

An older faculty friend suggested that this woman appeal to the grievance committee and she was assigned to an experienced counselor who helped her collect relevant data. It was shown that her superiors in the department had not even read her books and would not take her seriously. The prejudicial data was so clear that she was told to bring material to the civil rights lawyer of the university as well as to her dean. Having found the way to effective action, she won tenure immediately.

This illustrates how women often lack practical data on how to proceed. They fear using lawyers because the women might be called paranoid or litigious, and they are unprepared to handle the unjust, internal politics of large organizations. Both these women learned to fight their battles with dignity and self-respect that did not detract from their sense of womanhood. This type of appropriate professional stance is what professional women need to work for, using available methods and seeking experienced advice about tactics that succeed. New ones can then be improvised and eventually implemented.

Summary

Women in science are role-breakers who threaten the established order, and therefore they will continue to have difficulty in getting support from conservatives. Thus, they need unusual independence, tenacity, and a strong belief in themselves both as scientists and as women. They need great ego strength to stay firm in the face of prejudice and opposition, which will melt away slowly, alternating between progress and backlash. This is to be expected as characteristic of human development; change brings anxiety. Innovators have been punished, from Socrates to Galileo to Freud. Such historical perspective makes daily battles and losses easier to bear.

References

1. BERNARD, J. 1964. Academic Women. New American Library. Meridian Paperback. Second Printing. 1974.
2. G.A.P. REPORT No. 92. 1975. The Educated Woman: Prospects and Problems. Committee on College Student.
3. GADPAILLE, W. 1972. Research into the physiology of maleness and femaleness. Arch. Gen. Psych. 26(3):193–207.

4. HEINS, M. et al. 1977. Comparison of the productivity of women and men physicians. JAMA **237**: No. 23.
5. HENNIG, M.M. 1973. Family dynamics for developing positive achievement motivation in women: the successful woman executive. Ann. N.Y. Acad. Sci. **208**:76–81.
6. HORNER, M.S. & M.R. WALSH. 1973. Causes and consequences of existing psychological barriers to self-actualization. Ann. N.Y. Acad. Sci. **208**: 124–130.
7. JOHNSON, F.A. & JOHNSON C.L. 1976. Role strain in high commitment career women. J. Amer. Acad. Psychoanal. **4**:(1)13–37.
8. LERNER, H. 1978. Adaptive and pathogenic aspects of sex-role stereotypes: Implications for parenting and psychotherapy. Am. J. Psych. **135**:(1)48–52.
9. MACCOBY, E.F. Ed. 1966. The Development of Sex Differences. Stanford Studies in Psychology V. Stanford University Press. Stanford, Calif.
10. MOULTON, R. 1977. Some effects of the new feminism. J. Am. Psychiatric Assoc. **134**:(1).
11. MOULTON, R. 1977. Women with double lives. Contemp. Psychoanal. **13**:(1).
12. MOULTON, R. 1977. Fear of female power: a cause of marital dysfunction. J. Am. Acad. Psychoanal. **5**:(4).
13. MOULTON, R. 1978. Ambivalence about motherhood in career women. J. Am. Acad. Psa. **7**(2).

PART VII. Summation

An Agenda to Further Expand the Role of Women in Science and Technology

ETHEL TOBACH

*Curator, American Museum of Natural History
New York, New York 10024*

WHEN I THOUGHT that I would have the honor of introducing Estelle Ramey, I asked her what she would like me to mention, particularly in my introduction. "The ERA situation, of course," she immediately replied. And then, "But let me see where else I can do something on it." And, of course, she took the first opportunity she had to report on the latest crisis in the struggle and gave us a program for action. I think that in this, our last session, we should consider what should be our agenda for action upon leaving here.

In all the aspects of societal evolution and processes of change, techniques that bear directly upon control of the environment to make survival possible have been most significant and power-determining. The discovery of fire, the development of tools—sources of energy to tame the exigencies of nature though labor—made a sharp change in the history of changing relations among people, based on the control of those sources of energy. The effects of these changing societal relationships on gender roles are still with us today. There is no time here to go through the shameful history of oppression. The same purpose of controlling the products of humanity's harvest of natural goods underlay the brutalizing oppression of women and of groups of people, as in slavery. What is perhaps most relevant to our meetings these days is the growing awareness among women and minorities that the relation of people to the means of controlling the use of technology determines the value of those people to society. That is why the increasing entry of women and minorities into scientific and engineering fields concerns us today and should continually concern us. The characteristics of present-day technology are such that the expenditure of human energy is no longer the critical factor in controlling nature's exigencies. The number of individuals is not significant, nor is their physiological stamina or efficiency. It should be noted that when necessary, women have proved always to have that stamina and efficiency. Today when unemployment is high, the labor of women, not being necessary, is considered wanting in stamina and efficiency.

The source of energy today is based less on human labor than on technological instrumentation and control. The size of the population is seen as serious only when it outstrips the need for people to do the necessary work or when it falls below the level needed to buy the products produced. The importance of women and their activities stands and falls in direct relationship to the needs of society for labor or military power or for maintaining consumerism. This may be why women in the United States today are in the transitional process of finding it possible to win some battles and lose others. The societal demands on women are themselves not uniform or homogeneous. Thus, while women are finding it not always desirable for practical or philosophical reasons to have children, for a variety of reasons, industry and other societal groups are concerned that the population in the United States not fall too low. It has been suggested that insurance companies were very involved in the antiabortion campaign. Other societal decision-makers who see that there may no longer be as great a need for a pool of unemployed, however, are interested in helping women control the birth rate.

For example, military operations are such today that the victory in battle does not necessarily depend on actual personal fighting. Therefore, women are now being recruited by the Department of Defense for all phases of military duty, including combat. At the same time, this policy may withdraw young women from a dwindling job market, perhaps another reason why we are finding it easier to get into schools: it keeps us out of the employment agencies.

But when we get our training, we find that we are competing for a slice of a shrinking pie, as Dr. Marinez pointed out. I agree; we must enlarge the pie. The question is how.

The agenda for action requires us first to examine the realities of the world in which we live. Our first consideration in all our activities must be to consolidate our human resources, and in order to do this we must consider well all women and their situations. An example of this necessity comes to mind as I look over our audience. The statistics we have been hearing point to the fact that women scientists tend to be underpaid or unemployed. Did we do something about seeing that those underpaid, out-of-work women could come here and benefit from this Conference?

Another example: we have been talking about women getting into the opulent halls of industry and academia. How many of us have thought about the kinds of research and the societal meanings resulting from our activities there? The women's movements for freedom have always gained strength and victories when the women allied themselves with those who were concerned about all of society.

Do we have the time to think about the ideology of our science and technology? I think we may have to take the time. Too often in our schools we teach a kind of biology[1] and behavioral science[4] that tends to justify the pseudoscientific basis for discrimination against us. Should we lend ourselves to that? The hereditarianism of ethology, of Skinner, Jensen, and sociobiology is being proselytized in all the science courses in grade schools, high schools, and institutions of higher education.[3]

Let me give an example that speaks directly to us here. I recommend to you a report just issued by Fox and co-workers for the NIE on women and mathematics.[2] They have done an excellent review of existing research and have found that mostly poor science has been used to prove that women cannot be good mathematicians. They propose several lines of good research that need to be done. We must, however, examine all the assumptions that have been made in the course of finding "scientific" justifications for the gender role of women. Despite the extensive research in cognition and learning, the behavioral sciences still do not understand the basic processes that yield inventive, creative thinking and problem solving. Yet, the testing industry has devised guides for determining which people should be trained in science and engineering. On page 189 in the book cited, one finds the basic assumption that needs to be tested: how well founded is the concept that mathematical ability is the critical human faculty that makes for a good scientist or technician? The recent reexamination of the entire testing industry in regard to "intelligence" might be expanded to discover exactly what kinds of mathematical knowledge are needed for kinds of thinking that are most evident in science. Certainly for the biological science and the behavioral science that deal with physiology, ecology, and genetics, relatively few scientists and engineers involve themselves with the truly complicated mathematics that come into play in the theoretical formulations and the model building, be they women or men. The proposal in the NIE report says that all women need to know fundamental math and that perhaps some of them, just as only *some* men, may need to know higher mathematics.

Another example of basic processes in the sociology of science is the issue of peer review. It is not surprising that one of the most passionately defended bastions in the Science Establishment is that of the peer review system, particularly in regard to opening up such boards to nonscience members. The peer review system, as it operates at present, has been challenged because it tends to perpetuate the power of those who are already in decision-making positions in the scientific community. I suggest that, for women and minorities, the composition of those boards need to be opened to those representatives of society who will defend us. I regret to say that The New York Academy of Sciences, which has been partly trying to respond to the needs of women and minorities with regard to the scientific community, has resisted accepting a report on peer review. So, you see, the struggle needs to be engaged in on all levels in all professional and governmental institutions. Testing basic assumptions needs to be applied in all our work—on the job, in our professional societies, and in the women's movement.

Another assumption we have to test is the following: If women knew more of the substance of science they would, by the sheer force of their wisdom and brilliance, convince the powers that be, that they should be given freedom to pursue their activities in academia and industry. I think a test of that assumption would show that it is not enough. The winning of the right for all women and minorities to accessibility to this knowledge is a political fight, which requires psychological and political education. In every program we institute for science and engineering preparation, as well as actual education, we must include education for women and men as to the societal, psychological, and philosophical issues involved in changing social consciousness to do away with all oppressive discrimination. If one does not understand the basic causal processes of a phenomenon, one cannot control it or change it. The second point on our agenda for action then is to begin to pay even more attention to the theoretical base for understanding and changing the societal processes that lead to sexism and racism.

I know that in the discussion that follows you will be addressing yourselves to more specific points of action. Let me remind you of two that came to our attention the first morning of the Conference: 1) Increasing the number of women on the editorial board of *Science*. Dr. Abelson nominated Dr. Ramey, an excellent choice. 2) Having this convocation of women support NOW in its defense against the legal charge of conspiracy in restraint of trade.

Several good ideas for innovative approaches to our problems came out of the talks. I urge all of you to start finding ways of exploring them, putting them to the test, and joining with other people to implement them. First, join AWIS (Association for Women in Science) and see that your local chapter starts to deal with these issues locally and nationally. Second, join the women's caucus in your professional society. If there isn't one, form one. Three, get your organization to undertake an affirmative action program in its governance, in its public relations and governmental activities, and in its education and training plans.

REFERENCES

1. BRISCOE, A. 1978. Hormones and gender. *In* Genes and Gender: I. E. Tobach and B. Rosoff, Eds. Gordian Press. New York, N.Y.
2. Fox, L.H., E. FENNEMA & J. SHERMAN. Women and mathematics: research perspectives for change. NIE Papers in Education and Work: 8. Washington, D.C.
3. TOBACH, E. 1976. Behavioral science and genetic destiny: implications for education, therapy, and behavior research. *In* Genetic Destiny: Scientific Controversy and Social Conflict. E. Tobach & H.M. Proshansky Eds.: 142-158. AMS Press. New York, N.Y.
4. TOBACH, E. & B. ROSOFF, Eds. 1978. Genes and Gender: I. Gordian Press. New York, N.Y.

Equal Opportunity for Women in Science

SHEILA M. PFAFFLIN
*American Telephone and Telegraph Company
Basking Ridge, New Jersey 07920*

EQUAL OPPORTUNITY FOR women in science: a natural goal for our society, it might be assumed. America places great emphasis on science and technology, and it is proud of its egalitarian traditions. Moreover, science is viewed as an objective enterprise whose practices should be less dominated by the emotional biases that have operated against women in other areas.

Yet, if this Conference has one predominant message, it is how far we really are from achieving the goal of equal opportunity for women in science. In paper after paper, we find the same picture: women, underrepresented in tenured positions in the past, are still underrepresented; pay differentials between the sexes continue to grow as years of experience are accumulated; incidents of sex discrimination continue to occur; and currently we face a growing backlash that threatens the very concept of equality.

Not that the years of struggle have been useless. Increases, sometimes dramatic, in the numbers of young women training for scientific careers have been reported. Shocking though it is that it was necessary to sue the Department of Health, Education, and Welfare over the low numbers of women on scientific review boards, improvement has been achieved, and the more blatant forms of discrimination are disappearing. Few employers today would write a young women chemist that they do not hire women, as happened to Anna Harrison when she was starting her career. Nor would the American Psychological Association today publish descriptions of graduate programs with "men preferred" written in as they did when I was a student.

A climate has been created in which some of the pressures of discrimination have been lessened. The concept of conforming prejudice is important here. This simply means that many prejudicial actions arise at least as much from the perception that they are expected by one's peers as from strong personal emotions. In the past, the expectation that women should not be hired was a powerful influence even on men who had no strong feelings one way or the other. It was simply safer not to hire a woman. The only good excuse was that a woman candidate was overwhelmingly superior to all male candidates, and even then many institutions might view such an outcome with suspicion. The predominantly male structure of science still induces suspicion and hesitancy, but at least today there are countervailing forces in play that make equal treatment for women more acceptable.

Nevertheless, when all this has been said, serious problems remain. Discrimination today may be increasingly covert, but both statistics and individual experiences suggest that it is still powerful. It has proved extremely difficult to mobilize effective governmental action, especially in the case of academia. Individual lawsuits are sometimes effective, but as our experience with them increases, it has become clear that the costs, both in money and in damage to careers, are often prohibitive.

The difficulties still encountered make it clear that the optimistic view that equal opportunity for women scientists should receive strong support was based on incorrect assumptions. As Dr. Hall so eloquently described, science is not the objective, unemotional endeavor that is often portrayed. Scientific research takes place in a social context and is profoundly influenced by that context.

And the social context of American society is profoundly sex-typed. From earliest childhood, sex-role stereotypes are reinforced. And these stereotypes do not represent "separate but equal" if, indeed, such a concept is ever possible. Consider your own reactions to the following: a little girl playing with a toy truck; a little boy playing with a doll. Virtually everyone, whatever his/her professed views, reacts more negatively to the latter than to the former. The view that masculine activities are acceptable to a degree for women, but not the reverse, is but one reflection of our society's downgrading of the status of women and things associated with them. This is not the place to go into this more fully, but social scientists who have studied these issues have demonstrated that not only are women treated as a separate class, but they are a subordinate class and suffer the disadvantages of such a status.

Given this context, it was not to be expected that change would come readily in the sciences. On the contrary, greater resistance might be expected here for several reasons.

First, there is the insecurity of scientists. Science has two characteristics that contribute to this. First, it is intensely competitive, and in a very personal way. In many other occupations, competitiveness is modified by group settings of work. Decisions and implementation often involve many people, and responsibility for results is correspondingly diffuse. But a scientist takes the responsibility for her or his own work with, at most, a few, often changing, colleagues. Thus, if a male scientist is bested by a woman, he has fewer excuses, and the subordinate status of women often makes it more traumatic than being outclassed by another male.

A second problem is the difficulty academics face in identity. Surveys have shown that academic professionals are viewed as more "feminine" by the general public than many other professionals. Reaction against such implied feminization may contribute to the antagonism of academic scientists to the increasing numbers of women in science. Their masculine image is already under attack, so that association with women as equals is even more threatening than it is to the average man.

The elitism of the academic world has been noted at several points in this Conference as a contributing factor to continued discrimination against women in science. Far from having an egalitarian tradition, as is often naively assumed, our major academic institutions often seem to foster the view that their superiority places them above the rules that apply to lesser men in lesser institutions, and they seem to have been successful to a distressing degree in getting others to agree with them.

What conclusions are we led to from all this? First, we must accept the fact that we have fought only the first battles in what is going to be a long fight to achieve equal opportunity for women in science. We must not allow ourselves to become either discouraged or complacent. Laws against discrimination are a beginning, not an end in this struggle. We must mobilize the skills and resources in order to use them effectively over a long period to achieve real change.

We must address ourselves to the specific problems that have been identified at this Conference. We must develop more sophisticated methods for dealing with covert discrimination; better grievance procedures; stronger networks among women to counter the masculine social structures; stronger laws, which will no longer permit the universities to evade their obligations; and better enforcement of the laws we now have. Our conference participants have presented a compelling case for the urgency of action on these fronts.

But we must remember that the social context for science is important.

Women scientists cannot expect to achieve equality in a society that continues to view women as second-class citizens. It is necessary to work to eliminate sexism in all levels of our society. This is true in part because neither men or women scientists are insulated from this larger society. As long as women scientists are subjected to pressures from this society, in terms of unequal home and family responsibilities and in inadequate support for pursuit of careers, they will never reach their potential. Furthermore, as long as these biases exist, both men and women will enter the sciences conditioned by them, and the elimination of biases from science itself will be partial, at best.

Hence the stress on the need for efforts for broader change. Right now, of course, the overwhelmingly most important issue is passage of the Equal Rights Amendment, as several of our participants have stressed. Without this fundamental constitutional guarantee, future progress for all women, including women scientists, will remain precarious.